History, Power, and Identity

History, Power, and Identity

Ethnogenesis
in the Americas,
1492–1992

Edited by
Jonathan D. Hill

University
of Iowa Press
Iowa City

University of Iowa Press, Iowa City 52242
Copyright © 1996 by the University of Iowa Press
All rights reserved
Printed in the United States of America

Design by Omega Clay

Printed on acid-free paper

Library of Congress Cataloging-in-Publication Data
History, power, and identity: ethnogenesis in the
Americas, 1492–1992 / edited by Jonathan D. Hill.
p.   cm.
Includes bibliographical references and index.
ISBN 0-87745-546-5 (cloth), ISBN 0-87745-547-3
(paper)
1. Ethnic groups—America.   2. Ethnicity—
America.   I. Hill, Jonathan David, 1954–
E29.A1H57   1996
305.8'0097—dc20   95-52415
                                              CIP

01   00   99   98   97   96   C   5   4   3   2   1

01   00   99   98   97   96   P   5   4   3   2   1

Contents

History, Power, and Identity

Jonathan D. Hill

Introduction

Ethnogenesis in the Americas, 1492–1992

Cultural anthropologists have generally used the term *ethnogenesis* to describe the historical emergence of a people who define themselves in relation to a sociocultural and linguistic heritage.[1] In the following collection of essays, a number of cultural anthropologists are concerned to demonstrate that ethnogenesis can also serve as an analytical tool for developing critical historical approaches to culture as an ongoing process of conflict and struggle over a people's existence and their positioning within and against a general history of domination.[2] In this more analytical sense, ethnogenesis is not merely a label for the historical emergence of culturally distinct peoples but a concept encompassing peoples' simultaneously cultural and political struggles to create enduring identities in general contexts of radical change and discontinuity. For all the indigenous and Afro-American peoples whose histories are discussed in the following essays, ethnogenesis can be understood as a creative adaptation to a general history of violent changes—including demographic collapse, forced relocations, enslavement, ethnic soldiering, ethnocide, and genocide—imposed during the historical expansion of colonial and national states in the Americas.

Ethnogenesis is a useful concept for exploring the complex interrelations between global and local histories through focusing upon "the dialogues and struggles that form the situated particulars of cultural production" (Tsing 1994: 283). Ethnogenetic processes are intrinsically dynamic and rooted in a people's sense of historical consciousness, or "a reflexive awareness on the part of social actors of their ability to make situational and more lasting adjustments to social orderings . . . and an ability to understand that ordering as it is situated in larger, more encompassing spatiotemporal orders that include others who are socially different" (Hill 1988: 7). By defining ethnogenesis as a synthesis of a people's cultural and political struggles to exist as well as their historical consciousness of these struggles, *Ethnogenesis in the Americas* decisively breaks out of the implicit contrast between static local cultures and dynamic global history. None of the indigenous and Afro-American peoples discussed in the following essays can be understood as isolated local cultures, nor do their entanglements in broader relations of national and global power fully explain or determine the specific forms of ethnogenesis.[3]

In addition to a people's struggle to exist within a general history characterized by radical, often imposed changes, ethnogenesis is grounded in the conflicts within and among indigenous and Afro-American peoples. In contexts of colonial domination and structures of national power, ethnic groups become internally divided into factions struggling to control access to the dominant society's wealth and power (see Ferguson 1990; Whitehead and Ferguson 1992). Alternatively, factions can develop around the issue of how to cope with the dominant society.[4] Both kinds of factionalism can lead to ethnogenesis through a process of resisting not only a dominant social order but also other factions' ways of relating to that dominant order. Similarly, interethnic rivalries among indigenous and Afro-American peoples often formed part of ethnogenesis and ethnocide, especially in cases where competing colonial powers institutionalized such divisions into ethnic soldiering (see Whitehead, this volume).

Reconstituting Cultural Identities under Colonial Domination

Maroon societies of the circum-Caribbean area, or communities founded by escaped Afro-American slaves, offer what are perhaps the most dramatic illustrations of ethnogenesis in the Americas because of their radically uprooted origins as forced exiles from a great diversity of West, South, and East African societies. The diverse African peoples who founded Maroon societies had very little common ground upon which to embark on their struggles to create new communities, aside from their shared opposition to the inhumanity of colonial plantation societies that reduced Afro-American peoples to animal-like status.

Among the Aluku, a Maroon society of inland Surinam and French Guiana, shared historical origins through opposition to institutionalized slavery found expression in the practice of naming social groups according to the specific plantations from which their founding members had fled (see Bilby, this volume). These historically differentiated subgroups of the Aluku remained partially autonomous through the late eighteenth century, even as their leaders formed political and military alliances in order to fight the Dutch and their local allies, the Ndjuka Maroons. After their military defeat in 1793, the surviving Aluku united into a single ethnic group through worshiping a common set of religious oracles. Ritual and myth provided the central elements of Aluku political unification and ethnogenesis in the nineteenth century: "a god known as Tata Odun, said by the present-day Aluku to have come over from Africa along with the ancestors ... became the supreme tribal deity, to which all the different groups now owed obeisance" (Bilby, this volume). Whereas the historical experiences of slavery and escape into the remote interior forests of South America had produced an internally fragmented set of Maroon communities, shared religious beliefs and practices provided the Aluku with the raw materials for creating a new community by reaching deeper into the historical past of peoples and deities migrating across the ocean from Africa to America.

The importance of African, indigenous American, and European religions as cornerstones in the building of new ethnic identities emerges as one of the central themes in this collection of essays. In some cases, indigenous peoples revitalized precolonial symbols of ritual power, as in the building of the Seminole Confederation around ritual chiefs who controlled the sacred fire of mythic creation (see Sattler, this volume). In other cases, indigenous peoples formed new alliances and shaped new cultural identities through creative refashionings of formerly separate indigenous religions. The Kiowa, for example, owe their modern identity at least in part to their Jumano ancestors' adoption of ritual and ceremonial practices from the Crow, Hidatsa, and other northern Plains peoples with whom they entered into new patterns of trade and alliance during the eighteenth century (see Hickerson, this volume). Similarly, the Arawakan Wakuénai of interior South America formed new patterns of trade and alliance with their eastern Tukanoan neighbors as they fled from forced relocations and diseases along the lower courses of the Rio Negro into the relative safety of remote headwater areas (see Hill, this volume).

Also important were indigenous peoples' appropriations of European symbols of ritual power, especially in Andean regions, where Christian saints and deities became absorbed into a centuries-long process of constructing religious hierarchies (Silverblatt 1988; Dillon and Abercrombie 1988; Rasnake 1988). Although such appropriations of Christian ritual symbols were somewhat less prevalent in the South American lowlands than they were in the Andes, the nineteenth-century adoption of Christian symbols into indigenous religion among Carib-speaking Kapon and Makushi of Venezuela and Guiana provides an unusual example of ethnogenesis through actively appropriating religious symbols of the European colonizers (see Staats, this volume). In all these different cases, indigenous American, African, and European ritual and myth did not act as static cultural molds existing independently of changing historical conditions but as dynamic building blocks for the historical construction of new cultural identities.

Historical conditions for indigenous American peoples during the colonial period presented a grim picture of demographic collapse, slavery, warfare, and loss of control over lands and other resources. Within one century after the arrival of Spanish conquerors in the Andean highlands (ca. 1530), an indigenous population of approximately 9 million had been reduced to only 1 million (Cook 1981).[5] In lowland areas of South America, a precontact population of 8.54 million (Denevan 1976) had declined to about .5 million by the eighteenth century (Dobyns 1966) and continued to diminish throughout the nineteenth and early twentieth centuries. Indigenous North American population losses were equally devastating in proportional terms, falling from a precontact level of about 5 million to .6 million in 1800 and reaching a nadir of only .25 million between 1890 and 1900 (Thornton 1987: 90, 133). Thus, while indigenous Andean populations fell to about 10 percent of the precontact level, indigenous populations of lowland South America and the entirety of North America declined to only 5 percent of their strengths in 1492.[6]

Indigenous American survivors of the Great Dying during the colonial period faced many of the same problems as the Maroon societies of escaped Afro-American slaves. Although indigenous American peoples conserved many elements of sociopolitical organization, ecological adaptation, ritual, and myth that reached far into the precolonial past, the indigenous cultural identities that emerged during and after demographic collapse sharply diverged from precontact social formations. For example, the various Carib and Arawakan identities that emerged in colonial Surinam and the Guianas bore little resemblance to the regional chiefdoms that had spread across northern South America and the Caribbean Islands prior to the arrival of Europeans in the Americas (see Whitehead, this volume). Even in remote frontier areas located far away from the points of initial contact and early European colonization, indigenous peoples constructed new cultural identities as they adjusted to European diseases, technologies, and distant power struggles.

The voracious appetite for fertile lands, cheap labor, and material goods in colonial America affected indigenous and Afro-American peoples in very similar ways. The introduction of steel tools, firearms, and other European trade goods tipped the balance of power in favor of indigenous peoples who had the most direct access to centers of colonial wealth and power. Aside from the spread of contagious diseases, the most devastating effects of the colonial period were internecine wars aimed at capturing slaves to sell to or barter with the Europeans. In northern South America, for example, Dutch merchants offered Carib middlemen "10 axes, 10 machetes, 10 knives, 10 bands of glass beads . . . and sometimes a rifle, powder and lead molds" (Morey and Morey 1975: 12, translation mine) for each indigenous slave taken from the interior. In turn, the Carib middlemen needed only one axe, one machete, and four strings of pearls to acquire one indigenous slave from the interior. The indigenous slave trade did not end in lowland South America after its official abolition in 1767 but continued through the Rubber Boom of the late nineteenth to early twentieth centuries (Taussig 1987). Along the Caquetá and Putumayo Rivers in Peru and Colombia, Brazilian merchants traded steel tools, firearms, and other manufactured items to indigenous headmen, who canceled their debts by furnishing indigenous men, women, and children from neighboring groups. Except for greater emphasis on firearms, the terms of exchange were very similar to the payments that the Dutch slave traders had offered to Carib mercenaries during the early colonial period. "An infant costs the value of an American knife; a six-year-old girl is valued at one saber and sometimes an axe; an adult man and woman reached the price of one rifle" (Landaburu and Piñeda Camacho 1984: 27, translation mine). Although the trade in indigenous American slaves differed in many important ways from the massive African slave trade, both indigenous and Afro-American peoples suffered the same reduction to subhuman status in colonial America.[7]

Racist ideologies and practices against indigenous and Afro-American peoples buttressed the founding and expansion of Euramerican states in the colonial Americas. The common experiences of powerlessness, racial stereotypification, enslavement, and marginalization among indigenous and Afro-American peoples occasionally found historical expression in sociopolitical unification of escaped Afro-American slaves and resistant indigenous peoples. The Seminole Confederation of northern Florida is perhaps the most well documented case of such unification through resistance (see Sattler, this volume).[8] However, in the context of overwhelming Euramerican military force and material wealth, indigenous and Afro-American peoples more commonly found themselves internally fragmented and divided against each other in the service of colonial domination. The colonial powers bribed indigenous peoples to enslave other indigenous peoples from interior regions and hired indigenous mercenaries to prevent Afro-American slaves from escaping from coastal plantations into remote interior forests (see Whitehead, this volume). Ironically, the colonizers were even successful at obtaining the loyalty of Afro-American Maroons in military campaigns against other Maroons (see Bilby, this volume). In the colonial period, Euramericans created a Hobbesian "war of all against all" in which strategic considerations of military power and economic forces of material profit more often than not outweighed crosscutting ties based on resistance to domination.

In a 1991 study of Asháninka uprisings in the lowlands of eastern Peru,

Michael Brown and Eduardo Fernandez documented a complex variation on the interethnic relations that developed between indigenous and Afro-American peoples during the colonial period. During the early eighteenth century, Franciscan missionaries brought Afro-American slaves into their Amazonian mission settlements to serve as military defenders against indigenous attacks and uprisings. Black freedmen served as leaders of reprisal raids against rebellious Asháninka bowmen. When a major uprising began under the leadership of Juan Santos de Atahualpa in 1742, Afro-American freedmen and slaves switched their allegiance to the Asháninka. Many of Juan Santos's indigenous followers wanted to execute these renegade slaves and freedmen, but Juan Santos overrode their sentiments in favor of the Afro-Americans' strategic value in military resistance against the Spanish.

> Although Juan Santos saw blacks as an oppressed people . . . , he also had to contend with their role as occasional killers of Indians. It was probably the tactical skills of blacks . . . that convinced Juan Santos to put aside his prejudices and welcome them to the rebellion. He could ill afford to spurn their knowledge of Spanish weapons and fighting techniques. (Brown and Fernandez 1991: 49)

Also, by the 1740s, several Afro-American freedmen who had lived in the missions for many years had taken Asháninka wives and had thus become affinal relatives of the Asháninka (Brown and Fernandez 1991: 48).

Juan Santos was an indigenous highlander from Cuzco and was thus well suited to fit the mythic role of King Inca in an Asháninka messianic movement. The alliance of indigenous and Afro-American peoples under his command was able to successfully resist Spanish military forays into the eastern lowlands during the 1740s and 1750s. However, Juan Santos's messianic movement never stabilized into long-term processes of ethnogenesis, since he mysteriously died and his movement had disappeared by the late 1750s. Nevertheless, the story of Juan Santos's brief rise to power in the 1740s demonstrates how Afro-American and indigenous peoples were able to overcome their mutual suspicions as well as the colonial forces that set them in adversarial relations.

In the interior regions of North and South America, away from the diaspora of enslaved and escaped Afro-American peoples in southern North America, the Caribbean Basin, and coastal South America, the late eighteenth century was a period of intensified geopolitical competition among waning colonial powers and major challenges to the survival of indigenous peoples. On the southern Plains of North America, the Jumano faced new political and economic pressures from the Apache, Comanche, and other southwestern peoples during the eighteenth century. In order to take advantage of French trade networks to the east and north, some Jumano groups formed new relations of trade with indigenous groups of the northern and central Plains (see Hickerson, this volume). These shifting patterns of interethnic relations and colonial power gave rise to the modern Kiowa.

In the interior of lowland South America, the eighteenth century was a period of massive depopulation among indigenous peoples who had survived the diseases and warfare of the sixteenth and seventeenth centuries. Portuguese slave traders removed an estimated 20,000 indigenous people from the Upper Rio Negro region in the 1740s and 1750s, and the campaign of forced relocations to downstream locations, called *descimentos* (descents), further weakened indigenous peoples of the Amazonian interior in the last half of the century. In response to these Portuguese expansions into headwater regions of the Amazon Basin, the Spanish sent military expeditions and missionaries from the Andean highlands and the northern lowlands. As Spanish and Portuguese forces vied for control over the Upper Rio Negro region and its indigenous inhabitants, Arawakan peoples temporarily abandoned their ancestral lands along the Rio Negro and its major tributaries in order to flee to the relative safety of remote headwater areas to the south and west. These migrations forced Arawakan peoples to develop new ties of trade and alliance with the eastern Tukanoan peoples of the Vaupés River (see Hill, this volume). In the process, both Arawakan and Tukanoan peoples were forced to develop new forms of sociolinguistic and political organization, and new ethnolinguistic groups came into being along the boundary between Arawakan and Tukanoan territories.

The Rise of Independent States and the Geopoliticization of Indigenous American Identities

The essays in this volume build upon a number of recent studies that have broken away from past notions of indigenous American peoples as a conglomeration of static, isolated societies that were totally unequipped to deal with the massive changes set in motion during the colonial period (see, for example, Turner 1988; Whitten 1985, 1988; Wright and Hill 1986; Hill 1988; Whitehead and Ferguson 1992). In his anthropological vision of global history, Eric Wolf (1982) cleared the way for the emergence of critical historical approaches to ethnogenesis by replacing the earlier anthropological concept of precolonial America as a collection of isolated cultures, or "billiard balls," with a more sophisticated understanding of widespread regional systems of trade, warfare, and interethnic alliances. More recently, Whitehead and Ferguson (1992) advanced the concept of "tribal zone" as a sphere of interaction in which state-level expansion reduces multilingual, multicultural regional networks to territorially discrete, culturally and linguistically homogeneous "tribes." South Americanists replaced the Lévi-Straussian notion of Amerindian societies as "cold," "mythic," and ahistorical with a number of case studies demonstrating that indigenous Amazonian and Andean peoples had already formulated dynamic ways of understanding their historical pasts and that they were capable of transforming these indigenous modes of historical interpretation into coherent understandings of Europeans and their alien forms of disease, technology, and governance (Hill 1988). The essays in the present volume on ethnogenesis in the Americas continue in these recent and ongoing historical approaches and broaden them to include parallel developments in North Americanist and Afro-Americanist studies.

In the context of this growing rapprochement between anthropology and history that has so strenuously argued against linear, oppositional models of interethnic relations between states and indigenous (or Afro-American) minorities, the editors of a recent book entitled *Nation-States and Indians in Latin America* (Urban and Sherzer 1992) have resurrected the ahistorical notion of a fundamental contrast between "isolated Indian populations" and "ethnic groups." "Indians within Latin America can be located on a continuum from isolated, uncontacted Indian populations to full-fledged ethnic groups, on a par with other recognized ethnic groups within the nation-state" (Urban and Sherzer 1992: 5). This manner of setting up the issue brings back to life older dichotomies, such as traditional versus modern or pristine versus acculturated, under the new terminology of isolated Indian population versus ethnic group. Ethnicity, and hence also ethnogenesis and ethnocide, only comes into being after isolated Indian populations have become situated within states as interest groups that to some degree "accede to state sovereignty" (Urban and Sherzer 1992: 4). This linear model, or continuum, is intrinsically ahistorical and contributes to the reification of "Indians" as a category of peoples existing outside state-level political organizations and "ethnic groups" as indigenous peoples who have given up their cultural identities in proportion to the degree that they have accepted citizenship within Euro-American states. Extrapolating from this linear model of change back to precolonial times, the Americas appear as a checkerboard dotted with a myriad of isolated Indian populations (i.e., Wolf's billiard balls) which only came to develop a higher level of historical and ethnic consciousness through being incorporated into European or Euramerican states. Even a cursory reading of Albers's essay on the northeastern Plains of North America, Whitehead's account of colonial Surinam, Hickerson's essay on Kiowa ethnogenesis, or Hill's essay on northwestern Amazonia is sufficient to cast great doubt on the notion that precolonial America consisted of such isolated Indian populations. The concept of isolated Indian populations more faithfully reflects a Europocentric historical perspective on the Americas than the vast multilingual, multicultural regional networks that had developed prior to the Europeans' arrival in the Americas.

A typologizing model that starts out from the assumption of a basic dichotomy between isolated Indian populations and ethnic groups cannot be transformed at a later stage into a fully historical understanding of cultural identities, no matter how much special pleading to the effect that "none of the terms in our title, Indians, nation-states, and culture, are monolithic and static categories, but dynamic, in that they are constantly changing and adapting" (Urban and Sherzer 1992: 12). Urban and Sherzer recognize the fact that nation-state is a culturally specific concept of political organization that has an ambivalent relationship to cultural differences. They are also fully aware of the artificiality of the category "Indian": "Until the arrival of Europeans, there were no 'Indians.' The concept is a European invention" (1992: 12). However, just when Urban and Sherzer approach the brink of addressing the relations between states and indigenous peoples in a more complex, historical manner, they revert back to asserting that "a most fruitful way to conceive of the emergent quality of nation-state and Indian relationships is in terms of a continuum from Indian population to ethnic group" (1992: 12–13).

If such terms as "nation-states" and "Indians" are merely artificial European inventions, then why do the editors insist on preserving and promoting these terms not only in the title but as analytical concepts underpinning their theoretical model? One possible answer is that the promotion of a linear, dichotomous model of Indians and nation-states allowed the editors to circumvent the more challenging task of questioning relations of power as these have historically developed within and among indigenous American societies and in their interethnic relations with expanding European and Euramerican states. To do so would reveal the categorical term "Indian" to be not only a European invention but one that was, and still is, part of a broader process of symbolically removing indigenous American peoples from their histories and reducing them to stereotypic symbols of isolation and alienation from the colonial and independent states of the Americas.

Looking at the other end of the continuum, or ethnic groups situated within the state, the dichotomous model supports the dangerous misunderstanding that cultural differences among indigenous peoples are "potentially threatening to the sovereign jurisdiction of the state" (Urban and Sherzer 1992: 12). How and why such cultural differences pose a threat to state sovereignty are not even raised as questions, much less answered. Colonial and independent states in the Americas have always and everywhere encompassed a diversity of indigenous and other ethnic groups, and history provides no examples of this diversity threatening state sovereignty (although examples of the converse abound). By the end of the colonial period and the rise of independent states in the late eighteenth to early nineteenth centuries, indigenous American peoples had been so marginalized and demographically reduced that they could hardly be seen as a threat to state sovereignty. In the United States, the nineteenth century saw the reduction of 600,000 indigenous Americans to only 250,000 by 1900. "Meanwhile, the non-Indian population of the U.S. increased from about 5 million in 1800 to about 63 million in 1890 to over 75 million in 1900" (Thornton 1987: 133). How could anyone perceive a mere quarter of a million indigenous survivors of the Great Dying, divided into separate peoples and widely separated territories at the peripheries of Euramerican political power, as a threat to national sovereignty in such historical contexts?[9]

Population figures for indigenous peoples of lowland South America were comparable to those in North America during the nineteenth century. The total indigenous population in 1800 for all areas of what was soon to become the republic of Venezuela had fallen to a mere 258,000, a number which posed no real threat to the predominantly European, Afro-American, and mestizo majority (Grau 1987: 64–66). Throughout the northern lowlands of South America, the War of Independence and subsequent rise of independent liberal states created a power vacuum in which large landowners and mestizo colonists expanded into indigenous territories which the Catholic Church had formerly protected and managed. In the nineteenth century, the expansion of national states into the northern lowlands overwhelmed indigenous peoples in coastal and llano areas or forced them to seek refuge in inaccessible forests or across international borders. These marginalized groups of people lost their communal lands under new national laws mandating privatization of land ownership. Such refugees can only be understood as isolated Indian populations whose continued existence is "potentially threatening to the sovereign jurisdiction of the state" by removing them from the histories of colonial and national state expansion that originally produced their contemporary situations.

The danger of using ahistorical, linear models that dichotomize nation-states and Indians becomes even more apparent when its terms are applied to the contemporary political struggles of indigenous peoples in the Americas. In discussing indigenous rights movements in Latin America and the efforts of international organizations such as IWGIA, Survival International, and Cultural Survival to assist indigenous peoples, Urban and Sherzer assert that "the attempt by the Indians and their supporters is to deny one of the pillars of the state, namely, its autonomy with respect to other states" (1992: 9). This way of characterizing indigenous struggles for control over their lands and other resources is most unfortunate, since it attributes seditious motives to both the members of the movements and their international supporters.[10] Instead of aiming "to deny one of the pillars of the state," a more reasonable understanding of the aims of international groups supporting indigenous peoples in the Americas is that they are concerned with creating political spaces within the state which allow indigenous peoples to regain control over their lands and local forms of social organization and thus to have some measure of control over the manner in which they articulate themselves with national and international political orders.

From their very inception during the Wars of Independence in North and South America, the founders of liberal Euramerican states perceived indigenous peoples as potential equals only if they could be educated and brought into direct relations with Americans of European descent. The European concept of nation-state placed indigenous American peoples into a double bind. On the one hand, the liberal state promised civil and legal equality to all citizens within its borders. On the other hand, the rationalist, assimilationist, and individualist nature of this promised equality was extremely hostile to the older colonial policy of granting collective land rights to indigenous peoples as well as to the continuation of indigenous modes of economic production and social organization that had survived into or emerged during the colonial period. The rise of independent liberal states in the Americas placed indigenous peoples into contradictory social statuses: full citizens who received equal rights and lawless savages who must be educated and assimilated into the social life of the state.

The new nationalist rhetoric masked older colonial beliefs in the racial and cultural inferiority of indigenous and other non-European peoples. The principal architect of Latin American democracy, Simón Bolívar, was aware of the sociocultural diversity within Gran Colombia, but ultimately the Great Liberator himself could not transcend the racist stereotyping of indigenous and African Americans so common in the early nineteenth century. "These gentlemen have not cast their vision over the Caribs of the Orinoco, over the pastoralists of Apure, over the sailors of Maracaibo, over the merchants of Magdalena, over the bandits of Patia, over the indomitable Pastusos, over the Guahibos of the Casanare, and over all the savage hordes from Africa and America who, like male fallow deer, traverse the solitudes of Colombia" (letter from Simón Bolívar to General Santander, June 13, 1821; quoted in Grau 1987: 114, translation mine). Thus, even as the new republics gave official recognition to the equality of all their citizens, they remained rooted in colonialist ideologies of racial hierarchy that placed whites of European descent at the pinnacle of enlightened reason and African and indigenous Americans into a category of brutish "savage hordes." Throughout the nineteenth century, such racist ideologies and the political turmoil of the postwar period permeated the struggles among competing nation-states for control over remote border areas and their indigenous inhabitants.

The rise of independent states in the Americas failed to create a political space for indigenous peoples to survive and prosper as citizens within the jurisdiction of state sovereignty and as ethnic groups who were culturally and linguistically different. In their vision of democracy, the founders of American states saw no place for indigenous peoples except as remnants of a vanishing past (McGuire 1992). The primary reason for this institutionalized blindness toward indigenous American peoples was the adoption of the European concept of nation-state as the model for state formation and expansion in the Americas.

In a recent article called "The Nations of a State," Edward Spicer (1992) argued that the term *nation-state* is a misnomer insofar as the ideal model of a monolingual, culturally homogeneous, territorially bounded state has never existed, not even among the Europeans, who invented the nation-state concept and who unleashed it on the Americas and the rest of the world. With the possible exception of the tiny state of Denmark, modern European states emerged after the Renaissance through the rise of specific ethnic groups, or "nations," to positions of political and economic dominance over a plurality of other ethnic groups within bounded political territories (Spicer 1992: 33). The term "nation-state" obscures the internal cultural and linguistic diversity of states that could more accurately be called "conquest states."

> What remained hidden from the makers of state policy was that these peoples were living cultural lives of their own, that they had developed languages, or even that they spoke anything worthy to be called a language. . . . Either, it came to be believed, the subordinated peoples were inherently inferior or they might demonstrate their worthiness as human beings by discarding their outworn ways and becoming like the dominant peoples. (Spicer 1992: 29)

Spicer's approach offers a general vision of the dialectical articulations between ethnic homogenization and differentiation within conquest states, or the ongoing tensions between state-level ideologies asserting control over indigenous and other ethnic minorities through cultural assimilation and the potential resurgence of a plurality of unique ethnic groups within the borders of a single state. Cultural differentiation among ethnic groups is not "potentially threatening to the sovereign jurisdiction of the state" (Urban and Sherzer 1992: 12). Rather, the assertion of cultural differences threatens to reveal ethnocentric, racist beliefs and practices upon which conquest states were historically founded and thus to open up the possibility for a "nations-state" in which conquered and conquering ethnic groups enjoy equal rights without the threat of ethnocide or cultural assimilation into the dominant ethnic group.

As independent states expanded across the Americas in the nineteenth century, the European concept of nation-state informed state policies toward indigenous peoples at local and regional levels, resulting in a cultural landscape of relatively fixed ethnic, or tribal, groups. This process of tribalization (Whitehead and Ferguson 1992), or the geopoliticization of indigenous American cultural identities, was already in evidence during the colonial period in regions of sustained contact between European and indigenous American peoples. In the course of the nineteenth century, geopoliticization of indigenous cultural identities extended into regions that had continued to develop as multilingual, multicultural patterns of trade, warfare, and alliance during the colonial period.

The process of simplifying complex regional systems of interethnic overlappings, alliances, and mergers was clearly illustrated during the frontier expansion of Euramericans in the Great Plains of the United States and Canada. In the region north of the Missouri River, Cree, Ojibwa, and Assiniboin peoples entered into many different types of interethnic formation during the eighteenth and early nineteenth centuries. These shifting alliances were based in part on warrior societies that allowed Cree, Ojibwa, and Assiniboin peoples great flexibility in ecological adaptation to Plains resources as well as historical accommodation to changing economic patterns of European and U.S. trade (see Albers, this volume). Only after U.S. and Canadian military campaigns and subsequent treaties during the 1860s and 1870s did ethnonyms such as Cree and Ojibwa become concretized and associated with specific territories. As late as the early twentieth century, however, many Cree, Ojibwa, Assiniboin, and other indigenous peoples in northern Montana and North Dakota still remained officially "landless" (i.e., without official trust status in the United States) "because their hybridized ethnic backgrounds and identities did not match the picture of the policymakers, which was based largely on a notion of tribal blocs with exclusive memberships and territories" (Albers, this volume). The picture referred to here is that of the European concept of nation-state, and what was left out of that picture was the tremendous fluidity and sheer magnitude of interethnic relations among culturally and linguistically differentiated indigenous peoples.[11]

Although the nation-state model shaped official policies toward indigenous American peoples during the nineteenth century, these official discourses and practices often masked underlying currents of interethnic complexity that contained the seeds for long-term historical renewal and the emergence of new multilingual regional networks. Among the Makushi, Kapon, Pemon, and other Carib-speaking peoples of British Guiana and southeastern Venezuela, revitalization movements emerged during the 1840s and 1850s in the aftermath of massive dislocations and other traumatic changes during the War of Independence. With the end of African slavery in the British colony and the immigration of large numbers of South Asian peoples into coastal areas, indigenous Carib-speaking peoples of the interior lost the strategic significance they had had during the colonial period (Whitehead 1990a). The British continued the system of Dutch Postholders in the interior but greatly reduced the scale of gift giving to indigenous leaders (Menezes 1977). Meanwhile, Brazilian merchants backed by groups of armed thugs invaded Makushi settlements from the south and relocated some indigenous communities as forced laborers in agricultural projects along the Rio Branco. In this context of marginalization and geopoliticization, the Makushi and neighboring indigenous peoples created the Alleluia religion, both as a means of resisting Anglican missionaries and as a process of reconstituting a multilingual, regional network among Carib-speaking peoples of the Guiana Shield (see Staats, this volume). As the title of Staats's essay so aptly phrases the issue, "fighting in a different way" has continued to serve as a vital means for building communities and opposing the ethnocidal effects of gold mining, hydroelectric dam construction, fundamentalist North American missionizing, and other manifestations of late-twentieth-century state expansion.

1992 and the Struggles to Recapture the Historical Past

The double bind of equality at the expense of cultural identity that became concretized into nation-state policies during the rise and expansion of independent states in the Americas continues to engulf indigenous and Afro-American peoples in the late twentieth century. In contemporary Venezuela, Afro-Americans from the community of Curiepe have attempted to reassert their cultural identity within the state by giving recognition to the military importance of black freedmen and escaped slaves during the War of Independence (see Guss, this volume). What the people of Curiepe are trying to achieve is an alternative perspective on history that allows Afro-Venezuelans to have ethnic identities within a national context that denies the existence, much less the value, of such Afro-American identities. Official state ideology masks racial and cultural heterogeneity through "the myth of racial democracy," creating "a double bind situation wherein despite racial discrimination, blacks were unable to articulate it as the very category responsible, for this oppression was not recognized" (Guss, this volume; Wright 1990). Any individuals or groups who challenge this official ideology of racial democracy are quickly labeled political troublemakers: "if race did not exist as a recognizable category in this colorblind society, then all who spoke of it must be either foreign or subversive" (Guss, this volume). The dilemma of Afro-Americans in Venezuela is nearly identical to that of indigenous peoples who are caught between the twin ideologies of equality and the denial of racial and cultural differences within the state.[12]

As Guss points out, the people of Curiepe have been doubly removed from their ancestral African cultures, since the majority of Afro-Americans in Venezuela are descended from slaves brought from islands throughout the Caribbean or escaped slaves who sought refuge on the mainland. Faced with a doubly challenging task of recapturing their history, the people of Curiepe have appropriately chosen a double-stranded strategy of revitalizing African musical traditions and elevating the historical figure of Negro Primero, an Afro-American who gave his life in the War of Independence. This historical symbolism neatly finesses the charge that Afro-American cultural identity is subversive or threatening to national sovereignty by integrating African cultural origins with the political struggles that gave rise to the modern Venezuelan state.

In contemporary Ecuador, the leaders of indigenous and Afro-American social movements are seeking to move out of their state-defined statuses as marginalized, inferior peoples through "counterideologies . . . that seek to spark recognition of the falsity of the hypostatic ideological racialist structures [of the state]" (Whitten, this volume). In the confrontational arena of social opposition to the racial hierarchy of nation-state structure, indigenous demands for self-determination are met with official discourses portraying the movements as unruly behavior (*alzamiento*) that threatens national sovereignty. As Whitten correctly observes, the flurry of racist and racialist accusations against the indigenous rebirth (*levantamiento*) obscures the fact that the movement does not threaten national sovereignty but seeks to unmask the ahistorical, racist, and racialist ideologies that have placed indigenous and Afro-American peoples below and outside of the Euramerican dominated state. Again, the movements are not about "denying one of the pillars of the state" or "threatening the sovereign jurisdiction of the state" (Urban and Sherzer 1992) but about the creation of political spaces, or nations, within the state that allow people a degree of control over their lands and local forms of sociopolitical organization. This goal was made explicit in the Ecuadorian Levantamiento Indígena of 1990 by the indigenous leaders' demands for a constitutional change to designate Ecuador as a multinational, multiethnic state and by their consistent usage of "indigenous nationalities" as a term of self-reference. Their movement aimed at raising the possibility of a new kind of state, a nations-state instead of a nation-state, and the regaining of indigenous self-determination that had been progressively weakened by five centuries of colonial and national domination.

In the context of this politically charged resurgence of indigenous Ameri-

can ethnic identities, the 500th anniversary of European domination over indigenous and Afro-American peoples has taken on new symbolic meanings.
"Después de 500 años de dominación, autodeterminación en 1992!" [After
500 years of domination, self-determination in 1992!] (Whitten, this volume).
In the indigenous *levantamiento*, 1992 emerged as an epitomizing symbol for
the struggle to break out of static, racialist categories and to carve out new
spaces for indigenous and Afro-American peoples within the mainstream of
Ecuadorian political culture, no longer down and outside but up and inside.
1992 as epitomizing symbol is a symbolically overdetermined, historical metaphor for "the idea of people remaking the world and being in a world refashioned from the conquered one that the European 'discovery' . . . of 1492 began" (Whitten, this volume).

Drawing upon Comaroff's ethnography (1985) of African resistance to
colonial domination, Whitten interprets the recent indigenous and Afro-
American movements in Ecuador as "an unending struggle to take possession
of the sign" (Whitten, this volume). It is no coincidence that both indigenous
and Afro-American peoples have chosen to focus their political struggles on
history. For indigenous Americans, this semiotic struggle over history focuses
on 1992 as a metaphor for half a millennium of conquest, depopulation, enslavement, and marginalization as well as for the movement to transform this
symbol of ethnocidal losses into the creation of new ethnic identities that are
not vanishing from the Americas but reasserting their places in history. For
Afro-American peoples, the histories of escaped slaves and freedmen hold
profound significance as models of ethnogenesis in opposition to the brutally
racist, dehumanizing historical roots of the American states. To build communities such as Curiepe or the Maroon societies of Jamaica and Surinam in
the context of such institutionalized racism provides a metaphor for the resil-
ience and spontaneous creativity of Afro-American peoples.

The power to control and define the historical past is perhaps the ultimate
form of hegemony. Historicide, or the removal of peoples from their histories,
is radically disempowering because it obscures the historical processes that
have produced the racial hierarchies that prevail in the Americas today.

> Each nation-state saw itself in the center of the stage of history, and chronicles
> were written accordingly. As dominant peoples continued to write from this
> viewpoint, they became less and less able to discern the presence, even in
> their immediate theater of history, of any other peoples besides themselves,
> except as temporary obstacles to their own dominance, as disappearing rem-
> nants, or as persisting, backward peoples unworthy to be regarded as in the
> same category with the dominant nation. The standardization of history was a
> destructive process, eliminating from the sphere of historical knowledge hun-

dreds of peoples who, equally with the dominant peoples, had histories. It was more destructive than was the standardization of language, because it removed from general view cultural wholes, not just one aspect of a culture. (Spicer 1992: 43–44)

To successfully resist ongoing systems of domination, racial or ethnic stereotyping, and cultural hegemony, the first necessity of disempowered peoples, or of marginalized subcultural groups within a national society, is that of constructing a shared understanding of the historical past that enables them to understand their present conditions as a result of their own ways of making history.

The essays making up this volume cover a broad range of indigenous South American, Afro-American, and indigenous North American peoples in historical periods ranging from early colonial times to the present.[13] Like this introductory essay, I have chosen to organize the essays in a roughly chronological sequence from the early colonial period, through the rise of independent states in the Americas in the nineteenth century, to contemporary processes of ethnogenesis. This ordering of the essays is designed to stimulate a comparative, hemispheric understanding of ethnogenesis that transcends the divisions of cultural anthropologists into geographic areas of specialization. Also, a chronological ordering of essays more faithfully reflects the intrinsic historicity of ethnogenesis than an arrangement based on spatial proximity.

Notes

1. For a review of this literature, see Whitten (in press).

2. This approach to ethnogenesis builds upon Sider's recent definition of ethnohistory as "a name for struggles over the production and distribution of culture and, simultaneously, the existence of a people" (1994: 115). Sider's article grew out of a paper which was originally presented at the 1992 AAA session "Ethnogenesis in the Americas" in San Francisco and would have made an excellent contribution to this volume. Unfortunately, when I solicited the manuscript in early 1993, Sider had already submitted it to *Identities* for review.

3. Researchers investigating global and local power, transnational migration, and diasporas are grappling with this same problem of overcoming the tendency to work within implicit dichotomies between a "dynamic core" and a "static periphery." Tsing warns that "our analytic tools for studying global processes lead us back into the very dichotomy that we used them to try to escape: the division between a complex and transcontinentally active core and a static, locally bounded periphery. In the grip of this dichotomy, some places appear to generate the global, while other places seem stuck in the local. . . . With these dichotomies,

we can neither fully localize the concerns of European-origin peoples nor appreciate the global impact of the agency of non-Europeans" (1994: 282).

4. In his 1994 article, Sider lists "the increasing intensification of internal, 'factional' differentiation within post-contact native political communities ('nations,' 'tribes,' or 'towns') as one of five 'processes of differentiation and antagonistic separation.' . . . This differentiation often led either to civil war within the political community or to the formation of separate, 'new' political and cultural entities: for example, the Seminole emergence from a segment of the Creek—a segment that in part formed over irresolvable differences in strategies for coping with White domination" (Sider 1994: 110–111).

5. The population figures cited in this essay have been the subject of numerous debates. Whether to cite higher and lower estimates of precolonial population is irrelevant to the present essay, since there is no debate among serious scholars that proportions of the overall indigenous populations of North and South America lost during the colonial period were in the range of 90 to 95 percent.

6. Population rebounded in North America between 1900 and 1980, from .25 up to 1.4 million (Thornton 1987: 159 ff.). Unfortunately, the population of lowland South American peoples has not yet begun to rise, except in a few isolated cases.

7. It is important to note that not only African and indigenous American but also conquered European peoples were forced to enter the Americas as slave laborers during the colonial period. Under Cromwell's regime in the mid–seventeenth century, for example, several thousands of Irish Catholics, "including women and children, were transported to Barbados, Jamaica, and the mainland colonies. . . . in 1667 an account of Barbados described the Irish there as 'poor men, that are just permitted to live, . . . derided by the Negroes, and branded with the Epithite of white slaves'" (Miller 1985: 143–144).

8. Other examples include Chickasaw (Littlefield 1980a) and Cherokee (Littlefield 1980b) freedmen of North America and the black Carib. For a comparison of black Seminole and black Carib, see Bateman (1990).

9. Even in cases where several large ethnic groups compete for control over state power, as in the former Yugoslavia today, it is erroneous to argue that ethnic differences in any way cause conflict or threaten state sovereignty. In such tragedies, ethnic differences are used by the perpetrators of violence as attempts to rationalize or justify their actions, which are really motivated by political and economic factors.

10. For an illustration of how a Latin American military establishment accused indigenous rights groups of an international conspiracy aimed at undermining national sovereignty, see my analysis of the Piaroa land dispute of 1984 (Hill 1989) and its interrelations with a broader, hemispheric military process of enemy construction (Hill 1994).

11. Reinforcing one of the central themes of this volume, Albers also notes that earlier anthropological studies of indigenous Americans were formulated within the worldview of the nation-state "picture," and "it was customary to view

prestate regions as little more than epiphenomenal extensions of their autono-mous pieces" (Albers, this volume). Albers lists the culture area approach (Wissler 1927) and Steward's culture type perspective (1955) as examples of anthropologi-cal theories that have tended to reify tribal "puzzle pieces." Urban and Sherzer's "isolated Indian populations" also belongs on this list.

12. In an article called "The Selling of San Juan: The Performance of History in an Afro-Venezuelan Community," Guss (1993) explains that the comparison of the indigenous movement in Venezuela became part of a conscious strategy of cultural resurgence in the late 1980s. In part this strategy was stimulated by the film *Yo hablo a Caracas*, "a dramatic appeal by the Ye'kuana Indians to have their land and culture respected. . . . The language included in the *Culture Week* [in Curiepe] borrowed heavily from the indigenist literature just starting to circulate at that time" (Guss 1993: 461).

13. The majority of the essays were originally presented as papers in a 1992 session organized by John Moore and Norman Whitten on "Ethnogenesis in the Americas" at the annual meetings of the American Association for the Advance-ment of Science. A subsequent session on "Ethnogenesis in the Americas," orga-nized by Jonathan Hill at the annual meetings of the American Anthropological Association in 1992, contained later versions of some authors' papers. In addition, I invited Whitehead, Staats, and Guss to submit in early 1993.

Neil Lancelot Whitehead

Ethnogenesis and Ethnocide in the European Occupation of Native Surinam, 1499–1681

On the broad canvas of the native history of the Americas the Guianas region presents a number of social situations and cultural innovations that are relatively rare in other areas and often unfamiliar in the contemporary ethnography. Significant political contrasts between the trading-plantation settlements made by the Dutch, English, and French in this region and the territorial and evangelical ambitions of the Spanish and Portuguese in the rest of South America flow over into the relationships that were established between Amerindian leaders and the European colonizers, especially during the first century of contact (see also Whitehead 1993b).

The importance of these contrasting processes in Iberian and non-Iberian colonial occupation stems from the fact that such contrasts were critical to the ultimate survival, or destruction, of the different ethnic formations that were originally encountered in this area (see Whitehead 1992). By "ethnic formations" I mean to indicate the range of native political structures, economic systems, and cultural practices that went together to define the ethnicity of any particular group. By retaining this unitary framework for historical analysis it is possible to obviate various intractable theoretical problems as to sociopolitical typology, and we may then speak of the processes of ethnogenesis (and ethnocide), as well as the secondary phenomenon of tribalization (see Whitehead 1992). Moreover, this allows us to avoid the well-worn narrative trope of the clash of discrete, insulated "cultures," which produces a caricature of actual historical process and event. These historical processes of ethnic formation (ethnogenesis) thus involved Europeans, Africans, and Amerindi-

ans, and the groupings that emerged in the first decades of contact are therefore distinct from those that were initially encountered.

It was in reference to these new social formations, and in view of the demise
of earlier, precontact ones, that we may speak of ethnogenesis and ethnocide.
This fundamentally means that new group *identities* were created and old ones
fell into disuse, not necessarily that persons were themselves destroyed or
born. Although the question of the demographic impact of these processes is
obviously important (see Whitehead 1988 for a discussion of the Kariña case),
this essay is principally concerned with the historical context of how self-
representation and the definition of others work as synergetic processes for
the formation of group identity.

It has been proposed that the Guianas generally have formed a retreat area
for Amerindian groups that were threatened by the expansion of the Spanish
and Portuguese colonies to the south and north. While this is certainly the
case for the eighteenth century onward, it has been mistakenly assumed that
much the same can be said of the earlier period. In fact, much had already
changed among the Amerindians of this region between 1499 and 1681. Those
ethnic groups that we have come to know from the later colonial records and
more modern ethnographic accounts, such as the Carib, Arawak, Wayana,
Trio, and others, are not nearly so prominent in the sixteenth-century descriptions, if they are evident at all. This was only partly due to the fact that the
Europeans had an incomplete knowledge of the interior regions and relates as
much to the fact that the ethnic and cultural composition of native Surinam
has also undergone some 500 years of historical evolution. Just as the modern
states of Europe and the Americas are in some cases recent and unstable cre-
ations, so too the ethnic character of the peoples of modern Surinam have
emerged from earlier ethnic formations, and for this reason it is not possible
to simply project these modern ethnographic paradigms back into the past.
This consideration is underlined by the recent work on the human ecology of
Amazonia (Denevan 1992; Posey and Balée 1989; Roosevelt 1989).

It will be the purpose of this chapter to outline the historical conditions of
this transformation of native Surinam, a process that can be summarized as
resulting in a reduction of cultural variety and a general reorientation of native
political and economic systems toward the coast and away from the uplands
and their contacts with the Amazon Basin. As a result of these twin political
and economic pressures the range of ethnic self-ascription increasingly nar-
rowed into either Carib or Arawak identities or allegiances. At the same time
this process of indigenous identity re-formation was impacted by the direct
efforts of the European colonizers to actively promote stable ethnic groupings
with whom they could profitably interact, as in the use of Amerindians as a
mercenary military resource (Whitehead 1990a). Therefore, it will also be nec-

essary to look at the formation of Surinam as a European colony, since the distinctiveness of Surinam from the other Dutch colonies of the Atlantic Coast, Berbice and Essequibo, can in large part be attributed to differences in the relationships that developed with the native population in this early contact period, a point that colonial historians have overlooked when trying to explain such contrasts (Goslinga 1971: 420).

One further consequence of the complex nature of ethnogenesis and ethnocide in this region is an apparent lack of continuity between archaeological, historical, and ethnographic analyses of native societies. On the one hand, it is held that Surinam and the other Guianas were unfavorable environments for the development of effective agriculture, especially in the upland regions (Evans and Meggers 1960). But on the other hand, the contribution of foodstuffs by the Amerindians to the nascent colonies of the region was considerable, continuous, and critical to their eventual stability. Similarly, in the political sphere, without an appreciation of the past productivity of Amerindian agriculture, early descriptions of powerful chiefdoms in the Surinam region have been dismissed as the exaggerations of glory-seeking colonialists. Careful collation of a range of historical evidence suggests otherwise, however, and it is with descriptions of the earliest contacts along the Wild Coast, as the Atlantic littoral of the Guianas was first known, that our account of the ethnic transformation of native Surinam must begin.

First Contact: The Destructor Arrives

Although Columbus found his "Antilles," en route to Cathay in 1492, he did not reach the southern continent until 1498. It was 1499 before Vicente Yáñez Pinzón, who had accompanied Columbus on his first voyage, made the first report on the Wild Coast in the region of Surinam, saying that it was known to the natives as Paricora. This region had been sighted earlier in the year by the flotillas of Alonso de Hojeda and Amerigo Vespucci, but then, in the ominous words of Las Casas, "after Vicente Yáñez, another discoverer, or rather *destructor*, came out in the same month of December 1499 . . . Diego de Lepe" (1951, 2: 158, translation mine).

The low-lying mangrove coast of this part of northern South America offered no obvious haven or entrepôt for the further exploration of the interior. As a result, the discoveries taking place in the Caribbean and around its littoral sufficiently preoccupied the Europeans over the succeeding decades, and no settlement was attempted in this region. Indeed, the Amazon itself was virtually unknown until the 1540s, and the Orinoco was not occupied until the 1590s, despite its proximity to the prosperous colonies of the northern Venezuelan coast and Antilles.

As a result of these circumstances, our knowledge of the native societies of the region is largely intermittent for the first hundred years. But by the same token, the information dating from the 1590s onward illumines the character of a still autonomous native polity and economy as it grappled with the indirect effects of European occupations in the Caribbean and the southern littoral of Brazil, where the French, Dutch, and Portuguese were also active (see Whitehead 1993a). Nonetheless, the regional interconnections between native societies in the Guianas indicate that this was only a *relative* autonomy, and it should not be thought that the effects of European intrusion were not also manifest in the evolution of those groups on the periphery of initial contacts (Whitehead 1988: 73–81). Given the relatively late occupation of this region, the nature of the early European ethnology along the Wild Coast was often explicitly historical in character. This ethnographic interest was a direct result of the need to understand and cultivate native alliances in order to offset the existing Spanish presence in the Orinoco Basin and the Caribbean.

For the same reasons, Spanish historical sources are less ethnographically explicit, not just because the Spanish lacked an incentive to gather highly detailed information but also because they simply neglected to investigate this area. Nevertheless, the native regional links that connected the Amazon and Orinoco Basins, via the Rupununi savannas in the east and the Casiquiare watershed in the west, meant that at least diplomatic relations were necessary with the more eminent chiefs, known as *adumasi*, of the Wild Coast (Whitehead 1994). Such relationships were critical to Spanish efforts in settling the northern coast of Venezuela because of the role of the *adumasi* in supplying foodstuffs to the booming pearl fisheries on Margarita and the realization that native economic and political systems spread far into the interior of the continent.

It is probably because of its importance in these regional trade links that the river Surinam was so named by the Amerindians. In the language of the Karipuna (Island Carib), who habitually raided the *aruacas* (Arawak) for *caracoli* (golden artifacts), Sulinama was the country and river which gave access to the Amazon (Goeje 1931–1932: 519), as it was also a manufacturing site for the famous Amazon-stones, or *takua* (Boomert 1987: 40–41). This upland link to the Amazon Basin was also well known to the early Dutch traders, such as Amos van Groenewegen and Hendrickson, "merchants in those parts 27 years in quality a factor, with the upland Indians of Guiana" (Harlow 1925: 133). Dutch traders also participated in the exchange of steel tools for gold ornaments, using Surinam as their entrepôt (Purchas 1906: 409). This was probably managed with the Manoa of the Rio Negro acting as intermediaries for the sources of Amazon gold as far as the Rupununi savannas, the trade then being taken up by the Arawak (probably the Lokono) to the east and into Surinam proper (Edmundson 1906; Whitehead 1990a). This strategic position in a regional network of elite exchange was an economic basis for the political power of the Lokono *adumasi* in the early colonial era. Such interconnections over the Guiana Shield were quickly exploited by English, Irish, and Dutch traders from both the Guiana coast and Amazon Basin. For the Spanish the limited nature of this trade was outweighed by the search for military achievement and easy wealth in Peru and Colombia. Nonetheless, it is from the Spanish sources that the first direct and substantive information concerning the Amerindians of the Surinam region comes.

Information was first collected in 1519–20 for the Spanish crown by the *licenciado* Figueroa which vaguely indicated that *aruacas* were widely settled on the Wild Coast to the south of Orinoco. Some thirty years later, this region was more clearly described by Martin Lopez and again in the period 1560 to 1575 by Juan de Salas, Antonio Barbudo, and Rodrigo de Navarrete. These accounts relate that the Corentyn River formed the eastern limits of this Provincia de los Aruacas and describe a distinctly organized stratified group with a highly productive subsistence base. Rodrigo de Navarrete wrote that "it is well known that in their country no want of provision is felt [and] at the end of [each] month . . . two thousand loads of *Cacabi* [cassava bread] can be supplied, each load being more than two *arrobas* [= 50 lb./23 kg]. Thus they have frequently assisted us, and even at the present day they relieve the hunger of the people of that island [Margarita]" (CDI 1864–1885, 21: 221–239, translation mine). It is also noted that they grew maize and sweet potatoes, highlighting this use of an intensive agricultural system, reflected archaeologically in the form of various raised field and mound sites in ancestral Lokono territories (Boomert 1980; Versteeg 1985).

Aside from evidence of a highly productive economic base, there are strong indications that these *aruacas* operated a complex social system involving, for example, a shamanic elite, the Cemetu, who "recount the traditions and exploits of their ancestors and great men and also narrate what those ancestors heard from their forefathers . . . and in like manner they recount or preach about events relating to the heavens, sun, moon, and stars . . . Indeed, I consider that in many respects they are better acquainted with all those phenomena of nature, which the Christians hold in so much account, than we are" (CDI 1864–1885, 21: 225–226, translation mine).

Clearly, in a cultural sense, this group was ancestral to the Arawak (Lokono) of today. But the antiquity of the *aruaca* identity in this region is uncertain given both the contemporary testimony of the *aruacas*, as well as that of the Europeans. According to these accounts, "they came from the east in some ships, sailed all along that coast . . . and made friendship with the *caribes* that then possessed them. Noticing in time that the *caribes* were bad neighbors . . . they were against them, and after long and bloody wars succeeded from driving them out of the rivers [in the east] and remaining masters of the country, firmly establishing themselves therein" (CDI 1864–1885, 21: 222–223, translation mine).

The Europeans certainly played a role in this process, especially in the Essequibo and Surinam region, and so it should be appreciated, as in the case of the *caribes*, that even these early *aruacas* are not a simple equivalent of the Lokono of today. As the origin histories of the modern Lokono make clear (Im Thurn 1883: 175–186), they represent an alliance of clans and lineages, such as the Neekeari, Sceawani, and Panapi. These lineages differed somewhat in their natal language, as well as in their political orientations toward both each other and the Europeans. In this light a significant force for their unity as *aruacas*, under Lokono leadership, as paralleled by the *caribes* under Kariña leadership, was the profitable economic and political relations that the Lokono *adumasi* engineered with the Europeans. In short, the *adumasi* of the Lokono were among the most successful leaders in negotiating the pitfalls of the alien political conditions that the Europeans had created. More obdurate, or less pliant, groups such as the Yao, Suppoyo, Nepoyo, and Paragoto, despite their early importance in native political life, were eclipsed first by Spanish support for the *aruacas* and then by Dutch, French, and English alliances with both the *aruacas* and *caribes* (Whitehead 1990a, 1992).

Further complicating the identification of ethnic continuities between historic Amerindian groups and those in modern Surinam were cultural connections with the Arawakan groups of the Antilles, as well as this rise of the *caribes* as a significant native political force. Cultural connections to the Antilles are shown in the fact that the Arawakan Karipuna, referred to as Ipaio (i.e., "islanders" from Dominica), as well as Carepini in the early sources, were settled from the region of the Corentyn to the Malmanoury River in French Guiana. This has in itself considerably complicated the certain identification of Cariban groups, since the similarity of the name Carepini to *caribe* means that the early European sources often fail to distinguish this group from the Kariña. Further compounding these errors of identification, later sources, including modern ethnography, have perpetuated this confusion by referring to the Karipuna as Island Carib, which they certainly were not (see Whitehead 1995).

At the same time, the *caribes*, under Kariña leadership, developed extensive trade partnerships with the Europeans, thereby becoming very influential in the native economy, bringing many smaller or less well positioned ethnic groups, such as the Arawakan Karipuna, into dependent relationships, giving them their character as *caribes* (Whitehead 1988). The overall result of the interplay of these factors was that the Europeans lost sight of the more subtle ethnic distinctions between Amerindian groups, tending to lump all groups together as either *aruacas* or *caribes*. In this way both native self-ascription and the ethnological definitions generated by European colonialism worked together to cement the contrasting identities of *aruaca* and *caribe* into the native political networks of the whole northern South America region.

Since the Karipuna from the Caribbean islands straddled this tidy European distinction, by virtue of their Arawakan linguistic and cultural base but *caribe* political and military orientation, they became known as the Island Carib, notwithstanding the continued existence of satellite settlements on the mainland. But as the complexity of the foregoing explanation suggests, there is a continuing debate as to their role in the history of Amerindian politics in Surinam (see Allaire 1980; Boomert 1984, 1986, 1995; Hoff 1995; Whitehead 1995).

While the conflict of Carib (*caribes*) and Arawak (*aruacas*) has been an important narrative theme in the history of Surinam Amerindians, it cannot be simply equated with a conflict between Lokono and Kariña. Many other ethnic groups, now disappeared, were involved in this historical outcome, while the Europeans themselves exploited such emergent divisions among the Amerindians for their own purposes. As a result, the myriad of group identities referred to in the earliest accounts (e.g., Purchas 1906: 396) had all but disappeared by the middle of the seventeenth century, having been overshadowed by Spanish alliances with the *aruacas* in the sixteenth century.

One particularly good example of this process of ethnocide taking place in a context of regional ethnogenesis is the case of the Yao. According to the testimony of one of their chiefs, Wareo, reproduced by Lawrence Keymis,

> he was lately chased by the Spaniards from Moruca [River]; and that having burnt his own houses, and having destroyed his fruits and gardens, he had left his country to be possessed by the Arwaccas, who . . . for the most part serve and follow the Spaniards. He showed me that he was of the nation of Iaos, who are a mighty people and of late time were Lords of all the sea coast as far as Trinidad, which they likewise possessed. However, when the Spaniards first began to borrow some of their wives, they all agreed to change their habitation and do now live united for the most part towards the river of the Amazons. (1596: 4)

Some of these refugee Yao settled between the Cottica River and the mouth of the Maroni, where they formed towns with the Paragoto and Arawak. Although other Yao exiles were briefly dominant in the Oyapok region, both here and in Surinam they subsequently fade from the historical record. Whether this ethnic extinction was matched by a demographic one is unclear, as they may well have been absorbed as affines on one or the other side of the emergent Carib-Arawak hegemony. Whatever the case, their fate stands as a stark example of those processes of ethnocide and ethnogenesis that were occurring throughout the region at the start of the seventeenth century.

Trade and Settlement

The first traders and settlers in Surinam thus entered a complex political situation that was not resolved to the Europeans' satisfaction until the conclusion of the Indian War of 1681, which marked the definitive establishment of a Dutch Surinam.

In the interim, Surinam was the venue for intercolonial rivalry between the French, English, and Dutch. In these conflicts the Amerindians sometimes played a critical role as auxiliary troops (Whitehead 1990a), as they had done in consenting to settlement and trade in the first place. The Europeans soon realized that Lokono and Kariña leaders were particularly receptive to these purposes, and so, as mentioned above, it was they who came to dominate relations with the colonial authorities. Later in the seventeenth century this was to lead to formal treaties of peace and the exemption from slavery of those who participated in the Carib and Arawak identities. Those Amerindians that were not part of this status quo, such as the Paragoto and Suppoyo, tended to retreat from the coastal zone into the uplands, where their lack of a political connection to the European coastal zone meant they became the target of Arawak or Carib slavers supplying the burgeoning sugar plantations.

Until 1626 central Surinam was not a favored site for colonization within this coastal zone, the Oyapok, Cayenne, Maroni, Berbice, and Essequibo Rivers being preferred by the first Spanish, French, and English interlopers. In 1626, according to the manuscript of Major John Scott, a colony of some 500 men and women from La Rochelle was established on the Saramacca River but was deserted in 1629, "sickness falling amongst them and the Indians being troublesome." Ten years later the French returned to the Saramacca with nearly 400 persons, and although "they lived peaceably until the year 1642 . . . they grew careless, spread themselves to [the] Surinam [River] and Corentyn [River], had great differences with the Indians, and were all cut off in one day." Hard on the heels of this disaster, the English brought out a further 300 families in 1643 who settled on the Surinam, Saramacca, and Corentyn Rivers and "lived peaceably until the year 1645, at which time they espoused the quarrel of the French and were cut off by the natives." The French made one further attempt at settling the Saramacca, but the "greater part were cut off by the Careebs and Saepoyes [Suppoyo] Anno 1649" (Harlow 1925: 141, 142).

Contemporary with these efforts at the settlement of Surinam was the intermittent establishment of Dutch trading posts on the Surinam River, possibly entailing also some clearing of the land for sugar plantations on the Maroni and Commewine Rivers (Goslinga 1971: 419). It will easily be appreciated then that the disposition of the native population, as much physical as political, was a key element in the survival or destruction of these first colonies. By midcentury this was summarized by Scott as follows: "In Surinam, Commewine, Saramacca, Copename and Corentyn are about 5000 Careeb families, and there lives in Saramacca and the upper parts of Surinam about 1400 Turroomacs [Taruma] and up the Corentyn about 1200 Sapoyes. From the west side of Corentyn to Wina [Waini River] there live about 8000 families of Arawagoes, the best humoured Indians in America" (Harlow 1925: 137).

Although, as we have seen, the Suppoyo and Paragoto were still of some significance in the calculations of the colonizers, it is also evident that by this time the political preeminence of the Arawak and Carib had become well established. Accordingly, it is the development of adversarial identities between the Arawak and Carib which dominates native history in the latter part of the seventeenth century. It was in the context of Dutch and English rivalry over possession of the Surinam colony that the political and economic conditions were created for the emergence of relatively monolithic native power blocs under the control of coastal Arawak and Carib leaders.

As might be directly inferred from Scott's account of Amerindian settlement, the Carib were located far more extensively in Surinam than the Arawak. Yet it was the Arawak who were eventually to win the favor of the colonial authorities. The hostility of the Carib to almost all European settlement in their territories is evident enough from the successive failure of the various colonies up to the 1650s, and in fact this hostility never really ceased. Permanent settlement was only finally achieved as a result of the direct military and economic domination of the Carib population, facilitated by the military support of the Arawak from the Corentyn River.

In 1650, some 300 people were landed on the Surinam and Commewine Rivers under the command of Anthony Rowse, "a gentleman of great gallantry and prudence, and of long experience in the West Indies. His making a firm peace with the Indians soon after his landing, and reviving the name of Sir Walter Ralegh, gave the English firm footing in those parts, and it soon became a hopeful colony" (Harlow 1925: 142). According to Francis Willoughby, who initiated this colonization, "the gentleman which I sent [Rowse] hath brought with him to me two of the Indian kings, having spoken with several of them, who are willing to receive our nation, and that we should settle amongst them" (quoted in Williamson 1923: 153). Still extant in 1660, the English colony then adopted the name Willoughby-Land in recognition of Francis Willoughby's financial investment.

Despite this positive diplomatic beginning, contemporary descriptions of

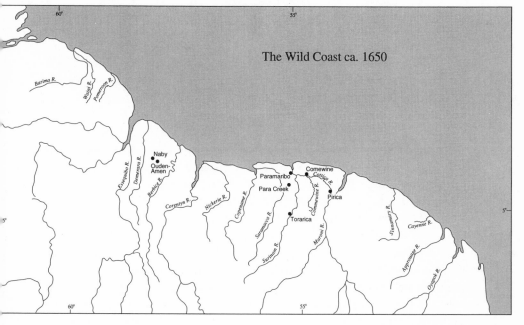

Figure 1. The Wild Coast, ca. 1650.

the English colony indicate that there was little cooperation from either side. Unlike the Arawak, who supplied the Spanish, the Carib appear to have given little assistance in fishing or hunting, while the upland groups remained altogether hostile (Warren 1667: 3–8). This is quite understandable in view of the English opinion of the Amerindians as "a People [who are] Cowardly and Treacherous, qualities inseparable" (Warren 1667: 23). Moreover, the economic orientation of the colony to sugar production meant that, in contrast to Essequibo, where direct trade with the Amerindians was the basis of a colonial economy, there was no real incentive to cultivate alliances with the Carib.

In 1665 Lord Willoughby himself arrived in the colony. "In the same year, and in the month of May, was this colony in its meridian, and after this month had its declination and went ever retrograde" (Harlow 1925: 199). This was caused by the first recorded epidemic in the colony, originating in the jointly settled European/Amerindian town of Torarica. Notwithstanding this and the "strange jealousies that possessed the inhabitants," various attacks were launched against the neighboring Dutch settlements on the Approuage, Pomeroon, and Essequibo in pursuance of the second Anglo-Dutch War of 1665–1667. Although a local neutrality was initially agreed between the French and

English, eventually the English were also ordered to attack the French at the Sinnamary and Cayenne Rivers, following the entry of the French on the Dutch side in the war in January 1666.

As we have seen, the local Carib did not actively oppose the English, but the support of the Arawak for the Dutch and French seems to have been far more important. In response to the threat of a joint raid by the Arawak and Dutch from the Berbice River, the English attacked two Arawak "warehouses," probably the fortifications at Ouden-Amen and Naby villages between the Demerara and Berbice Rivers; altogether some thirty Arawak were killed and seventy captured. As a result, contingents of Arawak assisted the French and Dutch in retaking the forts at Pomeroon and Essequibo. In Pomeroon the French "most inhumanely delivered them [English prisoners] to the cruelty of the Arawaks at the mouth of that river to be massacred" (Harlow 1925: 203).

Meanwhile, the Surinamese colony fared worse, in the words of Governor William Byam: "in August, God's Justice most sharply visited our transgressions, the sickness spreading throughout the colony" (Harlow 1925: 203). The indifference of the local Carib to the fate of the English colony, enhanced by its fast-deteriorating condition, stands in contrast to the persistent support of the Arawak for the Dutch in Berbice, Essequibo, and Pomeroon. Certainly some of the local Carib served as paddlers for the pirogues and even joined the English troops with "bundles of war-arrows" (Harlow 1925: 211), but lack of provisions meant they retired to their villages within a few days.

Such was the scene when in February 1667 the Dutch admiral Abraham Crijnssen appeared with a fleet before the fort of Paramaribo and demanded the English surrender. After Governor Byam refused, the Dutch attacked the following morning. A sharp fight followed, but the English surrendered. Significantly, the articles of capitulation recognized the role of the Amerindians in these rivalries. Article 11 states: "that the Charibees, our neighbours, shall be used civilly: & that care shall be taken, that we, & our estates shall not be damaged by the Dutch, French or *other Indian nations*" (Harlow 1925: 218, emphasis mine). Since the petition sent to Willoughby from the Assembly of the Colony of Surinam just prior to this attack makes explicit reference to the "fear of invasion of the Arawaca Indians, who will effect such mischief, as will consequently produce the inevitable ruin of us all," it seems clear that the advent of Dutch rule in Surinam would lead to the promotion of a corresponding dominance of their Arawak allies over the local Carib.

Although the English actually retook the colony six months later, Sir John Harman forcing the surrender of the Dutch on October 7, 1667, Articles 3 and 6 of the Treaty of Breda required that the colony be handed back to the Dutch. The English gained New York (New Amsterdam) in return. The definitive establishment of the Dutch in Surinam then completed the process of ethnic transformation that had been initiated by the English.

The Dutch Conquest

The "firm peace" that had been made with the Carib and the limited nature of the demands that the English colony, "planted at a distance and alone" (Oxenbridge, in Williamson 1923: 162) from the Carib, had made on the Amerindians meant that they had been relatively indifferent to its seizure by the Dutch. However, the Arawak clans that moved into Surinam under Dutch protection, particularly the Schotje, threatened to marginalize the powerful Carib chiefs of the Corentyn, Copename, Surinam, and Maroni Rivers. The ex-governor, William Willoughby, who had taken up his brother's titles after he had been lost at sea in a hurricane in 1666, belatedly tried to remedy this situation by commissioning one Major Needham to lead a punitive expedition against the Arawak in Corentyn and Berbice, pointedly referring to the torture of English prisoners by the Arawak "by the instigation of the Dutch" (CSP, Colonial Series, 1661–1668, no. 1812). However, diplomatic protests to Willoughby by Crijnssen prevented the execution of this plan, which Willoughby then disowned. Contemporary sources record that

> at the end of May arrived Serj.-Major Wm. Nedham [sic] and 20 English-
> men in a sloop with a commission from the Gov. of Barbados [William Wil-
> loughby] to act something upon the natives of this coast; whereupon the
> Dutch seized the vessel and sent Nedham and his company to Zeeland. This
> made some desirous to extricate themselves from the colony, and Major Ban-
> ister in particular demanded a licence to leave the colony with all his estate,
> which Crynsens [sic] denied. (CSP, Colonial Series, 1661–1668, no. 1814)

Although it was now in the interest of the Dutch conquerors to promote peace between the Arawak and Carib, which Crijnssen certainly attempted, it was disingenuous of him to suggest that it was only the English who promoted division between the Carib and Arawak (Archief Staten van Zeeland, 2035, No. 22, fol. 186). As we have seen, both the Dutch and French also promoted division among the Amerindian population where it served their interests. Crijnssen found he was unable to ignore past conflicts, and, following further incidents such as disputes between the Carib and Dutch traders on the Copename in 1675, open conflict with the Carib followed in 1678.

Undoubtedly these problems were aggravated by the lack of competent leadership after the departure of Crijnssen (Buve 1966: 16–17). In addition, there were attempts by William Willoughby and the other dons of Barbados to seduce the planters of Surinam to leave, as had happened even when the colony was English, since Barbados and Surinam plantations competed in the production of sugar (CSP, Colonial Series, 1661–1668, no. 577). The result of these overtures was that the white population steadily declined, presenting the Carib with a picture of decay that paralleled the deterioration of the English settlement just prior to Crijnssen's raid. Not surprisingly, Carib leaders saw this as an opportunity to rid themselves of the Dutch along with their Arawak allies.

In the latter part of 1678, the Carib attacked the European settlements at Pirica, Commewine, Torarica, and Para Creek, encouraging the black slaves to wreck the sugar mills and desert the plantations. This dealt a most effective blow to the already weakened colonial economy, and the Jewish and English planters clamored to be allowed to leave for Barbados immediately.

As Buve notes, in the middle of this chaos a new governor, Johannes Heinsius, arrived in December 1678 (1966: 17). He acted quickly, reinforcing the fort at Paramaribo and sending small detachments to Para Creek and Torarica. He also forbade the planters to leave and tried to reassure them as to the stability of the Dutch government by requesting reinforcements from the Netherlands. As these levies would take some time to arrive, he meanwhile tried to organize a *negercorp* from among the slaves. He also encouraged the Arawak from Berbice, under the command of Lucas Caudri, to join him in a joint attack on the Carib in the Para Creek area and along the Saramacca, with a second coordinate Arawak force, under their *adumasi* Warray, attacking the Carib in the Copename River.

Neither of these expeditions was particularly successful in achieving its military aims. In both cases the Arawak eventually refused to fight, clearly suggesting that the hostility of Carib and Arawak was very much a product of these European conflicts, rather than their cultural differences. In any case, as was discussed earlier, these identities as Arawak or Carib were themselves relatively recent and so obscured the heterogeneity of the ethnic origins of their members (see Whitehead 1990a).

Unable to simply play off Carib and Arawak, Heinsius pursued the policy of keeping up the military patrols of Dutch plantations, while trying by diplomatic means to divide the Carib settled in the central regions from those to the east in the Corentyn region and to the west in the Maroni area. In this endeavor he was reasonably successful, being permitted by the Carib chief Annassabo to construct a fort on the Corentyn in early 1679 and receiving a contingent of twenty warriors from the formerly hostile chief Tonay, thanks to the intervention of Annassabo (see Buve 1966: 20–22; Lichtveld and Voorhoeve 1980: 55–61).

Such overtures initially were less successful in the Maroni region since the activities of the *bokkenruylders* (Indian traders), always a difficult element to control for the colonial authorities throughout the Guianas, had alienated the Carib. However, once agreement was reached that certain named traders would not be allowed into the Carib villages again, permission was given to construct a fort at the junction of the Cottica and Commewine. This site was chosen in order to inhibit communication between the Carib of the central regions of Surinam and those of the Maroni River.

In April 1680 reinforcements of regular troops arrived from the Netherlands, effectively signaling an end to the need to further cultivate the outlying Carib communities. Although Heinsius died in July of this year, his strategy of attacking the Copename, Surinam, and Saramacca Carib only after having first secured the neutrality of the eastern and western groups was maintained by his successors (Buve 1966: 22–23). The fact that they now had European troops at their disposal also meant that there was no need to rely exclusively on Arawak assistance.

Those Carib that surrendered were well treated, not least because Carib aid to runaway slaves opened up the specter of a combined Amerindian and slave rebellion that could have overwhelmed the Dutch, as it nearly did in Berbice some ninety years later. However, the further pacification of the Corentyn Carib in 1684 and the resultant isolation of the Maroni chiefs meant that Dutch rule was never again explicitly challenged in Surinam.

Conclusion

It will be appreciated then that the subsequent evolution of political and economic relationships between the Dutch and Amerindians was heavily conditioned by the events of the first two centuries of contact. In certain areas the history of this period remains frustratingly opaque, especially when the continuous story of particular identities or individuals is sought. However, the same is often true as regards the history of European colonialism in the region, so the absence of certain kinds of information is not in itself fatal to historical study of native society and culture.

Furthermore, this period was one of often extreme and rapid change for the native population, so the apparent inconsistencies and unevenness of the historical information may be said to reflect this fact, rather than the general unreliability of this kind of evidence, as has sometimes been assumed (Meggers and Evans 1957: 583–589; Meggers 1992). In such a context the search for continuities between ethnic formations in the archaeological, historical, and modern eras is as much a contemporary political concern as it is a scientific one, just as the search for European tribal origins was undertaken to bolster the ideology of the nation-state.

This essay should not therefore be taken to indicate that there are no significant continuities between the Amerindian groups of past and present but rather that such continuities are not always at the ethnic level, despite persistence in cultural practices. As we have seen, the Arawak and Carib of today had their origins as much in the colonial struggles of the sixteenth and seventeenth centuries as they did in the fifteenth-century groups from which they arose, precisely as a result of the challenges posed to native autonomy by European contacts.

One important consequence of these considerations is that the Arawak and Carib of today, as well as the rest of the Amerindians, can be seen to be as Surinamese as any other of the European, African, or Asian ethnic groups that make up modern Surinam. They are all the product of a shared history and symbiotic social processes. It is to be hoped that a better understanding of this joint legacy will allow the Amerindians to take their rightful place in the continuing story of Surinam, just as our knowledge of the nature of ethnogenesis and ethnocide allows us to understand the historical sources of specific Amerindian identities.

Debate as to the meaning and origins of ethnic sentiment has tended to focus on the contrasts between what have been termed the *primordialist* and *instrumentalist* accounts (see Whitehead 1990a). But what is very evident from our consideration of the emergence of successive Amerindian identities here is that these analytical distinctions obscure the extent to which both kinds of process are at play. Barth's (1969) classic account tends to underplay the significance of the cultural base in determining the way in which specific ethnic identities are manufactured, while arguments for a strong continuity through the contact period are always in danger of a simplistic projection of present ethnic categories onto the heterogeneous data from the past. Clearly a combination of these understandings, coupled with the appreciation that both types of ethnic dynamic may coexist with a varying emphasis on one or another factor over time, is required for the adequate analysis of the genesis and extinction of ethnic identity through time.

It is for precisely these reasons that ethnogenesis and ethnocide have to be seen as complementary aspects of the same process of social and cultural change. Depending upon at which moment in time we choose to investigate this process, we will come away from that examination with an impression as to the dominance of one or another type of event. However, since we are really investigating the fate of forms of sociopolitical organization and their attendant cultural categories in the guise of ethnic identities, the processes of ethnogenesis and ethnocide are not necessarily indications of the demographic extinction or genesis of groups of people, only their identities as those groups. For these rather obvious reasons the investigation of the cultural aspects of ethnicity will only tell half the historical story. Until we also know how cultural actors are enmeshed in specific social relations that are the cause and motivation for cultural change (that is, until we also address the issue of power in conjunction with that of ethnicity), the historical process of identity formation will necessarily remain opaque.

Richard A. Sattler

Remnants, Renegades, and Runaways

Seminole Ethnogenesis
Reconsidered

With the publication in 1971 of the seminal essay "Creek into Seminole," William Sturtevant introduced the concept of ethnogenesis into American anthropology generally. It therefore seems appropriate to reconsider the Seminole case a generation later in a volume dedicated to examining that process.

Sturtevant's work remains an invaluable outline for the history of the Seminole and their emergence as a distinct ethnic group. Advances in anthropological theory and more recent research on the early historic period in the Southeast both support a reexamination of the topic. Likewise, Sturtevant's primary reliance on ethnographic models derived from the post-Removal Florida Seminole, rather than the majority Oklahoma Seminole, suggests the need for revision.

Earlier anthropological models of chiefdoms largely reflected functionalist and adaptationalist theories. These models emphasized relatively benign, organic integration and the role of chiefs as mediators in economic and political exchanges (Fried 1967; Service 1962; Steward 1955). More recent research on chiefdoms recognizes the inherent inequalities and conflicts within such political systems. These studies therefore examine elite strategies for maintaining power and emphasize the means by which elites finance these positions and recruit political support (Drennan and Uribe 1987; Earle 1991).

The accepted view of the southeastern Indians during the early historic period has been that they were organized as tribal societies, confederacies, or simple chiefdoms (cf. Hudson 1976). An explosion of research on the late prehistoric and early historic period in this region during the last decade has strongly challenged this view (Barker and Pauketat 1992; DePratter 1991; Hann 1988; Hudson 1990; Milanich and Hudson 1993; Smith 1987; Thomas 1990). As a result, a new consensus has emerged which dramatically alters our perceptions of these peoples.[1]

These recent studies of the sixteenth and seventeenth centuries in this region indicate that it was dominated by relatively large, complex chiefdoms, rather than tribal societies with largely autonomous villages (Hudson 1990; Barker and Pauketat 1992; Thomas 1990). These studies also provide important information on native sociopolitical concepts and models at the time of contact and suggest a new perspective from which to understand those of the late seventeenth and eighteenth centuries.

In the past, most ethnographic and ethnohistorical research has focused on the Florida Seminole. Their society underwent profound disruption and fragmentation during and after the Second Seminole War (1835–1843). By 1842, 90 percent of the Seminole had been removed to Indian Territory (modern Oklahoma), including almost all the established leaders. Further, the remnant Seminole had been driven south into the Big Cypress Swamp and the Everglades, where it was impossible to maintain traditional subsistence and settlement patterns. Refugees in these areas lived in dispersed family or clan settlements united in relatively loose coalitions under the leadership of the few remaining leaders. Given these circumstances, the post-Removal Florida Seminole provide an inappropriate model for understanding the earlier Seminole and proto-Seminole.

Ethnographic and ethnohistorical research on the Oklahoma Seminole reveals that they retained a strongly corporate, essentially Creek sociopolitical structure throughout the nineteenth century and into the present. Likewise, their sociopolitical groups show marked continuity throughout their history (Sattler 1987). There is also a marked similarity between modern Oklahoma Seminole and Creek sociopolitical concepts and those of the sixteenth century. Thus they should provide a better model for understanding Seminole ethnogenesis.

Sturtevant's analysis clearly reflects the earlier understandings of the southeastern Indians and chiefly sociopolitical organization. He views Creek and Seminole towns as generally autonomous and possessed of a natural tendency toward fission as population increased or as local resources became strained. When this is combined with an organic view of chiefly organization, the establishment of the Seminole settlements in Florida requires no more explanation than the opportunities offered by vacant lands and the pressures of European colonial expansion. His reliance on ethnographic models based on the Florida Seminole is also reflected in his analysis. While recognizing that they retained many Creek features, he views proto-Seminole settlements as random aggregations of individuals and families with less corporate forms of community and government.

Other analyses generally have shared these inadequacies (Swanton 1922; Craig and Peebles 1974; Fairbanks 1974, 1978; Wright 1986). Most have seen the process of proto-Seminole settlement as essentially random movements of individuals and families into Florida, requiring the creation of new and novel forms of community and government. The new forms generally are seen as more flexible and less corporate than their predecessors. These studies also give primacy to vague and generally exogenous forces in driving this movement.

The following essay attempts to refine the existing view of Seminole ethnogenesis. It draws on more recent historical and anthropological research and the perspective provided by ethnographic and ethnohistoric research on the Oklahoma Seminole. As such it is informed by improved knowledge of native sociopolitical models and a closer examination of political processes.

Eastern Muskogean Sociopolitical Organization

Bases of Elite Power in the Sixteenth Century. In order to understand Seminole ethnogenesis, it is first necessary to describe the nature of eastern Muskogean sociopolitical organization prior to the eighteenth century. The Seminole did not emerge in a vacuum, and their actions were shaped by existing patterns of behavior and thought which provided the basis for meaningful action.

At the time of European contact in the early sixteenth century, most eastern Muskogean peoples were organized into a number of competing hierarchical polities. These polities varied in size, complexity, and integration, ranging from simple chiefdoms along the northern Gulf Coast and the confederated chiefdoms on the Atlantic Coast to the complex paramount chiefdoms of the interior Southeast (Milanich 1990; Hudson 1990: 55–58). The larger, more complex polities possessed a three- or four-level political hierarchy with village headmen, provincial chiefs, and paramount chiefs. These polities incorporated multiple simple chiefdoms, using both peaceful incorporation and military conquest (Dye 1990: 213–214; Milanich 1990).

Organizationally, all of the sixteenth-century eastern Muskogean chiefdoms resembled what Southall (1988) has termed "segmentary states," though perhaps on a lesser scale. Rulers in these societies relied primarily on ritual hegemony to maintain political integration. As such, the paramount ruler's authority largely derived from sacred power and knowledge, often accompanied by claims of divine descent. The central ruler exercised little direct control over the outlying districts, which local rulers administered. The paramounts required only acknowledgments of suzerainty and the payment of tribute. Such polities are inherently unstable and given to rebellion and secession (Anderson 1990: 190–192; Hudson 1990: 57–58; Southall 1991; Trouwborst 1991).

The districts or simple chiefdoms, *italwa*s in Muskogee and "towns" in English,[2] were apparently the most stable units and internally self-governing. Each had a hereditary civil chief (*mikko*), a council of hereditary and appointive officials, and a body of military leaders. Each *italwa* contained a number of ranked matrilineal descent groups whose senior men served as heads (*achulaki*s) and sat on the *italwa* council (Hawkins 1848: 67–72; Nairne 1988: 32–36; Hudson 1990; Sattler 1987: 35–59; Swanton 1928a: 242–259).[3]

The sixteenth-century chiefs drew on various bases of power. Socially, they were the most senior men in their *italwa* (Sattler 1988: 14–15). Economically, the chiefs drew on both staple and wealth finance. They collected taxes and compelled corvée labor within the *italwa*, as well as tribute from subordinate polities (Brose 1989: 29; DePratter 1991: 132–133).[4] They also exercised at least partial control of foreign exchange, especially valuables (DePratter 1991: 155). Control over the distribution of these resources created important support. The war chiefs (*tastanaki*) provided an internal police force and specialized military force under the direct control of the chiefs. Paramount chiefs also employed military force to subdue rebellions (DePratter 1991: 48–52; Dye 1990: 213–215).

The most important source of elite power, however, was control over intangible assets. The hereditary chiefs (*mikko*s) and other officials were believed to possess inherent sacred power (*hiliswa*) similar to Polynesian *mana*. This power passed by matrilineal inheritance and, at least for the *mikko*s, extended outward through their descent group in diminishing degrees. During the sixteenth century, *mikko*s often based this sacred power on descent from the sun, a powerful deity. This power was combined with specialized sacred knowledge that enabled the *mikko*s and other officials to perform group rituals necessary to the prosperity and well-being of the *italwa*. These rituals centered on the sacred fire, which was the tutelary deity of the group and with which the *mikko*s had a special relationship (DePratter 1991: 57–72, 113; Hudson 1990: 50; Sattler 1987: 52–55).

Change and Continuity in the Colonial Period. Events during the sixteenth and seventeenth centuries profoundly affected these Muskogean chiefdoms. Some complex chiefdoms were already declining, owing in part to an unstable and deteriorating climate and to regional conflicts (Brose 1984: 167). European contact exacerbated this process through military action and the introduction of alien pathogens (Smith 1987: 54–112, 1989: 21–34). Some groups, such as the Guale and Apalachi, also came directly under Spanish domination and were subject to missionization.

By 1716, major changes had occurred. European diseases had produced massive depopulation in some areas. Older paramount chiefdoms, such as Kusa and Tascalusa, had collapsed and fragmented, and new alignments had emerged. Once populous districts were reduced to single settlements, and others had effectively disappeared. Significant dislocation accompanied this depopulation (Smith 1989).

The paramount chiefs relied heavily on sacred power to maintain their authority. This power was supposed to bring health and prosperity to their subjects. Epidemics and military defeats, therefore, called this power into question. It is significant that the chiefs apparently did not claim descent from the sun during the eighteenth century but still maintained a special relationship with the sacred fire, the sun's earthly representative (Anderson 1990: 192–199; Bartram 1927: 388–389; Hawkins 1848: 68–72; Hudson 1990: 55–58; Sattler 1987: 52–55).

The increasingly important deerskin trade also undermined the economic basis of chiefly power. The traders resided in the towns and dealt with individual hunters, rather than through the chiefs. The large number of these traders and the willingness of colonial governments to intervene on their behalf made it impossible for the chiefs to control them or the trade effectively. This situation largely undermined chiefly control over foreign trade, though the chiefs compensated by demanding large gifts from the traders residing in their jurisdictions and through coercing diplomatic gifts from the colonial governments (Sattler 1989).

International rivalries among the European powers also presented problems. While these rivalries offered major opportunities to skilled statesmen like Brim of Kawita, they seriously threatened less able leaders.[5] Representatives of European governments constantly intervened in the internal politics of the chiefdoms as they attempted to bolster their allies and undermine opponents. In the case of the British, the governments of different colonies competed against each other at times. Even private citizens intervened to further either national or private interests (Crane 1928).

Most researchers maintain that the older chiefdoms were replaced by simpler tribal societies during this period (DePratter 1991; Hudson 1990; Smith 1987). In contrast, I would argue that paramount chiefdoms continued to dominate the native political landscape through most or all of the eighteenth century, though in much weakened form.

Throughout the eighteenth century, the eastern Muskogean peoples were organized into named divisions, most importantly, the Talapusa, Apihka (also called the Kusa), Alabama, and Kawita (also called Apalachicola or Lower Creek). Membership in each division remained relatively stable throughout the century. The Apihka built towns on both the Coosa and upper Tallapoosa

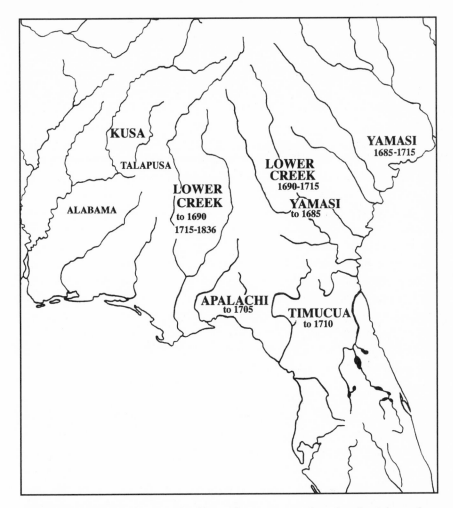

Figure 1. Eastern Muskogean chiefdoms, late seventeenth and early eighteenth centuries.

Rivers, and the Alabama settled on the lower Coosa and Tallapoosa as well as the Alabama River, indicating that these were not merely geographical divisions (see figure 1). Likewise, each division maintained a separate council with a recognized capital and exhibited general internal coherence of action and a degree of independence from each other (Farmar 1764; Fitch 1916; Glover 1725; Grant 1980: 15–17; Rivers 1874: 94; Swanton 1928a: 306–310; Taitt 1916).[6]

These divisions are best understood as successor chiefdoms. They lacked the power, wealth, and size of their predecessors but retained similar organizational principles and concepts of political legitimacy. Some of these chiefdoms, at particular periods, may not have been much more centralized or powerful than confederacies. Such fluctuations reflect the normal competition for power between central paramounts and district chiefs during periods of instability.

Within this context, paramounts, subchiefs, and others contended with each other and with the Europeans for power and prestige during the eighteenth century. The power of all chiefs had declined significantly after European colonization. Multilateral conflicts involving European powers and native polities, disease and depopulation, and repeated relocation of populations all contributed to the decline in chiefly power and increased political instability, as did the relative recentness of the new chiefdoms. Conversely, the manifest advantages of affiliation with larger and more powerful groups and with successful leaders promoted a degree of unity.

Seminole Ethnogenesis. The Lower Creek Kawita chiefdom provided the primary impetus for the formation of the Seminole, and the early settlers derived primarily from this chiefdom. Its complex history and heterogeneous composition promoted both instability and secession.

The available evidence indicates that this chiefdom was established in the early seventeenth century by towns from the former Kusa chiefdom who conquered an existing Apalachicola chiefdom on the Chattahoochee River.[7] The migration legend related by the Kawita chief, Chikilli, in 1735 describes this conquest by the Kawita, Kasihta, and Chickasaw (Gatschet 1969). The latter probably represent the Taskigi.[8] Archaeology and linguistics support this scenario, as do sixteenth-century documentary sources.[9]

After 1715, the Lower Creek also incorporated the Yuchi and Yamasi and conquered the Apalachi (see figure 2).[10] They thus constituted a multiethnic polity under the suzerainty of Kawita, which contained Muskogee, Apalachicola, Apalachi, Yamasi, and Yuchi elements (see figure 3). In part these groups formed separate *italwa*s, but Apalachi and Yamasi were also present in other towns (Boyd 1949, 1952; Fitch 1916: 182; Sattler 1992; Swanton 1922: 124, 141–143, 165–184, 216–230).

The Kawita apparently imposed religious and linguistic hegemony, as well as political control. Ritual practices and beliefs in all of the Lower Creek *italwa*s generally converged during the eighteenth century despite indications of earlier differences (Hann 1988: 70–95; Swanton 1928b).[11] Likewise, the Muskogee language dominated in relations between towns, and Hichiti emerged as the common language of the Apalachicola, Yamasi, and Apalachi towns (Swanton 1928a: 248–249).

Diego Peña and Tobias Fitch described intense political rivalries within the Lower Creek chiefdom between 1716 and 1725. During this period, the para-

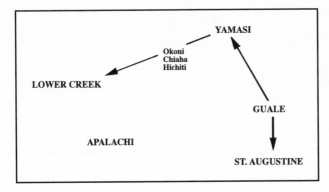

Figure 2. Ethnic mergers, 1680–1700.

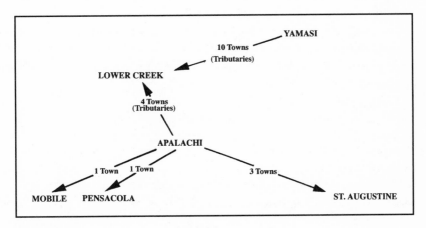

Figure 3. Ethnic mergers, 1700–1715.

mount chief, Brim of Kawita, actively pursued a policy of balanced neutrality and détente in regard to the British, Spanish, and French. A dissident faction led by his son, Simpukasi (Seepeycoffee), and his brother, Chilokilichi (Cherokeelechee), favored a stronger pro-Spanish alliance. This disagreement nearly produced armed conflicts on several occasions and resulted in threats of secession by dissident leaders (Barcía Carballido y Zuñiga 1951: 358; Boyd 1949, 1952; Fitch 1916). During the 1720s, the chiefs of Yufala Hopoya and Tamałi also pursued generally independent courses and frequently defied the authority of Brim, without making a complete break (Fitch 1916).

Most of the leaders and towns identified with these dissident movements were subordinate ethnic groups. Simpukasi was an Apalachi through his mother and was also married to an Apalachi woman (Barcía Carballido y Zuñiga 1951: 362). Likewise, the chief of the Apalachi Wakoka (Bacuqua),

Adrian, was another dissident leader (Boyd 1952). Chilokilichi and his town may also have had Apalachi or Yamasi connections (Barcía Carballido y Zuñiga 1951: 366). Two of the villages, Hichiti and Okoni, which intended to relocate to Apalachi have been identified by Swanton as Yamasi. Two more, Apalachikola and Sawokli, he identifies with the earlier Apalachicola chiefdom (Swanton 1922: 129–134, 141–143, 172–181). Likewise, both of these towns had strong associations with the Apalachi (Boyd 1949, 1952: 119). Tamaɫi and Yufala Hopoya also largely derived from the Apalachi and Yamasi.

These internal divisions and rivalries, both ethnic and personal, played a major role in Seminole ethnogenesis. Likewise, the larger geopolitical and economic conditions in the Southeast contributed to this process.

Proto-Seminole settlements initially appeared in three separate areas. These were the old Apalachee territory around Tallahassee, the Alachua region around modern Gainesville, and the forks of the Apalachicola River, where modern Georgia, Alabama, and Florida meet (see figure 4). Each area has a somewhat different history, though all areas share common elements. Their history can conveniently be divided into three periods: Colonization, 1720 to 1780; Separation, 1780 to 1822; Consolidation, 1822 to 1835.

Colonization, 1720 to 1780

The Colonization period extended from about 1720 until the end of the American Revolution. This period saw the colonization of northern Florida by people from the Lower Creek towns and the establishment of new chiefdoms there. These chiefdoms closely followed the older Muskogee patterns, though settlements may have been somewhat more dispersed.[12] While they established separate chiefdoms in Florida at this time, the proto-Seminole settlements still acknowledged Kawita's suzerainty, if somewhat distantly (Sturtevant 1971; Fairbanks 1978).

Apalachi Old Fields. The process by which the proto-Seminole settled the Apalachee Old Fields remains somewhat obscure. Several lines of evidence, however, indicate that this process began in the 1720s and that the Apalachi and the Yamasi played a central role.

Spanish authorities repeatedly reported new Apalachi and Yamasi settlements in this region between 1718 and 1738, though the number remains unclear, including one established by Apalachi refugees from Pensacola (see figure 5). The Apalachi and Yamasi villages named in Spanish sources included Amapexas, Hamasti, Tamaɫi, San Juan de Wakulla, and San Antonio (Barcía Carballido y Zuñiga 1951: 347–348; Benavides 1726; Bishop of Cuba 1728; Hann 1988: 291–294; Montiano 1738, 1747; Swanton 1922: 126–127). Some of these are probably different names for the same villages. In addition, the Spanish reported two settlements of Tocabaga on the Aucilla and Wacissa

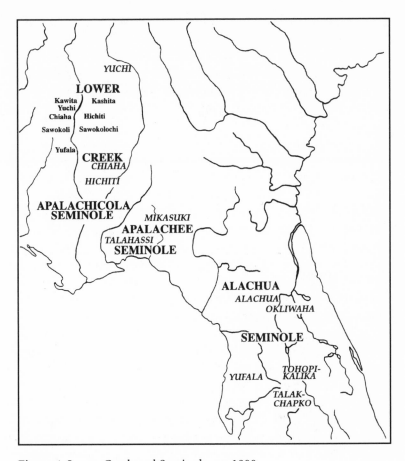

Figure 4. Lower Creek and Seminole, ca. 1800.

Rivers in 1718 (Primo de Rivera 1718). TePaske (1964: 206) has suggested that there were as many as six villages in the area in 1725, but the Spanish sources indicate no more than four and generally two—one Apalachi and one Yamasi (Hann 1988: 291–294). By 1739, only one village of Yamasi, Tamałi, was listed in the region (Montiano 1738).

The Spanish invited the Lower Creek and the Apalachi among them to settle Apalachee several times after 1716. While several towns said they would move, there is little evidence that they did so before 1720 (Ayala y Escobar 1718; Barcía Carballido y Zuñiga 1951: 378; Boyd 1952: 199; Hann 1988: 291–294; Primo de Rivera 1718). There are indications, however, that some people from the Lower Creek moved into the area during the 1720s.

Simpukasi, one of those who earlier promised to move, disappears from the historical record after 1726 (Porter 1948: 371).[13] For such a prominent and

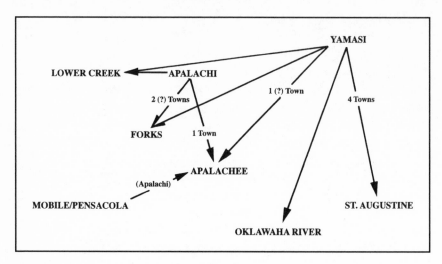

Figure 5. Ethnic movements, 1715–1720.

controversial leader to disappear without comment seems unusual. Importantly, Simpukasi is named as the founder of the Seminole in a tradition recorded in the mid-nineteenth century (Sprague 1847: 18–19).[14] Likewise, the Talahassi *mikko*, Tonapi, stated in 1777 that he was from Kawita, as was Simpukasi, and was taught to "love the Spanish" from infancy by his father. He further stated that he settled in the Apalachee region sometime between 1724 and 1740 (Boyd and Latorre 1953: 110–111).[15] The correspondence in town of origin and affinity toward the Spanish suggests a connection between Simpukasi and Tonapi. Interestingly, Tonapi also reports, in the same statement, that many of his people were Christians. The Apalachi and a few of the Yamasi constituted the only significant Christian element among the Lower Creek towns.

Additionally, a modern Oklahoma Seminole tradition names Talahassi, originally located in the Apalachee region, as the oldest of the Seminole towns.[16] This tradition must be viewed with some caution given the rhetorical use of "eldest" to indicate structural seniority and high prestige among the Seminole and Creek. If it accurately reflects Seminole settlement history, then Talahassi and the Apalachee region must have been settled prior to the mid-1740s, when the Alachua region was settled (see below).

Most or all of the Seminole settlements also apparently spoke Hichiti, rather than Muskogee (Sturtevant 1971: 103). Their language, however, is often described as corrupted and unintelligible to the Creek or as a mixture of Muskogee and Yamasi (Swan 1791: 200; Boyd 1958: 83). This is what would be expected if the Seminole primarily derived from conquered or otherwise incorporated Apalachi and Yamasi, rather than from the dominant Muskogee Kawita and Kasihta.

There is an apparent discrepancy between Spanish statements of the number of towns present and the evidence for additional Lower Creek settlements in the region. An examination of the nature of the Spanish statements partially resolves the problem. The Spanish authorities only list mission sites and towns loyal to the Spanish. There is reason to believe that there were also non-Christian Indians and Indians not firmly tied to the Spanish living in the area.[17] Likewise, Isidoro de León, commander of the Spanish fort at San Marcos, indicates a relatively large population in the region in the mid-1740s (Wenhold and Manucy 1957). The marked correspondence in these accounts suggests that the Apalachi and Yamasi first settled the Apalachi region beginning in 1718. The main emigration, however, apparently occurred in the 1720s and 1730s, involving Simpukasi and his followers (see Figure 6).

Maps from the 1740s through the 1760s indicate several settlements in the area, though some of these probably represent duplications under differing names, since the cartographers had no direct experience of the area (Delahaye 1740; Mitchell 1755; Jefferys 1761). More reliable sources from the 1760s and 1770s, after title to Florida passed from the Spanish to the British, indicate at least four towns: Talahassi near the modern city of that name, Mikasuki on the southwest shore of Lake Miccosukee, Okilakni (Ochlockonee) on the Ochlockonee River near the junction of the Little River, and Wasissa (Wacissa) on the upper Wacissa River. None of the sources listed all these towns, but each is well documented (Bartram 1927; Boyd 1934: 117–118; Boyd and Latorre 1953; Romans 1775; Stuart and Purcell 1778). In addition, other sources indicate more towns (Boyd 1941b: 204; Farmar 1764).

The exact relationship among these towns during this period remains ob-

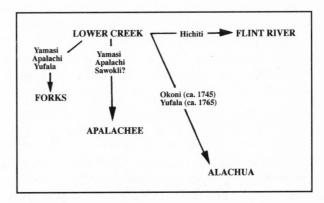

Figure 6. Ethnic movements, 1720–1780.

scure. They generally acted in concert, however, under the leadership of Tal-ahassi. The Talahassi chief, Tonapi, consistently represented all of them at talks with the British and the Spanish (Boyd and Latorre 1953; Covington 1961; Sattler 1987: 63–64). Despite a degree of independence, the Indians in this region remained under the control of Kawita prior to 1780 (Boyd and Latorre 1953: 113; Searcy 1985: 57).

Alachua. During the late 1740s or early 1750s, a group of Okoni under the Wakapuchasi (Cowkeeper) settled in the Alachua region around modern Gainesville, where they established several towns. They were joined over the next twenty years by other settlers from the Lower Creek (see figure 6). This group was the first designated as Seminole, also known as Alachua, and is the best documented of the Florida chiefdoms (Fairbanks 1978; Sturtevant 1971).

By the 1770s, this group comprised at least five towns: Kuskowilla (Cusca-willa) near modern Micanopy, Suwani Talahassochi on the Suwannee River,[18] Wichatukni on the lower Santa Fe River, Santafi Talofa (Santa Fe Talofa) on upper Santa Fe, and Itani at the head of Black Creek (see figures 4 and 5).[19] The Okoni also had incorporated, peacefully or by conquest, at least five other groups with an unknown number of villages: Talakchapko on the head of Pease River, Okliwaha at the bend of the Oklawaha River, Talofa Okhassi on Lake Apopka at the head of that river, and Chukochati at the south end of Annutiliga, or Big Hammock (Bartram 1927; Boyd 1934: 120; Romans 1775; Stuart and Purcell 1778).

The origins of the Talakchapko settlements are unclear, though they were later under the control of the Okmalki Chiaha and may have been from this town (Boyd 1958: 90–92). The Oklawaha and probably the Talofa Okhassi settlements are clearly Yamasi (Anonymous 1763; Bartram 1927: 164; Cohen 1836: 33; Jefferys 1761). The original Talakchapko settlements may also have been Yamasi, as statements by Okoni chiefs indicate that all of the settlements to the south were Yamasi (Candler 1910: 628; Bartram 1927: 164). The Chu-kochati settlers came from Yufala Hopoya on the Chattahoochee in 1767 (Romans 1775: 280–281).[20]

Various contemporary documents clearly state that the Okoni incorporated the Yamasi through conquest (Anonymous 1763; Bartram 1927: 117–123; Sattler 1987: 19–20). There is a reasonable probability that Wakapuchasi's Okoni were identical with the Ocute of the early Spanish accounts. They cer-tainly occupied the same area during the seventeenth and early eighteenth centuries, and the similarity of the names is significant.[21] If this is the case, then their movement into Florida represents an attempt to reestablish the in-dependent Okoni chiefdom. Their constant warfare with and conquest of the Yamasi in Florida may then reflect an attempt to reassert earlier hegemony over the latter.

By 1780, Wakapuchasi apparently exercised suzerainty over much of north-central Florida south of the Santa Fe River between the Suwannee and St. Johns Rivers. His successors maintained control through the nineteenth century (Bartram 1927: 117–124; Fairbanks 1974: 127–136; Sturtevant 1971: 104–105).

All the Alachua paramount chiefs succeeded to office through matrilineal inheritance and evidently primogeniture (Porter 1952).[22] They also employed strategic marriage alliances with subordinate chiefs to maintain their power (Sattler 1989).

The Forks. Throughout the eighteenth century, the people of the towns that had been settled well south of the other Lower Creek on the Chattahoochee (see figure 4) often pursued an independent course and defied the authority of the Kawita chiefs, but they did not make a complete break before 1780.

Chilokilichi, the previously mentioned brother of Brim, established a town at the forks on the lower Chattahoochee in 1715. This town was located on the site of the older Sawokli mission nearly 100 miles below the other Lower Creek towns. Chilokilichi's town was also known by the Spanish as Uchise and probably gave rise to the later town of Ochisi, which was originally located in the same area. In 1716 Diego Peña also reported another settlement, under Paypa Mikko, on the Flint River, one and a half miles from the forks. This is undoubtedly the Yamasi town in the same area referred to by other Spanish authorities (Barcía Carballido y Zuñiga 1951: 378; Boyd 1949, 1952; Wenhold and Manucy 1957).

In the late 1710s, Peña also described several Apalachi settlements on the Chattahoochee below the other Lower Creek towns (Boyd 1949, 1952). In the 1720s, Tobias Fitch places the Yufala Hopoya and Tamaɫi in this area (Fitch 1916). The similarity of the names of these towns and those of the Apalachi towns of Tama and Ayuwali (Ayuvale, Ayuville) is significant. Peña specifically names the Apalachi Tama (Boyd 1952: 116), and Ayuwali was among those settled on the Savannah River prior to 1715 (Salley 1926: 3–13, 1939: 13–16). Similarly, Yufala Hopoya and the Seminole towns derived from Tamaɫi contain several small clans, which are rare or absent among other Creek towns. Some of these clans can be directly linked to the Apalachi, while others may be indirectly linked.[23] On balance, both Yufala Hopoya and Tamaɫi were probably of Apalachi origin, though they may also have contained some Yamasi (Fitch 1916).

By the 1730s, these towns were located fifteen to twenty-five miles south of the others, which were generally separated by no more than two to five miles. Tamaɫi had moved into the forks of the Apalachicola by 1772. Both Yufala Hopoya and Tamaɫi also had established a number of outsettlements by that time, including Chowala, Ikanchati, and Ichiskatalofa (Farmar 1764; Coving-ton 1961: 47; Stuart and Purcell 1778; Bonar 1757; Taitt 1916).

The relationship among the various towns on the lower Chattahoochee at this time remains unclear. None of the evidence suggests unified leadership, but they tended to act cooperatively. All remained under the authority of Ka-wita but consistently defied that authority (Fitch 1916; McDowell 1958: 320; Taitt 1916: 546–547, 551–554).

Several factors contributed to the initial movement of people from the Lower Creek territory into Florida. Lower Creek and Yamasi raids on the Spanish missions had effectively depopulated northern Florida by 1710 (Nairne 1708: 196–197). The abundant and fertile vacant lands there offered an attractive economic resource for both chiefs and commoners, as did the large herds of feral cattle and horses and the extensive hunting territories. Eighteenth-century observers later described extensive fields and large herds among the Seminole which provided both subsistence and trade commodities (Blyth 1916; Bartram 1927: 115–132).

The Spanish presence was far smaller than that of the British, and they exercised less control over their territorial claims. The Florida chiefs, there-fore, suffered less from foreign intervention in internal political affairs. They also succeeded in restricting or eliminating the presence of traders in their towns, thus reestablishing a greater degree of control over foreign trade and reducing foreign interference in internal affairs. The Indian trade was of less importance to the Spanish than to the British and was primarily organized as an adjunct to diplomacy, rather than as a private commercial enterprise.[24] The dependency of the Spanish on Indian allies to maintain their frontiers with the British also made them particularly susceptible to demands for diplomatic gifts (TePaske 1964; Murdoch 1957).

By the time title to Florida passed to Britain in 1763, the Indians were well established. The British largely maintained existing arrangements, including limiting European presence in the Seminole towns, as they did not want an-other costly Indian war. The transfer, therefore, had little negative impact on the Florida chiefdoms (Gold 1969; Mowat 1943).

The greater abundance and lower cost of English trade goods provided new opportunities for expanded trade. Following the Spanish practice, the British traders maintained stores at prescribed locations outside of the Seminole settlements and only occasionally visited there. Thus the foreign presence in the Seminole towns was minimized. Under these conditions, the Alachua be-came the major suppliers of beef and horses to St. Augustine under the British (Parker n.d.: 7–9).

Separation, 1780 to 1822

The 1780s, ushered in by an unprecedented series of disruptive events, led to increasing separation and ultimately to full autonomy for the Seminole chiefdoms. The rising power and importance of the Creek Confederacy, the American Revolution, the usurpation of power within the confederacy by Alexander McGillivray, and the activities of the British adventurer William Augustus Bowles all contributed to this movement.

These events diminished the power of the *mikkos* and particularly of the paramount chiefs as the external demand and internal need for unified action by all eastern Muskogean groups shifted power away from the chiefdoms to the confederacy. Simultaneously, these conditions promoted dissent and factional disputes within the Muskogee. Withdrawal and independence provided a reasonable alternative for the geographically separated Seminole chiefdoms.

Specific conflicts of interest between the Florida chiefdoms and their northern relatives furthered the separatist trend. The Creek faced increasing pressures for land and other concessions after the American Revolution, primarily by the Americans. While the majority of the confederacy lay within the territorial claims of the new United States, the Seminole chiefdoms resided in territory claimed by Spain, which made fewer demands on the Indians. The focus of concern for the confederacy, therefore, diverged from that of the Seminole. The apparent willingness of the confederacy to sacrifice the property and prerogatives of more marginal groups, like those in Florida, to satisfy claims against the confederacy as a whole or to preserve the interests of the core groups increased this rift (Fairbanks 1974: 205–210; Sattler 1987).

The Alachua Seminole were the first to sever ties. Because they were distant from the centers of Creek power, Kawita's suzerainty had always been nominal there. During the American Revolution this group actively participated with the British in attacks against the Americans, in violation of official Creek neutrality (Boyd and Latorre 1953: 113; Searcy 1985: 20, 72, 108, 154). By the 1790s, the Alachua actively pursued an independent course, mostly by withdrawing from participation in Lower Creek and confederacy affairs. The succession of Payne as paramount chief following his uncle's death shortly prior to 1790 undoubtedly led to this policy shift (Caughey 1938: 124–125; Hawkins 1916: 317).

The abortive American invasion of East Florida in 1812 further contributed to the separation of the Alachua Seminole. While initially neutral in this conflict, the Alachua soon began attacking the American settlers and troops in northeastern Florida. The American response resulted in the destruction of three Alachua towns and severe injuries to Payne. Payne died of his wounds some time later and was succeeded by his brother Bowlegs. At this time, most of the Alachua withdrew farther south toward Tampa Bay. Bowlegs, along with about 500 of his people, moved to the site of Suwani Talahassochi (Davis 1930; Fairbanks 1978: 212–216; Sattler 1987: 73; Young 1934: 88).

The Mikasuki and Talahassi in Apalachee also began resisting Creek suzerainty after 1780. While this group generally followed the decisions of the confederacy at this time, they actively resisted the power of Alexander McGillivray,[25] instead early and actively supporting William Augustus Bowles, an English adventurer and opponent of McGillivray (Kinnaird 1931a, 1931b; Kinnaird and Kinnaird 1983; Wright 1986). Differences with the Creek increased to the point where these groups assumed full independence by 1804. Prior to this, the Apalachee Seminole had considered themselves bound by treaties and agreements made by the Lower Creek, sometimes without direct representation in the negotiations. During the 1790s, they more aggressively demanded direct representation in negotiations, and even the Lower Creek acknowledged Seminole autonomy by 1802 (U.S. Congress 1832–1861, *Indian Affairs* 1: 670, 673, 676; Sattler 1987: 71).

This increasing independence probably reflected another important change among the Seminole of this region. Tonapi of Talahassi apparently died shortly after 1777. He was succeeded as spokesman and leader by Kapicha Mikko (more commonly known as Kinhachi) of Mikasuki. Not only had a new leader emerged, but preeminence had shifted from Talahassi to Mikasuki. The nature and causes of this shift are unknown, but the effects were significant.[26] Regardless of the nature of the transition, the Mikasuki would remain dominant until the Second Seminole War, and the Apalachee settlements as a whole came to be known by their name (U.S. Congress 1832–1861, *Indian Affairs* 1: 127; Fairbanks 1974: 184).

Kapicha Mikko, in contrast to his predecessor, pursued a much more aggressive and independent foreign policy. Not only did he actively assert his autonomy from the Creek, but he also adopted an aggressive anti-American policy. Under his rule, the Apalachee Seminole opposed the United States on numerous occasions and engaged in a prolonged border feud with American settlements in Georgia between 1790 and 1818 (Fairbanks 1974: 194–228; Grant 1980: 453–456; Innerarity 1931: 105; Lockey 1949: 109–111; Sattler 1987: 83, 100–104).

The American Revolution also introduced a new component in the makeup of the Seminole chiefdoms. During the war, British authorities in Florida encouraged slaves from the rebellious colonies to escape by promising them freedom in Florida. At least some of these escaped slaves formed Maroon communities in the interior of Florida.[27] These communities forged alliances with the Seminole chiefdoms already there, paying an annual tribute to the chiefs. Most of the Maroons settled in the Alachua territory prior to

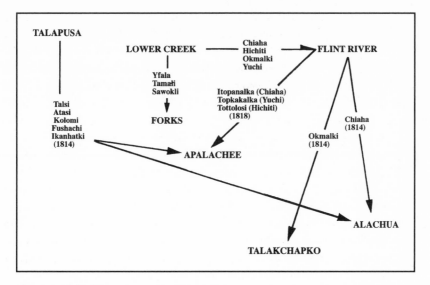

Figure 7. Ethnic movements, 1780–1822.

1814, where they formed at least two towns, allied with Payne and his sub-chief Imała, or Philip. Other blacks also lived in the Seminole towns either as slaves or as free men. Like the Maroons, most of them had come in during the American Revolution (Giddings 1858; Porter 1945, 1946a, 1946b, 1948, 1951a).

The Yufala and Tamałi continued their southward expansion after the American Revolution, though they retained a loose association with the Lower Creek. While the Yufala Hopoya remained in the same location on the Chattahoochee they had occupied in the 1760s, their outsettlements extended southward. The Tamałi migrated below the forks to the Apalachicola River, as did the Ochisi. The Yamasi also established settlements on the lower Chattahoochee, the upper Apalachicola, and the branches of the Ochlockonee River (see figure 7). Between 1780 and 1820, the Indians established at least twelve towns on the Chattahoochee and Apalachicola Rivers below Yufala (Olivier 1793; Westcott 1833a; Young 1934: 85–88).

By the 1810s, several of these towns had united under a single chief and assumed a common identity. At that time they comprised at least six towns: Ikanchati (Tohtohuiłi), Yamasi, Tamałi (Chukonikła), Ochisi (Ispaniwakki), and Yawohli (Iola), each of which maintained its own chief and square ground. The whole body was called Yamasi in 1818 and later referred to as the Apalachicola (Westcott 1833b; Young 1934: 85–88).

The Chiaha, Yuchi, and Hichiti also established several settlements on the lower Flint River beginning in the 1770s. By 1800, these numbered at least ten towns: the Yuchi towns of Pachilika, Intachkalka, and Topanalka; the Chiaha towns of Itopanalka, Amakali, Hotalihuyana, and Okmalki; and the Hichiti towns of Hichitochi, Chikasahachi, and Tottolosi Talofa (see figure 7). All these towns had their own chiefs and square grounds (Hawkins 1848: 61–66, 1916: 171–172; Young 1934: 85–88).

In the 1790s the towns on the Flint, Apalachicola, and lower Chattahoochee Rivers constituted at least four semiautonomous chiefdoms, each with several settlements. These included the Yamasi (Ochisi and Tamali), the Yuchi, the Hichiti, and the Chiaha. While they remained part of the Lower Creek, all began acting more independently and often in opposition to Kawita and the Creek Confederacy after 1790 (U.S. Congress 1832–1861, *Indian Affairs* 1: 309–310, 313–316, 373–374, 383, 669–670; Grant 1980: 427, 678–679; Westcott 1833b; Young 1934: 85–88). Clearly, the declining power and authority of the paramount chiefs, as well as conflicts of interest within the confederacy, encouraged minority groups within the Creek to assert greater independence. At this time the Americans and Spanish often referred to all of the Flint River and forks groups as Seminole (Green 1982: 35–38; Caughey 1938: 35–36, 286–287).

The aftermath of the War of 1812 and the Creek War of 1814 introduced significant changes among the Seminole. Most significant were a massive population increase and a change in the tribe's makeup from the inclusion of two new groups.

The defeat of the dissident Redstick Creek by the Americans and their Lower Creek allies produced a massive influx of refugees into Florida, mostly Upper Creek Talapusa (see figure 7).[28] While the earlier Seminole derived from Lower Creek towns and predominantly spoke Hichiti, the new immigrants mostly spoke Muskogee and outnumbered the older Seminole by perhaps two to one (Fairbanks 1974: 209–211).

Initially, most of the Upper Creek Redstick refugees settled in West Florida on the Escambia, Conecuh, and Choctawhatchee Rivers. In 1815, the Mikasuki, who had also joined the Redstick Movement, invited the refugees to join them, and many did so. These Redsticks established towns among the Mikasuki and Talahassi or settled in the area just to the east between the Aucilla and Suwannee Rivers. Other Redsticks settled at the abandoned Alachua territory, and some fled farther south to the Tampa Bay region (U.S. Congress 1832–1861, *Indian Affairs* 1: 838, 860; Boyd 1937: 260, 1958: 88, 93, 182; Carter 1956: 968–971; Fairbanks 1974: 210–211; Sattler 1987: 73–74).

Some of these Redstick towns were incorporated into the existing Mikasuki and Alachua Seminole polities. The alliance between the Mikasuki and the Talsi Redsticks was particularly strong and continued through the Second Seminole War. Other Redstick towns apparently remained independent or formed a separate chiefdom or confederacy in Florida. Unsettled conditions and a lack of records leave their situation unclear (U.S. Congress 1832–1861, *Military Affairs* 1: 681–701; Fairbanks 1974: 229, 231, 238–239, 249–250; Williams 1837: 214, 274; Young 1934: 83–84, 88).

The War of 1812 also brought a major new influx of blacks. During the war, the British established a fort at Prospect Bluff on the Apalachicola River, where they armed and trained escaped slaves and Maroons to fight the Americans. In response, blacks flocked to the area and established populous communities along the lower Apalachicola River. The fort was destroyed by American soldiers in 1816 as a result of continuing border conflicts and escaping slaves. The surviving blacks joined the Seminole and established communities among the Mikasuki and Alachua (Porter 1951a; Fairbanks 1978: 177–187; Sattler 1987: 81–82).

Events overtook the Seminole before the newcomers could be fully incorporated. The Mikasuki, Redsticks, and Alachua on the Suwanee River continued to follow the Redstick cult, producing much anxiety among the Americans. Likewise, hostilities between Florida Indians and Maroons and the Georgia settlers continued unabated. These hostilities involved elements of all three Seminole groups (Grant 1980: 698–699, 713–714, 717–718, 724–727, 763–764, 771, 773–774, 786–787; McReynolds 1957: 63–87; Young 1934).

These conditions provided Andrew Jackson with an excuse to invade Florida. During the invasion, Jackson's troops burned seven Seminole settlements: Tottolosi, Ikanchati, Attapalka, Talahassi, Mikasuki, and the two Maroon and Indian settlements on the Suwannee River. More important, both Kapicha Mikko of the Mikasuki and Bowlegs of the Alachua were killed in these engagements. They were succeeded by Takosa Imała and Mikkonapa, respectively (U.S. Congress 1832–1861, *Indian Affairs* 2: 409, 432; U.S. Congress 1832–1861, *Military Affairs* 1: 681–778; Young 1934).

Jackson's main purpose, however, was the conquest of Florida. After destroying the Mikasuki villages, he seized the Spanish fort at St. Marks on a pretext and proceeded directly from the Suwanee villages to Pensacola, which he besieged for the next five months. This siege actually lasted a month longer than the campaign against the Indians. The Spanish acknowledged reality and signed a treaty in 1819, transferring title to the Americans in 1821 (Fairbanks 1978: 183–185; McReynolds 1957: 73–87; Sattler 1987: 87–88). Despite his pretext of subduing the Indians, Jackson never negotiated a treaty with the Florida Indians. It was not until 1823 that such a treaty was finally signed. The Treaty of Camp Moultry set the stage for the next phase of Seminole history (McReynolds 1957: 88–101).

During the period 1780 to 1825, all three Seminole groups emerged as unified, independent chiefdoms. The political unification of the Alachua and Mikasuki clearly predated this period, and that of the Apalachicola Seminole may have also. The three chiefdoms achieved independence from the Lower Creek at different times, largely reflecting their proximity to the latter. The Alachua accomplished this earliest, being essentially autonomous by the end of the American Revolution and completely so by the 1790s. The Mikasuki and Tala-hassi achieved full independence by the beginning of the nineteenth century. The Apalachicola, closest to the Lower Creek settlements and the least numer-ous, only achieved full independence after 1818.

The Alachua Seminole were the most centralized and, prior to the arrival of the Redsticks, the largest of these chiefdoms. By 1820 they comprised five subchiefdoms, each with several villages, including Alachua, Tohopikalika, Okliwaha, Chukochati, Talakchapko, and Opilaklikaha (see figure 4).[29] The Alachua chief ruled as paramount chief over the whole body and took the title Mikkonapa, or top chief.[30] Either his brother or nephew served as paramount war chief and normally succeeded him. The paramounts also employed dy-nastic marriages to bind subordinate chiefs to them (U.S. Congress 1832–1861, *Indian Affairs* 2: 411–412; Fairbanks 1974: 242–272; Porter 1951b, 1952; Sattler 1987: 96–99; Williams 1837: 214).[31]

The Seminole in Apalachi, known collectively as Mikasuki, comprised at least six towns with numerous villages stretching from Lake Miccosukee in the east to the Ochlockonee and Little Rivers in the west and south to St. Marks. These towns were organized into at least two subchiefdoms, Talahassi and Mikasuki (see figure 4). The latter provided the paramount chief throughout the period 1780 to 1825, but little else was recorded regarding their internal organization. Following the Redstick War in 1814, this group also incorpo-rated the Redstick refugees from Atasi, Fushachi, Kolomi, and Talsi (U.S. Con-gress 1832–1861, *Indian Affairs* 2: 413, 439; Grant 1980: 708–709; Hambly and Doyle 1818; Sattler 1987: 100–104).

The Apalachicola Seminole also formed a unified chiefdom in 1820. The five towns making up this group (Ikanchati, Tamałi, Attapalka, Ochisi, and Yawohli) each had its own chief, but all acknowledged the authority of the paramount, who had the authority to depose a subordinate town chief. Like the Alachua, the Apalachicola paramounts used dynastic marriages to bind subordinate chiefs. Yellowhair of Tamałi was paramount chief in 1818 but was succeeded by Blount of Yawohli shortly afterward. The latter was succeeded by Nokus Yahola (John Yellowhair), chief of Tamałi and son of Yellowhair. This pattern of rotational succession is extremely unusual for the Muskogee but resembles that reported for the Guale and the Apalachi in the sixteenth and seventeenth centuries (Hann 1988; Sattler 1987: 99–100; Swanton 1922: 84–89; Westcott 1833b; Young 1934). This group achieved full independence only in consequence of the First Seminole War in 1818 and the Treaty of Camp

Moultry. The authority of Kawita, however, seemed rather nominal prior to that time. The other towns on the lower Chattahoochee and Flint Rivers either returned to the Lower Creek or joined the Mikasuki and Alachua in Florida (see figure 7) (U.S. Congress 1832–1861, *Indian Affairs* 2: 413, 439; McReynolds 1957: 73–87).

Following the American Revolution, the Florida Indians and some of those at the forks of the Apalachicola established separate identities from the Creek. While Americans and Creek referred to them collectively as Seminole, they lacked a unified identity at this time. Instead they possessed disparate identities as members of several paramount chiefdoms.

While there are no reports of conflicts between the Florida chiefdoms, there is no evidence for any unifying organization either. In fact, the three groups each showed considerable independence of action and actively pursued independent courses (Fairbanks 1974: 74; Sattler 1987: 83).

Conflict and Consolidation, 1822 to 1835

The period immediately following the American conquest of Florida was one of considerable turmoil for the Indians. Several towns had been destroyed, and residents of a number of others had fled into the unsettled regions to the south and east. More important, the American government insisted on treating the Indians as a single, unified tribe. As such, the Americans intended to relocate all of the Seminole onto a single reserve, whose location was not decided until 1822.

In response to American demands, the disparate Seminole groups formed a unified council to deal with them. This council included all the Redstick towns, the Alachua, the Apalachee Seminole, and the Apalachicola Seminole. One Hichiti town, Tottolosi Talofa, participated as well. This council existed, initially, simply to deal with the Americans and to negotiate a new treaty with them. It had no enforcement powers, and its only official was a speaker. This office, largely symbolic and honorary, was given to Hiniha Imała, *mikko* of Tottolosi Talofa, in recognition of the fact that his was the first town burned in the late war (Fairbanks 1974: 265; Sattler 1987: 104–105).

The treaty, signed in 1823, clearly reveals the lack of unity. Under its provisions, virtually all the Seminole were to be located on a single reservation in central Florida near the existing Alachua settlements. Separate reservations for six Apalachicola chiefs and their followers were established on the Apalachicola River. Hiniha Imała was one of these chiefs, but most of his town seems not to have joined him there (McReynolds 1957: 88–102).

Various difficulties beset implementation of the treaty, including opposition by the Indians. Those in the Apalachee region and on the Apalachicola had no desire to be removed. Conversely, the Alachua, in whose territory the reservation was located, did not welcome an influx of people from other chief-doms who did not recognize their suzerainty. In consequence, it was not until 1825 that Indians from the Apalachicola River and Apalachee were removed to their new homes (U.S. Congress 1832–1861, *Indian Affairs* 2: 618, 620–621, 625–626).

This conflict over removal to the new reservation further revealed the in-substantial nature of the Seminole council. In 1824, Governor Duval of Flor-ida Territory deposed Hiniha Imała for resisting the removal efforts and re-placed him with the Mikasuki *mikko*, Takosa Mikko (John Hicks). Not only did the Seminole tolerate this unprecedented and unique event, they unani-mously approved it (U.S. Congress 1832–1861, *Indian Affairs* 2: 689–690; McReynolds 1957: 106). The Seminole clearly placed little significance on this council, other than as a mechanism for dealing with the Americans, since such interference in internal politics was never tolerated in any other context.

The council was transformed into a true government after the northern towns removed to the new reservation. In 1825, an election was held, and Takosa Imała of Mikasuki was selected paramount chief of the whole body. George McCall, who witnessed the event, described the installation of the new paramount as an elaborate affair with more than 100 participants and 2,000 spectators. After he was installed, Takosa Imała pledged to enforce the laws and punish violators who broke the laws of either tribe, and shortly after had two violators punished (McCall 1974: 152–156). Conflicts between the Alachua and Mikasuki continued, however, and Takosa Imała was replaced by Mikkonapa, paramount chief of the Alachua, in 1833 (U.S. Congress 1832–1861, *Indian Affairs* 2: 630–631, 636–637, 694; McCall 1974: 157; Sprague 1847: 79; Sattler 1987: 105–106).

The new Seminole council grew progressively unified and effective between 1825 and 1835. In part, this evolution reflected the need for greater coopera-tion on the restricted reservation. Increasing pressure by the United States on the Seminole to sell their Florida lands and remove west of the Mississippi also contributed to growing unification.

The powers of the chief and unity of the council were well illustrated by the execution of Charley Amarthla (Chali Imała) and actions early in the Second Seminole War in December 1835. The council ordered Charley Amarthla's execution for cooperating with the American removal effort. A party of war-riors from several different towns under the command of Osceola (Asi Ya-hola), war chief of the Talsi, carried out the sentence. Several military actions early in the Second Seminole War involved close cooperation and coordinated action by diverse elements of the Seminole. The ambush of Dade's command near Tampa Bay and the simultaneous execution of Wiley Thompson, U.S. Indian agent, at Fort King involved 400 to 1,000 warriors in locations ninety miles apart. The Battle of the Withlacoochee with U.S. troops under General Gaines in February 1836 likewise involved several hundred warriors from several different towns (U.S. Congress 1832–1861, *Military Affairs* 6: 561–563, 565; Potter 1836: 94–97, 102–116, 143–147; Sprague 1847: 88–93, 110–111).

In form the Seminole national council resembled those of the paramount chiefdoms and that of the Creek Confederacy. It consisted of the chiefs and principal officials of each of the Seminole towns and had a principal chief, speaker, war chief, and other officials like the towns and paramount chiefdoms. The office of principal chief remained hereditary in the line of the Alachua paramounts until 1885. American observers reported that the principal chief had absolute authority over the whole, as did the other chiefs in their own towns (Bemrose 1966: 15; Harney 1837: 870–871; McCall 1974: 156, 221; Perryman 1817: 8; Simmons 1973: 71, 77; Sprague 1847: 88, 93).[32] Clearly, the Seminole followed earlier sociopolitical models in developing this new government.

One innovation was the appointment of Takosa Imała as principal war chief after Mikkonapa's accession to office. This pattern of appointing the war chief from the Mikasuki chiefdom continued through the Second Seminole War (Hitchcock 1837: 518–531; Sattler 1987: 105–107, 141–146; Westcott 1833a: 96–97).[33]

This development marked the first emergence of a unitary Seminole identity. Unity, however, was fragile, and dissidents were common and often followed independent courses. The separation of the tribe into friendly and hostile factions during the Second Seminole War clearly revealed these divisions. Only after removal to Indian Territory did this unified identity become fixed and encompass the Apalachicola as well (McReynolds 1957: 159–173, 243–289; Sattler 1987: 106–107, 176–214).[34]

Among the Florida Seminole after 1840, fragmentation and dislocation resulted in the creation of novel sociopolitical relations. Earlier political ideologies influenced these new forms, but reduced circumstances and altered material conditions precluded following older practices. As a result, Florida Seminole ethnic identity became more diffuse and relied more on kinship and ritual bases (Fairbanks 1978; Sturtevant 1971).[35]

Conclusion

The eastern Muskogean people retained the same political models and forms in the eighteenth century that they had had in the sixteenth century. Events during the intervening period and conditions in the eighteenth century, however, had weakened the power of the chiefdoms and the paramount chiefs. These conditions increased divisions within the chiefdoms, particularly the multiethnic Lower Creek, and encouraged dissidents to secede. The presence of vacant lands in northern Florida and weak Spanish control over the region provided a vital opportunity for secession. The success of the Kawita paramount chiefs in international affairs and the protection offered by the emergent Creek Confederacy, however, kept the dissidents from completely severing ties.

After 1720 immigrants from the Lower Creek colonized northern Florida. Corporate groups, primarily incorporated Apalachi and Yamasi, apparently initiated this immigration. The immigrants established new chiefdoms in Florida which closely followed older Muskogee patterns, though settlements may have been somewhat more dispersed.[36] While they established separate chiefdoms in Florida at this time, the proto-Seminole settlements still acknowledged Kawita's suzerainty, if somewhat distantly (Sturtevant 1971; Fairbanks 1978).

Changing geopolitical and world economic conditions following the American Revolution increased both centralization and conflicts within the Creek Confederacy, while eroding the power and authority of the paramount chiefs. As their interests diverged from those of the confederacy, the Seminole paramounts pursued a more independent course, resulting in full autonomy and separation. Other minority groups within the confederacy followed similar, though less successful, strategies of independence.

Unification of the Seminole occurred only under external pressure from the United States, although it also reflected the need for greater internal cooperation and the resolution of disputes between chiefdoms in a more restricted area. Consolidation, however, followed existing Muskogee models, and the new tribal government resembled those of the older paramount chiefdoms. Unification also met some opposition as paramounts and subchiefs sought to preserve their own power or pursued personal and group interests. The Seminole took thirty years to complete the process, and then only after the defection of several chiefs and their followers.

The process of Seminole ethnogenesis and unification must be seen within the context of the interaction of aboriginal sociopolitical models and shifting geopolitical situations. Native elites contended for power and prestige, pursuing personal and group interests, within this context. In doing so, they largely maintained the earlier sociopolitical models, rather than replacing them and developing novel modes of organization. These aboriginal models, in force in the sixteenth century, retained much of their force and legitimacy among the Seminole and Creek at least until the 1850s and to some extent to the present in Oklahoma.

Seminole withdrawal and later separation represented rebellions and secession, rather than sociopolitical transformation. Subordinate chiefs, largely from conquered or incorporated minority groups, sought to expand their power and independence at the expense of the paramount chiefs of Kawita. In the process they challenged the legitimacy of the paramounts but not of the sociopolitical models, which they replicated in their new locations. In mobilizing support for their claims, these rebellious chiefs employed numerous strategies, including ethnic identity, kinship, and economic or political advantage.

Such rebellions were not new and were documented for the early-sixteenth-century southeastern chiefdoms, as well as for similar polities elsewhere. The reduced power of the eighteenth-century paramount chiefs, owing to reduced populations and resources and increased geopolitical instability, fostered such separatist movements by subordinate chiefs. Because of the recent formation of their chiefdom and externally induced disruptions, the paramounts of Kawita also had not consolidated their position and were particularly susceptible to challenge. Many dissident chiefs sought to reconstitute earlier independent paramount chiefdoms, albeit in new configurations or locations. These new chiefdoms were frequently multiethnic, but this situation also reflected older patterns. Even the formation of multiethnic communities was not novel.

The new chiefdoms in Florida assumed different names, thus creating new ethnic identities, also in keeping with aboriginal practice. Ethnic identity in the aboriginal Southeast largely reflected political unity along with shared language, ritual, and descent. The dynamics of chiefly sociopolitical organization in the region imposed linguistic and religious unity, while fostering intermarriage and shared descent.

Descriptions of Seminole towns from the eighteenth and nineteenth centuries clearly indicate the existence of square grounds and regular Muskogee institutions and forms of government (Bartram 1848, 1927; Porter 1952; Young 1934; U.S. Congress 1832–1861, *Military Affairs* 1: 681–749, 6: 56–80, 450–574, 7: 870–871). Most direct observers of both groups in fact make no distinction between the two and indicate that Seminole practices are identical to those of the Creek.

Assumptions that the Seminole created novel forms of social and political relations rest on several grounds, all suspect. First, Lower Creek leaders and European or American observers, all of whom were politically interested parties, frequently stated that the Seminole towns were "made up" and derived from several different Creek towns. Second, all three of the Seminole regional groups contained towns of differing ethnic origins.

Reports that the early Seminole towns were made up of people from various towns likely indicate that they drew Apalachi and Yamasi previously incorporated into other towns, as well as their relatives and friends, rather than a lack of corporate structure and identity. Similar accusations were made concerning the Tamaɫi and Yufala Hopoya, who were clearly corporate and followed established Creek patterns (Swanton 1922: 181–184, 261–263). Such accusations that a town is invented or improperly constituted remain a central element in Oklahoma Seminole and Creek political rhetoric as a means of discrediting political rivals.[37]

Likewise, multiethnic chiefdoms were not uncommon in the sixteenth century and clearly represent a longstanding pattern in the region, rather than an innovation (Hudson 1990; Hann 1988: 24–69). As mentioned, however, paramounts imposed a degree of linguistic and ritual hegemony over subject chiefdoms. Over time this process would create unified ethnic identity within the chiefdom. Multiethnic settlements were also common, at least by the early eighteenth century. Most of the Lower Creek towns contained people from other groups at this time, and several Apalachi settlements were also multiethnic in the seventeenth century (Hann 1988: 24–69). The important factor in determining identity in these communities and chiefdoms was the composition of the core populations, particularly the elites.

All the major Seminole groups showed considerable continuity through time. Talahassi, Mikasuki, Ochisi, Alachua, Yufala, and others exist throughout the period prior to Removal and continue among the Oklahoma Seminole. If the Seminole were less corporate than the Creek there should have been more fluidity and less permanence. Furthermore, the Oklahoma Seminole today hold to Creek political models and clearly did so throughout the nineteenth century (Sattler 1987).

Traditional Muskogee concepts of political legitimacy imposed important constraints on group formation and claims to rulership. As stated previously, legitimacy derived from lineage and control over intangible assets, primarily inherited sacred power and knowledge (Sattler 1987: 52–55, 1992; Hudson 1990: 50).[38] Establishing a new town required access to a sacred fire, which could not simply be invented or created, and to its rituals (Sattler 1987: 44–45, 52–55, 1992).

Dissident leaders who wished to found new towns therefore had to establish publicly acknowledged access to sacred power and knowledge. Such access was largely determined by descent and lineage. Leaders also had to recruit the support of others who could fill other essential leadership positions, principally those of the *hiniha* and priest. These positions also depended in part on descent as well as on specialized training, and the *hiniha* office belonged to a clan other than that of the *mikko* (Bartram 1848: 21–27, 39–41, 1927: 388–392, 399, 400–401; Hawkins 1848: 67–75; Sattler 1987: 51–52, 55–57).

These conditions largely limited leadership to those of demonstrable "royal" lineage. Among the Lower Creek this group included both those belonging to the clans of the existing *mikko*s and those of formerly royal Apalachi and Yamasi lineages. The former may have been less likely to secede since they partially shared the power of the *mikkos* and had opportunities for high office. This was particularly true during the early eighteenth century, when Lower Creek population reached an initial nadir. Not only was the total population of the towns low, but royal clans were not normally the largest. Junior members of the royal lineages or members of junior lineages within the royal clans were probably responsible for establishing the numerous "daughter towns" and outsettlements in the late eighteenth century after the population rebounded. Incorporated Apalachi and Yamasi, however, generally enjoyed no such benefits and faced limited opportunities for advancement. Even where they controlled separate towns, these were subordinate to Kawita and the Muskogee towns. It is therefore not surprising that the identifiable leaders and towns involved in the early formation of the Seminole derived from these groups. Immigration thus reflected a counterhegemonic response by ethnic groups and leaders subordinate to Kawita's suzerainty.

Dissident leaders derived support through a variety of other mechanisms. Kinship clearly provided a basis for recruiting followers and would have included both consanguinal and affinal relatives.[39] Shared ethnic identity provided another source, as did promises of economic and political advantage.

While these polities derived primarily from the Apalachi and Yamasi, they were undoubtedly multiethnic. Both groups intermarried extensively with each other and with other Lower Creek towns (Fitch 1916; Taitt 1916). The new settlements would have drawn affinal relatives from other groups, as well as friends and associates seeking the greater economic or political opportunities available there.

In both Alachua and Apalachee, the immigrants also seem to have incorporated earlier settlements of refugee Apalachi, Yamasi, and probably Timucuan, none of whom had joined the Lower Creek after 1715. Most authorities have assumed that all the refugee populations were either absorbed by the Creek or settled near St. Augustine, Pensacola, and Mobile following the Yamasee War of 1715. The population data make this unlikely, however. A comparison of population estimates for the Lower Creek, Apalachicola, Yamasi, and Apalachi from 1715 in Carolina and Georgia with those of the known settlements in the twenty years following the war shows a marked disparity (Rivers 1874: 94; Boyd 1949; Glover 1725). Such a massive population loss would require far higher mortality among the Indians than is indicated in the records of the war.[40]

Ethnic identity among the Seminole, and in the Southeast generally, therefore largely reflected political alignments. Political ideology remained conservative over three centuries, though political realities shifted markedly. Leaders both manipulated older bases of power and created new ones within the context of this ideology but remained vulnerable to challenge. Consequently, political affiliation, and with it ethnic identity, remained rather fluid.

Notes

1. While not all scholars agree with the interpretation presented here, it does represent the majority of recent research.

2. The Muskogee term *italwa* actually refers to any self-governing polity and applies equally to simple chiefdoms, district chiefdoms, and paramount chiefdoms, as well as nation-states. To avoid confusion, this term will be employed here to designate the minimal self-governing units, known as "towns" or "bands" in English. Larger units will be referred to as chiefdoms, and villages under the direct control of another town will be referred to as settlements. The latter term also applies to villages whose status is uncertain.

3. While these descent groups included lineages, clans, and phratries by the beginning of the eighteenth century, the evidence does not indicate the nature of the earlier descent groups. The universality of matrilineality among the Muskogean peoples argues that this descent rule pertained earlier.

4. Household contributions to the public granaries are often treated as voluntary contributions to the commonweal. There is no indication, however, that anyone ever failed to contribute. During the nineteenth century, the *tastanaki* enforced such contributions, as well as participation in corvée labor (Reynolds 1867: 328). Under such conditions, these are more realistically termed taxes.

5. Brim of Kawita was paramount chief of the Lower Creek from before the Yamasee War to the early 1730s and a primary architect of the Creek Confederacy. He was unquestionably one of the greatest statesmen of the era. His successors have maintained his foreign policy but seem less successful at domestic policy (Fairbanks 1974: 101–105; Juricek 1987: 78–85, 110–118, 181–193).

6. The minor shifts in membership, which were not always accompanied by relocation of the towns, also argue that these were primarily political rather than geographic divisions. Likewise, shifts in power among towns within the divisions reflect processes common in chiefdoms and other centralized polities.

7. The Lower Creek temporarily relocated to the Okmulgee and Oconee Rivers between 1690 and 1715 but returned to the Chattahoochee following the Yamasee War (Bolton 1925: 55; Crane 1928: 168–179, 254).

8. The origins of the Taskigi remain somewhat obscure, though they are supposed to be from the north (probably the Tennessee River) and to have originally spoken a different language (Swanton 1922: 207–211). Diego Peña referred to this language as the "*diamaza* tongue" in 1716 (Peña 1716). This may be a copying error for Chickasaw. In the latter half of the eighteenth century, they were frequently associated with the Alabama and Koasati, described as refugees from

the north by Marcos Delgado in 1686 (Delgado 1686). From this and other indications, the Muskogee originally may have referred to all Tennessee River Muskogean as "Chickasaw."

9. The archaeological evidence suggests a relationship between the four northernmost towns on the Chattahoochee (Kawita, Kasihta, Taskiki, and Kolomi) and settlements on the Upper Coosa and Tallapoosa Rivers, while the remaining towns are related to the Fort Walton groups to the south in Florida (Schnell 1971; Schnell, Knight, and Schnell 1981: 130). Linguistically, these four towns are Muskogee speakers, while the other Chattahoochee groups speak Hichiti (Swanton 1922). While Kawita does not appear in the sixteenth-century exploration documents, both Kasihta and Taskiki are mentioned as subjects of Kusa in the Coosa-Tallapoosa drainage (Hudson 1990: 104).

10. The Yamasi were a successor to the sixteenth-century Ocute chiefdom on the Upper Altamaha, Okmulgee, and Oconee Rivers. By 1715 they had incorporated remnants of the Guale from the Georgia coast and had relocated to the South Carolina coast above the Savannah River. Following their defeat in the Yamasee War of 1715, the Yamasi towns dispersed widely. In addition to those who joined the Lower Creek, several towns settled near St. Augustine, and some settled farther south along the Oklawaha River (Delahaye 1740; Jefferys 1761). The Apalachi originally occupied northwestern Florida between the Ochlockonee and Aucilla Rivers and were missionized by the Spanish in the 1630s. In 1704, a combined force of South Carolina colonists, Lower Creek, and Yamasi conquered the Apalachi and destroyed their towns. The survivors were widely dispersed. A significant number were enslaved by the Carolinians. Others fled to St. Augustine, Pensacola, and Mobile. The majority, however, relocated northward, where they settled either in the Lower Creek towns on the Okmulgee and Oconee Rivers or in four towns on the Savannah River. The latter comprised over 600 people in 1715. Like the Yamasi, they were defeated and dispersed following the Yamasee War. Those who were captured were enslaved and shipped out of the colony. Many joined other Apalachi at the Spanish and French settlements or among the Lower Creek, but many remain unaccounted for in the records (Hann 1988: 264–318).

11. I would suggest that the eight-day-long Apuskita or Green Corn Ceremony reported for Kawita and other "Mother" (capital) towns reflects this ritual hegemony. Other towns held four-day ceremonies, and the longer ceremonies in the capitals likely allowed representatives of subordinate towns to attend (Swanton 1928b: 546–611).

12. Other authors (Sturtevant 1971; Fairbanks 1978) have assumed that these settlements abandoned the older Creek forms of organization and government. The available direct descriptions from the eighteenth and early nineteenth centuries, however, indicate the existence of square grounds and regular Muskogee institutions (Bartram 1848, 1927; Porter 1952; Young 1934).

13. While Porter (1952) identifies Simpukasi with the later figures, particularly

with Sampiaffi (Muskogee, Simiapaya), I feel this identification is erroneous. Both names are properly titles, rather than personal names. Simpukasi means "with the leader," while Simiapaya designates an official who acted as a representative of the *italwa* (Hewitt 1939: 138–139). A twenty-year absence from the records seems unlikely given his earlier prominence and the fact that his uncle Chilokilichi remains prominent as Chikilli during this period.

14. The recorded version is somewhat garbled and wrongly identifies Simpukasi with the Alachua Seminole but is still significant.

15. In a statement made in Havana on December 22, 1777, he specifically says that "ever since he learned how to manage firearms, he came to live with them at the before mentioned fort San Marcos de Apalachee, where he remained." This would indicate an age of about fifteen, when Creek and Seminole boys became designated gunmen. Since he earlier stated he was nine or ten years old during the governorship of Antonio Benavides, this would place his emigration to the area between 1724 and 1740. He also states he acted as a courier for the Spanish commander at St. Marks for about twenty years, clearly placing him in the area by 1743.

16. Because this tradition was collected from members of several different Seminole towns, some not closely tied to Talahassi, it carries some weight. Had it come only from Talahassi or from members of towns closely tied to it, the statement would be rather suspect.

17. Barcía indicates that there may have been Apalachi settlements in the area around Apalachee, though north of the former Apalachi settlements and the later site of St. Marks, as early as 1718 (Barcía Carballido y Zuñiga 1951: 366). Governor Dionisio de la Vega reported in 1728 that the Indians in Apalachee had revolted the previous year and that those who remained hostile had withdrawn from the area of the fort (Swanton 1922: 127). Other statements that there were only a few Indians at St. Marks also leave open the possibility of British-allied Indians in the region (Auxiliary Bishop of Florida 1736).

18. William Bartram's description of this town in 1775 seems to conflate it with the Talahassi town in the Apalachee region (Bartram 1927: 180), but it also appears on the Stuart-Purcell map of the road from Pensacola to St. Augustine (Stuart and Purcell 1778).

19. Bartram also describes at least two other unnamed villages on the St. Johns River (Bartram 1927: 95–96, 180).

20. Swanton assumes this town was established by the Upper Creek Yufala town, but the evidence really does not support this interpretation. While Romans states that Chukochati was settled from the Upper Creek Yufala, he uses the term rather loosely in places to include the Lower Creek. Likewise, while the population of this town decreased by 50 between 1764 and 1793, that of Yufala Hopoya dropped by 100 (Farmar 1764; Olivier 1793).

21. The name may be properly Okonni and is often spelled with a double *n* in early English documents. The geminate *n* in Muskogee is often heard as a *d* or *t* by speakers of European languages.

22. By at least 1804, the paramount chief of the Alachua was known by the title Mikkonapa (top chief).

23. Apalachi clans can only be reconstructed by inference from family names (see Hann 1988: 70–95, 365–369; Scarry 1992). The Creek Chikota clan corresponds to the Apalachi Chuguta, Ispani to Esfan, and Kowi or Koi to Cui. Likewise, Nokfilha clan, whose name has no meaning in Muskogee, translates as "good things" in Apalachi (Haas 1975: 288). Some or all of the reported but largely extinct Creek clans Osana (otter), Asun(wa) (Spanish moss), and Sonaki (toad) may correspond to the Apalachi Osan(ac) (Swanton 1928a: 159–161).

24. Only two traders were located in Seminole towns at Alachua and Suwani Talahassochi. The remaining trading posts were established on the borders of the Seminole territory and at the Spanish fort at St. Marks. The Spanish government's desire to control and regulate trade, particularly to prevent illegal trade with the British colonies, thus converged with the desires of the Seminole chiefs.

25. Alexander McGillivray, the son of a Scots trader and an Alabama woman, was the most powerful man in the Creek Confederacy during the 1780s. Despite the fact that many referred to him as the "chief" of the confederacy, the only office he held was that of war chief, a subordinate position. He manipulated this position, an appointment as Spanish "commissary" to the Creek, and a silent partnership in Panton, Leslie and Company, who dominated the southern Indian trade, along with impressive personal wealth bequeathed by his father, to dominate the confederacy (Sattler 1987: 64–66).

26. This may have reflected either normal matrilineal succession or a more significant usurpation of power. While Kapicha Mikko's parentage is undocumented, his mother may have been a "sister" of Tonapi. Dynastic marriages were a regular feature among the Florida chiefdoms. In such cases women went to live with their chiefly husbands rather than follow the normal matrilocal pattern (Sattler 1987: 72–73, 1989). Conversely, the Mikasuki had been at the center of various conflicts with the Creek authorities. They were prominent among Bowles's supporters in 1804 and active Redsticks after 1812 (Kinnaird 1931a; Kinnaird and Kinnaird 1983; Sattler 1987: 72–73). Such actions may represent an assertion of power and influence in opposition to Talahassi.

27. While Maroon communities existed in Florida earlier under the Spanish prior to 1763, there is no evidence that they formed any connection with the Seminole or that they formed a part of the later Seminole Maroons. The available evidence indicates that the earlier Maroons in fact left with the Spanish in 1763. Most references to the later Maroons indicate that they had moved to Florida during or after the American Revolution (McReynolds 1957: 23, 84; Mulroy 1993: 6–12; Sturtevant 1971: 106–108).

28. In response to embassies by the Shawnee leader, Tecumseh, the nativistic Redstick Movement emerged among the Upper Creek. This movement soon became a full-fledged civil war opposing the Redsticks, mostly Alabama and Talapusa, against the Lower Creek and the other Upper Creek towns. American forces under Andrew Jackson joined the Lower Creek and defeated the Redsticks at

Horseshoe Bend (Tohopikalika) in 1814. Several of the Flint River towns also joined the Redstick Movement, as did the Mikasuki. The latter, however, were not involved in the military engagements (Halbert and Ball 1969).

29. The origins of all these groups, except the Tohopikalika, can be identified readily. The Alachua were the descendants of the original Okoni settlers under Mikkonapa. The Oklawaha, under the chief Yaha Hacho, represented the older Yamasi population. The Chukochati, under Halpata Hacho, originated from the Yufala Hopoya. The Hotalihuyana, also called Talakchapko, were Okmalki-Chiaha settled on the Pease River under Opony, who probably settled there in part in the 1790s. The Opilaklikaha were Maroons under Abraham. The Tohopikalika, under the leadership of Philip or Imała, are of unknown derivation but may represent the earlier Talofa Okhassi. They also included a Maroon community under John Caesar (Bemrose 1966: 70; Porter 1946a).

30. While this is generally considered the personal name of the Alachua chief during the 1820s and 1830s, his uncle, Payne, also employed this title in 1802 (Morales 1802).

31. Philip of Tohopikalika, Abraham of Opilaklikaha, and Huti Imała (Jumper) all had wives given them by Payne or Mikkonapa.

32. The same reports also state that the chiefs were marked by particularly sumptuous dress.

33. This ascendancy of the Alachua also may reflect older sociopolitical models, as the reservation was in their territory.

34. Even after Removal, Seminole identity remained fluid, and many towns vacillated between Creek and Seminole identity. It was not until the late 1850s that the Seminole achieved their final configuration, when dissident elements, including most Redsticks and some Apalachicola, rejoined the Creek.

35. It is noteworthy in this regard that most of the remaining Seminole leaders in Florida after removal were war chiefs (*tastanaki*) and priests (Sprague 1847).

36. A more dispersed pattern of scattered hamlets around a smaller central village was typical both earlier and later in more favored conditions. In Florida there was abundant land, low population density, and little likelihood of attack. Such dispersal does not require or imply less political integration.

37. Creek and Seminole in Oklahoma maintain a distinction between modern, Western-style governments and traditional forms, referring to the former as *ahaka* (made, manufactured), with the clear implication that these are artificial, fake, or imitation. Within towns, similar accusations are employed to question the legitimacy of a rival's claims to leadership.

38. Such power was inherent in the *mikko*s and their lineages and extend outward in diminishing degrees to their entire clan and perhaps phratry. There were several other bases of power. Socially, they were the most senior men in their *italwa*. Economically, they collected taxes from within the *italwa* and tribute from subordinate polities. They also drew on wealth finance through at least partial control of foreign exchange, especially valuables. Redistribution and generosity in expending these resources created important support. The war chiefs (*tastanaki*)

provided an internal police force and specialized military force under their control. Paramount chiefs also employed military force to subdue rebellions (Sattler 1987: 52–55; Milanich 1990; Dye 1990).

39. The eighteenth-century tradition concerning the foundation of the Yuchi town by a Kasihta chief, his siblings, and his Yuchi wife's relatives provides a model for this process (Hawkins 1848: 62).

40. Likewise, later population figures for the Florida settlements are not fully reflected by declines in the populations of the Lower Creek towns (Toro 1738; Montiano 1747; Swanton 1922: 434–437; Georgia Council 1761; Farmar 1764; Bartram 1927; Olivier 1793; Hawkins 1848; Young 1934; Dexter 1823 [1958]; Duval 1824). Reconciling these would require far higher fertility rates among both the Creek and the Florida groups than is likely or supported by the data. A more likely explanation is that many refugees established settlements in the interior of Florida, where Spanish presence and control were essentially nonexistent.

Nancy P. Hickerson

Ethnogenesis
in the South Plains

Jumano to Kiowa?

It may be useful to think of ethnogenesis as a process which can be logically divided into three phases, not neatly sequential but in principle comparable to phases in life-cycle transitions: separation, a liminal period, and reintegration. For persons or groups who are to constitute a new ethnic entity, separation amounts to the negation or severing of their existing group loyalties. In the liminal phase, surviving—usually dysfunctional—social and/or economic ties wither away, and alternative connections are initiated or strengthened. Reintegration means that a new identity is consolidated, affirmed through ritual and the adoption of a validating mythology. This phase sets the course for future collective consciousness; it may obscure all traces of the earlier history (or histories) of the population and even promote a belief in a miraculous origin or special creation. While the term *ethnogenesis* itself would seem to imply a special attention to the third phase, the formation of the new identity, it is obvious that the prior phases are also crucial to the process. In fact, research interest has more often been directed toward the discovery of previous identity and the consequences of cultural death than to the history and circumstances of reintegration.

In essence, ethnogenesis can be no more than an outcome of the universal workings of culture change, which are constant and ongoing. Economic and social relations are frequently in flux, a fact which is reflected in shifts in social alliances and in the formation of new political groupings. However, it is rapid and wholesale changes of this sort which appear as apparent discontinuities in the historical record. These bring an air of mystery to the subject in the guise of "lost civilizations" and new tribes which seem to "emerge" out of nowhere, without obvious predecessors. Examples of such seeming discontinuity can readily be recalled worldwide (e.g., the demise of the Maya Old Empire, the appearance of the Scythians), but among the tribes of the Great Plains, at the dawn of history, it seems to have been the norm. Between the identifiable prehistoric cultures and the historic tribes of the region there is an interval of a century or more, typically characterized by rapid overall change and the intermingling of previously disparate cultural traits and complexes.

In his book *The Cheyenne Nation*, John Moore (1987) posits the existence, in late prehistoric times, of three independent Algonkian-speaking villages which, in the course of the seventeenth century, shifted westward from the Great Lakes region into the Plains and in so doing adopted a seminomadic style of life. Moore traces the transition of these groups to the full nomadism of hunting bands and documents their conjunction, with segments of allied tribes, in the formation of the Cheyenne camp circle. He thus reveals the Cheyenne tribe to be a complex whole built of diverse components and brought, in the changing political setting of the northern Plains, to a nation-hood formalized by the adoption of a charter and symbolized by the organization and performance of the Sun Dance.

Moore suggests that other Plains peoples are the products of similar pluralistic origins. I believe that those whom we know as Kiowa have undergone experiences of separation, transition, and reintegration during a history which can be shown, in a general way, to parallel that of the Cheyenne. However, the details of these histories are evidently quite different; cultural resemblances between the historic tribes may be seen as a kind of convergence, under the leveling influence of similar ecological and political milieus.

In this essay, I attempt a preliminary formulation of Kiowa ethnogenesis. As the initial phase, I examine the cultural death of one ethnic entity, the Jumano of the South Plains. The Jumano were well known to Spanish explorers and colonists in the sixteenth and seventeenth centuries but disappeared from the historical record soon thereafter. I infer the possible course of events during a liminal period which began as Jumano identity eroded and which brought the surviving population into new geographical and social settings. In the reintegrative phase, a century after the Jumano diaspora, I suggest that eastern remnant bands formed the nucleus for the emergence of the Kiowa nation.

The Jumano at the Dawn of History

Sixteenth- and seventeenth-century accounts of Spanish exploration and colonization often mention a wandering *nación* which inhabited much of the South Plains east of the Rio Grande. This people, the Jumano,[1] were a conge-

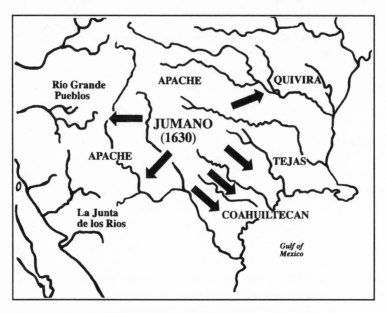

Figure 1. The South Plains showing the location of the Jumano,
ca. 1630, and major trade routes with neighboring peoples.

ries of interrelated bands indigenous to this region, evidently corresponding
to a continuation of the late prehistoric Jornada culture (Campbell n.d.). Their
likely linguistic affiliation, Tanoan, links them to the eastern and southern
Pueblo tribes of New Mexico (Hickerson 1988). Sites associated with the Jornada, a marginal extension of the southwestern Mogollon tradition, show
traces of a late transition to bison hunting and indications of trade contacts
both with the nuclear Southwest and with agricultural tribes of the eastern
Plains. Similarly, the historic Jumano were known to the Spaniards as bison
hunters and traders.

A series of regional trade partnerships linked individual Jumano bands to
agricultural communities from New Mexico to La Junta de los Rios, the confluence of the Rio Grande and the Río Conchos. They moved seasonally between their hunting grounds in the South Plains and the Rio Grande Valley,
where certain frontier villages were centers for their trade. In the Plains, the
Jumano were also in contact with a number of eastern and southern tribes;
they are known to have traveled as far as Quivira, beyond the Arkansas River,
and the Hasinai (or Caddo) in eastern Texas.

Since their contacts extended into Mexico, it is possible that the Jumano
had some knowledge of horses prior to 1570, when a Spanish exploring party
left a horse in a Jumano village near La Junta de los Rios. A few decades later,

at the time of Salas's expedition, the Jumano in the Plains east of New Mexico may have been partly equestrian. By 1680, in any case, the Jumano were conducting a large-scale trade in horses and were evidently using horses and wagons to haul goods eastward from La Junta de los Rios. At this date, late in their history, they—like the Kiowa two centuries later—followed a way of life which hinged on bison hunting, horse pastoralism, and trade.

The role of the Jumano as traders probably originated as an extension of a long history as nomadic hunters. By the time of the Spanish *entradas*, they were already specialized in this role to a degree. There were Jumano enclave communities in gateway locations in the pueblos, at La Junta, and at the border of Quivira (the *gran población* encountered by the Oñate expedition). The processing and warehousing cadres at these sites were seasonally augmented by increments from the Plains, as nomadic hunters and itinerant traders arrived and departed. At rendezvous sites in the High Plains of West Texas, contacts between Jumano bands would have been the occasion for exchanges of goods; this increased the circulation of exotic trade wares (such as New Mexican turquoise and mineral pigments, Mexican copper bells and macaw feathers, Alibates flint, western obsidian, Rio Concho pearls, and seashells from the Gulfs of Mexico and California).

Through the seventeenth century, the Spanish colonies evidently considered the Jumano to be an important economic and political power, valued especially as a link to the Nations of the North, the Caddoan tribes and confederacies. During these years, the name "Jumano" was evidently used in two related senses. First, and earliest, it was a generic term which the Spaniards applied to people of a certain cultural and linguistic type who were widespread along and east of the Rio Grande and in the South Plains. In a narrower sense, the term referred to Indians of this type in their role as traders. In this capacity, they could be found far from their bases near the Rio Grande and well outside of their hunting range in the South Plains. This second usage had become predominant in the last decades of the seventeenth century; by this time, the Jumano people had abandoned or been driven from most of their earlier territories, and their presence is principally documented in peripheral areas, both east and west.

Separation: The Jumano Diaspora

The late seventeenth century was the period of the rapid decline of the Jumano which so intrigued Bandelier (1890), Hodge (1911), Bolton (1911), and others. The "mystery" of Jumano disappearance from the historical record continued to be a popular topic of scholarly speculation until 1940, when Scholes and Mera went so far as to propose, in effect, that such a tribe had never really existed; the name, they argued, was simply a synonym for *rayado* (striped or painted people) (1940: 275). For several decades, this formulation has been widely accepted as a solution to the "Jumano problem."

Such rumors to the contrary, however, my research indicates that the Jumano were an authentic people who did not disappear mysteriously. Rather, their territories were preempted and the survivors became scattered as a consequence of more than a century of intermittent warfare. In this struggle, which was already in progress during the years of Spanish exploration and colonization, the contending parties were, on one side, a wave of invading Apache and, on the other, the Jumano and their allies. The confrontation continued sporadically through the sixteenth and seventeenth centuries, with the invaders advancing from the north and west, while the aboriginal groups lost ground and were either displaced or incorporated by their conquerors.

The Jumano-Apache war was not simply a contest over hunting grounds and territory—it also concerned trade routes and access to trade centers. Early intimations of this war appear in the accounts of the Coronado expedition, which reported that the "Querechos" (Apache) and "Teyas" (Jumano) were embattled just east of the northernmost pueblos. Five decades later, Oñate's troops found Apache "Vaqueros" trading at these villages (Taos and Picuris), while battling their enemies the Jumano farther south, near Pecos pueblo. Thirty years after this, the Apache controlled the trade at Pecos, and the Jumano had withdrawn over 100 leagues to the east.

In the 1660s, the Seven Rivers Apache disrupted Jumano trade in the Tompiros, their last remaining foothold in the pueblos. Loss of this port of entry ended direct Jumano access to the colony of New Mexico, although the Spaniards continued to make annual expeditions to deal with them in the Plains, and the trade continued at El Paso and La Junta de los Rios. However, the southern trade route, linking La Junta with Jumano *rancherías* in central Texas, was broken sometime during the 1680s; the Upper Colorado Valley became Apache territory soon thereafter. At this point, Apache dominance of the South Plains was complete, and the Jumano were a conquered and displaced people.

Much of the recorded information on the Jumano and their struggle against the Apache in the South Plains derives indirectly from their efforts to win Spanish assistance to the native resistance movement. Two occasions stand out, early and late in the century. In the 1620s, Jumano emissaries came repeatedly to the Franciscan mission at Isleta, begging for missions in the region to the east. This eventually led fray Juan de Salas to make the long trek into the Plains described in Benavides's memorial of 1630 (Ayer 1900–1901). The upshot of Salas's efforts, however, was not the stabilization of the Jumano position, which the Indians evidently desired, but a missionary-assisted retreat and resettlement of refugees in the Estancia Valley, east of the Tompiro pueblos.

More explicit appeals for Spanish military support were made at El Paso in 1681 and 1682 by the Jumano chief Juan Sabeata. The accounts of the subsequent Lopez–Dominguez de Mendoza expedition, which included both clergy and a military force, provide detailed information on the route between La Junta de los Rios and the river that the Spaniards called "Rio Nueces" in central Texas and document the existence of a chain of Jumano settlements along the way. One important base was situated near the confluence of Toyah Creek and the Rio Pecos; another was located on the Rio Nueces itself, probably the Concho near its confluence with the Colorado of Texas. It was in the Plains between these two locales that the Jumano pastured the horses they traded to the Nations of the North. The journal of Captain Juan Dominguez de Mendoza records both the concern of the Jumano for the safety of their herds and the very real threat of Apache raids, which resulted in the theft of both Jumano and Spanish horses (Bolton 1908: 331–335). However, the colonial government of New Mexico did not commit forces to the cause of the Jumano and their allies, and fray Nicolas Lopez subsequently failed to obtain support for a proposed campaign of mission building in the Plains.

A few years after this failed expedition, depositions taken at Parral in Nueva Vizcaya, from Juan Sabeata and other native leaders, describe the annual wars of the Jumano with the Apache and their struggle for continuing access to the herds of buffalo in their traditional hunting grounds (Hackett 1926: 261–277). The region must have fallen soon thereafter, with any remaining Jumano settlements abandoned or destroyed. In the early eighteenth century, the entire region was occupied by the Apache, who were soon trading and raiding at San Antonio and other new Spanish settlements in central and southern Texas.

The Eastern Frontier

The foregoing account of Jumano decline and fall reflects the perspective of Spanish observers based in New Mexico and Nueva Vizcaya. Their reports document the position of the Jumano in relation to the Spanish colonies; however, little is known about the actual extent of native trade and diplomacy in the east, beyond the limits of direct Spanish rule. Indications of the nature of these contacts are rare, especially in the earlier period, when very few Europeans visited the South Plains and eastern Texas.

One of the earliest indications of long-distance trade of the sort conducted by the Jumano is the mention, by the Gentleman of Elvas, of woven textiles and turquoise which the De Soto expedition found in the territory of Guasco, evidently on the Brazos; these things "were brought from the direction of the sunset" (Hodge 1911: 246–247). The narrative of Cabeza de Vaca also documents the operations of a trade network which reached as far as the Karankawa and Coahuiltecan and reveals the presence of specialized traders who had freedom of passage among feuding tribes and bands (Covey 1961: 67–68). Interestingly enough, Cabeza de Vaca and his companions sojourned for a time with a band of traders who carried bows and arrows into central Texas from the west, just as the Jumano did a century later. Like the Jumano, these traders contacted their clients during intertribal gatherings at the time of seasonal events such as pecan or prickly pear harvests.

Jumano claims of trade in Texas are echoed in French documents of the late seventeenth century. Members of La Salle's colony learned about the visits of Jumano traders, both from the Hasinai (Tejas) and from a neighboring tribe (Cox 1922: 231–233). In 1686 and 1687, representatives of the French colony were able to purchase much-needed horses in Hasinai country, noting that the animals had been brought there by the Choumane (Jumano) (Cox 1922: 93–94).

The Manrhout and Gatacka

Two letters written several years earlier by La Salle himself from the Illinois country are of special interest in relation to the trade in horses. These letters are fragmentary and undated; however, internal evidence suggests that one was written just prior to, and the other subsequent to, his 1682 voyage to the mouth of the Mississippi (about the time of the Lopez–Dominguez de Mendoza expedition in Texas). In the earlier, as part of a general discussion of problems of travel through the interior of the continent, La Salle raises the possibility of obtaining horses from a native source. There are many, he indicates, to be found among the "Pana, Paniassa, Manrhout, Gatacka, Panimaha and Pasos." La Salle seems uncertain about the location of these groups, which are located "a bit farther than one might wish"; but he appears to believe that they can readily be reached, via the Missouri or, alternatively, by land, the intervening country being open (Margry 1974 [1879], 2: 168).

In the second letter, La Salle recounts events of the voyage of exploration during which he took possession of the Mississippi. Here, in an aside concerning the rivers and peoples of North America, he again mentions the Pana and their "neighbors and allies," the Manrhout and Gatacka. This time, La Salle seems to be on surer ground and indicates the source of his information: a Pana of around eighteen years of age, one of a group of young men sent to him by their families to be educated à la françoise (Margry 1974 [1879], 2: 201).

It can be assumed that this Pana youth represented native economic interests compatible with the development of the trade to which La Salle also aspired. His people, La Salle was told, live "more than two hundred leagues to the west, on one of the branches of the Mississippi" in two adjacent villages. The Gatacka and Manrhout are located to the south of these villages. They sell horses to the Pana, which (La Salle assumes) they "apparently steal from the Spaniards of New Mexico." He goes on to convey a good deal of information about the Indians and their horses: the horses could be very useful because of their hardiness. The Indians use them in war, in hunting, and to carry their possessions; they do not use them in farming. The horses can live out of doors, even in the snow, and need no other food than pasturage. They are strong, of great endurance; they can carry the meat of two buffalo. Finally, he adds that his *petit Pana* informant has seen, in his country, certain stones which may be turquoise; La Salle finds this to be a confirmation of a trade connection with the west (Margry 1974 [1879], 2: 202).

For present purposes, the most important information is perhaps the locations of the Pana, just over 200 leagues[2] from La Salle's headquarters of Fort St. Louis, and of the Manrhout and Gatacka, an unspecified distance to the south of the Pana. The series of names "Pana, Paniassa . . . Panimaha" suggests the scattered Caddoan groups west of the Mississippi. The locale, on "one of the branches of the Mississippi," is vague but indicates at least that it was not on the Missouri, a river with which La Salle was already well acquainted; perhaps the specific stream could not be identified from the information given by the Pana youth. French maps of 1700 to 1720 show the Paniassa in locales which later came to be identified with the Taovaya and Wichita.[3] In this case, the young man's estimate of distance would be confirmed: from Fort St. Louis, a radius of 200 leagues (roughly 530 miles) intersects the Arkansas River twice, just above and just below the earliest documented location of the Taovaya and Wichita. In this connection, the reference to "two villages, side by side" is of special interest. In 1719, Claude du Tisne visited two such Paniassa villages which lay roughly one league apart on a tributary of the Arkansas. There were, all told, around 300 horses in the villages at the time; silver work and other goods testified to past trade contacts, direct or indirect, with the Spanish colonies. Horses were evidently in short supply, since the villagers were reluctant to sell them to the Frenchmen. A few individuals claimed to have visited the Spanish settlements, years past, in the company of the traders; at the time of Tisne's visit, however, the way was blocked by the Comanche (Margry 1974 [1879], 4: 311–314).

Who were the traders, the source of the Paniassa horses? In 1682 (or thereabouts), the most likely purveyors of horses to the Taovaya and Wichita—the people of Quivira—would certainly have been the Jumano. They held territory south of the Arkansas, carried on an active trade in horses, and dealt both with the Spanish colonies and with Indian tribes located east of the Apache frontier. As already indicated, there were Jumano *rancherías* and horse herds along the Upper Colorado of Texas; other Jumano bands, with their herds, may have been spread over a wider area, perhaps as far north as the Upper Brazos. Jumano friendship with Quivira was documented by Benavides as early as the 1620s. In 1683, Juan Sabeata claimed two great Caddoan confederacies or "kingdoms"—Quivira and Tejas—as allies. Sabeata's Jumano made annual expeditions to trade with the Tejas (Caddo or Hasinai), transporting horses as well as clothing, weapons, and other goods of Spanish manufacture. Delegations from the Tejas sometimes accompanied the Jumano on visits to La Junta de los Rios; representatives from Quivira (Wichita) may have done so as well.

There is no evidence that the Jumano, in the late seventeenth century, regularly raided or stole large numbers of horses from the Spanish colonies. Rather, it would seem that they had become true horse pastoralists and that their herds in the South Plains were at least partly self-sustaining. The Jumano did steal horses from their enemies, the Apache, as the Apache stole from them. But they were at pains to maintain good relations with the Spanish colonies. Late in the century, circa 1685 to 1691, Juan Sabeata was named by the royal governor of Nueva Vizcaya as "governor of the Cibolos, Jumano, and Nations of the North" (Hackett 1934: 138; Hackett 1926: 263). In this capacity, he and his followers were active agents of the colonial administration, serving as messengers and information-gatherers as well as traders in Spanish relations with the village peoples of the eastern Plains, notably the Caddoan tribes.

But what of the names "Manrhout" and "Gatacka"? James Mooney may have been the first to call attention to the significance of the La Salle letters and to propose an identification of these groups. He must immediately have recognized Gatacka as the long-established name of the people also known, in recent times, as the Kiowa Apache. Reasoning from this positive identification and bearing in mind the long association of the Gatacka with the Kiowa, he went on to suggest that "Manrhout . . . may possibly be some obsolete name for the Kiowa themselves" (1979 [1898]: 248). Mooney made this inference, in part, on the basis of nomenclature but also with an eye to geographical location and to the cultural implications of the La Salle text—particularly the references to the horse culture.

For present purposes, Mooney's reasoning may be provisionally accepted, leading to the following propositions: (1) The Gatacka, or Kiowa Apache, can be securely identified as an Athabascan-speaking group. If (2) the Manrhout are posited as ancestral Kiowa, they were, perforce, Tanoan-speaking. Since (3) the Jumano were Tanoan-speaking, the Manrhout are best identified with the Jumano. Thus, the La Salle letters provide support for the premise that (4) the Jumano of the eastern frontier, at the end of the seventeenth century, were a likely founder population for the Kiowa nation and indicate that their alliance with the Gatacka, or Kiowa Apache, was already established at this early date.

The Liminal Phase: 1700 to 1800

Between these references and a continuous historical record of the Kiowa, beginning around 1800, there is a century of mystery. The liminal phase would have begun with the destruction of Jumano integrity, in several stages: displacement from their more northern territories and from trade with New Mexico by 1670; loss of hunting grounds between the Pecos and the Colorado a decade later; displacement from the Colorado Valley and termination of the trade at La Junta, perhaps a decade after that. The last straw may have been the outbreak of hostilities between the Caddo and Spain, beginning in 1693. This temporarily brought an end to Spanish involvement in Texas and coincided with Apache expansion eastward. It signaled the end of Spanish sponsorship of Jumano trading expeditions and may have forced various Jumano bands to choose between submitting to their longtime enemies, the Apache, in the west or joining forces with their longtime allies, the Caddoan tribes, in the east.

Juan Sabeata, the Jumano chief and governor, was disappointed at the failure of his efforts to win Spanish support against the Apache. In a petition for help which he addressed to New Mexican officials at El Paso in 1682, Sabeata had raised the possibility of a French presence in Texas—a constant bugaboo in New Spain—and hinted that trade contacts may already have taken place in that quarter. Spanish fears of French encroachment were realized a few years later, when La Salle planted his colony on the Texas coast. During an encounter in a Hasinai village, the Jumano solicited trade with members of the French colony, and a Jumano leader—probably Sabeata himself—even approached La Salle with a proposal for a joint attack on Spanish settlements on the Rio Grande. La Salle's colony was short-lived, however, and the Jumano overtures came to naught. However, they clearly give notice of conflict and instability in economic relations and reveal a Jumano leadership which was weighing both international and regional geopolitics in a desperate search for alliances.

As the Apache advanced eastward to occupy the valleys of the Colorado and Brazos, there were repercussions along the Rio Grande. As early as 1685, Posada reported that refugees from central Texas, Jumano included, were seeking shelter in the Spanish missions below El Paso. Posada went on to suggest, as part of an ambitious proposal for the development of a port at the Bay of Espíritu Santo (Matagorda Bay), that the Jumano be resettled on the Colorado, to help protect the port against Apache encroachment. They would, he suggested, defend this territory because "it is their land which the Apacha nation took away from them and whom they hold as enemies. Their desire for vengeance . . . will impel them to remain faithful" (A. B. Thomas 1982: 65–67).

Thus, on the west, there was some movement of the Jumano from the Plains toward the Rio Grande, where the missions provided temporary security. Some years later, when the Apache invaded the Rio Grande Valley south of New Mexico, most of these missions were abandoned. Eventually the surviving Jumano, like other remnant groups, were at least partly absorbed into the Apache population. References cited by Bolton indicate the presence of bands of "Apaches Jumanes" in western Texas and northern Mexico. Bolton saw in this the solution to the mystery of the disappearance of the Jumano from the historical record—they had merged with their former enemies (1911: 84).

But was this the whole story? Was withdrawal westward the only recourse open to the Jumano of the eastern frontier? What of their herds and the trade in horses? Might not a part of this population have removed eastward rather than westward, seeking new pastures and hunting territory ahead of the advancing Apache and closer to their Caddoan allies? These allies were, at the time, already looking to France as a potential market for their furs and a new source of trade goods. The east-west routes had fallen, but the opportunity was at hand for a reoriented trade network in which the erstwhile Jumano could find a new role and a new identity.

I hope eventually to present a more complete scenario of the transition from Jumano to Kiowa but can now only posit a possible course of events and suggest some considerations which may be of significance when a complete chronology can be written.

Changing Jumano Nomenclature

As already noted, "Jumano" appears to be a Hispanization based on a number of cognate native appellations. Used as a generic term, subsuming much geographical and cultural variation, it thus represents, from the beginning, an extension of aboriginal usage. In this generic sense, the Jumano consisted of a loosely organized network of territorial divisions or bands. A number of names of these divisions are known (though not always clearly distinguishable from allied groups which were often found in the company of the itinerant Jumano). For example, in 1582, one chronicler, Espejo, referred to a string of communities along the Rio Grande between La Junta and El Paso as "Jumanos" (Bolton 1908: 168–192); another member of the same expedition, Luxan, distinguished, from south to north, the "Otomoacas," "Caguates," and "Tanpachoas" (Hammond and Rey 1953: 153–212).

A century later, the native captains who accompanied Juan Sabeata on the road east from La Junta represented the "Cibolos," "Caguas," and "Cholomes" (Hackett 1934: 137). The Cibolo (the "Cow Nation" earlier encountered by Cabeza de Vaca) were the predominant Jumano group in the hinterlands east of La Junta and were (as the name suggests) primarily buffalo hunters. The Cholome were part of the farm belt at the confluence of the Rio Grande and Río Conchos. Scattered references to the name Cagua (cf. Caguate) or Caigua are found throughout the history of the Jumano trade. This diffuse group may have been more integrally involved in the trade itself than were the others, and their name—whether it denoted a band, a kinship grouping, or a status category—gives the most obvious hint of a connection to the later Kiowa. It appears that while the use of Jumano declined, Caigua endured; it recurs from time to time in the eighteenth century and reappears as the principal designation of a new tribal entity in the nineteenth.

Only a tentative explanation can be offered for the name Manrhout, used by La Salle, which does not obviously resemble any known tribal designation in the South Plains region. It could have originated in the Spanish word *manso* (or, in the seventeenth century, *manxo*), meaning "docile" or "tame," an adjective most often applied to domesticated animals but also commonly used in the Spanish colonies to characterize friendly Indians—in contrast to those who were unfriendly or "wild."

The Spanish term was apparently incorporated in a borderlands pidgin. As early as 1598 it is recorded in Oñate's account of an encounter near El Paso with Indians who surrendered with the words "Manxos . . . Micos!" [(We are) peaceful . . . Friends!] (Hammond and Rey 1953, 1: 315). It is, incidentally, retained as the name of the Manso tribe, historically located in that same region. The term could well have been applied, descriptively, to the Jumano, based on their reputation for trade and other friendly dealings with the Spanish colonies.[4]

The Gatacka or "Kiowa Apache"

As already indicated, the Gatacka alliance with the Kiowa is longstanding and may even predate the liminal period. Their origin, like that of the Kiowa, presents a mystery; in this case, the mystery hinges on whether the ancestral population was eastern Apache (historically, enemies of both Jumano and Kiowa) or a segment of another, unidentified Athabascan population. The degree of linguistic distance between Kiowa Apache and other Apache groups—all of which, according to Hoijer (1971), speak dialects of a single language—suggests that the separation of the Gatacka from these southwestern Athabascan is relatively ancient.[5]

I concur with Hyde (1959: 43) in favoring a link between the Gatacka and the Escanjaque, whose presence in the Plains is first noted at the time of Oñate's expedition to Quivira. In the 1650s, these people were evidently antagonists and trade rivals of the Jumano on the Rio Nueces. However, an alliance between the two groups could have arisen out of their common involvement in the Caddo trade, as well as their shared experience of losing lands along the Colorado River to the eastern Apache (ancestors of the Mescalero and/or Lipan) (A. B. Thomas 1982: 57).

In the nineteenth century, the Kiowa and Gatacka were frequently encountered together, sometimes appearing under the generic name of "Trading Indians." The Gatacka came to be called "Kiowa Apache" in recent times, probably because of their inclusion in the Kiowa camp circle during the summer tribal assembly; this indicated a formal political union, as well as an economic alliance.

The Caddoan Tribes and Confederacies

The earliest Spanish references to the Jumano east of New Mexico give evidence of their friendship with Quivira (presumed to be the ancestral Wichita people). To the southeast, the Jumano were closely allied with the Tejas (Caddo or Hasinai) of eastern Texas. These alliances were clearly reflected in Spanish policy, which, throughout the seventeenth century, repeatedly sought to use the Jumano as intermediaries in maintaining economic ties and friendly (if distant) relations with the Caddoan confederacies. The Caddoan were, in turn, seen as potential buffers against encroachments from the east by France or other European powers.

After the turn of the century, the Caddoan groups evidently continued their friendship with the erstwhile Jumano and may have actively sponsored the reorientation of their trade along a north-south axis. The northern terminus of the new network could have been another Caddoan group—perhaps for a time the Pawnee but eventually the Arikara, whose villages on the Missouri were a major focus of trade up to the 1790s. At that time, according to Hyde, there was a "league of tribes" in the northern Plains which united the Arikara, Kiowa, and Gatacka (1959: 185). Throughout the nineteenth century, neither Kiowa nor Kiowa Apache were ever in a prolonged state of war with the southern Caddoan; their cordial relationship with the Wichita, in particular, is reflected in the continuing cooperation of these tribes in the treaty period.

The Trade in Horses

The Manrhout location apparently lay along the Upper Colorado River of Texas, a zone of natural pasturage which, years later, was famous for its abundance of wild horses. This is the region in which Spanish sources document the presence of large Jumano herds. It is likely, however, that other Jumano bands, also with horse herds, were spread over a larger area, perhaps as far north as the Upper Brazos.

Until shortly after 1700—about the time the Apache became established on the Colorado and Brazos—the Wichita villages on the Arkansas lay at the northern limit of the trade in horses. By midcentury, horses were found throughout the Plains, at least as far north as the Crow and Blackfoot (Haines 1938: 434). In the interval, the ancestral Kiowa and Gatacka must have shifted location and extended their movements toward the north. This shifting may, in part, have been motivated by the expansion in the South Plains of a new and highly aggressive people, the Comanche, who challenged and eventually gained precedence over the Apache.

North of the Comanche-Apache frontier, Kiowa bands then spread through the country between the Arkansas and the Platte, a region ideally suited for their pastoral way of life. They pastured their herds north and west of the villages of their Wichita allies, who were relocating toward the south and east for better contact with French trading posts in Louisiana. The Kiowa were now in position to become middlemen between the French-Wichita trade and the northern Plains tribes. They became known as a hunting and trading people, moving between the Arkansas and the villages of the Arikara and Mandan. The pattern of their movements must have resembled that of the old Jumano, who gravitated between their camps in the Plains and the villages of their eastern and western trading partners. It might be noted that the proposed connection to the Jumano implies a long history for the Kiowa horse complex, dating to the 1570s, if not earlier.[6]

Reintegration: The Kiowa Nation

When modern Kiowa recount their own past, they usually begin with an account of their ancestors' emergence out of an underworld onto the earth's surface. The events are set in a cold land in the far north. The place of emergence is thought to be in the Yellowstone River Valley, close to the camps of the Crow. The Kiowa have many place-names for mountains and other geographical features of this region, and they recall a trail of southward migration that led them to their historic territory between the Arkansas and Platte Rivers.

It has often been pointed out that the tradition of the Kiowa northern homeland is at odds with the evidence of language, which provides an obvious link to the Tanoan Pueblos in the Southwest; Kiowa origins therefore pose a problem (Davis 1979). The Kiowa emergence myth itself appears to be a variant of a well-known southwestern type, exemplified in Zuni and Hopi accounts of the ascension of clan ancestors through a series of underworlds to the earth's surface. Newcombe, considering a somewhat broader spectrum of "their varied and complex social and ceremonial life . . . their societies, traditions, and their artistic sense," also posits a southwestern cultural origin for the Kiowa (1969: 220–221). R. Lowie (1953) and Erminie W. Vogelin (1933), though not arguing for a southwestern affiliation, specifically discounted Kiowa traditions of northern origin and alliance with the Crow tribe on the basis of comparisons of culture traits and folklore motifs.

Despite the hard evidence of such etic comparisons, however, the Kiowa myth rings true in emic terms.[7] Like other sacred stories of creation and cultural origin, it celebrates a real beginning, the coming into being of a new ethnic entity. However, it must be admitted that such entities do not really spring into existence fully formed, out of nothingness. In this case, the mythic northern emergence may be read as a metaphoric expression of the actual emergence of the Kiowa people into a new level of political reality; it marks their birth as a tribal nation.[8]

The Kiowa nation, like the Cheyenne, was undoubtedly diverse in its sources, incorporating both Kiowa-speaking bands and other elements drawn from incorporated and allied groups. Besides having maintained a long political alliance, the Gatacka and Kiowa undoubtedly intermarried over many generations. Kiowa families also trace descent from Crow, Arapaho, and Sarsi ancestors, as well as the many Mexican, Texan, and other "captives" who were part of the tribe.

A suggestion of the composite nature of the Kiowa nation in its earlier days may be found in the plan of the 1867 Sun Dance circle, as recorded by Mooney in 1896. One place in the circle belonged to the Kʰato, or Biters, a name which refers to the Arikara. Another place was reserved for the Ga'igwu, or Kiowa proper. Three places were assigned to the Kobui, or Elk; the Kinep, or Big Shields; and the Kontallyui, or Black Boys. The sixth place, of course, was that of the Semat, the Gatacka or Kiowa Apache. There is also a tradition of an extinct seventh band, the Kuatda, or Pullers, who spoke a "peculiar dialect of Kiowa" (Mooney 1979 [1898]: 228–230). Reportedly, in earlier days, these bands had their own chiefs, as well as distinctive ritual paraphernalia, religious societies, and so on (Boyd 1981: 40–42; Nye 1962: 30). It is not unreasonable, then, to suppose that these segments of the Sun Dance circle can be traced to originally disparate groups—Kiowa-speaking and non-Kiowa—which made

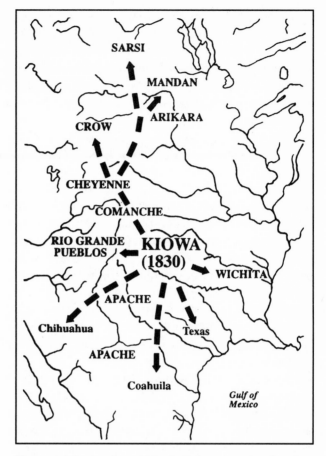

Figure 2. The South and North Plains, ca. 1830, showing the location of the Kiowa and major trade routes with other peoples.

up the Kiowa nation. In addition, an ancient separation of northern and southern tribal divisions, or moieties, may be recalled in the designations of T'okinahyup, or Northerners (literally "Cold People") and Guahalego, Southerners (named for the Kwahadi, or Comanche, with whom they were affiliated) (Mooney 1979 [1898]: 227).

The Crow

It is clear that a close relationship with the Crow constituted an important influence on the Kiowa in their formative period. The Kiowa recall especially friendly relations with the Crow people, as well as with the Arikara, Mandan, and Hidatsa. A special tradition of Crow fosterage of Kiowa children was reported by Mooney: the children were, reportedly, left with the Crow for long periods of time in order to maintain a knowledge of the Crow language—a practice undoubtedly related to the Kiowa role in trade (Mooney 1979 [1898]: 156). A number of prominent Kiowa, including Chief Kicking Bird, have claimed Crow ancestry (Boyd 1981: 12).

More to the point, perhaps, is the tradition that the Sun Dance was acquired, directly or indirectly, from the Crow. More basic, and perhaps more significant than adoption of the Sun Dance itself, however, was the acquisition of a new style of tribal organization. This innovation, which greatly facilitated cooperation in hunting and warfare, amounted to the formal linkage of disparate bands and families into a single integrated political body—a tribal nation. The annual gathering of bands amounted to an affirmation of national unity, dramatized in the performance of the Sun Dance. This innovation was undoubtedly a response to the pressures engendered by colonialism and, especially, by the westward expansion of the United States in the post–Civil War period. The new form of political organization became established in the northern Plains before spreading, in a more diffuse form, to adjacent regions. My own cursory comparison of features of social and political organization shows the largest number of similarities between the Kiowa and tribes of the North Plains and Plateau areas. This area of congruence stands out in contrast to other cultural and linguistic traits which betray the older and more deep-rooted connection to the South Plains and Southwest.[9]

When the Lewis and Clark expedition ascended the Missouri River in the summer of 1805, they reported that the "Kiawa," in seventy tents, were located on the headwaters of the Platte, very near to the Yellowstone Valley, the territories of the Crow, and the traditional place of Kiowa emergence (Coues 1965 [1893], 1: 58–60). The seventy households—likely the northern moiety but not the entire Kiowa population—could have been assembled to participate in a Sun Dance, perhaps under the sponsorship of the Crow. The tradition that the *taime* idol, a stone effigy figure that is central to Kiowa Sun Dance symbolism, was a gift from the Crow (or, alternatively, from an Arapaho who received it from the Crow) suggests that there was a formal, ritualized transfer of the ceremony, along with its sacred artifacts.

In their early years of trading in the north, the Kiowa could have been witness to a wave of spectacular ceremonial events, as the Sun Dance complex spread through the tribes of the region. They became friends and trading partners of the Crow, lived among them for periods of time, and eventually intermarried. When the Crow assembled for their summer ceremonials, the visitors may have been given a place in their camp circle (as the Gatacka would be part of the Kiowa circle). Eventually, the Kiowa also adopted these ceremonies and adapted them to their own needs. This process was completed when the Kiowa Cold People, after sojourning in the north, eventually re-united with their southern congeners. They brought with them a vision of a new type of tribal unity, promoted by an annual gathering of bands and heightened by the drama of a great ceremonial. Thus, sometime around 1800, the Kiowa assimilated a political and religious complex which was already current among their northern neighbors and allies.

U.S. Traders and Trading Companies

Throughout the eighteenth century, there is no indication of French or Span-ish recognition of the Kiowa, a tribe which is first acknowledged as a political entity in the Louisiana Territory under U.S. rule. On the other hand, there can be little doubt that trade relations, direct or indirect, were maintained throughout this period. The history of relations between Plains tribes and Francophone traders, from La Salle's exploration of the Mississippi to the Lou-isiana Purchase, is obscure and may never be fully documented. U.S. trading companies, based in New Orleans and St. Louis, undoubtedly built on the contacts begun under French and Spanish rule. As already noted, Jumano-French relations were established in the 1680s; it is likely that such relations (at times direct, at times through the Caddoan) continued to influence the movements of the Jumano and their eighteenth-century descendants.

Around 1800, the earliest U.S. references to the Kiowa already indicate an inclination to establish and maintain close relations with trading company representatives. Meriwether Lewis himself remarked on their penchant for barter and suggested that the Kiowa "might be readily induced to visit the trading establishments on the Missouri" (Coues 1965 [1893], 1: 58). In the same period, around the turn of the nineteenth century, an American trader, James Purseley (or Purcell), was evidently closely associated with the Kiowa, since he was with members of the tribe on the Upper Platte River in 1803 and also is known to have accompanied a delegation of Kiowa to New Mexico two years later (Weber 1971: 37; Mooney 1979 [1898]: 171).

After Lewis and Clark, U.S. traders rapidly expanded operations in the new territories. The movements of the Kiowa were likely orchestrated to meet the needs of certain St. Louis–based traders who established posts on the Arkan-sas River and its tributaries. The tribe had a working relationship with the Chouteau family and its operatives beginning in the 1830s, if not earlier; this relationship continued through the treaty period.[10]

The Comanche

From the perspective of recent Kiowa history, the most important allied tribe is undoubtedly the Comanche. The entry of this Uto-Aztecan people into the Plains was roughly concurrent with the Jumano diaspora; it may even be hypothesized that pressures initiated by the Comanche precipitated the eastward surge of the Apache, which in turn drove the Jumano from their lands in central Texas. Although there is no record of direct Jumano contact with the Comanche, they or their Great Basin congeners may be found—as "Yutas"—among the nations which Juan Sabeata named as allies, based on their common opposition to the Apache (Hackett 1931: 138–139).

As to subsequent relations between the Kiowa and Comanche, Kiowa tradition indicates an early period of hostilities. This warfare may initially have forced the Kiowa toward the north and then have temporarily blocked intercourse between northern and southern Kiowa bands. Prior to 1800, however, the Kiowa and the Kwahadi band of Comanche became allies; reportedly, the alliance was negotiated by a Mexican rancher or trader (Mooney 1979 [1898]: 162; Boyd 1981: 16). The alliance was lasting and served the Kiowa well, as it opened the way around 1805 for trade access to New Mexico.

More important, the Kiowa, with the Comanche as their allies, were now able to extend their territorial base south of the Arkansas and Canadian Rivers and to rediscover the old Jumano routes for raiding and trading deep into Texas and Mexico. In a very general sense, the Kiowa—as the cultural heirs of the Jumano—now had come full circle. They could reoccupy territory which their ancestors had been forced to abandon two centuries earlier, and they regained a role in trade with New Mexico and other provinces. They had preserved and maintained their traditional role as hunters, horse-pastoralists, and traders while escalating this role to a new level of complexity in the cultural flux of the nineteenth-century Great Plains.

Notes

Many of the insights and interpretations expressed in this paper have been developed in previous papers and a recent book (Hickerson 1988, 1990, 1994). I am grateful to Texas Tech University for academic leave in 1986 and 1992, which gave me time for research and writing, and the National Endowment for the Humanities and the Newberry Library for additional support.

1. The name actually appears in a number of variant forms, including Jumane, Xumane, Humana, Sumana, and Choumane. The geographical distribution of the variants is touched on by Sauer (1934).

2. This passage is quoted incorrectly by Mayhall (1962: 23), with the unfortunate result that the Pana location is indicated to be only 100, rather than 200, leagues from the Illinois River site of Fort St. Louis.

3. See, for example, the rough map of ca. 1700 said to be based on Tonti's evidence; or the De Lisle map dated 1718 (Tucker 1942, plates 15, 19).

4. La Salle's "Manrhout" would have been, phonetically, approximately [manR^{h}o]. If it was, indeed, a reflex of *manxo*, it was probably filtered through two or more Indian languages.

5. Based on linguistic evidence, Hoijer suggests that "the migration south-ward . . . took place first by the groups we now know as the Navajo, San Carlos, Chiricahua, and Mescalero, followed by but still in contact with the Jicarilla and Lipan. The Kiowa Apaches clearly came much later" (1971: 5). This interpretation is a reversal of his earlier (1938) view that the division of the Apache took place within the Southwest and South Plains.

6. Other aspects of Kiowa culture may eventually be interpreted in light of the proposed connection with the Jumano. For example, early Kiowa participation in the peyote complex, as well as their historical role as intermediaries in the trade in peyote, may become more understandable when it is realized that Jumano trade extended into peyote-producing regions of Mexico in the seventeenth century.

7. *Etic* refers to culture traits (material, social, folkloric, etc.) treated analytically, as discrete entities, for purposes of cross-cultural comparison and generalization; *emic* implies that such traits have value and significance only in a specific cultural context.

8. I have followed Moore (1987) in using the term *tribal nation* to indicate a degree of political unification which goes beyond the more informal ties of territoriality, kinship, language, and sense of common identity which constitute the usual definition of a tribe. Periodic gathering of bands and performance of inclusive rituals, such as the Sun Dance, are associated with this type of organization.

9. From Murdock (1967), the following columns were tabulated: 7, 12, 14, 19, 20, 22, 24, 25, 27, 28, 30, 31, 32, 33, 67, 72, 73, and 80–84. Those omitted are those in which Kiowa data were lacking or which are noncontrastive for the tribes compared. The highest number of correspondences were Kiowa/Teton Dakota (11) and Kiowa/Flathead (11); in the South Plains, the highest number was Kiowa/Comanche (8).

10. The Kiowa traded at A. P. Chouteau's fort on the Canadian River in 1839; they may well have been acquainted with Chouteau operatives decades earlier, in the Rocky Mountains. It might be noted that in 1819 Joseph Brazeau, a longtime agent of Berthold and Chouteau, was familiarly known as "Cayowa" (Hafen 1982: 31).

Patricia C. Albers

Changing Patterns of Ethnicity in the Northeastern Plains, 1780–1870

Over twenty years ago, William Sturtevant introduced the idea of ethnogenesis to American anthropology in a pioneering study of the sociopolitical processes by which the Seminole became differentiated historically from the Creek (1971: 92). Although he defined ethnogenesis in this work simply as "the establishment of group distinctiveness," his study actually touched upon broad transformational processes in ethnic group identification. These involve the long-term movements by which the ethnic identities of human communities get changed, and as such they are historical and evolutionary in scope (Moore 1987). But no matter how it is specified, ethnogenesis is an important idea that needs to be recovered and included in any conceptual discourse on ethnic phenomena. It is also a concept whose myriad dimensions require further exploration and explication.

Although ethnic phenomena have drawn a great deal of scholarly interest over the past few decades, the concept of ethnogenesis has gotten buried and lost under the more inclusive rubric "ethnicity." In the literature on historic North American Indian populations, for example, considerable attention has been paid to the scope and variety of ethnic identities and interethnic relations (Elmendorf 1971; Anastasio 1972; Albers 1974; Davis 1974; Trigger 1976; Sharrock 1977; Ewers 1975; Weist 1977; Blu 1980; Wood 1980; Fromhold 1981; Ford 1983; Muga 1984, 1988; Albers and James 1986; Bishop 1987; Hanson 1986, 1987; Albers and Kay 1987; Tanner 1987; Miller 1989; Milloy 1988; White 1991; Quinn 1993; Miller and Boxberger 1994). However, only a few studies (Sturtevant 1971, 1983; Sharrock 1974; Wood and Downer 1977;

Greenberg and Morrison 1981; Moore 1987; Albers 1993) actually address how local groups changed their ethnic identities as a result of their relationships with others or reveal how ethnogenesis involved a variety of different transformative processes.

Many of the better-known examples of ethnogenesis result from conflict and fission, but there are a number of interesting cases where transformations in ethnic identities were based on cooperation and fusion. As a form of ethnogenesis, neither interethnic fusion, hybridizaton, or merger has been as well described as other historical processes of ethnic change (Albers 1993: 112–122). The situation of the Plains Assiniboin, Cree, and Ojibwa, as originally reported in the pioneering study of Susan Sharrock (1974), is one notable exception. Throughout much of the eighteenth and nineteenth centuries, these populations jointly occupied a large area of territory in the northeastern Plains, and in varying ways and degrees they intermarried and collaborated in a range of activities from combat and trade to subsistence and ceremony. Segments of these populations also lived together, eventually forming composite residence groups in which new ethnic identifications developed over time.

The historic situation of the Plains Assiniboin, Cree, and Ojibwa did not conform to typical tribal models where territories were divided, claimed, and defended by discrete ethnic groups, nor did it fit descriptions in which political allegiances were defined primarily in exclusive ethnic terms. Ethnicity in the generic and highly abstract sense of a "tribal" name did not always function as marker of geopolitical boundaries. Given a pluralistic pattern of land use and alliance making, most of their ethnic categories did not have a high level of salience or any a priori power to organize and distribute people across geographic space. What appears to have been more important in defining the geopolitics of access to land, labor, and resources were social ties based on ties of kinship and sodality in their varied metaphoric extensions and expressions. Indeed, it was only after the imposition of U. S. and Canadian sovereignty that their ethnic names took on any real importance, and then it was only because these were invested with the legal power of treaties written by nation-states (Sharrock 1974; Albers and Kay 1987).

In addition to serving as an important challenge to conventional representations of American Indian ethnicity and geopolitics, their case also provides an apt illustration of the variable paths ethnogenesis takes. In particular, it highlights instances of ethnogenesis where processes of merger rather than separation dominate ethnic change. Merger is one of a continuum of accommodations that groups of different ethnic origins make to each other's presence, and, as described at length elsewhere (Albers 1993: 112–122), it is a type of interdependence involving the mutual use and protection of a shared land base. As an accommodation that ethnic groups make to each other's presence, merger assumes a variety of different structural configurations and associated patterns of ethnic identification, ranging from loosely knit alliances among ethnically distinct groups to tightly integrated coalitions where ethnic differences are dissolved.

Building upon the seminal contributions of Sharrock's study (1974), this essay describes how interethnic merger entailed a variety of transforming patterns within the ranks of Plains Assiniboin, Cree, and Ojibwa. Not only does it discuss the regionally varied and historically changing characteristics of these patterns on the northeastern Plains, but it also defines some of the conditions that fostered a widespread process of ethnic hybridization and that contributed to the emergence of new cultural groups and ethnic identifications during the eighteenth and nineteenth centuries.

Merger and Its Structural Variations

In many earlier ethnographic writings on the historic Plains, tribes were identified as either friends or enemies, and the relations between them were described as either peaceful or hostile. This kind of division, as Katherine Weist (1977: 43) astutely noted, obscures the complexity of relations among populations of different ethnic origin. On the friendly, peaceful side of the divide, Plains Indian populations were linked to each other in various ways. On the one hand, they were connected through different kinds of symbiosis, where relationships were formed out of functionally differentiated positions in production and/or distribution. In these relations, peoples of diverse ethnic origins formed alliances against common enemies, collaborated in trade and ceremony, and even intermarried. Notwithstanding their interdependence and coparticipation in a variety of activities, groups maintained their ethnic integrity and separateness through various structural mechanisms (Albers 1993: 100–111). On the other hand, Plains Indian populations were tied to each other through relationships of merger where ethnically distinct groups stood on more or less common grounds in relation to the means of production. Under merger, groups not only intermarried and jointly collaborated in subsistence, ceremony, and military activity, but they freely traveled and resided within each other's nominally designated areas of occupation. In the process, ethnic differences were often minimized (Albers 1993: 112–121).

In contrast to the past, when it was customary to view the Plains as little more than an epiphenomenal extension of its autonomous tribal pieces, more recent perspectives (Albers 1974, 1993; Sharrock 1974; Ewers 1975; Weist 1977; Wood 1980; Hanson 1987; Moore 1987) see the area as consisting of a series of regional formations that were greater than the sum of their ethnic parts. In these arrangements, local ethnic groups were connected to each other through complex ties of symbiosis and merger. When Plains Indian populations stood on common grounds and held shared interests in a setting of merger, their relationships produced a variety of structural patterns which can be represented heuristically by a four-stage continuum which marks a series of different structural positions along the road to ethnogenesis.

One end of this continuum is represented by a *polyethnic alliance formation*, in which different ethnic groups share territory, engage in joint military action, and collaborate in a variety of ceremonial and subsistence activities. Alliances of this order are highly varied in terms of both the character and degree of interlinkage between constituent groups, but for the most part, local groups retain some level of residential and ethnic distinctiveness (Sharrock 1974; Ewers 1975; Hanson 1987; Albers 1993: 113–114). This contrasts with other patterns of merger, where separateness breaks down at a residential level and where, as a result, the ethnic markers identifying local groups change.

At the other end is the *emergent ethnic community*, where the process of ethnogenesis has reached completion. Here groups that were once distinct are now joined. Indeed, they become so intermingled that they are virtually indistinguishable from each other in a cultural and social sense. In the process, they not only form a political entity that is separate from their parent populations, but they also assume an ethnic identification that is distinctive as well. It is an identity that emphasizes unity and solidarity over any differences from their ethnic pasts.

Toward the middle of the continuum are two different, but often overlapping, merger patterns. One, the *ethnic bloc confederation*, is associated with situations where politically dominant ethnic blocs retain their integrity and simply absorb "foreign" ethnicities into their ranks. This kind of pattern sometimes evolves when a small population becomes incorporated into the body politic of a larger group and, in the process, does not give up the identity of its separate origin (e.g., Kiowa-Apache in the ranks of the Kiowa, or Sarcee in the Blackfoot confederation) (Jenness 1932; Bittle 1971; Albers 1993: 113–115). In another form, members of equally large, powerful, and contiguous ethnic blocs intermarry, share territory, and collaborate in warfare and other activities, and in the process some of their residence groups, especially those situated in border zones, develop bicultural heritages. The groups with dual backgrounds, however, remain affiliated politically and ethnically with one or the other parent bloc (i.e., bands of Lakota ancestry in the Cheyenne tribal circle) (Moore 1987). In this kind of pattern, merger begins to penetrate the core of local settlements; however, intermarriage and coresidency are not widespread enough to alter political arrangements at the level of either parent bloc.

The other pattern at the middle of the merger continuum is the *hybridized group coalition*. Here intermarriage and coresidency become so pervasive and widespread that local settlements with dual ethnic origins begin to constitute a sociopolitical body whose interests and actions stand apart from those of either parent bloc. In the process, they take on hybrid ethnic identities as well (Sharrock 1974: 111–113). At this point, ethnogenesis is not yet completed because the hybrid populations still retain some sort of umbilical connection (i.e., in language preference, economic dependence) to either or both parental blocs.

In historic times, the merger patterns of the Plains Assiniboin, Cree, and Ojibwa were historically changing and regionally varied. In one way or another, their patterns of merger represented the full breadth of the four-stage continuum just described. How these were manifested in different locations and at changing points in time is a central concern of the following discussion.

Early Movements and Historic Antecedents

Contrary to earlier interpretations (Secoy 1953; Ewers 1974; Sharrock and Sharrock 1974; Mandelbaum 1979), the Assiniboin and Cree moved to the prairies and High Plains of North America from a variety of forest and parkland locations which spanned a vast area between the Red River on the east and the North Branch of the Saskatchewan River on the west (Wright 1965: 189–227, 1981; Hlady 1970: 278–279; Ray 1974: 4; Syms 1977; Smith 1981; Russell 1991). From the seventeenth century onward, their migrations and adaptations happened gradually when frontier populations from the parklands of Manitoba and Saskatchewan became more dependent on a grassland subsistence cycle and remained in prairie locations for extended periods. Eventually, many of the immigrants moved deeper into the prairies and onto the High Plains, where they were joined by additional waves of Assiniboin, Cree, and later Ojibwa from parkland and forest habitats (Ray 1974; Milloy 1988; Russell 1991; Peers 1994).

By the mid–eighteenth century, Cree and Assiniboin populations coexisted over a widespread and ecologically varied territory. The most southerly located Assiniboin, and some of the Cree as well, were adopting horses and beginning to occupy prairie lands on a permanent basis. The transition of some Cree and Assiniboin to a grassland subsistence pattern was accompanied by the emergence of distinct ethnic markers. Not only did the Native populations make distinctions among themselves along ecological lines, but fur traders in the region increasingly identified and separated groups according to the kind of environments in which they lived (Sharrock 1977: 7–21). The name "Strong Wood" was applied to Cree and Assiniboin involved in a parkland-forest subsistence cycle with a seasonal use of the prairies. These populations traveled primarily by canoe, worked as trappers for the fur trade, and became the groups most dependent on the trade for their means of production (Ray 1974:

144). The other label, "Meadow," was used for Cree and Assiniboin who were adapted to a grassland cycle. These people were equestrian, buffalo hunters and traders, who neither liked nor were especially good at trapping (Sharrock 1977: 11; Ray 1974: 147). Their dependence on the fur trade was marginal and confined primarily to the acquisition of guns and ammunition and other sundry items for which these groups increasingly exchanged meat provisions (Ray 1974: 147). By the late eighteenth century, even though the Assiniboin had come to be associated with the grasslands more often than the Cree (and vice versa), representatives of both were intermingled across forest, parkland, and grassland environments in varying ways and degrees.

Wherever these two populations located themselves, they appear to have lived with each other largely in peace. After establishing trade with the British at Hudson Bay in the seventeenth century, several groups of Cree and some Assiniboin developed into middlemen who traveled the river systems over long distances to exchange peltries for guns and other European goods (Ray 1974: 51–71; Thistle 1986: 3–32; Milloy 1988: 5–20; Russell 1991: 87–91, 187–199). In the western reaches of Cree and Assiniboin occupation, these bands established trade alliances with their ethnic congeners and with the neighboring Piegan-Blood-Blackfoot-Sarcee who lived on the prairie's edge between the North and South Branches of the Saskatchewan River. Every year, Cree and Assiniboin traders would meet these neighbors in a trade fair located at the junction of the North and South Branches. After more than a century of trading in which the Assiniboin (but especially the Cree) were sole suppliers of guns and other European goods to the Blackfoot-Piegan-Blood-Sarcee, these various ethnic groups became linked to each other not only through ties of trade but marriage as well (Milloy 1988: 16).

To the east, a similar trade complex was developing between Assiniboin and Cree and the Mandan-Hidatsa of the Upper Missouri River. Those trading directly with the Missouri villagers were a prairie/parkland people who received European commodities from ethnic congeners following a woodland/parkland subsistence cycle (Ewers 1968: 14–33; Ray 1974: 55–57, 87–89; Milloy 1972: 47–48; Wood 1980: 98–109; Albers 1993: 100–112). In a pattern paralleling developments farther west, the eastern Assiniboin and Cree became the primary suppliers of European goods to the Missouri villagers in return for hides, corn, and, later, horses. But unlike the more westerly trade chains, the Missouri River complex was much more unstable politically. This was probably because the Missouri villagers had access to competing lines of trade, including ones that bypassed the Cree/Assiniboin's British trade chains and linked them with the Ojibwa/Dakota's French connections. Indeed, until the early eighteenth century, there is indirect evidence (Burpee 1927: 109; Bowers 1965: 217–218, 476, 482; Wood 1971: 2, 58; Ray 1974: 5–6, 12–19;

Syms 1977: 112–113, 1979) that the trade competition and hostility between Cree/Assiniboin and the Ojibwa/Dakota spilled out into the Plains and in all likelihood contributed to Hidatsa, Crow, and Cheyenne villagers abandoning their settlements in eastern North Dakota and taking up residence on the Missouri. After the Ojibwa broke off their trade with the Dakota in the 1730s and became allied with the Assiniboin and Cree, most of the Mandan-Hidatsa's access to European goods was restricted to one or more of their Ojibwa-Cree-Assiniboin trade connections (Hickerson 1970: 65–66, 81–86, 1974: 58–59; Ray 1974: 4–12).

As an extension of their partnership in long-distance trading, the Cree and Assiniboin were military allies across the entire expanse of their joint territorial range. In the west they were united in an unremitting war with the Atsina-Arapaho, and they also joined together with Blackfoot-Blood-Piegan to fight the Shoshone-Flathead-Kootenai (Milloy 1988: 12–16; Russell 1991: 187–189). Farther east they were engaged in warfare with the Atsina as well, but they were also enemies of the Lakota and Crow. In addition, there was intermittent hostility with Hidatsa and sometimes even Mandan (Milloy 1988: 41–46). Finally, in their most easterly locations they remained allied in a war against the Ojibwa-Dakota until the 1730s, when the latter's trade connections disintegrated. Thereafter, the Ojibwa entered the alliance camp of the Cree and Assiniboin, and they shared the same enemies over much of the region that all three groups commonly traveled and occupied (Hickerson 1956, 1970; Vogelin and Hickerson 1974: 17–159).

From the late seventeenth until the middle of the eighteenth century, details about the character of relationships between these populations are very sketchy. From what is known, however, a couple of general points can be made. First of all, it is apparent that throughout much of their area of occupation the Cree and Assiniboin were shifting from relationships resting on symbiosis and a functional differentiation in trade to ones based largely on merger (Sharrock 1974: 103–106). Throughout their co-occupied and ecologically varied territories, many followed similar subsistence strategies and held the same position in regional trade chains (Ray 1974: 27–115). But whether ties between particular groups of Cree and Assiniboin were based on symbiosis or merger, it is clear that over the entire reach of their shared territories they constituted a polyethnic alliance formation (Albers 1993: 112–122). At this time in history, however, there is little evidence of merger much beyond the level of loosely amalgamated trade and military alliances within territories that were jointly traveled and occupied. Local settlements, even when interspersed, were still being separated and identified as either Assiniboin or Cree. Although intermarriage was reported and probably widespread, it was not of sufficient magnitude to break down preexisting ethnic markers.

It was into this polyethnic alliance formation that the Ojibwa entered in the mid–eighteenth century, adding to the already complex patterns of merger in the region at large.

Evolving Patterns of Merger: 1780 to 1830

The years between 1780 and 1820 mark a time when increasing numbers of Assiniboin and Cree along with a small but growing population of Ojibwa moved onto the prairies and became fully adapted to a Plains way of life (Ray 1974: 94–103; Sharrock 1977: 11; Milloy 1988: 21–37; Peers 1994: 27–97). In the late eighteenth century, much of their movement was precipitated by changing economic conditions. As described in much greater detail elsewhere (Ray 1974: 125–182; Thistle 1986: 51–80; Peers 1994: 63–84, 99–112), these entailed a declining involvement in the fur trade and an increased participation in the meat provision, robe, and hide traffics. In order to maintain economic viability in the region's changing markets, many of the groups located in parkland environments moved onto the prairies, where they adopted the use of horses and engaged in a competitive production of food provisions and hides for European markets (see figure 1).

While this shift was taking place, Euramerican traders were also changing their locations and opening up posts within reach of the prairies. In doing this, they undercut some of the important and powerful middlemen positions that Assiniboin, Cree, and Ojibwa occupied in the peltry and gun trade (Ray 1974: 130–133; Jackson 1982: 11–19; Milloy 1988: 52–64). With this change, many of those who were primarily trappers and/or traders were pushed or drawn into the production of food provisions to sustain their position in the marketplace (Ray 1974: 137–148, 157–160; Peers 1987: 111–138). But even though changes in the fur market and in the locations of traders may have motivated many groups to focus more of their productive activity around a grasslands environment, their ability to make the prairies a primary homeland and resource base rested on other factors as well, including the acquisition of horses through either trading or raiding (Peers 1987: 77–79, 110–114; Milloy 1988: 47–64).

The ability of the Assiniboin, Cree, and Ojibwa to enter the prairies and remain there on a sustained basis also had important demographic aspects. One of the most significant of these was the impact of the 1780–1782 smallpox outbreak (Taylor 1977; Trimble 1986). In its aftermath, many of the parkland/woodland Assiniboin, Cree, and Ojibwa gained a foothold in depopulated prairie zones whose earlier occupants were unable to retain their territories. Entry into some of these zones was gained through force and warfare. In others, however, entry took place peaceably through marriage and coresidency (Morton 1929: 63–64; Ray 1974: 105–106; Taylor 1977; Green-

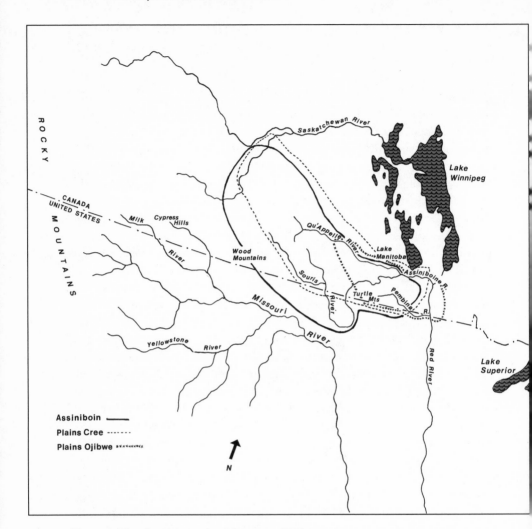

Figure 1. Overlapping territorial ranges, 1800.

berg and Morrison 1981; Thistle 1986: 63–65; Milloy 1972: 57–58, 1988: 12–13; Peers 1994: 20–21; Schilz 1988).

Since the territorial expanse of prairie-adapted Assiniboin, Cree, and Ojibwa was vast, extending in a northwesterly direction from the Red River to the North Branch of the Saskatchewan, these economic and demographic transitions had different consequences for them depending on their particular geographic locations and their social positions within regionally organized systems of trade and alliance (Milloy 1972, 1988). This, in turn, affected how various patterns of merger evolved across the territorial landscapes they occupied between 1780 and 1825.

Eastern Locations. In the most easterly reaches of their prairie range south of the Assiniboine River, between the Pembina and Souris Rivers, the settlements of Assiniboin and Cree were interspersed. As revealed in the accounts of Alexander Henry (Coues 1897, 1: 119, 152, 166, 191, 196, 198, 204, 228, 243–244, 413, 419) and John Tanner (James 1956: 37, 71, 77, 137, 142), among other early sources (Harmon 1911: 78, 81, 85, 88; Hickerson 1956: 278; Ray 1974: 96–100; Sharrock 1974: 109–110; Sharrock and Sharrock 1974: 35–38, 46–47), these two populations covered the same territory, intermarried, occupied joint camping places, utilized identical vision questing sites, and collaborated in winter bison hunts. Moreover, they traveled together on trading expeditions to the Mandan villages on the Missouri as well as to European trading posts on the Assiniboine and Red Rivers (Coues 1897, 1: 119, 140, 185, 190–191, 203, 228, 429; Hickerson 1956: 280–282, 285; James 1956: 50–51, 277; Ray 1974: 157–160; Sharrock 1974: 109–110; Milloy 1988: 50–58). They also joined together on war expeditions against the Dakota, Atsina, and intermittently the Mandan/Hidatsa (Coues 1897, 1: 135, 159, 165; Hickerson 1956: 280, 287; James 1956: 57–58, 63–64, 86–87, 96–98, 137–143, 203–207; Milloy 1972: 107–127, 1988: 57–58). Here ethnic merger continued to take on the appearance of a polyethnic alliance formation in which local bands held separate ethnic identities but cooperated in advancing their common interests over land and trade routes.

In the years between 1790 and 1810, the Ojibwa were just beginning to make their presence felt in this region (Coues 1897, 1: 53, 57; Hickerson 1956: 274–293; Peers 1987: 27–61). When they arrived on the prairies west of the Red River, they did so gradually and usually in small family groups (Ray 1974: 99–102; Thistle 1986: 70–71; Peers 1987: 47–60). They lived peaceably among resident Assiniboin and Cree, sometimes intermarrying, camping with them, sharing in subsistence and ritual, and fighting against common enemies (Coues 1897, 1: 191, 196, 257, 269, 429; James 1956: 57–58, 63–64, 70, 78, 86–87, 96–98, 132, 137, 142; Peers 1987: 53, 71–84). Laura Peers (1987: 71–73) argues that the Ojibwa were able to penetrate the prairie regions dominated by Assiniboin and Cree because they posed no economic threat to either. There was no competition, because these groups were functionally differentiated. The Ojibwa were primarily trappers of small game, whereas the Assiniboin and Cree were mostly big game hunters (James 1956: 73–75; Ray 1974: 125–135, 168–175). Where the Ojibwa intermingled with the Cree and Assiniboin, their relations appear to have been built on merger rather than symbiosis. Despite the contrasts in their productive orientations, these differ-

ences did not constitute a basis for any major organized system of trade between them. At any rate, the division was short-lived, because within a decade
or two of their arrival on the prairies, many Ojibwa were no longer trappers
but equestrian buffalo hunters whose way of life was inseparable from that of
.the Assiniboin and Cree among whom they lived (Howard 1977: 17–20).

Until the 1820s, the Ojibwa were still a minority population on the prairies,
and their presence was probably welcomed by the eastern Assiniboin and Cree
as a source of recruits to fight the ever-present danger of enemy populations
like the Dakota, Hidatsa/Crow, and Atsina (Peers 1987: 71). This is especially
likely in light of the losses these Assiniboin and Cree suffered in the 1780–
1782 smallpox outbreak. Indeed, the magnitude of this epidemic was so great
that in some regions of their occupation, especially those east of the Red
River, the Assiniboin and Cree no longer retained an identifiable presence.
What actually happened to them is a source of debate, but it is likely that
some of the survivors remained in their home territories, where they became
incorporated into the ranks of the resident and inmigrating populations of
Saulteaux and Ojibwa (Tyrrell 1968: lxxv–lxxvi; Vogelin and Hickerson 1974:
17–159; Ray 1974: 104–108; Greenberg and Morrison 1981). Others, however, probably moved west, where they joined forces with a large vanguard
population of Assiniboin and smaller but closely associated groups of Cree,
both of whom were consolidating and expanding their prairie holdings from
the Assiniboine to the Pembina and Souris Rivers (Coues 1897, 1: 314, 408, 2:
516, 522–523; Thwaites 1904–1905: 221–222; James 1956: 70, 132, 142; Masson 1960, 1: 272; Ray 1974: 96–100; Sharrock 1974: 109–110; Sharrock and
Sharrock 1974: 35–38, 46–47).

After 1780, the ties connecting the southeastern Assiniboin and Cree were
clearly linked to a long history of coresidency, trade collaboration, and military alliance making (Russell 1991). Now, however, their alliances appear to
have been more dense and tightly knit in response to the losses each sustained
from epidemic diseases (Sharrock 1974: 109–110; Taylor 1977; Trimble 1986).
Nevertheless, both still maintained ethnic integrity at least from the stand-
point of those outsiders who reported on their identities and whereabouts.

Central Locations. In the years between 1780 and 1830 and throughout the
previous century, a combined and growing force of Cree and Assiniboin became adapted to a Plains way of life on the prairies south and west of the
Touchwood Hills. From the Qu'Appelle River to the South Branch of the Saskatchewan River, Assiniboin and Cree were populating the parklands and adjacent prairies not only from the northern forest areas of Manitoba and Saskatchewan but also from the parklands and prairies along the Assiniboine
River in the east (Coues 1897, 2: 5; Harmon 1911: 72; Morton 1929: 63–64;
Ray 1974: 96–97, 99–101). Here, as elsewhere, a picture of devastation and

population decline followed in the footsteps of the 1780–1782 epidemic and, in all likelihood, contributed greatly to the realignment and increased merger of the area's populations (Ray 1974: 109–111; Taylor 1977). It also probably opened up avenues for the combined forces of Cree and Assiniboin to expand into the less-populated and well-defended prairie regions of other ethnic groups, including the Atsina and Hidatsa (Morton 1929: 34–35, 63–64; Flannery 1953: 9–16; Milloy 1972: 102–106, 1988: 33, 51; Ray 1974: 105–106; Thistle 1986: 63–65; Schilz 1988: 41–56; Russell 1991: 200–209).

By contrast, movements into prairie regions once occupied by depopulated segments of the Blackfoot-Blood-Piegan were much more peaceful and an extension of this population's long-standing kinship, trade, and military alliances with the westernmost Cree and Assiniboin (Milloy 1988: 5–20; Russell 1991: 187–191). The ability of Cree and Assiniboin to travel and move peaceably beyond the South Branch of the Saskatchewan onto the lands of kin and friends among the Blackfoot-Blood-Piegan, however, came to an end in the early nineteenth century, when trade connections between these populations were undermined by the establishment of European posts on the western reaches of the North Branch of the Saskatchewan River (Milloy 1988: 31–40).

After a history of close collaboration in trade and military affairs, the merger relationships of Assiniboin and Cree in the Qu'Appelle region had advanced a step further (Sharrock 1974: 108–109). As described by the trader Daniel Harmon (1911: 40–41), the two populations were so intermixed that it was impossible to distinguish them. Local residence groups were bilingual and bicultural, and they held dual ethnic affiliations as well (Harmon 1911: 42–44). In addition, Cree and Assiniboin were reported in large, mixed encampments on the South Branch of the Saskatchewan River, and there were other multiethnic bands covering much of the prairie/parklands from there to the Qu'Appelle River as well (Coues 1897, 2: 522–523; Harmon 1911: 78, 81, 85, 103–104, 120; Ray 1974: 96–97, 99–100; Sharrock and Sharrock 1974: 23–33).

In contrast to Assiniboin and Cree settlements elsewhere, which were distinguished along ethnic lines, the bands in this region were described in hyphenated ethnic terms as "Cree-Assiniboin" (Coues 1897, 2: 597; Harmon 1911: 78, 81, 85, 103–194; Sharrock 1974: 111–112). Here the process of merger went beyond the level of regional alliance making and even an intermittent pattern of coresidency among ethnically different kin and friends (Sharrock 1974: 108–109). It now reached the very makeup and structure of local bands over a fairly large stretch of territory, and in doing so it started to take on the characteristics of what Sharrock called a "fused ethnicity form" (1974: 111), or what is identified here as a hybridized group coalition.

While there is no question that bands in the Qu'Appelle and South Branch regions were becoming ethnically hybridized, it is hard to determine at this date whether they formed a distinct body politic that was separate from either of their respective parent groups and, if they did, how many of them were so involved. Depending on their locations and prevailing historical circumstances, many of the hybridized, Assiniboin-Cree or Cree-Assiniboin bands still appear to have been connected to their larger parent populations, forming ethnically distinct enclaves within each bloc (Ray 1974: 96–100). As a result, their situations probably corresponded more faithfully to that of an ethnic bloc confederation. Whatever the particular case, it is certain that there was a much more complex and completely integrated pattern of ethnic merger in this region than in the other areas of joint Cree and Assiniboin occupancy between 1780 and 1820.

Again, the merger patterns of this region were further complicated when the Ojibwa entered the scene. As in regions along the Assiniboine and Red Rivers, they arrived in the Qu'Appelle River Valley vicinity in small trapping groups (Harmon 1911: 72). Before the 1820s they followed and mostly occupied the forest zones, which were becoming depopulated of Cree and Assiniboin, who were now more dependent on parkland/grassland subsistence cycles. But no matter where the Ojibwa moved in this vast region, their early settlements and trapping territories were largely intermixed with those of the Cree and Assiniboin (Ray 1974: 101–103).

Western Locations. In their newly occupied lands between the South Branch and North Branch of the Saskatchewan River, the Cree and Assiniboin were reported once again to cover much of the same territorial range and to participate jointly in trading parties and raiding expeditions (figure 1) (Milloy 1972: 94–10; Sharrock 1974: 111; Russell 1991). In this general region, however, they appear to have formed encampments that were more ethnically separate and distinct than those in the Qu'Appelle area (Coues 1897, 2: 522–523; Ray 1974: 96–97, 99–100; Sharrock and Sharrock 1974: 23–33). Also, in contrast to many areas farther east, where Cree and Assiniboin were interspered across the same landscape in more or less equal numbers, there was a spatial divide in the far west (Ray 1974: 107–113). Here the vast majority of Assiniboin were prairie dwellers, whereas most of the Cree lived in the parklands and forests (Morton 1929: 47; Ray 1974: 148–155; Russell 1991:181–186). Not surprisingly, the cultural divide that distinguished the two populations was more obvious here as well.

West of the Battle River's junction with the North Saskatchewan, the Cree and Assiniboin were primarily forest-adapted trappers. They covered much of the same territory, but here the Cree far outnumbered the Assiniboin. Their local groups were smaller, widely dispersed, and more ethnically distinct, but once again, these were interspersed over a common territorial range. Also, at the turn of the nineteenth century, the Ojibwa were brought into the area by European traders from places as far east as Sault Sainte Marie (Coues 1897, 2: 603, 653, 703–705). Along much of the North Branch of the Saskatchewan River, the expansion of Cree, Assiniboin, and later Ojibwa onto the prairies was impeded by the presence of Blackfoot-Blood-Piegan and Sarcee (Sharrock and Sharrock 1974: 21), and, as a result, few of these populations were recruited to a Plains way of life until a much later period.

Aside from the fact that the western Cree and Assiniboin were distributed unequally across adjoining ecozones, there were also other conditions that kept them more separated than groups farther east. One of the more important of these was that the Cree, especially those along the North Branch, were much more dependent on trade, alliance, and intermarriage with neighboring Blackfoot-Blood-Piegan (Milloy 1972: 49–63, 73). Even after hostilities erupted with these groups in the early nineteenth century, the North Branch, or "Upriver," Cree were the ones most often involved in peace-seeking efforts (Milloy 1972: 96–106, 200–206). In subsequent years, they often took political stands that were different from the South Branch, or "Downriver," Cree, who were more adapted to the prairies and more closely aligned with the Plains-oriented Assiniboin in trade and in an unending pattern of warfare with the Atsina and Blackfoot-Blood-Piegan (Milloy 1988: 31–40, 83–102, 103–118).

In the far west as elsewhere, trade and military alliances connecting the Assiniboin and Cree reached back many generations. In the early decades of the nineteenth century, however, the merger pattern between these two populations was much more amorphous and loosely woven than in regions farther east. Intermarriage and coresidency were reported, but generally not in the same degree. Here a polyethnic alliance formation existed, but the social networks that supported it appear to have been less dense and by extension less compelling than those evolving in the eastern and central portions of the Assiniboin's and Cree's territorial range. Ironically, however, the first historical reference to the name "Cree-Assiniboin" as a distinct ethnic ascription comes from the record of Alexander Henry's travels in this region during 1808 (Coues 1897, 2: 597). This ethnically mixed band, which was observed at Fort Vermillion, was rare in the area at this time and in all probability was traveling here from a home location in the vicinity of the Qu'Appelle River, where such groups were common.

New Patterns of Merger: 1830 to 1870

The years between 1830 and 1870 mark another period when significant change took place in the lives of native peoples in the northeastern Plains. First of all, groups who once traded with the British at entrepôts along the

Assiniboine and Qu'Appelle Rivers were turning their sights to the Americans establishing posts at Fort Union near the confluence of the Yellowstone and Missouri Rivers (Sharrock and Sharrock 1974: 68–69; Ray 1974: 147–154, 207). Bison were becoming harder to find and starting their precipitous decline in the eastern grasslands (Ray 1974: 205–207, 229–233; Vogelin and Hickerson 1974: 127–128). Moreover, increasing numbers of Metis were entering the prairie regions as full-time freedmen hunters and traders (Hickerson 1956; Ross 1957: 255–257; Ray 1974: 205–207, 229–233; Vogelin and Hickerson 1974: 114–125; Peers 1987: 124–127, 147–153, 1994: 154–156). Finally, smallpox epidemics were sweeping across the region, decimating several populations in their path (Denig 1961: 71–73; Ray 1974: 188–192; Taylor 1977; Trimble 1986). Taken together, these events triggered a variety of changes in regional patterns of merger and in the ethnic affiliations of local groups.

Eastern Regions. In the first half of the nineteenth century, the eastern prairie region occupied by the Assiniboin, Cree, and Ojibwa underwent a major change in its ethnic composition. In the first half of the nineteenth century, increasing numbers of Ojibwa moved into the area, and as they did so they became widely incorporated into the Cree-Assiniboin body politic (Vogelin and Hickerson 1974: 122, 126–127; Howard 1977: 5–12). By the 1840s they had moved from being minor players in the region's Cree-Assiniboin melting pot to becoming its dominant population after Cree and Assiniboin numbers were severely depleted during the smallpox epidemic of 1837 to 1838. Mirroring what had happened in other areas sixty years earlier, much of the prairie region south of the Assiniboine River became Ojibwa in the face of these population losses (figure 2) (Ross 1957: 269–272, 324–325; Denig 1961: 71–73; Ray 1974: 187–192; Howard 1977: 21–23; Vogelin and Hickerson 1974: 103–104, 117, 120–137; Peers 1987: 135–178).

The growing prominence of the Ojibwa, however, was not a simple process of one ethnic group replacing the others; rather, it involved a complex process of amalgamation in which ethnic groups indigenous to the area and new arrivals as well formed at least two emergent ethnic communities. In one, the Ojibwa, along with a small population of Cree and Assiniboin, became closely affiliated with the Metis, who were beginning to occupy much of the same territorial range (Ross 1957: 269–272, 324–325; Denig 1961: 110–111, 123–131; Vogelin and Hickerson 1974: 77, 96, 103–104, 117, 122). As described in detail elsewhere (Ross 1957; Sprenger 1972; Dusenberry 1985), the prairie Metis were themselves a newly emergent ethnic community, with people of predominately mixed French/English, Ojibwa, Cree, and Assiniboin ancestry. After the fur trade collapsed, many of them joined together to take up buffalo hunting and to become independent traders and transporters. After the 1840s

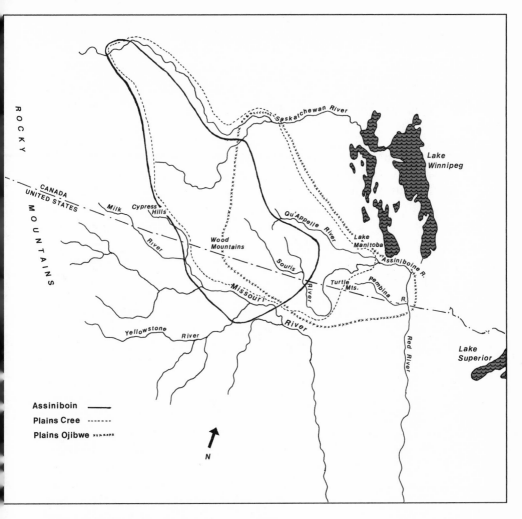

Figure 2. Overlapping territorial ranges, 1840.

they constituted a recognizable ethnic bloc with a political agenda and interests that often differed from the Indian and European groups with whom they were related.

Some of the eastern Assiniboin, Cree, and Ojibwa traveled, hunted, and traded with the Metis and generally sided with them in battles against the Dakota. They also shared commercial connections to British and American interests along the Red River, and their settlements were often intermixed as well. After the smallpox epidemic of 1837 to 1838, the Metis became the dominant population in areas northeast of the Turtle Mountains (Stevens

1859: 148–149; Giraud 1945: 820–821; Howard 1977: 46–51; Ross 1957: 84, 248, 255–257, 411–412; Sprenger 1972: 52–55; Ray 1974: 205–207; Vogelin and Hickerson 1974: 84–85, 93, 98–99, 115, 119, 123, 126, 128–137). But even though the Cree, Assiniboin, and Ojibwa were now minority populations in this region, they still retained a vested interest in territories that reached to the Assiniboine and Red Rivers (Ross 1957: 411–412). This common interest was aptly described by Father Belcourt, who stated that "the Crees and Assiniboins regard themselves as *equally masters* of these lands with the Chippewas, having acquired them jointly with the latter, at the expense of their blood" (quoted in Vogelin and Hickerson 1974: 117, emphasis in original). Thus, notwithstanding a change in this area's ethnic composition, there was still a strong sense that it was a jointly held territory.

As in earlier decades, the region's ethnically diverse residents were merged and connected to each other through kinship and marriage (Vogelin and Hickerson 1974: 100, 111–120, 126, 129). Until the 1840s they continued to form a tightly knit polyethnic alliance formation. Thereafter, and largely as a result of population losses sustained by the Cree and Assiniboin, merger patterns in this area took on a new appearance. The Cree and Assiniboin, who were not absorbed into the emergent ethnic community of the Metis, remained in the area in considerably reduced numbers either as small remnant communities or as members of ethnically mixed bands of Ojibwa. In either case, they constituted minority segments within an ethnic bloc confederation where the Ojibwa and their Metis relatives dominated the scene.

Beyond the Turtle Mountains to the valley of the Souris River, another pattern of merger was evolving. When the hide market developed along the Missouri River in the 1820s, Assiniboin and Cree, along with some Ojibwa in their midst, began to trade with the Americans (Kurz 1937: 55–56; Howard 1952; Denig 1961: 81–82; Ray 1974: 147–154). In addition to the attraction of new trade opportunities, joint forces of largely Assiniboin and Cree pushed their territorial ranges farther south and west as the size and dependability of bison populations declined in the east. By the 1830s, many of the allied Assiniboin-Cree and a growing population of Ojibwa newcomers were reported spending much of their time hunting and camping in the region of the Souris River (Ross 1957: 255–257; Ray 1974: 205–207; Sharrock and Sharrock 1974: 68–69; Vogelin and Hickerson 1974: 127–128).

After the 1837–1838 smallpox epidemic, however, the Ojibwa became a dominant ethnic presence on the prairies between the Turtle Mountains and the Souris River. In contrast to what happened farther east, however, an emergent ethnic community emerged out of the combined forces of Assiniboin, Cree, and Ojibwa. Although this population is usually called the Plains Ojibwa in modern ethnographic sources, its ethnic origins were actually much more diverse (Howard 1977: 21–23). Some of its members were descended from the Ojibwa/Saulteaux/Bungi of western Ontario, while others traced their ancestry back to the mixed communities of Chippewa, Huron, Ottawa, and even Menominee from northern Michigan, Wisconsin, and Minnesota. Whether their roots reached back to the northern or southern shores of Lake Superior, the Ojibwa who were located on the Plains west of the Turtle Mountains lived among and intermarried with Cree and Assiniboin (Howard 1977: 117–123; Peers 1987: 73–87, 101–102, 1994: 20–21). Indeed, the very diversity of their roots has led to disagreement among scholars over whether they constitute a branch of the Ojibwa or the Cree (Howard 1977: 5–11). Even within the ranks of their modern-day descendants on the Turtle Mountain and Rocky Boys Reservations, consensus is lacking over whether they belong to the Cree or Ojibwa (Dusenberry 1962: 52; Howard 1961, 1977: 5–11; Fox 1983: personal communication).

Much of the confusion stems, at least in part, from the fact that the western Ojibwa who lived on the prairies covered a vast territorial range, and, as a consequence, they were not a uniform population either in terms of their culture or the sociopolitical alliances they maintained with outside groups (Skinner 1914; Howard 1977; Peers 1987, 1994). Those who eventually spent most of their time west of the Turtle Mountains were probably the most ethnically mixed of the Ojibwa populations on the prairies. In fact, they were so intermingled with Assiniboin and Cree that they came to be identified with them in name. Indeed, if ethnographers and historians followed the path of indigenous ethnic naming practices, it would become apparent that local systems of ethnic classification were quite different from those that have become standardized in the literature. One implication of this difference is that indigenous naming practices mark a distinct ethnic group that gets lost in conventional scholarly classifications.

The name these "Ojibwa" called themselves is Naka.wiyiniuk, which means "speakers of a foreign language" (Howard 1961, 1977: 6). The Algonkian-speaking Cree also called them Nahka.wiyiniwak (speakers of a foreign language) as opposed to the generic name they gave themselves, Ne.hiyaw, which translates as "those who speak the same language" (Smith 1981: 267–268; Mandelbaum 1979: 8). This, incidentally, is the same meaning as the name Shiya-iyeska, applied to them by neighboring Assiniboin and Dakota speakers (Albers 1974: 54–55). Shiya-iyeska is also a name given to Assiniboin bands of Cree-Ojibwa ancestry, and when used in this context the name is translated either as "Cree-talkers" or "Cree-speakers" (Kennedy 1961: lxxii–lxxv). Such a consistency in naming practices indicates that these Ojibwa were well nested in polyethnic alliance formations with the Cree and Assiniboin, but it also suggests that within this alliance some were forming a separate and ethnically distinct population. Ethnographic descriptions (Skinner 1914; Howard 1977; Albers, Ahlers, and Howard in press) of their historic culture and social organization clearly support this view, and it also suggests that although they were related to Ojibwa (Bungi) living on the prairies north of the Turtle Mountains, they were different from them in many critical respects (Howard 1977: 5–11).

One of the bands from this newly emergent ethnic community was led by Little Shell, who lived for many years in the Fort Peck area of Montana. He did so because close relatives were enrolled at this agency, including a maternal uncle, Red Stone, who was identified as Assiniboin. He was also related to the Cree-Assiniboin Broken Arm, who was a member of the Shiya-iyeska division, many of whom settled at Fort Peck. It was this Assiniboin division whose members were intermarried with the Ojibwa who called themselves Naka.wiyiniuk. Indeed, some of the descendants of Little Shell, who eventually settled on the Turtle Mountain Reservation, carry the surnames "Cree" and "Assiniboin" (Bottineau 1900: 99, 114; Delorme 1955: 132–134; Howard 1977: 5–25; Fox 1983).

The Central Regions. In the late 1820s, combined forces of centrally located Assiniboin, Cree, and Ojibwa were also pushing their territorial reach farther south and west onto the High Plains (Pilcher 1824: 453–457, 1838: 474; Larpenteur 1898: 92; Sharrock and Sharrock 1974: 61–62). Besides the establishment of an American trading presence at Fort Union on the Missouri River, there were other factors which precipitated this movement. One of the most important was the Atsina's abandonment of lands north of the Missouri River (Flannery 1953: 12–13), and another was the opening of peaceful relations with the Hidatsa and Crow. Trade and military alliances established with the Crow in the 1830s, plus a peace accord reached with the Hidatsa in the 1850s, laid the groundwork for movements south of the Missouri along the Yellowstone River (Milloy 1972: 42–43, 163–164, 211, 216; Weist 1977: 45–49).

After the 1830s, the largest concentrations of Assiniboin, along with smaller numbers of Cree and Ojibwa, were located west of the Souris River in an area extending to the Wood Mountains and then south along the Poplar River to the Missouri (figure 2) (Maximillian 1906, 22: 387–388, 23: 14–15, 190; Sharrock and Sharrock 1974: 68–69; Ray 1974: 96–98, 104, 207–212; Vogelin and Hickerson 1974: 117). Only three decades earlier, some of those residing in the Wood Mountains were reported in the vicinity of the Turtle Mountains (Maximillian 1906, 23: 201–202; Campbell 1963: 108). In addition to migrations from the east, there were also reports of groups moving to this area from the Qu'Appelle region (Denig 1961: 81–82). Here, as in their more easterly locations, growing numbers of Assiniboin, Cree, and Ojibwa were leaving their former homelands and moving west because of changing market opportunities and declining bison populations (McKay 1858; Ray 1974: 207–208).

Much of the area along the Missouri and Yellowstone Rivers was inhabited primarily by Assiniboin. By contrast, the neighborhood of the Wood Mountains was more equally populated by representatives of each of the three ethnic groups. It can be surmised from a variety of sources that the Wood Mountains–Poplar River region, much like the Qu'Appelle area thirty years earlier, was a highly integrated zone with polyethnicity reaching beyond the level of regional trade and military alliances to the very fiber of local residence groups. In their newly inhabited lands in the Wood Mountains–Poplar River region, Assiniboin, Cree, and Ojibwa settlements were interspersed across the same geographic landscapes. These populations also intermarried, traveled and encamped together, and fought on the same side against Atsina, Lakota, and now the Blackfoot-Blood-Piegan (Hamilton 1834a, 1834b, 1835a, 1835b, 1835c, 1835d; McKenzie 1835a; Maximillian 1906, 22: 387–388, 23: 14–15, 17–18, 190, 201–202; Abel 1932: 390–391; Larpenteur 1898: 155–164; Kurz 1937: 202; Denig 1961: 80, 82, 110–111; Campbell 1963: 23, 108; Sharrock and Sharrock 1974: 74, 79, 80). Indeed, some Euramerican observers (Maximillian 1906, 23: 15–16; Sharrock and Sharrock 1974: 79–83) who came to this area in the 1830s reported that these groups not only shared the same territory but that they were largely indistinguishable in their appearance and customs.

This area certainly conformed to a polyethnic alliance formation, yet it also took on many of the characteristics of a hybridized group coalition. This is suggested by the writings of some Euramerican observers who consistently blurred the ethnic origins of the populations who wintered in the Wood Mountains. Thus, bands associated with such figures as Iron Child and Broken Arm were identified as Cree sometimes and at other times as Assiniboin even within the same source (Hamilton 1835c; McKenzie 1835b; Maximillian 1906, 23: 16; Larpenteur 1898: 155–164; Kurz 1937: 202; Denig 1961: 80, 82, 110–111, 114; Campbell 1963: 23; Boller 1972: 125–126, 138–144).[1] This apparent confusion in ethnic identity cannot be attributed simply to observer error. It was more likely a consequence of the dual, and in some instances triple, ethnic affiliations of the bands located in this region.

In the 1830s, many of the hybrid Assiniboin and Cree bands described in the Qu'Appelle region in earlier decades were also migrating in southwesterly directions (Sharrock 1974: 111). By the late 1840s, some of their winter camping sites were located at the eastern edge of the Cypress Hills, and their hunting grounds extended from the Milk River north to the Prickly Pear (or Cactus) Hills (figure 2) (Denig 1961: 71–73). These hybrid bands were the ones identified in the ethnographic literature as the Young Dogs, or Nehiopwat in Cree (Fraser 1963: 8–9; Sharrock and Sharrock 1974: 90–91; Mandelbaum 1979: 9–10). Although much of this Cree-Assiniboin population was destroyed in the epidemics of the 1830s (Denig 1961: 71–73) and 1850s (Sharrock and Sharrock 1974: 136–137), they still constituted a distinct ethnic force in 1868, when Issac Cowie (1913: 302–303) described them as parties to a large buffalo hunt in the Cypress Hills.

As Susan Sharrock (1974: 112–113) writes, Cowie's account (1913: 302–303) clearly separates the ethnic identities of Assiniboin, Cree, and Saulteaux (Ojibwa) from the "semi-Stony and Cree 'Young Dogs.'" During the 1860s the Young Dogs were part of a larger polyethnic alliance formation in southern Saskatchewan, in which member groups traveled a common territory, hunted together, and allied with each other for military purposes. Yet it is also clear that the Young Dogs were described as being a politically and ethnically distinct group within the alliance and as being closer to the Assiniboin than the Cree (Cowie 1913: 308–317). Not only did they have a distinct location in the camp circle, but they also maintained their own warriors' lodge (Cowie 1913: 308–309, 331).

The case of the Young Dogs is clearly an example of a hybridized group coalition. The collective ethnic ascription for this group is very informative, insofar as it is derived from a warrior society ascription (i.e., Young Dogs or Big Young Dogs of the Assiniboin and Big Dogs of the Cree) that was common in the Plains (Lowie 1909: 79; Mandelbaum 1979: 110–120). That this ethnically hybrid population came to be identified with a sodality-like name is not surprising, since warrior societies were a principal means of bringing about cohesion and support within and across local ethnic group boundaries (Albers 1993: 119–122). In a manner not dissimilar to the Dog Soldier division of the Cheyenne, described in detail by John Moore (1974, 1988), the Young Dog bands were at the frontiers of Cree and Assiniboin expansions into contested territorial zones. Indeed, it might even be argued that it was the sodality alliances of Young Dog warriors among the Assiniboin and the Cree that advanced the process of structural integration between these two ethnic blocs and that, in so doing, paved the way for interethnic ties in other areas of social life, especially marriage and coresidency (Albers 1993: 121).

As in the past the Qu'Appelle region continued to be at the crossroads of polyethnic alliance formations. Now, however, the ethnic composition of the region was changing. The Ojibwa were becoming a dominant ethnic presence, especially in areas north of the Qu'Appelle River, while their numbers were smaller and intermingled with Cree, Assiniboin, and Cree-Assiniboin to the south. There were also a number of groups evolving a mixed Ojibwa and Cree heritage, and by the 1860s they had come to dominate this region's ethnic landscape (Palliser 1863: 202; Cowie 1913: 302–303, 308–310; Denig 1961: 110–111; Fraser 1963: 19–26; Hind 1971: 46, 53; Ray 1974: 96–100; Sharrock 1974: 113).

More so than the Saskatchewan River populations farther north, many of the ethnically mixed Assiniboin-Cree, Cree-Assiniboin, Cree-Ojibwa, and Assiniboin-Cree-Ojibwa populations who traveled the country between the Qu'Appelle and Assiniboine Rivers in the northeast and the Wood Mountains and Cypress Hills in the southwest were wiped out in the smallpox epidemics of the 1830s and 1850s (Denig 1961: 71–73; Ray 1974: 188–192). Most of them were too depopulated to retain a politically independent status, and as a result some of their historic uniqueness as hybrid groups was eventually lost. In later decades they tended to affiliate politically and identify ethnically with one of their parent ethnic blocs.

After the 1870s, for example, the Nehiopwat were identified primarily with a Cree ethnic bloc. Even though Issac Cowie (1913: 308) had linked them politically with the Assiniboin, they were eventually included among the Namihkiyinawak, or "Downstream" Cree, ethnic divisions (Fraser 1963: 4; Mandelbaum 1979: 1). They appear to have become more associated with Cree, not because they were any less Assiniboin than their relatives farther south but because they tended to take more of their trade north to posts in territories dominated by Cree (Milloy 1972: 163–164). In addition, after their numbers were severely depleted by the epidemics of the 1830s and 1850s, the more northerly hybrid groups probably recruited new members from the ranks of the Cree, who were now a much larger population in the area (Hind 1971: 46, 53; Sharrock and Sharrock 1974: 90–91).

By contrast, the hybrid bands in the Wood Mountains became more closely linked to one of their parent ethnic groups, where they were known as the Shiya-iyeska. This happened not only because they traded, traveled, and intermarried with predominately Assiniboin bands on the Missouri River but also because, in later years, it became more expedient politically for them to emphasize the Assiniboin side of their identity. Here, as they did farther north, epidemic population losses contributed directly to realignments in merger patterns and associated ethnic identities. In both of the areas where ethnically mixed Cree and Assiniboin had once formed hybridized group coalitions, they were now embedded in the *ethnic bloc confederations* of their respective parent populations.

Western Regions. Although the sociopolitical divide between Assiniboin and Cree along the North Branch of the Saskatchewan River was still obvious by the mid–nineteenth century, it was not as pronounced as it had been in earlier decades (Palliser 1863: 202; Fraser 1963: 11–42; Milloy 1972: 223–229). In this period increasing numbers of parkland-adapted Cree and Ojibwa were leaving their homelands to become full-time prairie dwellers, and they were doing so for many of the same reasons as Cree and Ojibwa in regions farther east (Milloy 1988: 95–99, 103–118). With this influx, some of the earlier distinctions between the Plains Assiniboin and Cree began to break down. While each still retained a unique language and cultural practices, reports of their intermarriage and coresidency abound, as do references to the sharing of territory and collaboration in communal bison hunts (Cowie 1913: 317; Sharp 1954: 29–30; Hind 1971: 107; Milloy 1972: 232–237, 249–250, 256–260; Dempsey 1984: 39, 45, 59). Also, most of the Plains Cree, including those along the North Branch, were more firmly and uniformly on the side of the Assiniboin in what had now become a largely uninterrupted wave of raiding and war with the Blackfoot-Blood-Piegan and their allies, the Atsina (Milloy 1972: 167–199, 1988: 95–99). With the strengthening of military ties, increased intermarriage, and coresidency, as well as more frequent collaboration in productive pursuits, the social networks that supported polyethnic alliance formations in this area became much more ramified and tightly knit.

In fact, after the 1840s many of the Cree, Assiniboin, and Ojibwa who lived along the North Branch of the Saskatchewan River were extending their hunting forays farther south. In these movements, the territorial ranges of the northern Assiniboin, Upriver Cree, and Ojibwa were starting to overlap those of the Cree-Assiniboin, Downriver Cree, and other populations in the south (figure 2). In the 1860s, all these populations were reported to hunt together and live in common encampments in the vicinity of the Cypress Hills (Cowie 1913: 308–310; Bennett 1969: 142–155; Dusenberry 1954, 1985; Sharrock 1974; Dempsey 1984). These groups, and other ethnically mixed populations from locations in the northeast, moved to the plains of southern Saskatchewan and adjoining areas in northern Montana because of diminishing economic opportunities in their home locales. By the 1870s, this entire area had become a haven and a melting pot for a wide variety of native ethnic groups in search both of a livelihood and of independence (figure 3) (O'Connell n.d.; Rodnick 1938: 20, 77; Sharp 1955: 213–218; Sharrock 1974: 111–113; Spry 1976; Vogelin and Hickerson 1974: 153–163; Dusenberry 1954, 1985; Dempsey 1984).

Added to the increasing complexity of interethnic relationships in the region was the addition of Crow and Hidatsa to local polyethnic alliance formations. Newly established trade relationships with the Crow and Hidatsa created an even larger expanse of territory in which groups could peaceably live and travel. After 1870, the Assiniboin, Cree, and Ojibwa range extended from the North Branch of the Saskatchewan in Alberta to the Yellowstone and Musselshell Rivers in Montana (figure 3). Relations between the Hidatsa-Crow and Assiniboin-Cree were generated and solidified through intermarriage, adop-

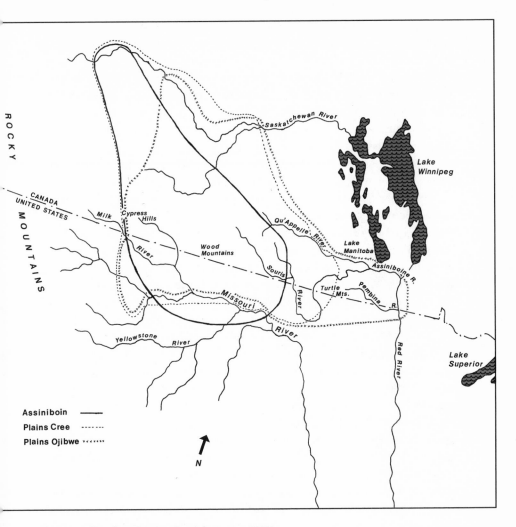

Figure 3. Overlapping territorial ranges, 1875.

tion, and sodality "brotherhood," and they contributed to an even greater ethnic diversification in band membership (Bowers 1965: 5–6, 217–218, 260, 287, 295; Milloy 1972: 42–43, 163–164, 223, 229; Dempsey 1984: 25–84; Weist 1977: 39–41). In Saskatchewan, for example, one band, whose ancestry was predominately Cree but mixed with Assiniboin and Ojibwa, was led by a Crow-Hidatsa known as Sweet Medicine (Dempsey 1984: 29). In Montana, a leader of Cree-Ojibwa-Assiniboin ancestry named Little Poplar was married to a Crow woman. He and his followers spent much of their time hunting and living in regions south of the Missouri River until U.S. military forces intervened in the 1880s and forced them to relocate in Canada (Dempsey 1984: 59). Throughout the northwestern Plains, ethnic hybridization was penetrating more deeply into the roots of kinship formations and affecting a larger number of local residence groups. Whether local bands identified with single ethnic names or hyphenated ascriptions, their ancestries were becoming more complex and ethnically mixed.

By the middle of the nineteenth century, the polyethnic alliance formations in which the Assiniboin, Cree, and Ojibwa were nested gave these populations uninterrupted access to at least three major sources of Euramerican trade, including the Hudson Bay Company entrepôts along the river systems of Canada, the American fur-trade posts on the Missouri, as well as a variety of small independent outfits that operated an overland trade route connecting St. Paul with the Red River and then onto the plains of North Dakota and Montana (Howard 1977). Their expansive territorial range also encompassed diverse grassland, parkland, and forest habitats, and until the 1850s it gave them access to three of the large bison populations in the northern Plains. Finally, with the growing inclusion of Crow and later Hidatsa in their political coalitions, they had access not only to new territory and a steady supply of horses but also additional manpower to protect the territories in which they lived and traveled (Anonymous 1940: 130; Milloy 1972: 42–43, 163–164, 223, 229).

In the years between 1840 and 1870 the process of merger had become even more widespread and complex. Bands traveled and settled over much wider areas, extending their territorial reach, diversifying their economic opportunities, and expanding their social ties (Vogelin and Hickerson 1974: 221–224; Dempsey 1984: 25–55; Albers and Kay 1987: 67–74). Widening the range of contacts and resources to which local groups had access was a sensible strategy for accommodating the rapid political, economic, and demographic changes taking place in their midst. That this pattern continued well after the formation of reservations, even in the face of forces which denied its existence, speaks to its strength as a strategy for adapting to rapid change.

Further Ethnic Realignments in Postreservation Times: 1870 to 1890

In the 1870s reservations were established in northern Montana at the Fort Peck and Fort Belknap agencies for Assiniboin occupancy. No reservation, however, was created for the Plains Cree and Ojibwa in the United States, nor had reserves been established in Canada for these groups or the Assiniboin. Since the United States was preoccupied politically and militarily with the Lakota and Cheyenne during the 1870s, little was done during this decade to address the situation of the nontreaty Assiniboin, Cree, and Ojibwa who inhabited the plains of North Dakota, Montana, and adjoining areas in Canada. As a consequence, many of the nontreaty Assiniboin-Cree-Ojibwa traded at and took rations with their Assiniboin, Crow, and Hidatsa relatives who were affiliated with U.S. reservations (Simmons 1871: 140; Alderson 1873–1875; Bogy 1874–1879; Lincoln 1878, 1879; Rodnick 1938: 20, 70). At the same time, these Indians, along with those "officially" under U.S. trust, traveled to places like Fort Walsch to take rations in Canada (Sharrock and Sharrock 1974: 127–139). In the years after 1870 most of the Ojibwa, Cree, and Assiniboin continued to jointly occupy and opportunistically use their territories as they had in previous decades (Morris 1881; Kline 1882; Sharrock and Sharrock 1974: 127–139; Dempsey 1984: 25–55, 92–97, 102–110).

Notwithstanding the imposition of U.S. and Canadian sovereignty over this region, which included the establishment of international boundaries and tribally fixed treaty borders between Lakota, Crow, Atsina, Piegan, and some Assiniboin (notably those who lived south of the Missouri River under the leadership of Foolish Bear), many of the Plains Assiniboin, Cree, and Ojibwa continued to cover their territories, most of which were now concentrated along the international line, in a hybridized fashion (figure 3). Since neither the United States nor Canada had the means to enforce any of its imposed boundaries, local Indian populations dispersed themselves across the region using organizational strategies to which they had become accustomed and largely ignored the borders, which were still only paper abstractions.

The continued movement and settlement of Cree, Assiniboin, and Ojibwa on both sides of the international line, however, was increasingly politicized after it became apparent that some of the Metis bands in their midst were arms suppliers to the Lakota and Cheyenne (Freeman 1872; Vail 1872; Merritt 1876). Since the military believed these arms came from Canada (even though many were trafficked out of networks originating in St. Paul), it put pressure on Canada to take treaty and scripts with the Indians who the United States presumed were "Canadian," which meant, by and large, Cree, Ojibwa, and Metis (Bennett 1969: 142–155; Sharrock and Sharrock 1974: 127–139; Dempsey 1984: 59, 92). Although Canada did so and removed many of the border Assiniboin-Cree-Ojibwa to reserves farther north along the Qu'Appelle and Saskatchewan Rivers, several mixed bands continued to remain in the border areas of Montana, not only because bison were still to be found in these areas but also because many of them were closely related to the Assiniboin, Crow, and even Blackfoot populations already enrolled on U.S. reservations (Dusenberry 1985; Dempsey 1984: 92–97, 102–110).

When U.S. hostilities with the Lakota subsided, the military turned its attention to the ethnically mixed populations of Assiniboin, Cree, and Ojibwa, along with related groups of Metis, who were staying in Montana and adjoining areas of southern Saskatchewan. For a wide variety of reasons, these groups became identified generically as either Cree or Canadian. No matter what their real ethnic origins happened to be (and many of them had been born and lived most of their life in the United States and had little or no Cree ancestry), they became subject to years of military harassment, which included the destruction of their settlements and their forced removal to Canadian soil. However, these groups resisted military harassment and returned to the United States, where they encamped by themselves or among reservation-based relatives (Kline 1925; Dusenberry 1954, 1962, 1985; Dempsey 1984: 96–105).

By the 1880s, there were still several groups of Indians without any official trust status in northern Montana and North Dakota. Some of them were members of full-blood bands of Assiniboin, Cree, and/or Ojibwa, but the vast majority were members of the region's growing Metis community. Much of this population remained landless not because their native origins were denied but because their ethnic ancestry did not fit preconceived notions about the dispersion of American Indians across the geographic landscape. They were identified consistently as Cree, an Indian tribe for whom the United States assumed no trust responsibility under the assumption that it had never occupied American soil. Although many had Cree ancestry, they were also Assiniboin and Ojibwa and even Crow, Hidatsa, or Blackfoot. Ironically, most of them had close relatives who were fully enrolled on reservations in the area. Because their hybridized ethnic backgrounds and identities did not match the picture of the policymakers, which was based largely on a notion of tribal blocs with exclusive memberships and territories, some of these ethnically mixed groups remained landless until the twentieth century (Bottineau 1900; Dusenberry 1954, 1962, 1985).

Conclusion

Some scholars (Smith 1969; van den Berghe 1973; Skinner 1975) have viewed ethnic pluralism as a condition unique to the state, arguing that only states have structures which can contain as well as control the varied and at times conflicting interests of diverse ethnic groups. To assert that the historical social formations of the Ojibwa, Cree, and Assiniboin were not ethnically pluralistic is like saying there is no religion without a church, no politics without a state, and no economy without a market. The issue is not whether pluralism exists outside the state but rather how different kinds of social formations incorporate and integrate ethnically diverse populations in structurally distinct ways.

The alliance formations of the Plains Assiniboin, Cree, and Ojibwa constitute one sort of pluralistic structure based on a process of merger. Between 1780 and 1870, their patterns of integration ranged from loosely structured alliances in territorial use, trade, and military affairs among ethnically separate residence groups to highly integrated and ethnically hybrid coalitions. In some areas these even reached a stage where new ethnic groups were formed, including the Nehiopwat and Naka.wiyiniuk. The diversity of merger patterns that evolved defy easy generalization, except to say that they were in a constant state of flux and becoming. Not only did these configurations change from one locale to another, but they were also transformed within each geographic area over time. Even though they were responsive to historically specific forces, it is clear that epidemic disease coupled with changing economic opportunities were important in bringing about their transformation (Albers and Kay 1987: 74–80; Albers 1993: 115–119).

During the nineteenth century, a growing competition over access to horses, territory, and trading opportunities contributed to the emergence of interethnic coalitions over the entire Plains. For the most part these coalitions took on the appearance of clustered network formations built around segments of different ethnic groups whose members banded together and jointly protected shared territorial ranges and trade routes (Sharrock 1974; Ewers 1975; Weist 1977; Albers and Kay 1987; Hanson 1987; Moore 1987; Albers 1993). In many important ways, these clustered structures differed from the chainlike configurations that had evolved in and dominated the region during the previous century (Albers 1993: 100–112). As Sharrock (1974: 112–119) so skillfully demonstrated, these polyethnic formations were organized segmentally, with local groups forming large political and economic blocs and subdividing into smaller ones as circumstances warranted. One of the most important characteristics of these formations was their flexibility, which enabled groups to rapidly rework their relations and even identities as local situations demanded.

Although segmentary patterns of alliance making under merger were widespread in the Plains, there were important structural differences from one locale to the next. Among the Cheyenne and Lakota, for example, these formations were more centralizing and less amorphous than those of the Cree, Ojibwa, and Assiniboin, a difference which may reflect other widely reported contrasts in the social organizations of these groups (Oliver 1962; Moore 1974, 1987). Indeed, it might even be hypothesized that the ethnic bloc confederation pattern of merger was much more pronounced and enduring among the Cheyenne and Lakota as a result of a greater formality and stability in the organization of their councils and soldier sodalities, whereas the hybridized group coalition pattern was more widespread among the Ojibwa, Cree, and Assiniboin because their councils and soldier sodalities were less centralized and more informally constituted (Oliver 1962; Moore 1974, 1987; Albers 1993). If this was the case, it might also help us understand why ethnogenesis appears to have followed contrasting paths for these populations as well.

However particular patterns of merger evolved in the Plains, it is clear that one of the more significant challenges facing students of American Indian ethnohistory is a greater understanding of the changing complexity of relationships that interconnect ethnically diverse populations across the geographic landscape (Quinn 1993). In an intellectual climate where essentialist theorizing has been rejected in favor of highly particularistic reconstructions, little has been done to compare and explain the character and dynamics of interethnic relations across different empirical settings. Yet there is a growing need to do this. Not only is it important for reaching more comprehensive understandings of regional integration, ethnic pluralism, and ethnogenesis in regions such as the Plains, it is also necessary for developing more sophisticated theories of interethnic articulation on a global scale.

Note

1. Contrary to John Ewers's (1974: 43–44) writing on the matter, there is compelling evidence to indicate that the Assiniboin Broken Arm and the Cree Broken Arm of the Wood Mountain area were one and the same person, while the Broken Arms reported in the vicinity of the North Branch of the Saskatchewan River and at Red Lake in Minnesota were different men (Kane 1968: 49; Milloy 1972: 163–164; Vogelin and Hickerson 1974: 148).

Kenneth Bilby

Ethnogenesis in the Guianas and Jamaica

Two Maroon Cases

The term *ethnogenesis*, though it entered the English language only a few decades ago, has become well established in the social science lexicon. The growing currency of the term in anthropology reflects an increasing awareness of the fact that sociocultural systems and identities are rarely as static or as closed as was once thought.

In current usage, *ethnogenesis* most often denotes a gradual process through which older ethnic categories and boundaries are redefined. Sometimes it is also used to refer to the transformation or shifting salience of pre-existing cultural identities as they become politicized in new contexts. Only rarely is the term applied to cases of full-fledged, truly new ethnogenesis; that is, the rapid formation of entirely new societies and cultures when individuals of diverse backgrounds are suddenly thrown together by fate and forced to create societies afresh. Perhaps this is because these societies are more the exception than the rule in human history.

Such societies have been characterized by anthropologists as neoteric or cenogenic, for they cannot be said to have grown entirely, or even primarily, out of any previously existing society; they embody unique and unprecedented biological and cultural blends (Gonzalez 1970; Bilby 1988). Many of these new societies owe their existence to the major upheavals and displacements of persons associated with European conquest and expansion during the last five centuries, with the African slave trade playing a particularly prominent role. Because of their relatively recent and rapid formation and their typically small scale, these societies provide us with a unique opportunity to explore some of the ways in which groups of uprooted and displaced individuals have managed to construct new social orders and cultural identities out of multiple pasts.

Among the new peoples that sprang into being as a result of European conquest and colonization are the Maroon societies of the Americas. These societies are composed of descendants of enslaved Africans who escaped from plantations and created new societies and cultures beyond the reach of the European colonial powers. Maroon communities were once spread across the slaveholding areas of the Western Hemisphere, but only a few have survived to the present.[1] The Windward Maroons of Jamaica and the Aluku, or Boni, of French Guiana and Surinam are two such present-day Maroon peoples. This essay compares the Jamaican Maroon and Aluku cases, focusing on processes of ethnogenesis and examining how economic factors, religious ideology, and cultural notions of kinship have intersected in the construction of new identities and new forms of solidarity.[2]

The Jamaican Case: The Early Years

The first major groupings of Maroons in Jamaica emerged when the British wrested the colony from Spain in 1655 and large numbers of Spanish slaves took advantage of the turmoil to flee to the mountainous interior. Some groups sided with one or the other of the European adversaries, while others remained aloof from the conflict.[3]

Among these early Maroons were both Africans, veterans of the transatlantic voyage, and Creoles, born in Jamaica. In later years the original Spanish Creoles were joined by Creole slaves born and raised in what had become a British colony. The African-born Maroons, judging from both historical and contemporary evidence, represented a complex spectrum of geographical and cultural regions, ranging from Senegambia and the Gold Coast down through the Congo-Angola area and even into East Africa.[4] Although individuals belonging to certain broad ethnolinguistic categories, such as those labeled "Congos" or "Coromantees" by the Europeans, may have been numerically dominant at different periods, there were always smaller numbers of individuals from a wide variety of other African ethnic groups present, and the ethnic balance continued to shift over time. At any rate, it is certain that many different African languages and cultural backgrounds were represented among the Maroons throughout the late seventeenth and early eighteenth centuries (Kopytoff 1976a: 37–42).

Very little can be said with certainty about how the early rebels who escaped from the plantations and banded together in common cause organized themselves politically and how they actually coalesced into new societies. Nonetheless, a few general statements can be made based on our limited knowledge of life among the Maroons prior to 1739, the year of their landmark peace treaty with the British.

First, initial groupings tended to grow out of military alliances. Political authority among the early Maroons was typically vested in a handful of military leaders who had gained respect as able fighters and skillful strategists and had become recognized as chiefs (Kopytoff 1973: 70–79, 1978; Schafer 1973: 60–61, 64–65; Campbell 1988: 50–52). Political authority also had a religious dimension, and in some cases ritual specialists, Obeah men and women, who did not necessarily play an overt military role nonetheless exercised considerable political influence (Kopytoff 1973: 83–89, 1978: 298, 301; Campbell 1988: 51, 123, 176–177; Hart 1985: 80–81).

Early Maroon social and political organization was relatively unstable. The formative period was characterized by shifting alliances and fluctuating boundaries of group identity, with new members continually being added through recruiting and raids on the plantations (Kopytoff 1976a: 42–46, 1978: 295–296). In some communities, an imbalance of the sexes, with men greatly outnumbering women, caused internal tensions and served to increase instability (Kopytoff 1973: 79–80, 1976a: 43, 1978: 301–304; Schafer 1973: 76).[5]

For their subsistence, the Maroons depended on a form of domestic production based on slash-and-burn horticulture in which women played a central role (Edwards 1796: xxx; Dallas 1803: 106–108; Kopytoff 1973: 161–163). One can assume that over time this led to the development of more stable domestic groups tied to a land base. Fixed settlements emerged in the general vicinity of primary areas of cultivation, and the inhabitants of these new communities established territorial claims over the villages they built and the lands they cultivated (Kopytoff 1973: 69). By the early eighteenth century a number of major Maroon towns existed in the Blue Mountains of the eastern part of the island, the most famous being Nanny Town, named after the legendary female religious leader of the Windward Maroons.

Nanny Town appears to have been at the center of a series of shifting alliances during the early eighteenth century that led to the formation of a loose-knit federation that included several dispersed Windward Maroon communities. It is not clear to what extent Nanny and her followers exercised actual authority over these other villages in daily life, but her preeminence as a religious (and possibly political) leader seems to have been recognized by virtually all the eastern Maroon groups. In any case, each Windward Maroon village was under the leadership of its own chief or chiefs and operated in a more or less autonomous fashion, although military cooperation and some exchange of personnel between different villages is known to have taken place (Kopytoff 1978: 298–301; Campbell 1988: 49). Windward Maroon attempts to forge military alliances reached their greatest extent in the 1730s, when the eastern Maroons, under increasing pressure from the British, who had recently seized their main town, sent a group to the Leeward Maroons and their chief, Kojo (Cudjoe), more than a hundred miles away on the opposite side of the island, to propose a cross-island confederation (Kopytoff 1973: 38–39, 53; Hart 1985: 86–87; Campbell 1988: 70, 92–94). The attempt failed, possibly, in part, because of British intervention, and the Windward and Leeward Maroons have maintained separate identities until today. In contrast, the three present-day Windward Maroon communities of Moore Town, Charles Town, and Scot's Hall recognize common historical origins and a largely shared cultural heritage.

Jamaican Maroon ethnogenesis unfolded through a number of interdependent processes. In the first instance, new group identities must have grown organically out of the social and biological bonds that were generated by ongoing face-to-face interaction in the early Maroon settlements. It is quite possible that some actual or fictive kinship relationships were carried over from the coastal plantations, as some aspects of kinship ideology undoubtedly also were (see Mintz and Price 1992: 43–44, 66–67); but the creation of new family units, however these were defined, must have been at the foundation of the new shared identities that began to emerge in the forest. This process was no doubt closely linked with the gradual definition of territorial claims and boundaries, for the recognition of rights over land gave concrete expression to social identities already rooted in domestic relations. At a later stage, political relationships superseding these local kin-based groupings would also come into play, as larger social identities were constructed out of political alliances. Thus, emerging definitions of ethnic identity (that is, who was included in one's primary group of identification and who was not) came to reflect not only actual relationships of kinship and, in later years, descent but also extra-local political and military alignments.

Religious ideology, derived largely from African models and principles, constituted a powerful social cement, not only for relationships based on kinship, descent, and coresidence but for broader political coalitions lacking such a foundation in local social relations. It is known that African-derived ritual oaths were used to induct new recruits into Maroon communities, seal political alliances between distinct groups, and even consecrate the treaties made with the British in 1739, which remain sacred to the Maroons to this day.[6] Moreover, as we shall see, present-day evidence suggests that the syncretic Afro-Jamaican religion developed by the Windward Maroons was family-based, with ceremonial life revolving around possession by the spirits of ancestors, who were called upon to help resolve community problems.

The Role of Religion in Jamaican Maroon Ethnogenesis:
A Closer Look

Unfortunately, historical documentation of land tenure and kinship structure in the pretreaty Maroon communities is almost entirely lacking. Ethnographic data gathered in recent times cannot be used to construct a reliable picture of social and economic organization in the early days, since these communities were radically transformed by the 1739 treaties, which in effect created Maroon reservations, thereby setting in motion fundamental social, political, and economic changes (Kopytoff 1973, 1976b; Campbell 1988: 126–163). Yet the traditional religion still practiced in the eastern Maroon communities retains many features that must have characterized Maroon religion during the formative period. Since Maroon religion has resisted external pressures for change by remaining closed to outsiders and has been kept separate from Christianity through a process of compartmentalization (Bilby 1981: 53–55), this is the one area in which contemporary ethnography can be used to help recover certain aspects of the process of ethnogenesis not revealed in the written record. When we examine contemporary Windward Maroon religion from this perspective, we begin to see the close relationship between religious ideology, kinship, and the social meaning of land. This in turn allows us to imagine more clearly how such linkages must have operated more than two centuries ago to bring a new people into being. Let us take a closer look, then, at traditional religion in the Windward Maroon community of Moore Town.

Traditional religion in Moore Town is centered on the ceremony known as Kromanti Play or Kromanti Dance. Central to Kromanti Play are the ties maintained between living Maroons and their ancestors through spirit possession, or *myal*. Although in theory any Maroon can become possessed by an ancestor, it is the specialized medium known as the *fete-man* (or, if female, *fete-uman*) who serves as the chief intermediary between the living and the dead. The *fete-man* cultivates special relationships with a number of individual human ghosts, some of whom were spirit mediums during their own lives. These ghosts devote themselves to the *fete-man* and carry out his bidding in exchange for offerings and favors.

A good portion of any Kromanti Play involves interaction between possessed spirit mediums and the other Maroons in attendance, who remain unpossessed (*kliin yai*). This ongoing interaction between living Maroons and their ancestors reinforces a strong sense of continuous community identity across generations, even as it allows local social and political relationships to be aired, negotiated, and redefined in a public setting. It also renews and helps to maintain sacred ties to the lands on which the ancestors are buried.

The question of burial has traditionally been an important one for Maroons. For one thing, a *fete-man* must sometimes visit the graves of those Maroons whose spirits he relies on in order to make offerings, properly care for the burial site, and otherwise ensure that these spirits' demands are met.

As far back as present-day Maroons can remember, Moore Town has had a special rule governing burial. This rule dictates that all burials within the boundaries of the communally held Maroon treaty lands must take place within a specially designated, centralized public cemetery. (This contrasts with the general rural Jamaican pattern of burial within private yards or on separate family plots.) Originally, the community burial ground of Moore Town was located at a place called Bump Grave, next to an area near the center of the village known as the *asafo* ground or *asafo* house, where major Kromanti Play ceremonies were once regularly held. Long ago, however, the cemetery was moved to the Anglican churchyard nearby. Although this change of location says much about the increasing influence of the Anglican church, it did nothing to diminish the importance of the ties between the living and the dead maintained through Kromanti Play. Kromanti Play continued to be practiced separately, and the old rule of centralized burial was simply carried over from the original sacred Maroon burial ground to the new Anglican cemetery. Even today, only Maroons are normally buried in this community cemetery. This mode of burial serves to sustain a collective sense of Maroon identity, rooted in notions of common descent and communal ownership of land, while endowing this identity with a sacred dimension.

The sacred relationship between land and the ancestors buried on it is not unique to Maroons. Elsewhere in rural Jamaica it has been shown that the common practice of burying kin on family plots contributes to the creation of inalienable "family land." Clarke (1966: 65), writing of this custom, reports that "the religious association of land is strong: the spot on which the ancestors are buried is sacred and land containing their graves should not be permitted to pass into alien hands." In other words, the creation of such family land establishes sacred, inalienable ties between individual parcels of land and the groups of cognatic kin who inherit them. All descendants of the original owner inherit rights to the land, and some of those who activate these rights may themselves be buried on the land when they die. Thus, over the generations a sort of landholding corporation composed of cognatic descendants of the original owner comes into existence (Besson 1988: 48).[7] "Any member of this family 'through the name or through the blood' has rights of use which are not lost through non-exercise for any period" (Clarke 1966: 44).

The burial practices of Maroons have served to create and maintain a similar concept of sacred family land, although in the Maroon case this family land extends beyond individual yards or plots to encompass the entire territory held by the community (i.e., the collectively held Maroon treaty lands). All members of the Maroon community, whether actual ties of kinship can be traced or not, are said to belong to a single family by virtue of their common descent from an original ancestress, Grandy Nanny, who is sometimes characterized as the "mother of the Maroons" (Martin 1973: 53–57; Bilby and Steady 1981: 458; Bilby 1984b: 11–13).[8] In addition to being remembered as a great ritual specialist and leader during the time when the Maroons were at war with the British, Grandy Nanny is also conceptualized as the original "owner" of the Maroon treaty lands.[9]

Membership in the Maroon family is passed on bilaterally from Maroons to their children, who automatically inherit "Maroon blood" at birth. Interestingly enough, the main material consequence of possessing Maroon blood is that it confers upon an individual guaranteed rights of usufruct over a portion of the communally held Maroon lands; all of Grandy Nanny's descendants (called Nanny's *yoyo* in the Maroon Kromanti ritual language) are entitled to a share of this land. If a person's claim to membership in the Maroon community—or Maroon blood—is acknowledged, then the individual may acquire a parcel of land by applying to the colonel, or chief, and the Maroon council (*kamati*), who are obligated to accommodate the request.

But Maroon blood has spiritual consequences as well, for possession of such blood entitles one to participate in the ceremony of Kromanti Play. This ceremony is the main site where the mystical notions of descent that define the social boundaries of the Maroon community are put to a sacred test. It is believed that the ancestors who possess mediums at Kromanti ceremonies are able to "smell" the presence of non-Maroon blood, which they find intolerable. Should a non-Maroon (called *obroni* in Maroon Kromanti language), even an invited one, be present when possession occurs, the medium invariably becomes enraged by the outsider's foreign smell and instantly attempts to attack the non-Maroon intruder. This response is conceptualized as an involuntary, almost physiological, reaction to *obroni* blood, and there are no exceptions to it. The *obroni* will be forced to leave. If he is able, however, to secure the help of a specially assigned Maroon protector who agrees to guide him through a series of ordeals and rituals intended to assuage the enraged spirit, his presence will eventually become acceptable, and he will be able to stay during episodes of possession. (This applies, however, only to possessions by the individual spirit or spirits to which he has been personally introduced, and no others.) This complex ritual drama, which is enacted whenever non-Maroons visit Kromanti Play for healing, as they frequently do, constitutes the clearest and most powerful symbolic representation in Maroon culture of the line dividing Maroons from non-Maroons (Bilby 1981: 76–80). It serves to remind Maroons that the division between them and others is an immutable part of the natural order (Bilby 1984b: 14).

We see, then, how religious ideology, notions of kinship, and land tenure are closely interrelated in the Jamaican Maroon case. The Maroon blood that allows unchallenged entry to Kromanti Play, thought to have been inherited from a common ancestress, symbolically embodies the family relationship shared by all Moore Town Maroons (as well as the boundary dividing Maroons from non-Maroons). Membership in this family in turn guarantees access to the communally held Maroon treaty lands. This collectively owned material base continues to serve as one of the main foundations of Maroon ethnic identity in Moore Town. The sacred relationship between the Maroon family (Nanny's *yoyo*), the communal lands, and the ancestors buried on them is embodied by the centralized Maroon community cemetery. This symbolized nexus of ideas about kinship, land, and cosmology is at the heart of Maroon identity in Moore Town.[10]

It is always risky to project from what is known of the present back into the past. Yet with a little imagination, it is easy to see that the general concepts of shared blood, family land, and ancestral presence, which survive in modified form today, must have been central to the initial process of ethnogenesis in the Jamaican Maroon case.

The earliest ancestors of these Maroons—those who first broke away from the plantations and fled to the forest to start a new life—began their adventure as collections of individuals who banded together in order to survive. These fugitives, taking their chances in a largely unfamiliar wilderness, started out in a condition that can be characterized as something close to an absence of "society." While the collective effort to survive might have led them almost immediately to begin the construction of what could be called a new society, based on shared experience and common understandings, the genesis of a new *ethnic* identity would have required another generation at least. Only through an initial process of biological reproduction could shared blood be created and incorporated into an ongoing process of social reproduction. Meanwhile, subsistence practices, including cultivation, would require a division of labor and the devising of domestic arrangements of one kind or another. These domestic arrangements would come to be associated with rights over land and the food produced on it, and these in turn would create a link between shared blood and the specific sections of land over which groups of kin, however defined, had come to have recognized rights. Thus would family land of one kind or another come into being. To judge from contemporary ethnographic data, such family land would likely have been defined partly in religious terms, and the burial of ancestors on such land would likely have played a part in this process.[11] A "community" (or family) identity based on common descent and a shared territory would gradually emerge out of these evolving relationships. Once this occurred, an initial process of ethnogenesis could be said to have taken place. Ethnic identities formed in this way might then merge with others, for instance, through marriage outside of the original family or community or as a result of political alliances.

To summarize: the limited evidence that we have suggests that Jamaican Maroon ethnogenesis depended on the interplay of three primary factors: the availability and disposition of land, the emergence of localized kin groupings sharing a territorial base, and the development of a religious ideology that reflected and supported the emerging social order. Let us now briefly consider the Aluku Maroons of French Guiana and Surinam to see how their origins compare with those of the Jamaican Maroons.

The Aluku Case: The Early Years

As in the Jamaican case, we have very little certain knowledge about the earliest days of the Aluku.[12] While some of their ancestors are known to have escaped into the forest as early as 1712, the majority fled from coastal Surinamese plantations during the mid–eighteenth century, hiding out in the unsettled swamplands of the Cottica River region. Following a protracted war with the Dutch colonists, they moved across the Maroni River to French Guiana in 1776. In 1793 they suffered a major defeat when their leader, Boni, was killed by a party of Ndjuka Maroons who had allied themselves with the Dutch. In 1860 they were finally recognized by a French-Dutch treaty as a free people with the right to travel without restrictions in both French Guiana and Surinam. Since this time the majority of Aluku have been considered French subjects and since 1969 have been full French citizens.

The African ancestors of the Aluku, like those of the Jamaican Maroons, came from many different regions, had widely varying cultural backgrounds, and spoke a large number of different languages. The early Aluku also included Creoles among their numbers, individuals who had been born and raised on Surinamese plantations. Although there is evidence that at least one of the groups that banded together in the forest after escaping was composed primarily of Kromanti (or Kormantin) individuals originating from the same general region of West Africa, most groups were highly mixed, and these varied origins are still reflected in certain aspects of present-day Aluku culture, such as religious structure (Hoogbergen 1990: 203–207).[13]

Like the early Jamaican Maroons, the earliest ancestors of the Aluku, those who escaped into the forest and banded together, organized themselves into a series of politically autonomous groupings with their own military headmen and their own settlements and cultivations (Hoogbergen 1990: 23–51). They

too relied upon slash-and-burn methods and a system of domestic production in which women eventually came to play a key role (Hoogbergen 1990:
18–19). From time to time these autonomous communities joined together
and collaborated in military expeditions against the coastal plantations. As in
Jamaica, political alliances were usually ratified by sacred blood oaths; reports of such ritual oaths abound in the historical literature (Hoogbergen
1990: 17–18).

Like the Windward Maroons of Jamaica, the ancestors of the Aluku came
to constitute a loose federation, characterized by shifting alliances between
local chiefs and a certain amount of intermarriage and movement between
communities. Like Nanny in Jamaica, a central figure emerged in this federation, a military and religious leader named Boni. A great strategist and particularly courageous fighter, Boni coordinated and led most of those military
efforts in which chiefs and warriors from more than one Maroon community
participated. Despite the numerous long-term political and military alliances
Boni helped to establish, the various communities and chiefs maintained their
political autonomy throughout the war period (Hoogbergen 1990: 199). It was
only after the devastating defeat of the 1790s that the remnants of the different
groups came together and formed a single sociopolitical unit displaying most
of the elements of Aluku social structure as it exists today. The final political
unification of the separate bands into a single "tribe" or "nation" seems to
have been effected through the subsuming of the different groups under the
authority of a single set of religious oracles; namely, the oracles controlled by
the oldest group of rebels, those led by a chief named Asikan and, after him,
by Boni. The divinity originally worshiped by this particular group—a god
known as Tata Odun, said by the present-day Aluku to have come over from
Africa along with the ancestors—thus became the supreme tribal deity to
which all the different groups now owed obeisance (Bilby 1990: 118).

The settlements formed by the early ancestors of the Aluku were even less
stable than those of the early Jamaican Maroons, for the Aluku ancestors
changed the locations of their villages often, making mobility a part of their
strategy of evasion (Hoogbergen 1990: 199–201). Even so, the evidence suggests that the processes through which group identity was constructed were
similar in the Aluku and Jamaican cases. Early on, for example, coresidence
became an important governing principle, and the social identities that began
to emerge out of face-to-face interaction, domestic relations, and shared experience gradually became anchored to territorial concerns.

The Aluku ancestors, however, blended this process of defining territorial
claims and boundaries with an organizing principle that apparently had no
counterpart among the Jamaican Maroons. In the Guianese forest the various
emergent communities of rebels identified themselves collectively with the

specific plantations from which their founding members or leaders had escaped. As an expression of a *new* corporate identity tied to collective ownership of land in their new forest environment, the members of each band
adopted the name of this plantation of origin (or, sometimes, the plantation's
owner or the region in which it was located). As more stable kin groups began
to develop and to stake territorial claims based on settlement and first cultivation of an area, a principle of uterine descent began to be applied to the
already operative concept of collective ownership of natural (or other) resources. With the advent of new generations, membership in these collectivi-
ties was passed on in the female line, and full-blown corporate matriclans,
known as *lo*, eventually emerged (Hoogbergen 1990: 207–215).[14]

Like the Jamaican Maroons, the ancestors of the Aluku came to possess a
religious ideology that had developed in tandem with, and both mirrored and
supported, emerging social identities. Not only villages, cultivated land, and
natural resources but certain important ritual possessions came to be collectively owned by the clan. For example, each village acquired its own shrine to
clan ancestors, along with its own mortuary house, where major rites for deceased clan members were performed.

The Role of Religion in Aluku Maroon Ethnogenesis:
A Closer Look

As in the Jamaican case, present-day Aluku Maroon religion provides us with
important clues to the process of ethnogenesis. Aluku society today is divided
into six primary named, corporate matriclans, or *lo*, each of which "owns"
one or more villages, the surrounding lands and natural resources, and the
horticultural camps and areas of cultivation established by clan members in
more distant locations (Hurault 1961: 18–20; Bilby 1990: 145–146). In many
ways the *lo*, which operates as a politically autonomous corporation in most
contexts, resembles a distinct "ethnic group." It is at the level of the clan that
the Aluku acquire their primary social identity and feel the strongest sense of
group loyalty, and it is at this level that religious ideology, notions of kinship,
and ownership of land intersect most neatly.

Most of the Aluku clans are localized in single villages, although a few,
having undergone fission, are now divided between two or more villages. Like
the Jamaican Maroons, the Aluku maintain close ties with their ancestors.
However, the Aluku do not communicate with the spirits of ancestors primarily in the context of ceremonies featuring spirit possession,[15] nor do graves
or cemeteries serve as the primary locus of such communication.[16] Most in-
vocations of ancestors occur, rather, at a central village shrine called the *faaka
tiki*. The *faaka tiki* consists of one or more wooden posts, the oldest of which
is said to have been "planted" in the ground by the village founder, the person

who originally "cut the village" (cleared the land for settlement). There fellow clansmen assemble on various occasions to pour libations and request favors or protection from clan ancestors. Like the central cemetery for Jamaican Maroons, the Aluku *faaka tiki* symbolizes the sacred, inalienable ties between the ancestors, their living descendants, and the lands they hold collectively; at a more general level, it stands for the corporate identity of the clan. Also symbolic of this connection is the mortuary house (*kee osu*) that every village possesses. Here all clan members belonging to the village are brought when they die to be consulted through divination, honored with offerings, and feted with music and dance before being taken to the appropriate cemetery in the forest for burial. Although inactive most of the time, the mortuary house stands in a prominent location, usually near the *faaka tiki*. As the main site of the transition from the world of the living to that of the ancestors, it too constitutes a powerful symbol of the sacred relationship between land, ancestors, and descendants.

The shared essence thought to be inherited by members of the same clan, rather than being conceptualized as "blood" (as it is by members of the Jamaican Maroon community of Moore Town), is represented with the term *bee*, meaning "womb." To say that two people "are *bee*" is to say that they are related through uterine links: at some point in their ancestry, whether one generation ago or ten, they are thought to share a "common womb." At the highest level of generalization (and the only level that corresponds to a corporate identity), a person's *bee* (matrilineal kin) and *lo* (clan) coincide (and at this level the two terms can be used interchangeably).[17] All the members of a *lo*, whether genealogical relationships are known or not, are held to be related by virtue of common descent from an original band of runaways and/or an original ancestress to whom links are no longer traceable.

Land, valued ritual possessions, and other material assets belonging to the clan are owned collectively by all descendants. As among Jamaican Maroons, land use is governed by a system of usufruct; and although rights to use of particular plots are transmissible across generations within families or clan segments, the land remains inalienable and cannot be given away or sold to persons outside the clan.

We have seen how each village has its shrine to clan ancestors and its mortuary house, both of which symbolize the corporate identity of the clan. But there is yet another distinct sphere of religious activity that is peculiar to each clan. This important sphere comprises a special category of gods and spirits called *kunu*. Much like the idea of Maroon blood in Jamaican Kromanti Play, the Aluku concept of *kunu* defines and represents, in religious terms, the "natural" boundaries between those who are of a clan and those who are not. A *kunu* is an avenging spirit created by an act of wrongdoing against a human being, spirit, or god. A victim of murder, for instance, may come back as a ghost to haunt the murderer and other members of the murderer's clan with illness and misfortune. Likewise, a god that once inhabited the body of a *papa* snake may return to exact vengeance from the clan of the individual who caused its death while burning a patch of ground in preparation for cultivation. Spirits of several different kinds, when offended, may become *kunu* in this way.[18]

What all *kunu* share is that, once created, they are thought to remain attached to a clan eternally. Furthermore, they are thought to strike indiscriminately within the clan, without regard to individual guilt or responsibility for the original act of wrongdoing. This means that all clan members, in theory at least, are equally vulnerable to attacks by such avenging spirits.[19] In addition, each *kunu* limits its attacks strictly to its chosen clan, and in principle, members of one clan need never fear an attack from another clan's avenging spirits.

Despite their fearful nature, *kunu* have a positive side as well which becomes evident only when they possess mediums and begin to communicate through them. This opens the way for a process of "taming," whereby the avenging spirit may be turned from a threatening force into a source of aid whose powers can be used to benefit rather than harm the community. This positive transformation can only be maintained, however, by periodic offerings and collective prayers intended to "cool the heart" of the spirit. These observances often bring together large numbers of fellow clansmen at the *faaka tiki*, the aforementioned shrine to the ancestors that symbolizes the corporate identity of the clan. A particularly old and venerable *kunu* may even have a post of its own planted at this central shrine, merging the notions of common descent and spiritual unity within a single sacred structure. Thus, in its "tamed" form, a *kunu* both serves as a positive expression of corporate clan identity and defines the boundaries of that identity, since members of other clans are excluded from the community of worshipers defined by common vulnerability to that avenging spirit.

This brief description should serve to show that in the Aluku case, as in the Jamaican Maroon case, religious ideology, kinship, and land tenure remain closely linked. The spiritual essence in which all members of a clan are thought to share is conceived as having been inherited through descent from a common womb. This shared essence is manifested in the common vulnerability of all clan members to the same *kunu*. By virtue of their common descent, clan members inherit not only a shared set of avenging spirits but also rights to the land and other resources held collectively by their clan. The corporate identity of the clan, as a territorial unit, is represented by the central village shrine to the ancestors, planted in the earth by village founders, as well as the mortuary house, where clan members undergo the transformation from living persons to ancestors who from then on will be addressed, like those of earlier generations, at the *faaka tiki*, the village shrine.

In Aluku religion, as in that of the Jamaican Maroons, we can still detect the key elements that contributed to Aluku ethnogenesis, and we can imagine how the linkage between these elements must have been at the foundation of this process. The parallels with the Jamaican Maroon case are apparent. In a sense, those who ran away and banded together in the Guianese forest were forced to start from scratch. They came from a wide variety of different African backgrounds, and although it is known that the Creolized slave culture to which they had been exposed on coastal plantations provided some basis for common understandings, they nonetheless found themselves in a largely unfamiliar environment without a preexisting social structure, fully shared culture, or sense of collective identity. These they were forced to construct anew, while struggling to survive in the forest.

As in Jamaica, the process of ethnogenesis—as opposed to simple consociation, coresidence, and military alliance—began with biological and social reproduction. Both archival and contemporary ethnographic evidence suggests that the first generation of women among the runaways played a crucial role in this process. Their children formed the first kin groups to whom the property acquired and controlled by the initial bands of runaways could be transferred. A primary resource was land, which came to be cultivated in large part by women, and rights established through first cultivation would have become attached over time to kin-based domestic groups. As it turned out, membership in these groups quickly came to be defined through a principle of uterine descent, which over the generations led to the development of corporate lineages and clans (conceptualized as being descended from a common womb) with rights of ownership and use over the territories first settled or cultivated by their matrilineal ancestors (as well as the valued ritual possessions handed down from these ancestors).

Along with corporate identities, the property-holding descent groups that began to emerge from this process acquired *lo nen* ("clan names," generally derived from the plantation-related names used by the original bands of runaways), and the evolving social structure was reflected in the emerging religious ideology. Descent groups evolved their own exclusive cults of *kunu*, or avenging spirits, while the sacred relationship between these corporate groups, the land they held in common, and the ancestors became embodied in a standardized set of community shrines consisting of the *faaka tiki* and the *kee osu*. It was the formation of these initial corporate descent groups that was at the foundation of ethnogenesis among the ancestors of the Aluku; the political alliances that eventually caused these descent groups to be merged into larger political units, thus expanding the boundaries of ethnic identity, as well as the religious adjustments that came to reflect these expanded identities were secondary.

In summary, the general similarities to the Jamaican Maroon case are evident. Aluku ethnogenesis appears to have depended on the interplay of three primary factors, namely, the existence and domestication of an available land base, the development of localized kin groupings linked to territorial claims, and the growth of a religious system that reflected and undergirded the newly emerging sociopolitical structure.

Differing Outcomes of Ethnogenesis in the Two Cases

In spite of the initial similarities, the societies of the Jamaican Maroons and the Aluku eventually took on rather different shapes. This can be attributed not only to the longer and greater isolation of the Aluku from the coastal society but to the fact that the building blocks of ethnic identity in the two cases, similar as they were in a general sense, were conditioned by unique cultural and ecological factors and were combined in politically different ways.

Since at least the late eighteenth century, the primary unit of social organization and ethnic identification among the Windward Maroons of Jamaica has been the politically self-contained individual settlement, each governed by its own headmen and councils and none subject to a higher authority other than that of the colonial government. In effect, ethnic identity and community identity have long been coterminous for Jamaican Maroons. In contrast, among the Aluku, while the primary unit of social organization is the localized clan, ethnic identification occurs at a higher level of political organization that outsiders sometimes refer to as the "tribe." In other words, ethnic identity overarches community identity in the Aluku case. While each of the six main Aluku clans has its own village chiefs, and each village operates in most situations as a politically independent unit, ultimate political and religious authority is vested in a paramount chief, known as the *gaanman.*

In comparing the contemporary societies of the Jamaican and Aluku Maroons, it becomes apparent that the structure of the single-community Jamaican Maroon ethnic group, viewed as a whole, parallels that of the Aluku localized clan in several interesting respects. For reasons that are not yet entirely clear, the Jamaican Maroons appear never to have adopted a principle of unilineal descent that might have generated corporate clans or lineages similar to those of the Guiana Maroons. Nevertheless, the Windward Maroons of Jamaica, as we have seen, still think of themselves as a large, clanlike family, all of whose members are related through descent from a common ancestress, the legendary Nanny, even though the genealogical links can no longer be traced. This is not unlike the conceptualization of the Aluku clan, or *lo*, which is imagined as being descended from an original band of runaways and/or an apical ancestress, although the genealogical links cannot be specified.

The parallel can be carried further. Membership in an individual Jamaican Maroon community, which is acquired automatically at birth, confers upon the individual his ethnic identity, his rights over communally held land and the natural resources controlled by that community, and his eligibility to participate in that community's traditional religious system, embodied in the ceremony of Kromanti Play, from which non-Maroons are excluded. Similarly, membership in the Aluku clan, which is automatically inherited from one's mother, determines an individual's primary social identity, his rights over the collectively owned material resources of the clan, including land, and his participation in a community of worshipers united by their common vulnerability to a number of *kunu*, or avenging spirits. When all these similarities between the two societies are taken into account, the typical ethnic unit developed by the Windward Maroons of Jamaica—the self-contained ethnic community defined by territory, common descent, shared spiritual essence, and ideals of social and political solidarity—begins to look something like the localized Aluku clan writ large.

Indeed, one can surmise that had circumstances been right, the individual Aluku clans might have ended up, at least for a time, as self-contained, single-community ethnic groups bearing some resemblance to those in Jamaica. This could have happened, for instance, if the initial bands of runaways had failed to ally themselves with other bands and had continued to develop in isolation. On the other hand, had conditions been favorable in Jamaica, the political alliances initially forged between separate bands and communities could have eventually led to a permanent overarching political authority and an expansion of both territory and ethnic identity.

The most important factors militating against either of these outcomes appear to have been political and ecological. In the Aluku case, the separate bands were finally forced together by adversity, their numbers having been greatly reduced by war, their most important leaders killed, and their crops destroyed. The survivors had no option but to pull together and salvage what was left of their fledgling societies (which by that time already included the beginnings of the descent groups that were to evolve into today's Aluku clans). In the Jamaican case, on the other hand, permanent political mergers between the various Maroon communities were prevented by both British intervention and the lack of an adequate land base. The treaties of 1739 included relatively small grants of tax-free lands to individual Maroon settlements, resembling reservations. Later in the eighteenth century a few additional land grants were made to communities in other areas that had been settled by related groups of

Maroons. (Such land grants amounted to a form of official government recognition that the inhabitants of a settlement were Maroons.) Since then each individual community has continued to hold its own treaty lands in common, and this communal land base has helped define and maintain these officially recognized Jamaican Maroon communities as distinct ethnic entities, furnishing them with corporate identities not unlike those of the landowning Aluku clans.[20] In the Jamaican case, however, land has never really been freely available. Over the years territorial expansion became less and less feasible as lands in the vicinity of the Maroon communities were claimed and occupied by the British crown, private interests, and the expanding peasantry. Unlike the Jamaican Maroons, the Aluku, who inhabit a vast, largely unsettled rain forest, have always been surrounded by an abundance of readily available land on which new claims and settlements could be established as needed. Throughout most of Aluku history, there has been little to stand in the way of any social or political impetus for territorial expansion.

Conclusion

The two cases of recent ethnogenesis briefly examined here throw light on the double-sided nature of ethnicity as a social process. On the one hand, the ethnic identities of the Jamaican Maroons and the Aluku are ultimately rooted in notions of common descent and shared substance and have grown organically out of actual kin-based communities through a largely endogenous process of daily face-to-face interaction and negotiation. On the other, they must also be seen, at least in part, as precipitates of larger political and economic forces. The treaties with the British government and the associated land grants, for example, played a profound part in the definition of Jamaican Maroon ethnicity, hastening the development of corporate ethnic identities and influencing the path this process took. Among the Aluku, interaction with colonial governments played a less obvious role. Yet, had it not been for their eventual alliance with the French, the ancestors of the Aluku would probably have been absorbed by their more numerous Ndjuka Maroon neighbors, in which case they probably would not have survived to the present as a separate ethnic group (Lenoir 1975: 314; Bilby 1990: 574). Today the Aluku are undergoing yet another kind of ethnogenesis as their ethnic identity becomes increasingly politicized and its boundaries more pronounced in response to the rapid incorporation of their territory into the French state over the last two and a half decades (Bilby 1990).

As this last statement suggests, the term *ethnogenesis* has not always been used to mean the same thing. Although a distinction is sometimes made in the literature between primary ethnogenesis (the process whereby a new ethnic community or group comes into existence) and secondary ethnogenesis (the development of ethnic consciousness caused by social mobilization), the term is often used without specifying which of these processes is meant, thereby creating a potential for confusion (see Riggs 1985). The distinction between primary and secondary ethnogenesis is an important one, however, for it corresponds roughly to two contrasting approaches or perspectives in the study of ethnicity, one of which has come to be labeled "primordialist" and the other "situationalist" (also sometimes called "circumstantialist" or "instrumentalist").[21] On the one hand, cases of secondary ethnogenesis— since they tend to be linked with shifts in political and economic circumstances that have suddenly rendered ethnicity useful as an organizing principle for the conscious mobilization of interest groups—quite naturally lend themselves to one-sided analyses emphasizing the situational nature of ethnicity in an ethnographic present. On the other hand, cases of primary ethnogenesis, which involve the gradual emergence of wholly new peoples or ethnic groups over time, reveal more clearly the complementarity and interdependence of situational and primordial factors in the historical construction of ethnic identities.

This is easily seen in the two cases of primary ethnogenesis we have examined here. Viewed from one perspective, new peoples such as the Jamaican Maroons or the Aluku dramatically exemplify the situational nature of ethnicity, since they can be shown to have come into being as a direct result of large-scale political and economic processes and conditions, such as capitalist expansion, warfare, slavery, conquest, displacement, and mass migration. If it were not for such exogenous forces, these new ethnic groups would never have sprung into existence. From another point of view, however, these peoples also demonstrate quite clearly the primordial nature of ethnicity—its cognitive basis in emotionally charged notions of common origin, shared historical experience, kinship, and shared substance. Indeed, the evidence suggests that if such a primordial basis for ethnicity does not exist to begin with, a newly forming collectivity, as part of the process of becoming not just a group with common interests and goals but an *ethnic* group, will certainly create it. As Bentley remarks, "Ethnogenesis, the formation of an ethnic group where none existed before, requires 'primordialization' of group identity, consensual acceptance of some primordial ancestor, event, or place as the common 'root' of identity" (1983: 9). In the case of the Jamaican Maroons and the Aluku, the beginnings of this process of primordialization came about spontaneously as a consequence of the biological, social, and political bonds through which diverse individuals and groups merged to create new collective identities rooted in kinship and territorial rights. Out of this process emerged, along with these new collective identities, religious ideologies and forms of historical consciousness that are as primordial—which is to say as compelling, ineffable, and irreducible to political or economic strategies of the moment—as any in the world.[22]

Our comparison of ethnogenesis among escaped slaves and their descendants in two different parts of the Americas clearly shows that ethnic identities and sentiments need not be associated with an ancient or immemorial past in order to be backed by the force of primordial ties and loyalties. As recently as 350 years ago, neither the Jamaican Maroons nor the Aluku existed. This much cannot be doubted. No one, not even these peoples themselves, would argue that their origins trail off into an ancient, immemorial past and vanish into the mists of time. Yet the ethnic identities of these two peoples are not lacking in depth. On the contrary, they are profoundly rooted in the same sorts of seemingly primordial ties and sentiments that lend ethnic identities their affective power elsewhere in the world.

As we have seen, the Jamaican Maroons and the Aluku, in creating new societies, very successfully primordialized their historical experience. Ethnogenesis depended on an actual meeting and union of real individuals and a process of social and biological production and reproduction that was complemented by the growth of a religious ideology reflecting the emerging social structure. As time went on, the new peoples born of this process couched the political alliances and extralocal relationships through which their nascent societies began to expand in metaphors and symbols of kinship and breathed cosmological life into them. The resultant ethnic identities, Jamaican Maroon and Aluku, are no less profound and genuine, nor any more contrived or mythical, than those of peoples who, in absolute historical terms, are known to be much older. Like human beings everywhere, the Maroons of Jamaica and the Aluku have both invented, and been invented by, their worlds.

Notes

1. For a general overview of Maroon societies throughout the Western Hemisphere, see Price (1979). See also Bilby and N'Diaye (1992).

2. The discussion that follows draws on my field research among both the Moore Town Maroons of Jamaica (1977–78, 1991) and the Aluku Maroons of the Lawa River region along the border of French Guiana and Surinam (1983–87, 1990, 1991). I am grateful for the support provided by the Organization of American States (1977–78), the Fulbright Hays program (1983–84), the Wenner-Gren Foundation (1985), the National Science Foundation (1986–87), and the Smithsonian Institution (1991).

3. Detailed summaries of seventeenth-century Maroon activity in Jamaica may be found in Schafer (1973: 5–26), Parris (1981: 187–193), Hart (1985: 1–21), and Campbell (1977, 1988: 14–43). The eighteenth century is covered extensively in Williams (1938), Kopytoff (1973), Hart (1985), and Campbell (1988).

4. Although most of the Africans imported to Jamaica came from West and Central Africa, it is known that a significant number of slaves from Madagascar joined both the Leeward and Windward Maroons at various points during the seventeenth and eighteenth centuries (Kopytoff 1976a: 38–39).

5. Price (1979: 18–19) points out that severe shortages of women were an endemic problem for early Maroon communities, not just in Jamaica but in many other parts of the Americas.

6. For more on sacred oaths among eighteenth-century Jamaican Maroons, see Kopytoff (1976a: 44), Hart (1985: 64, 104), and Campbell (1988: 50, 113, 115). For an excellent discussion of the Jamaican Maroon treaties as sacred charters sealed by blood oaths, see Kopytoff (1979). The significance of sacred oaths among Maroon peoples in several parts of the Americas is discussed at greater length in Bilby (1994a).

7. Jean Besson's groundbreaking work on the concept of family land in the Caribbean has done much to enlarge our understanding of both the symbolic significance and the socioeconomic functions of this customary form of land tenure (see Besson 1984, 1987, 1988). Among her many contributions to the study of agrarian relations in rural Jamaica is her finding that "burial on family land, generally followed by 'tombing,' places an individual kinsman within the wider context of the ancestors of the family line and also fuses this line with the immortal land" (Besson 1988: 48). See also Carnegie (1987: 95–96) on this question.

8. Although Leann Martin was told repeatedly that all Maroons in Moore Town belong to a single "family" or "clan," she apparently did not encounter the related tradition of common descent from Grandy Nanny. Her claim that "the relationship is thought to result from intermarriage among descendants of the small original group rather than from sharing a single common ancestor" (Martin 1973: 53) conflicts with the statements of many of my informants, who said that it is not only because of this early intermarriage but because all the Maroons of Moore Town are Grandy Nanny's *yoyo* (descendants) that they belong to a single "family."

9. Fragmentary archival evidence suggests that the eighteenth-century Windward Maroon leader Nanny actually did obtain legal title to at least a portion of the lands that now belong to the Moore Town Maroon community. In 1740, the year after the treaty, a grant of 500 acres in the vicinity of Moore Town was made by the governor of Jamaica to "a certain Negro woman called Nanny and the people now residing with her." The wording of the registered land patent, now housed at the Jamaican Government Archives in Spanish Town, specifies that the grant was made not only "unto the said Nanny and the people now residing with her" but to "their heirs and assigns" (Campbell 1988: 174–180; see also Kopytoff 1973: 137–140).

10. The foregoing description of Windward Maroon ideas about communal land, descent from Nanny, and the ancestral presence represents an ideal picture abstracted from the statements of many different informants. Like most such abstractions, it glosses over a number of complexities, including occasional excep-

tions to the stated rules. For example, despite the general rule of burial in the central Anglican cemetery of Moore Town, there exists a smaller graveyard in the outlying district called Seaman's Valley, near the border of the Maroon communal lands, where both Maroons and non-Maroons have long been buried. More recently, a number of other churches in Moore Town have begun their own separate burial grounds, a trend which seems to be gaining increasing acceptance. I even know of a few Maroon individuals living on communal land (though not near the center of town) who have buried relatives in their own yards (for which they have been strongly criticized). Despite such conspicuous exceptions, the notion that the Anglican churchyard is (as the cemetery next to the *asafo* ground once was) the "proper" and "best" place for a "true-born" Maroon to be laid to rest is still widely held and constitutes the official position of the Maroon council that governs in Moore Town.

The capsule description of Maroon descent ideology offered here, though accurate enough as an abstraction, also neglects to mention a number of ambiguities. For one thing, some Moore Town Maroons question the tradition of common descent from Nanny, reasoning that the men and women who fought alongside this founding ancestress must have produced family lines of their own. Some go so far as to state explicitly that the tradition is but a figurative representation and should not be taken literally. Furthermore, the idea of a "shared blood" exclusive to Maroons (whether derived from Nanny or some other source) is challenged by a long and complex history of intermarriage and sexual unions between Maroons and other Jamaicans. Despite these apparent contradictions, the myth of Nanny as mother of all Maroons continues to function effectively at a symbolic level. Whether or not it is believed to be literally true, it embodies the corporate identity of those Windward Maroons who continue to hold land in common, practice their Kromanti religion in private, and claim to belong to a single family or clan. The boundaries of this identity, though not always entirely clear in other contexts, continue to be sharply drawn at Kromanti ceremonies, where those believed to share Maroon blood are symbolically separated from those believed to be without it. (In actual practice, how a possessed medium ends up behaving in the presence of a visitor of uncertain blood tends to be worked out in advance through a complex process of negotiation involving members of the larger community.)

The fact that the ideological abstractions discussed above are sometimes contradicted by a more complex reality does not detract from their value as lingering symbolic reflections of a past social order—reflections which, I believe, may be used to throw light on the processes through which this order came into being.

11. This process would undoubtedly have been influenced by two cultural principles that Mintz and Price describe as being among the "widespread fundamental ideas and assumptions about kinship in West and Central Africa"; namely, "the emphasis on unilineal descent, and the importance to each individual of the resulting lines of kinsmen, living and dead, stretching backward and forward through time" and "the use of land as a means of defining both time and descent,

with ancestors venerated *locally*, and with history and genealogy both being particularized in specific pieces of ground" (1992: 66).

12. This historical summary, as well as some of the analysis that follows it, is based on a careful reading of Hurault (1960), de Groot (1975), de Beet (1984), and Hoogbergen (1984, 1985, 1990), which are the best sources to date on the history of the Aluku. See also Price (1976: 29–39) and Stedman (1988).

13. The group composed primarily of Kormantin individuals was headed by a chief named Kormantin Kodjo. Hoogbergen says of this group that "their ethnic origin nearly always traced back to the Kormantin and Gangu peoples" (1990: 47). In this essay I do not examine in any detail the process of cultural Creolization that played a crucial part in the ethnogenesis of both the Aluku and the Jamaican Maroons, having chosen to focus instead on the relationship between land tenure, kinship, and certain general features of religious structure and ideology. Obviously, the African cultural backgrounds of those who created these new societies contributed to the process of ethnogenesis in many ways and at many levels. The complicated question of African cultural continuities, however, cannot be adequately treated in the amount of space available in this paper. See Mintz and Price (1992) for an illuminating discussion of several of the theoretical problems involved.

14. The initial bands of runaways that joined together in the forest were known by the term *lo*. The same term was applied to the corporate matriclans that emerged later out of these original bands. The question of how exactly the Aluku and other Guianese Maroons came to settle on a unilineal (specifically, matrilineal) principle of descent in forming corporate kin groups has yet to be resolved. See Mintz and Price (1992: 69–71) and Hoogbergen (1990: 216–219) for two contrasting points of view.

15. Although it does not play the central role that it does in Jamaican Maroon religion, direct communication with ancestors does occur among the Aluku through the occasional possession of mediums by the *yooka* (ghosts) of deceased clan members. Such possession takes place in a variety of contexts.

16. Nonetheless, cemeteries continue to symbolize the sacred ties between clan territories, the ancestors buried on them, and their descendants, even though they are located in the forest, away from human habitation. Each of the several cemeteries in the Aluku territory is associated with specific villages and clans. As I noted in an earlier work, "the dead . . . are revered, and their final resting places, though far removed from the villages, are among the most potent symbolic locales rooting the Aluku in their territory" (Bilby 1990: 361–362).

17. Aluku social structure differs in certain important respects from those of the other Surinam Maroon societies. Unlike the *lo* of societies such as the Ndjuka and Saramaka, the Aluku *lo* is not further divided into named corporate lineages known as *bee* (see Köbben 1967; Price 1975). Among the Aluku, the terms *lo* and *bee* are used interchangeably to refer to the corporate clans that form the basic unit of Aluku social structure, although the former term is the more common one. The term *bee*, as already suggested, is also sometimes loosely used to refer to

matrilineal descendants of a common ancestress who have no corporate identity as such or even to siblings, so long as they have the same mother.

18. Detailed discussions of the workings of *kunu* among the contemporary Aluku may be found in Hurault (1961: 221–235) and Bilby (1990: 146–147, 362–363). The very similar *kunu* system of the neighboring Ndjuka Maroons and the *kúnu* system of the Saramaka Maroons have been described by Thoden van Velzen (1966) and Price (1973).

19. See Price (1973) for a discussion of the flexibility of the *kúnu* concept as it operates over time among the Saramaka Maroons. Among the Aluku, as among the Saramaka, there is a substantial difference between theory and practice as regards the behavior of avenging spirits.

20. Interestingly enough, none of the branch communities settled at a later point by Maroons migrating away from one or another of the towns previously granted "treaty lands" have succeeded in splitting off and becoming the same kind of self-contained, politically autonomous ethnic units. Instead, settlements such as Comfort Castle, Ginger House, and Brownsfield (all settled many generations ago by Maroons originally from Moore Town), despite substantial populations, have developed into satellite communities that are granted political representation on the Moore Town council. Although many of the Maroons in these branch settlements evince a strong sense of Maroon identity, sharing many cultural traditions with Moore Town people and participating to some extent in ceremonial life there, they do not live on communally owned lands. Like other rural Jamaicans, they typically bury close relatives on their own modest parcels of family land.

21. The primordialist-situationalist dichotomy (which has often been labeled with other sets of terms, such as instrumental-affective, mobilizationalist-primordialist, or situational-cognitive) is summarized in Glazer and Moynihan (1975: 19–20) and Casiño (1985: 25). It has spurred many debates and continues to turn up in the literature on ethnicity from time to time.

22. For studies of historical consciousness among Maroon peoples, see Price (1983) on the Saramaka Maroons, Bilby (1984a) on the Jamaican Maroons, and Bilby (1994b) on the Aluku. Bilby (1995) compares Jamaican Maroon and Aluku oral historical narrative.

Jonathan D. Hill

Ethnogenesis
in the Northwest Amazon:

An Emerging Regional Picture

Prior to the 1980s, the ethnology of northwestern Amazonia focused almost entirely upon the eastern Tukanoan-speaking peoples of the Vaupés Basin in Colombia and Brazil. Several outstanding monographs and numerous shorter publications on eastern Tukanoan peoples provided in-depth perspectives on indigenous social organization, subsistence economics, mythology, ceremonial exchange, and sacred ritual (Goldman 1963; Reichel-Dolmatoff 1971, 1975; C. Hugh-Jones 1979; S. Hugh-Jones 1979). This rich ethnographic literature depicted a complex tapestry of riverine, fishing, and horticultural societies held together by the practice of language group exogamy and internally organized into patrilineal, patrilocal sibs that grouped themselves into larger, ranked confederations, or phratries. Despite these common underlying principles of linguistic exogamy and serial ranking of patrisibs, there were also numerous variations and dissimilarities among eastern Tukanoan peoples that called for comparative analysis and interpretation. Perhaps the most significant of these differences was the fact that the Cubeo, a relatively large eastern Tukanoan-speaking people of the Cuduyarí River, did not practice language group exogamy like other eastern Tukanoan peoples but instead divided themselves into three exogamous phratries within a single language group.[1]

In the 1990s we have reached a new level of understanding that allows us to raise questions and hypotheses about the historical and political processes which gave rise to the unique configuration of multilingualism and ranked social organization in the Northwest Amazon region as a whole. Three areas of investigation during the 1980s have brought us to this new level of understanding: (1) analysis of the eastern Tukanoan regional system as a flexible process that was in many respects analogous to "dispersed hunter-gatherers, with their local group interdependencies, fluidity in territorial boundaries, and fluctuations in local group membership" (Jackson 1983: 6); (2) intensive ethnographic and historical studies among the various phratries and language groups of northern Arawak-speaking peoples living along the Upper Rio Negro and its tributaries immediately to the north and east of the Vaupés Basin (Wright 1981; Hill 1983; Gonzalez Ñ. 1980; Vidal 1987; Journet 1988); and (3) the adoption of new approaches to indigenous histories among both eastern Tukanoan and northern Arawakan peoples (Wright and Hill 1986; Hill and Wright 1988; Chernela 1988, 1993; Hugh-Jones 1988; Reichel-Dolmatoff 1985; Vidal 1993). Each of these three developments has made significant contributions to our current understanding of history and social organization in Northwest Amazonia. Taken together, these three new areas of investigation lead to conclusions very different from the pre-1980 ethnographic literature.

Regional Analysis of Eastern Tukanoan Social Organization

Jackson's comparative study (1983) of eastern Tukanoan social organization in the Central Vaupés Basin was a masterpiece of sociolinguistic analysis and the first major synthesis to demonstrate that the extralocal, regional ties among eastern Tukanoan language groups were much more flexible and dynamic than previously imagined. Although the principle of language group exogamy was almost perfectly adhered to in Jackson's survey of intermarriage patterns,[2] marriage strategies ranged from an ideal of sister exchange between closely related affinal groups all the way to symbolic bride capture among distantly related groups with little or no prior history of intermarriage (Jackson 1983: 81 ff.). These divergent marriage strategies resulted in statistical clusterings of pairs of closely related language groups embedded within a broader, regional set of alliances that were open, fluid, and dynamic. In a similar manner, relations of mythic descent that united several language groups into extralocal ranked confederations through the idiom of common brotherhood were also fluid and negotiable rather than fixed and agreed upon. Jackson (1983: 86–92) provides numerous examples of disagreement over phratric organization, leading her to conclude that "phratric membership is probably epiphenomenal" (1983: 86) and that "it is fruitless to try to construct exclusive groupings based on phratric principles derived either from known marriage practices or statements by informants" (1983: 88).

Jackson's analysis of regional social organization in the Vaupés Basin provided a foundation for asking new questions about the historical coming-into-being of language group exogamy and ranked phratries among eastern Tukanoan peoples. At a regional level, the principle of language group exogamy resulted in the integration of separate language groups into wider, geographically dispersed networks of trade and intermarriage. At a macroregional level, language group exogamy defined a clear yet permeable boundary between eastern Tukanoan peoples and "others" who failed to practice language group exogamy. "The Cubeo on the northern boundary of the region are at times excluded in discussions of 'real people' " (1983: 97) because they marry among phratries within the same language group. This example demonstrates how the principle of language group exogamy serves as a means for defining the social boundaries of the eastern Tukanoan regional system, yet it still does not explain why eastern Tukanoan peoples chose to use language as the primary building block of their collective identities. The existence of shadowy, dispersed phratries in the Central Vaupés is even more mysterious. Why did eastern Tukanoan peoples develop such ranked groupings of language groups if they served no apparent political or economic purposes?

Recent Research on Northern Arawakan Phratries

Preliminary answers to these questions began to emerge in the 1980s through intensive research among the northern Arawak-speaking phratries inhabiting the Içana-Guainía drainage area immediately to the north and east of the Vaupés Basin. In-depth studies among the Hohodeni phratry of Brazil (Wright 1981), the Dzáwinai and Wariperidakena phratries of Venezuela (Hill 1983), and the Adzaneni phratry of Colombia (Journet 1988) demonstrated the existence of strongly hierarchical patrilineal phratries that were (and to some extent still are) localized within distinct riverine territories. The principle of serial ranking of patrisibs within these phratries was amplified through linkage to marriage rules so that men of highly ranked sibs in one phratry married only with women of highly ranked sibs in other phratries (Hill 1983, 1987). Like the eastern Tukanoan peoples of the Vaupés Basin, the northern Arawakan phratries to the north and east considered shared language to be a crucial marker of collective identity. However, instead of magnifying language differences through a rule of language group exogamy, the northern Arawakan phratries minimized linguistic differences by giving emphasis to the mutual intelligibility of widely different dialects (named after different ways of saying yes and no) within a single, regional ethnolinguistic community. This larger regional identity, called Wakuénai, or People of Our Language (Hill 1983), resembles a greatly expanded version of Cubeo sociolinguistic organization, or a single language group divided into exogamous, internally ranked phratries. The Cubeo population of approximately 1,500 to 2,000 (Jackson 1983: 87) is concentrated in a single riverine territory along the Cuduyarí River, whereas the Wakuénai phratries number at least 8,000 people spread

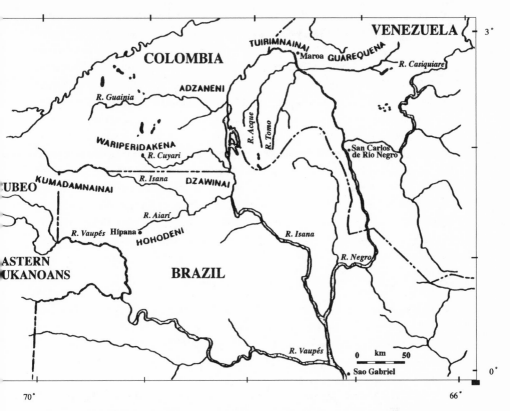

Figure 1. The Northwest Amazon region in Venezuela, Colombia, and Brazil. The ancestral lands of Wakuénai phratries are along the Isana, Aiarí, Cuyarí, and Guianía Rivers.

across several different riverine territories in Brazil, Venezuela, and Colombia (see figure 1). The strong resemblance between Wakuénai and Cubeo socio-linguistic organization receives further confirmation from Goldman's observation that "a possible translation of the Cubeo self-name Pamíwa is 'people of the language'" (cited in Jackson 1983: 84). In other words, the Cubeo self-name is probably an exact eastern Tukanoan translation of the northern Arawakan self-name Wakuénai, or People of Our Language.

Research on the northern Arawakan, or Wakuénai, phratries during the 1980s demonstrated that the eastern Tukanoan regional system of language group exogamy and ranked phratries could no longer be understood in isolation but only as part of a much larger region that included both eastern Tukanoan and northern Arawakan phratries. Comparison of the two subregions revealed a clear contrast between localized, exogamous phratries among the

Wakuénai and dispersed, "epiphenomenal" phratries among eastern Tuka-noan peoples (Hill 1985). Paralleling this basic contrast was the fact that the Wakuénai preference for linking marriage to inherited rank within phratries was either not practiced among the eastern Tukanoan (Jackson 1983: 75) or actively discouraged (S. Hugh-Jones 1979: 206). The contrast is also expressed in the symbolic realm of religious beliefs: the Wakuénai phratries all claim to have descended from ancestor spirits that emerged from the ground beneath the rapids at the center of mythic space, whereas eastern Tukanoan peoples explain their origins in terms of a more mobile, decentralized process of jour-neying ancestral "Anaconda-Canoes" (Wright 1981; Hill 1983, 1985). Even without an examination of history, the comparison clearly indicates that ranked social organization is much more fully developed among the Wakuénai than it is among the eastern Tukanoan. Simple logic points to the hypothesis that the mysterious epiphenomenal phratries found among the eastern Tuka-noan are the result of interethnic relations with the Wakuénai phratries to the north and east.

The comparison is not complete, however, without a consideration of the transitional forms of linguistic and social organization found along the boundary between eastern Tukanoan and northern Arawakan phratries. The Cubeo, who speak an eastern Tukanoan language but do not practice language group exogamy, are located in the intermediate area between the Wakuénai and the Central Vaupés. Like the Wakuénai, the Cubeo divide themselves into exogamous phratries and directly link the principle of inherited rank to mar-riage practices (Jackson 1983: 75). Another eastern Tukanoan people who live in the intermediate area between the Central Vaupés and the Içana-Guainía drainage area are the Wanano of the lower Vaupés River, and they also have localized phratries and link marriage preferences to inherited rank (Chernela 1983). In other words, localized phratries that play a direct role in shaping intermarriage patterns and other forms of exchange are found among the Wakuénai and only those eastern Tukanoan peoples who live along the north-ern and eastern limits of eastern Tukanoan territory. Farther away from this area bordering on territories of the Wakuénai phratries, eastern Tukanoan peoples do not have localized phratries and do not link the principle of rank-ing to marriage preferences.

New Approaches to Indigenous Histories

Perhaps the most enduring legacy of anthropology in the 1980s was the ad-vancement of new ways of approaching indigenous histories. Eric Wolf's pow-erful synthesis of global history (1982) brought a definitive conclusion to the study of small-scale societies as isolated "billiard balls" by demonstrating how the global spread of colonial powers had in one way or another transformed the political-economic conditions of even the most remotely situated peoples. Other influential researchers called for a reevaluation of indigenous oral histories as a valid source of insight into the various ways that small-scale societies have struggled to cope with the contradiction betweeen forced incorporation into state-level societies and the persistence of autonomous cultural identities (Rosaldo 1980; Sahlins 1981; Price 1983).

The ethnology of Amazonian societies, and especially that of the Northwest Amazon region, played a very active role in the emerging rapprochement of history and anthropology during the 1980s. The Lévi-Straussian characterization of Amazonian societies as "cold," "mythic" structures had not only blinded researchers to the possibility of studying indigenous understandings of the historical past but had preempted such studies by asserting that Amazonian societies actively suppressed any concern for knowing the historical past. As improbable as it may seem from today's vantage point, a leading authority on Amazonian social organization wrote as late as 1981 that "this kind of thinking is typical of the ideology of a Lévi-Straussian 'cold society' . . . a mythic timeless order is in each generation re-established" (Kaplan 1981: 159). In that same year, Robin Wright's dissertation on "History and Religion of the Baniwa Peoples of the Upper Rio Negro Valley" (Stanford University, 1981) demonstrated that ritual specialists and other elders among the Hohodeni (a Wakuénai phratry living along the Aiary River in Brazil) had a complex tradition of oral histories that encompassed historical events and processes dating back to at least the early nineteenth century. Wright's archival research on the forced removals of indigenous peoples from the Upper Rio Negro region during the late colonial period fully and specifically corroborated the Hohodeni elders' historical memories. The edifice of Lévi-Straussian structuralism and other ahistorical modes of anthropological theory began to crumble under the weight of growing empirical evidence that Amazonian peoples had developed a rich variety of oral histories that were grounded in mythic beliefs and ritual practices but not frozen into a "mythic timeless order."[3]

Having read an early draft of Wright's dissertation before going to do my doctoral fieldwork among the Wakuénai phratries of Venezuela in 1980–81, I was alert to the possibility that my indigenous interlocutors would express an active interest in talking about the historical past of the region. They did not disappoint me in this expectation, and shortly after completing my dissertation (Hill 1983) I began a series of collaborative writing projects on indigenous history, ritual, and myth with Robin Wright (Wright and Hill 1986; Hill and Wright 1988).[4] In a nutshell, we demonstrated that the Wakuénai phratries had experienced a long history of interethnic relations with expanding colonial and national societies of Latin America and that this history was actively remembered through an array of narrative discourses and ritually powerful ways of speaking. Even the most sacred of mythic narratives, or the story of how the trickster-creator had raised the ancestral spirits from beneath the rapids at Hípana, was not an attempt to freeze or deny historical changes but a dynamic mode of historical interpretation that actively sought to reconcile indigenous forms of ritual power with the alien forms of power and domination that Europeans and their descendants had brought into the region.

Concurrent with our collaborative works on Wakuénai ethnohistory, other researchers began to study and publish works on the ethnohistory of other northern Arawakan peoples (Gonzalez Ñ. 1986; Vidal 1987) and on the eastern Tukanoan peoples of the Vaupés Basin. Reichel-Dolmatoff published an important analysis (1985) of Desana and Tukano narratives about the Tapir-People, or the Arawakan peoples living to the north of the Tukanoan. "From the analysis of textual sources it seems rather improbable that this [Yuruparí] ritual complex is of Tukanoan origin; it seems rather to have been taken over from the Arawakan tribes" (Reichel-Dolmatoff 1985: 113–114). Reichel-Dolmatoff's analysis adds further support to the assertion that the eastern Tukanoan regional system cannot be understood in isolation but must be approached from a comparative perspective that includes a concern for long-term historical patterns of warfare, trade, and intermarriage between eastern Tukanoan and northern Arawakan peoples. Goldman's observation that "one Cubeo phratry was, in fact, once Arawakan" (1963: 26) indicates that the "trading" between eastern Tukanoan and northern Arawakan peoples included not only ritual practices and wives but also entire language groups and phratries. Although it is impossible to pinpoint the precise time when this integration took place, there is strong ethnographic and historical evidence upon which to base some probable hypotheses about when and how these macroregional ties began to develop.

Overview of Wakuénai Ethnohistory: Interethnic Relations with Colonial and National Polities

Prior to the eighteenth century, the Wakuénai were at the center of a vast area of riverine territories inhabited by northern Arawak-speaking peoples, ranging from the Manao along the Lower Rio Negro all the way to the Achagua and Maipure along the Middle Orinoco and its tributaries (see figure 2). The Upper Rio Negro is strategically situated at the intersection of the two largest river systems in South America, the Orinoco and the Amazon, a factor that contributed to the emergence of widespread networks of trade and intermarriage.

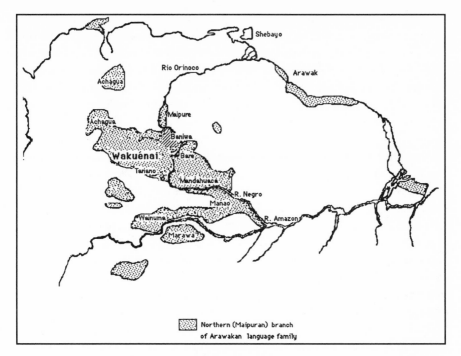

Figure 2. The geographical distribution of Northern Arawakan language groups prior to 1492. Adapted from Key 1979: 74.

Interregional networks of trade between the northern Andes, the Caribbean Basin, and the Amazon Basin centered around the Middle Orinoco Basin, where the abundance of turtle eggs and fish during dry-season months brought together indigenous peoples from llanos areas to the north and west as well as from forested areas to the south and east. Radiating outward from the core region along the Middle Orinoco were three major chains of trade. To the north and east, Carib-speaking peoples traded such forest and coastal products as blowguns, arrows, baskets, poison, pigment, and pearls in exchange for *quiripa* (shell money), turtle oil, smoked fish, gold, and salt (Morey and Morey 1975: 18). These predominately Carib-speaking trade networks channeled products from the llanos and Middle Orinoco Basin throughout coastal areas of Venezuela, the interior forests and coastal plains of Guiana, and up into the Antilles. To the west, Achagua and other Arawak-speaking peoples traded products of the llanos and forest with the Muisca and other Chibcha-speaking peoples of the northern Andes (Rausch 1984: 11). Gold, salt, and cotton cloth were the principal trade goods obtained from Andean peoples (Morey and Morey 1975: 18–19). To the south, Saliba- and Arawak-speaking peoples of the Upper Orinoco and Rio Negro traded forest products, such as curare poison and resins, in exchange for turtle oil, smoked fish, and shell money. Trade networks criss-crossing the northern lowlands centered around the production of surplus fish and turtle oil in the Middle Orinoco Basin, but there is no historical evidence of powerful chiefdoms that dominated this central region. Instead, the Middle Orinoco had developed into a zone of intercultural trade and contact among a variety of linguistically different peoples. "The Andean Cordillera, the Upper Orinoco (tropical forest, Amazonia), and Guayana interconnected themselves with the llanos by means of trade. . . . The commercial relations with the Andes, the upper Orinoco, and Guayana appear to have passed across the llanos but not toward the llanos" (Morey and Morey 1975: 27–28, translation mine). Political relations among various indigenous peoples in the Middle Orinoco Basin consisted of horizontal ties "in which no one group dominated the others" (Biord Castillo 1985: 96, translation mine).

It is important to situate the Wakuénai and other remaining northern Arawakan peoples in the context of this broader, interregional system of trade across northern South America and the Caribbean Basin. Prior to the traumatic changes of the eighteenth century, northern Arawakan peoples controlled the entire stretch of riverine, tropical forest territories from the central hub of trading along the Middle Orinoco River all along the Upper Orinoco, Casiquiare, and Upper Negro and down into the Central Amazon floodplains surrounding Manaus. This macropolitical system of riverine, Arawakan peoples formed one of the three indigenous centers of northern South America. They were the primary source of tropical forest products to northern Andean and circum-Caribbean chiefdoms as well as the recipients of gold, salt, textiles, shell money, and other products passing through the llanos. The Wakuénai phratries of the Upper Rio Negro region were strategically situated at the center of the northern Arawakan diaspora and controlled the flow of trade goods circulating through the narrow passages connecting the Middle Orinoco Basin to the Lower Rio Negro and the Central Amazon floodplain.

Perhaps due to their remote location at the frontier between two expanding empires, the Wakuénai remained numerous during the colonial period at the same time as Arawak-speaking peoples to the north and south were decimated by disease, slavery, and warfare. However, after the expulsion of Jesuit missionaries in 1767, the Portuguese government launched a campaign of forced relocations to downstream sites that greatly reduced Arawakan and Tukanoan peoples living along the Lower Içana and Vaupés (Chernela 1988; Wright 1981; Wright and Hill 1986). Compounding the impact of these forced descents, or *descimentos*, was the arrival of successive waves of epidemics of flu, measles, smallpox, and other exogenous diseases in the 1780s. The survivors fled to remote, inaccessible areas at the headwaters of the Içana and Rio Negro (Guainía). Large, permanent settlements along the Lower Vaupés, Içana, and Negro Rivers were left totally abandoned for several years.

The collapse of the Portuguese colonial government at the end of the eighteenth century gave indigenous peoples of the Upper Rio Negro region an opportunity to recover from their losses under the *descimento* policy. Along the Lower Içana and its tributaries, Wakuénai groups reconstituted their internally ranked phratries and renewed their subsistence economy of fishing, manioc gardening, and hunting (Wright 1981). The period of recovery lasted well into the nineteenth century but came to an end in the 1840s, when the newly independent state of Brazil began to implement a policy called the Directorate, which gave local administrators authority to force indigenous groups to perform "public service labor." Resistance to the new policy was met with military force, and in the 1850s the program resulted in widespread abuses of indigenous labor.

The millenarian movement led by Venancio Camico arose against this background of hunger and deprivation along the Rio Negro in Venezuela and the abusive Directorate policy of public service along the Içana River in Brazil.[5] In 1858 Venancio began to prophesy that the world would end in a fiery conflagration on St. John's Day. Venancio was captured and returned to San Carlos but later escaped from prison and fled to the Aki River (a tributary of the Guainía River). Although the millenarian movement of 1858 had ended in abrupt military defeat, Venancio Camico continued to preach resistance to the whites' economy until his death in 1903. By 1900, the shaman-prophet's vision had become incorporated into the ritual advice given during male initiation: "The white men are thieves who buy our wares cheap and sell their merchandise to us at high prices. That is why they are rich and we are poor. Know that the whites are your enemies. Hide your hatred because it's strong, and treat the whites with distrust because they are traitors" (Matos Arvelo 1912: 86, translation mine). Venancio's movement was a historical rite of passage for the Wakuénai, Baniwa, and other Arawak-speaking peoples of the Upper Rio Negro region. The colonial political economy of indebtedness and military force could no longer be regarded as a purely alien power, external to the indigenous social order, but had to be exorcised from within.

The first two decades of this century were a period of catastrophic losses of life and autonomy for indigenous peoples of the Venezuelan Amazon. A rubber baron turned dictator, Tomas Funes, created a reign of terror in which thousands of indigenous laborers and their families perished. The Wakuénai, whose ancestral lands along the Guainía and Içana Rivers straddled the borders between Venezuela, Colombia, and Brazil, migrated to safety in Brazil or remote headwater areas of Colombia.

In the post–World War II era, the Rio Negro–Guainía was resettled by Wakuénai groups whose ancestors had fled into Colombian and Brazilian territories to escape Funes's dictatorship. By the early 1980s, the Wakuénai and Yeral had formed villages and moved into towns throughout the westernmost areas of the Venezuelan Amazon territory, from Coquí and San Carlos in the south to Puerto Ayacucho and the llanos in the north.

The history of interethnic relations in the Upper Rio Negro is not characterized by a smooth, progressive incorporation of indigenous Arawakan peoples into colonial empires or nation-states but by periods of intense change followed by periods of recovery during which indigenous peoples returned to their ancestral lands to form new alliances. The late eighteenth and late nineteenth centuries were periods of intense state-level expansion into the Upper Rio Negro and major irreversible changes to indigenous societies of the region. Each of these periods of heightened change was followed by periods of declining state-level power that allowed indigenous societies to recover from losses of population, land, and autonomy. It was precisely during these periods of recovery after major, traumatic changes that ethnogenesis flourished in the Upper Rio Negro region.

Some Key Features of an Indigenous Arawakan Model of History

Wakuénai understandings of the historical and mythic pasts are embodied in narrative discourse and ritual performances of sung and chanted speech, called *málikai*, that instantiate powers of mythic creation and shamanistic transformation. One of the main challenges of developing an indigenous model of history is to find (or invent) a vocabulary of key terms that does not reduce the semantic complexity and poetic musicality of indigenous mythic and ritual discourse to a set of soundless abstractions or visual-spatial metaphors.

Anthropology and related disciplines have largely failed to develop a vocabulary that is adequate to the task of describing these poetic naming processes in their full complexity. Paul Friedrich's definition of poetry as "the symbolic process by which the individual mediates between the music of a natural language and the (nuances of) mythic meaning" (1986: 39) comes close to capturing the dynamic interactions between musicality and semanticity that pervade Wakuénai ritual performances. In my attempts to interpret these verbal performances, I have found it useful to relativize, or activate, the interrelations between musicality and mythic meaning by focusing on the relative importance of either musicality or semanticity in any specific performance. *Mythification* is the term I use to denote the process of using semantic categories of language to constrain the musicality of speech into relatively steady, tonally and rhythmically stable ways of chanting or singing. Wakuénai ritual specialists refer to mythification as "We heap up the names in a single place" [Wakétaka nakúna papínirítsa], a verbal activity in which a large number of specific names, or souls, are invoked (i.e., "heaped up") within a single generic category of mythic being. Ritual performances of this process are acts of pure signification, social continuity based upon perfect transmission of meaning from mythic ancestors to human descendants and the creation of socialized individual human beings, or "persons." Through mythification or "heaping up the names in a single place," the Wakuénai poetically construct an idealized concept of the person as a living instantiation of collectively shared mythic ancestors.

Mythification defines the concept of persons at the individual level, but the full meaning of personhood must allow also for the individual's capacity to actively participate in the historical construction, transformation, and reproduction of the social order. I use the term *musicalization* to denote the process of using dynamic features of musicality to transform semantic classifications of being into an expanding world of peoples, places, species, and objects, all in perpetual motion. Wakuénai ritual specialists refer to this process as "We search for the names" [Wadzúhiakaw nakúna], a musical process of moving rapidly through a number of generic categories of mythic being and, at the same time, "journeying" through a number of distinct musical "places" (tones, tempos, timbres, rhythms, and volumes). In ritual performances, musicalization embodies the power of communication between persons, or groups of people, to expand and open up the relatively closed, bounded identities established through language and myth. In myth, musicalization originated in the struggle between men and women for control over the sacred musical instruments of the mythic ancestors. Musicalization transforms social identities through constructing and mediating between categories of Otherness, or naturalized social being.

The complex interrelations between mythification and musicalization are most vividly demonstrated in the long sets of *málikai* songs and chants performed during male and female initiation rituals. These social events are complex rites of passage in which chant-owners and other senior kin of the initiants symbolically construct Kuwái's second mythic creation of the world. The collective construction of the world as an expansion, or opening up, is applied directly to the transformation of children, who are associated with the mythic primordium and Kuwái's first mythic creation, into fully socialized adults who participate in the social world of exchange relations between kin groups. A long series of *málikai* songs and chants performed over the initiates' sacred food (*káridzámai*) forms the central core of ritual activities for both male and female initiations.

These performances consist of an opening song, a long series of chants, and a closing song that musicalize the mythic descent of Kuwái from the sky to the ground at Hípana, the horizontal displacement of Amáru and Kuwái across the surface of the world, the return of Amáru and Kuwái back across the world to Hípana, and the return of Kuwái from down on the ground back up to the sky. The musical, horizontal opening up of the world in initiation rituals creates a sociogeographic image of the world of peoples and places occupying an immense region of riverine territories. The process begins and ends at Hípana, the place of mythic emergence and the center, or "navel," of the world, where mythic beings are linked to the world of human beings via a cosmic umbilical cord (*hliépule-kwa dzákare*). Between opening and closing songs, a long series of chants outlines a horizontal journey across the world through the naming of places along the Aiary, Içana, Vaupés, Negro, Atabapo, Orinoco, Guaviare, Inirida, Guainía, and Cuyarí Rivers. In these chants, the Wakuénai musically construct a mythic map of their world as the center of a much larger region, which corresponds almost exactly to the distribution of the northern, or Maipuran, subfamily of Arawakan languages prior to the colonial period (see figure 2). The musical naming of places in *málikai* embodies a historical consciousness of a past when the ethnopolitical situation of the Wakuénai differed profoundly from that of the present.

The horizontal opening up of the world is also directly embodied in the organization of musical sounds in *málikai* songs and chants. The opening and closing performances are sung rather than chanted or spoken, and by making use of exactly the same pitches, the two songs provide a stable, vertical tonal center around which the more dynamic chants, or "journeys," gravitate. Musical movements between vertically distinct pitches in the opening and closing performances of *málikai* poetically construct the mythic space-time of relations between powerful mythic ancestors in the sky-world and their living human descendants in this world. These vertical musical movements also embody the power to control movements within human society between developmental stages in the life cycle and between older and younger generations.

Between these two songs, the names of all places and animal species are chanted in a long series of performances that lasts for many hours. Horizontal movement, or displacement from the center of the world, is expressed in a variety of musical dimensions. The chants begin on different pitches, and the starting pitch is gradually sharpened through microtonal rising so that the final verses end up on a totally new pitch. The tempo is percussively sounded by striking *kadápu* whips on a basket that covers the initiates' sacred food (*káridzámai*), and the initial tempo is gradually increased during each chant.

The chants also exhibit contrasting dynamics between loud and soft sounds, since the principal chanter's voice is doubled at the end of each verse by a second chanter. From time to time, the chanters' voices are accompanied by a collage of sounds made on the sacred flutes and trumpets. In short, the musicalization of mythic power uses tonal variation, microtonal rising, acceleration, and instrumental heterophony to directly embody the processes of horizontally journeying to other places, or becoming other peoples, and back. Musicalized mythic power is the poetic construction of a historical space-time through movements away from and back to the center of mythic and tonal space.

An Indigenous Arawakan Model of Ethnogenesis

Through the complex of narratives and ritual language outlined above, the Wakuénai view themselves as the principal makers and keepers of a sacred regional history which subsumes the origins of the white people and their culture in the Upper Rio Negro region. The following version of the myth of sib ancestor emergence comes from a Dzáwinai chant-owner of the Lower Guainía River in Venezuela (Hill, field notes). The bulk of his narrative consists of a simple listing of Wakuénai sib names and their corresponding male and female tobacco spirits. Excluding the list of names, the narrative is reducible to the following underlying sequence of actions:

1. The white men were the first people to emerge from the hole beneath the rapids at Hípana, and Iñápirríkuli gave them all a single name (*yárinárinái*) and tobacco spirit (*hérri hálepíwanai iénipe*). "Later we will go to search for the names [*nanáikika*] of these people," explained the trickster-creator.

2. Iñápirríkuli searched for the names of all the Wakuénai sibs and gave them each a pair of tobacco spirits.

3. After giving names and spirits to all the Wakuénai sibs of the Içana and Guainía Rivers, Iñápirríkuli continued to search for the names of Arawakan and Tukanoan groups of the Vaupés (Tariano, Wanano, and Cubeo). Although these groups formed part of the same search for sib names by Iñápirríkuli, they are distinguished from Wakuénai sibs by the phrase "after the white men" [*hnetédali yárinárinái*].

4. Iñápirríkuli ran out of names, for "there were too many people" [*néni ñétim yúhakawa*]. "Let's heap up these people and give them the spirit-name 'liwakétanhim dzáwi-ñápirríkuli' (the heap or pile of Iñápirríkuli)." Iñápirríkuli gave the white men the name *yárinárinái*, and he named the places where they were to live Colombia, Venezuela, and Brazil.

In this narrative, the twin processes of mythification and musicalization in *málikai* becomes a means for giving cultural form to an indigenous interpretation of the history of Indian-white relations in the Upper Rio Negro region. The arrival of the white men is not expressed as a passive experience that "happened to" the Wakuénai but as part of the same active process through which Iñápirríkuli, the trickster-creator, brought into being the ancestral spirits of the Wakuénai. The trickster-creator raised the white men's ancestors from the ground at Hípana before raising the sib ancestors of the Wakuénai and other indigenous groups, but he did not give the white men powerful sib names that must be actively "searched for." Iñápirríkuli announced his intention to search for the sib names of the white men later, after searching for those of the Wakuénai and their neighbors. As is so often the case in narratives about Iñápirríkuli, the trickster-creator's words and deeds are in the final analysis shown to be clever deceptions which must be interpreted rather than taken at face value. In the final episode of the narrative, when Iñápirríkuli has run out of names because the white men were too numerous, the real intentions of the trickster-creator are revealed: to heap up the white men as *liwakétanhim* (heap or pile) rather than to search for their sib names (*nanáikika*). This denouement makes explicit the contrast between higher- and lower-level naming principles and the analogous contrast between indigenous peoples (*hwá nawíki*) and the white men (*yárinárinái*). The contrast is not a simple binary opposition of the Lévi-Straussian sort (i.e., Indian : white :: dynamic : static) but a continuum of more-to-less dynamic.

In the concluding episode of the narrative, Iñápirríkuli runs out of names because there are "too many people," and he names the places where the white men are to live: Colombia, Venezuela, and Brazil. The indigenous view of history presupposes smallness of social scale but not rigidity. Sib names for several indigenous societies of the Upper Rio Negro region are added to Iñápirríkuli's search "after the white men," but the white men themselves are simply too numerous to include in this mythical process. The trickster-creator does, however, name the places where the white men are to live. Given the central importance of spatial movements and the naming of places in Wakuénai ways of thinking about the past, Iñápirríkuli's naming of white men's places is better understood as a metaphor of the active creation of a historical space-time which the Wakuénai have shared with the white men for the past 250 years rather than a static, atemporal arrangement of space into a mythic order. The division of Wakuénai ancestral lands among Brazil, Colombia, and Venezuela was a historical process of great significance to the Wakuénai, for the spatial movements back and forth between river systems has been a key strategy for coping with the white men's diseases, economic oppression, military force, and missionary activity.

Beyond serving as a metaphorical vehicle for indigenous understanding of the ambiguities of power relations that have historically developed between colonizing and colonized peoples in the Upper Rio Negro region, the narrative of mythic ancestral emergence symbolically reformulates the chronological sequence of major historical periods beginning with the arrival of Western peoples, technologies, and diseases in the eighteenth century. The colonial period brought massive social, demographic, and ecological changes to the Upper Rio Negro region, and the overwhelming significance of these changes is recognized in the narrative by placing the whites as the first category of people to emerge at the center of mythic space. At the same time, the narrative gives recognition to the historical decline of Western colonial power at the end of the eighteenth century by explaining that the whites were not given sacred names but "set aside until a later time." In both political and mythic history, the end of colonial governments in the region was followed by a period during which the white colonizers were "set aside" or did not play a significant part in the region's history. This period is elaborated upon in the second and third episodes of the narrative through the trickster-creator's search for the spirit-names of various Arawakan and Tukanoan groups of the Upper Rio Negro region and adjacent portions of the Vaupés Basin. The narrative acts as a historical and mythic explanation of the coming-into-being of hierarchical, internally ranked political confederations of patrilineal sibs among the Arawakan Wakuénai. Keeping in mind that the metaphor of "going in search of the names" refers to processes of social and geographic expansion through migration and exchange between affinally related groups, it makes sense to interpret these two episodes as an indigenous model of ethnogenesis, or the coming-into-being of the Wakuénai peoples as a process of recovery and reconstitution in the aftermath of colonial domination and accompanying losses of population, land, and other resources. As the narrative of mythic emergence implies, this process of ethnogenesis included a reorientation of Arawakan phratries toward neighboring eastern Tukanoan peoples living along the Vaupés River and its tributaries.

It takes only little historical imagination to understand how and why this shift in regional interethnic relations took place during the early nineteenth century. By the end of the eighteenth century, larger, more sedentary riverine groups of Arawak-speakers, such as the Manao, Baré, Maipure, and Achagua, had become so completely assimilated into colonial systems of mission settlements (called *reducciones*) that the Arawakan peoples living in the headwater regions of the Rio Negro were cut off from their former trading partners. Downstream areas which had been major points of intersection in the vast network of northern Arawakan peoples stretching from Manaus to the Central Orinoco became centers of colonial control, epidemics of contagious disease, and economic exploitation of indigenous labor. Arawakan peoples of the headwater regions survived the colonial period by moving farther upstream to more protected, remote locations, and this movement brought them into increasingly permanent contact with the eastern Tukanoan of the Vaupés and its tributaries. The initial movement of Arawakan peoples into Tukanoan areas was almost certainly a period of interethnic competition and warfare, and these conflicts may have been the political reason for the historical emergence of ranked phratries among the Wakuénai. With the decline of colonial governments in the region, competitive pressures eased as many Wakuénai sibs returned to downstream areas along the Içana and Negro Rivers. Not all Wakuénai sibs returned to downstream areas; some remained in the Vaupés Basin, where they became Tukanoan. If this analysis is correct, then the most probable time that this fusion of Tukanoan and Arawakan peoples took place was the period of recovery from colonialism during the early nineteenth century.

The period of recovery lasted several decades into the nineteenth century but ended with the expansion of the newly independent states of Brazil, Venezuela, and Colombia into the Upper Rio Negro region. In the 1840s and 1850s, the Brazilian government began to implement its Directorate policy, giving more authority to local administrators to force indigenous laborers to perform "public service." In Venezuela, Arawakan peoples were increasingly ensnared in exploitative relations of debt peonage with white or mestizo traders. These political and economic conditions set the stage for indigenous revitalization movements and other forms of resistance that overtly expressed indigenous peoples' desires to free themselves of the whites' domination. Revitalization movements, among other things, made clear the indigenous population's sense of being overloaded by alien political controls and economic exploitation. In the new context of expanding and competing independent nation-states, the Wakuénai and their eastern Tukanoan neighbors were becoming increasingly powerless. The narrative of mythic ancestral emergence expresses this growing sense of disempowerment in the fourth and final episode. "There were too many people" and "not enough names," so the trickster-creator gave the whites a single name and "heaped them up" in one place. In this context, names are not just representations or labels but social identities and the corresponding natural places that the mythic ancestors created for the survival of their living descendants. With the rise of independent nation-states and their expansion into the Upper Rio Negro region in the mid- to late nineteenth century, the indigenous model of ethnogenesis as a process of using language to define distinct social identities and musicalized language to reproduce, transform, and create new identities was overwhelmed. Revitalization movements helped indigenous peoples to survive traumatic changes during the Rubber Boom of the late nineteenth and early twentieth centuries, but this second major crisis in Wakuénai history redefined the social meaning of the twin processes of mythification and musicalization. After the Rubber Boom the Wakuénai were no longer able to define themselves as simply the living descendants of the mythic ancestors and the affinal allies of the Cubeo, Wanano, and other eastern Tukanoan peoples. From the period of the Rubber Boom forward, the Wakuénai had also to struggle with their historical disempowerment within nation-state systems of political control. By the twentieth century, the Wakuénai had become the survivors of a holocaust, and the twin processes of mythification and musicalization had become part of a deadly serious game of recapturing a viable historical past in the aftermath of genocidal oppression and a culture of terror that had destroyed entire indigenous peoples of the Upper Rio Negro region in less than a single generation.

Conclusion

The ethnohistory of Northwest Amazonia has taken new directions as researchers have adopted more broadly comparative, regional approaches (Jackson 1983; Hill 1985) and as they have experimented with new ways of studying indigenous models of history. Our current understanding of the complex social and historical forces that led to the formation of the Northwest Amazon region's unique configuration of exogamous language groups and ranked patrilineal phratries will undoubtedly undergo further refinement and revision as new studies continue to appear (e.g., Vidal 1993).

Today there is a general consensus that the northern Arawakan phratries of the Upper Rio Negro region formed part of a macroregional diaspora of riverine, Arawak-speaking peoples that spanned the Orinoco and Negro Basins and that was fully established long before eastern Tukanoan peoples arrived in the Vaupés Basin. Through combining the insights of Jackson (1983), Goldman (1963), Wright (1981), Chernela (1983, 1988, 1993), Reichel-Dolmatoff (1985), and myself (1983, 1985, 1993), I have concluded that the eastern Tukanoan practice of language group exogamy originated as an adaptation to the historical interrelations with the set of northern Arawakan phratries who collectively identify themselves as the "People of Our Language." Language group exogamy can be understood as an eastern Tukanoan strategy of resisting the migratory waves of northern Arawakan phratries by inverting the latter's practice of dividing the language group into several ranked, exogamous phratries. By creating a mirror image of these sociolinguistic patterns, or the building of ranked phratries through language group exogamy, the eastern Tukanoan constructed a regional boundary that clearly distanced them from the Wakuénai and that also allowed for a zone of interpenetration along the northern and eastern borders of the Vaupés Basin. Sustained interethnic relations between eastern Tukanoan and northern Arawakan peoples most likely began in the late colonial period (ca. 1740–1810), when the external pressures of disease, forced labor campaigns, and missionization were driving the Wakuénai phratries and remnants of downstream peoples to migrate to places of relative safety in the remote headwater areas of the Vaupés, Içana, and Guainía Rivers.

Notes

1. Goldman provided a tantalizing bit of evidence that has subsequently turned out to be highly significant when he observed that "one of the Cubeo phratries was, in fact, once Arawakan" (1963: 26).

2. Only 1 out of 534 marriages in Jackson's sample violated the principle of language group exogamy (1983: 94).

3. Simultaneously, Fabian (1983) and other theorists launched major critiques of structuralism and other ahistorical theories that removed the subjects of anthropological research from history.

4. The edited volume *Rethinking History and Myth* (Hill 1988) broadened the critique of "cold societies" to a wide range of indigenous Andean and Amazonian societies.

5. Venancio Camico was an indigenous Baniwa man from the Río Guainía in Venezuela. For a detailed reconstruction of Camico's biography, see Wright and Hill (1986). For interpretations of historical and mythic narratives about Venancio Camico, see Hill and Wright (1988).

Susan K. Staats

Fighting in a Different Way

Indigenous Resistance
through the Alleluia Religion
of Guyana

While I was studying the Akawaio language with the Charles family, whose compound forms one of the small, dispersed settlements along the Middle Mazaruni River, fairly frequently someone would remove a plastic envelope from a basket hanging in the rafters and hand me a paper to read. They had tucked away decades of birth certificates, marriage licenses, and vaccination records. Victor, the old man who led the Alleluia services, had concurrent membership cards from no fewer than three of Guyana's major political parties. Sometimes I was asked to comment on a child's health record or to calculate someone's age, but usually this was a means of teaching me about Akawaio life. My friends had rightly perceived my dependence on paper (I rarely, for example, could recall words that I failed to enter in my notebook), and so their documentary history added to my understanding of personal and regional history.

Still, I was rather surprised one day when a young fellow casually unfolded a certificate and handed it to me. Printed at the top was the inscription "Jizes Klaish, Alleluia Sochei," and below, "Jesus Christ, Alleluia Church." What followed was the record of John Winston's baptism at Amokokupai, the central holy place of the Alleluia religion, in Akawaio with English interlinear translations.[1]

Jengbadaugwazak Sochei dak Amokokupai
Baptized in the Church at Amokokupai

Mazuling Yawuluta, Guyana yau
Upper Mazaruni River, Guyana

Baptismal records have multiple functions in Guyana's interior. Certainly, the record indicates that the bearer has a prior commitment to one church in the midst of many, including the Anglican Church and Protestant evangelicals like Seventh Day Adventist, Wesleyan, and Pilgrim's Holiness. Besides signaling spiritual affiliation, baptismal records serve as identification papers necessary for such things as admission to primary schools. Religious membership is also a prominent topic when negotiating partnerships in the back-stabbing world of gold and diamond mining. Finally, the record summarized a century and a half of negotiated spiritual authority, a dialogue in which the leadership of the Alleluia Church had adopted a fundamental sign of European religious institutionalization.

John Winston had been baptized in 1968 at the age of ten by Aibilibin, the last of the great Alleluia prophets, who takes his name from the Alleluia phrase meaning "God's Power." The document additionally recorded Winston's parents' names, address, and the number which indexes his entry in the baptismal register at Amokokupai. It ended with the declaration:

Seyla: ji seyla: enabailung jengbadaugwapa: kalidai John Winston
This is a true copy of the baptism record of John Winston

jengbadaugwazak lepa: tuna ke Paba ika:iba:na: ezek yau Imu
baptized with water in the name of the Father, the Son,

Yawala: nela:.
and the Holy Spirit.

The politics of religious revitalization is vigorously contested when indigenous people appropriate Christian ideology and signifiers. The familiar approach of isolating within religious practices a dialectic of resistance and accommodation was recently given depth with the suggestion that revitalization movements may respond as much to conflicts among indigenous people as to colonial domination (Brown 1991). Social and ideological differentiation is a commonplace at most times and locations, and so any religion that develops as an ethnogenetic movement must bring meaning to people following a variety of life strategies. A central problem in the study of religious revitalization is to find the means by which a religion deals, through its organization and ideology, with the enduring conundrum of unity in the presence of difference, of resistance that tolerates factionalism.

In the following essay I will document the development of the Alleluia religion as an ethnogenetic movement of resistance and discuss the treatment of social difference through Alleluia symbolism and performance. Symbolic and performative considerations are keys to understanding that Alleluia is, for its adherents, a means of "poetically constructing a shared understanding of the past that enables them to understand their present condition as the result of their own ways of making history" (Hill 1992: 811). While reaffirming regional interethnic bonds, the followers of Alleluia were obliged to set upon, literally, a "way of making history," an abstract model of the passage of Amerindian culture through time.

To see that Alleluia is rightly considered an ethnogenetic movement, it is necessary to specify the way it came to mold some aspect of social identity. Many identities vie for importance in daily life in Guyana. The commonly recognized social categories in this Land of Six Races are Indo-Guyanese, Afro-Guyanese, Portuguese, Chinese, Amerindian; the final category is generally given as either white or mixed. To be Amerindian is to be culturally suspect, to face in ordinary relationships the expectation that one's life choices should augment the development of all native people, an assessment in which, not surprisingly, sophistication equals fluency in coastal culture.

Beyond national models of race, there are a number of ethnic groupings that have their greatest influence in the Guyanese interior. The table mountain Roraima marks not only the triple frontier of Guyana, Venezuela, and Brazil but also the center of an ethnically, linguistically, and historically complex group of indigenous South Americans (Butt Colson 1983–1984; Thomas 1982). Arawak-speaking Wapishana live in the South Rupununi Savannas and Carib-speaking Makushi live in the North Savannas. Speakers of other Carib dialects include the eponymous Carib north of the Pakaraima Mountains, the Pemon, and the Kapon. The Pemon, most of whom live in the Gran Sabana to the west of the Kapon, include the Arekuna, Kamarakoto, and Taurepan. Kapon refers to the Akawaio in the Mazaruni River region and the Patamona to the south. In addition to membership in one of these linguistically distinct groups, people strongly identify with communities on the river or creek of their birth. Identities based on heritage aside, religion and class indicators such as literacy, fluency in English, degree of education, and occupation have considerable divisive force in daily life.

The Alleluia religion developed in the mid–nineteenth century among the Makushi and has remained remarkably influential, particularly in many Akawaio and Patamona communities.[2] Some Pemon communities follow the related religious movements Chochimuh and San Miguel that developed in the 1950s and 1970s (D. Thomas 1976, 1982). It is not the case that the religion supplies a biogenetic charter through which Akawaio adherents see themselves as a unique and bounded people distinct from, say, Seventh Day Akawaio. Alleluia expressive culture nonetheless has implications for ethnic consciousness. Alleluia followers affirm, through daily worship, a representation of the meaning of Amerindian culture, in the recognized presence of other definitions, through hymns, prayers, and the historical tales that illuminate their significance.

Alleluia Culture: A New Tradition for Earth's Last Days

The heart of Alleluia worship is song. Early in the morning, while everyone lies asleep or dozing in their hammocks, one of the Alleluia leaders begins to sing and carries through until sunrise prayers. During the day, people sing Alleluia to purify freshly killed game, request safe passage for travelers, assist in the growth of crops, and cure the sick. In keeping with the egalitarian ethos of most communities, leaders include both men and women (Forte and Melville 1989; Jordan 1980). The strongest Alleluia followers obtain songs through dreams. Community members learn the short texts quickly, and during services, with their eyes tightly closed or with a hand covering the face in a personal meditation, they sing the hymns in unison over and over. Alleluia songs often speak of personal redemption and the coming destruction of the world.

> Earth-maker God is coming,
> Mist-maker God is coming.
> (Butt 1960: 73)

> Take me up to heaven, Father,
> Let me touch my bench there.
> Take me up to heaven, Father.
> (Henfrey 1964: 134)

People say that when they sing these songs, they feel great solemnity because the performance reveals to them the beauty of heaven, and they are sad that they must continue their lives of hardship and struggle on earth. In all-night dances, men and women lock arms and march as the soldiers of God, chasing away evil. They realize that on the eve of the destruction of the world, the heart or life-force (*yewang*) of all entities and objects will disappear: in the last days, a righteous person may offer a suffering companion food and drink, but it will not satisfy his or her body. Creeds during morning and Sunday services profess the guidance Alleluia will provide in the days of chaos.

> Alleluia sela yagalu bukare sela yewang sela
> Kompas mailundelu
> Sela aibilibin mu yawalulu

> Waku yewang mokaning
> Nong yewang mokaning

Tuna yewang mokaning
Morouk yewang mokaning
Torong yewang mokaning
Ok yewang mokaning
Tuma yewang mokaning
Egi yewang mokaning

[This Alleluia is my being. This wisdom, this spirit
Is like a compass, it is my strength.
This is God's power; it is right mind.

Good spirit leaving
Earth spirit leaving
Water spirit leaving
Fish spirit leaving
Bird spirit leaving
Game spirit leaving
Food spirit leaving
Cassava spirit leaving]

Alleluia believers recall the origins of the religion as much as they anticipate
the millennium. The stories of the divine revelations to prophets reinterpret
the history of missionization so that unequal access to knowledge was reversed
through immediate contact with God. A summary of Butt Colson's version of
the origin story follows.[3]

The first Hallelujah prophet, a Makushi named Bichiwung, worked for a
white parson in a mission school. The parson took Bichiwung to England.
Bichiwung had learned some English, and so he was able to discover that the
parson was withholding God's words, a source of strength, from him. One
day, the whites left him alone in their house to look after their great wealth.

During this time, Bichiwung decided to meet God and find out if the
whites' teachings were true. He set off on the trail to God which the whites
had shown him, and reached heaven. At first, God wouldn't let Bichiwung
into heaven, but after Bichiwung explained his purpose, God gave him a tour.
God said that the whites were deceiving him, and that Hallelujah was good.
God gave Bichiwung Hallelujah, a bottle of white medicine, words and songs,
and a piece of paper that was the Indian Bible. Bichiwung sealed all these
things inside a canister. He wanted to stay in heaven, but God refused, as
Bichiwung had not yet died. So Bichiwung returned the way he had come. He
stopped reading the white man's Bible, knowing that he had got Hallelujah
from God *on his own* (original emphasis).

When Bichiwung returned to Georgetown, he was met by Makushi friends. He had sent for them to help him carry back all his wealth. As Bichiwung had directed, they sold parrots, baskets, and other things to get money to buy trade goods.

Back at his village, he began to teach Hallelujah. His wife, refusing to observe the Sabbath, went to work in her gardens. Left at home with his daughter, Bichiwung slept and his spirit went to heaven, and he found Hallelujah there once more. His daughter also slept and went to heaven. His wife returned to a locked door several times and accused her husband of incest. He denied the allegation, and finally converted her. Bichiwung and his family preached among the Makushi: some believed him, and some thought he was a liar. He had several helpers: Plegoman, Enewali, Pratalu, Wakowyamu, and Jesik. Believers prayed all the time until they got the right words from God.

Sorcerers became jealous of Bichiwung's plentiful gardens, and one day they attacked him. Bichiwung died. His wife rubbed his body with the medicine he had received from God and he returned to life. Later, sorcerers killed him and cut him into two or three pieces. His wife gathered together the pieces and resurrected him with the medicine again. Finally, Bichiwung was killed and cut into many small pieces. The sorcerors scattered the pieces all around. Because some pieces were lost, Bichiwung could not be revived. He died and went to heaven.

People began to forget what Bichiwung had taught them, mixing up Hallelujah songs and dances with traditional ones. Then Abel, the founder of Akawaio Hallelujah, got good Hallelujah from God and gave it to the people.

The negotiation of tensions between inherited and invented tradition is a central theme in Alleluia origin tales, prompting the question of whether new perspectives on the past implied a repudiation of indigenous cultural practices. Many of the Alleluia prophets, for example, are said to be reformed shamans (*piaimen*) or *kanaima*s, indigenous sorcerors who are believed throughout the circum-Roraima area to be the cause of most deaths. As is commonly the case, *piaimen* in this area arouse distrust because they have the ability to kill as well as to cure. While some prophets switched their specialization from *piai* to preaching, Alleluia leaders generally did not aim to curtail the practice of indigenous curing. Butt Colson's work in the 1950s indicates that Akawaio followers of Alléluia did not abstain from shamanic ritual. She observed that "all present shamans are believers, and many are enthusiastic adherents, taking part in church activities and feasts" (1977: 45). Among the Patamona, Alleluia dances partially replaced shamanic performances, but *piaimen* still practiced and attended to the local condition of the community along with Alleluia leaders, who sought the ultimate source of power (Butt Colson 1971). Indeed, the Alleluia prophet who follows a trail to heaven during dreams retraces the soul flight of a *piaiman*. Although only a few people in the Mazaruni today would call themselves *piaimen*, many people know and use some *piai* techniques, evidence that the practice has undergone transformations partially independent of Alleluia. During much of its tenure, then, the Alleluia religion has coexisted with indigenous curing practices.

Kanaima violence, a source of terror in the region for decades, seems to be even more resilient than shamanism. *Kanaima*s often act out of jealousy or the desire for revenge and inflict upon their victims devastating damage to the tongue, anus, and joints that is almost always fatal (im Thurn 1883; Wavell, Butt, and Epton 1966; Whitehead 1990b). This form of violence may be a relatively recent assassination cult that developed in the nineteenth century as a result of demographic collapse and diminished Carib leadership (Whitehead 1990b: 166); at any rate, the threat of *kanaima* attack is a major source of factionalism throughout the circum-Roraima region. Family histories cycle around a byzantine pattern of *kanaima* attacks and reprisals. The threat of *kanaima* attack also arises during disagreements on political issues such as strategies for gaining land title. Even if *kanaima*s threaten society and culture in Alleluia origin tales, they are just as much a part of indigenous life today. The religion has not limited their activities substantially.

The traditional practice that receives more ambiguous treatment in these narratives is not *kanaima* violence or shamanism but the *parishara* dance festivals that led to the loss of Alleluia knowledge among the Makushi. The Patamona, like the Makushi, from whom they learned Alleluia, drank too much in a spree one night and lost the knowledge again (Butt Colson 1971). These *parishara* festivals are superficially similar to Alleluia worship: both involve night-long singing and dancing, and performers are fortified with plenty of cassava drink like *paiwari* and *cassiri*. Although organized festivals are not common, people still sing and enjoy *parishara* songs; many people find the songs' sexual and naturalistic imagery wicked but compelling. An Alleluia leader explained, "They're like Sparrow music," comparing *parishara* to the popular and prurient compositions of the Calypsonian Mighty Sparrow. Alleluia worship probably took some of its performative organization from *parishara* festivals, and so the critical issue for followers is the separation of sacred and secular genres and not a denial of tradition.

As can be appreciated from this discussion, the Alleluia religion was not, in intention or in result, concerned primarily with the repudiation of indigenous culture. It does not appear to have addressed factionalism that may have been caused by shamanic violence, nor did it curb the greatest sources of fear, *kanaima* attacks. The problems that Alleluia sought to redress were based on broader social processes.

Historical Beginnings: The Currents of Revitalization

Bichiwung's revelatory vision cannot be dated precisely; the earliest traveler's observation of Alleluia occurred in 1884, recorded by Sir Everard im Thurn on his trip to Mount Roraima: "The Indians around us, under the influence of a most remarkable ecclesiastical mania which had just then spread in a wonderful way into those distant parts raised—as they kept Christmas with much drinking, without intermission from sunset to the next dawn—an absolutely incessant shout of 'Hallelujah! Hallelujah!'" (im Thurn 1885: 266, quoted in Butt Colson 1985: 107).

It was common from the earliest periods of contact for indigenous people to be taken to England as curiosities for the audiences of the conquest. Robert Schomburgk, an explorer and colonial administrator in British Guiana, took a Makushi, a Warrau, and a Paravilhano to England in 1839 (Butt 1960), and so the story that Bichiwung received his earliest visions and "got Hallelujah" in England may be literally true. At any rate, Colson accepts im Thurn's suggestion that Alleluia was new in 1884 and sees this decade as the period of the origin of the religion, in contrast to Henfrey, who lists the 1840s as its beginning (1964: 128).

What is clear, in spite of these ambiguous beginnings, is that the emergence of Alleluia was a response to drastically changing interethnic relations in the early post-Emancipation period. An appreciation of the turbulent interval from the 1830s to im Thurn's observations of 1884 suggests that the daily lives of Makushi and other indigenous people were shaped by the nation-building efforts of several colonial governments. The original followers of Alleluia found themselves in a convergence of political collapse, economic restructuring, and international border disputes.

In the early seventeenth century Dutch settlers in Essequibo, Demerara, and Berbice, the three colonies that made up British Guiana, allied themselves with indigenous people to insure safety and trade for the new colony, just as neighboring Spanish colonies were allied with the Lokono of the Orinoco (Menezes 1977; Whitehead 1988). They traded steel implements and cloth for forest products and, increasingly, indigenous slaves. By the late seventeenth century, the shift from a subsistence to a plantation economy stimulated the slave trade and began a major transformation in international and local relationships that entwined the lives of indigenous and Afro-American peoples. As in other plantation societies, Maroons proved to be a major problem for the Dutch colonial government. By 1744, the director-general of Essequibo noted that there were at least 300 Maroons living in the northwest of Essequibo, and from 1796 to 1803 the number of slaves doubled from around 30,000 to 60,000, drastically outnumbering the 10,000 planters (Menezes

1977: 6, 6 n, 52). As a means of providing regional security, the Dutch adopted the twin policies of military recruitment and presentation of annual gifts. Their use of indigenous peoples to capture runaway slaves and to put down slave rebellions involved the Arawak and other groups but was directed primarily at the Kariña, or "True Carib," whose political and economic position relative to other indigenous peoples was augmented as a result.

Near the turn of the century, international power struggles resulted in the transfer of the three colonies to the British. Although indigenous groups continued to protect the plantation system, British authorities proved to be disappointing partners who were much less trustworthy in their remuneration than the Dutch (Menezes 1977: 49). The period of Emancipation, from 1833 to 1838, created intense dissatisfaction and disorganization of indigenous peoples in the colonies. In 1837, when the return of Maroons was no longer necessary, annual presents were discontinued. The resulting collapse of Carib dominance coincided with decreased interethnic hostilities, which nevertheless became entrenched in indigenous folklore. Farabee (1924: 14) writes that during his expedition early in the twentieth century, open warfare had ended, but the Makushi remembered violent conflicts with the Wapishana, Carib, and Arekuna. Many indigenous groups were obliged to find alternative sources of income, especially in the emerging timber industry. Income was likewise the preeminent issue for the colonial government, which now found itself devoid of productive labor on the plantations. Before new immigration policy brought contract laborers from India, Southeast Asia, and the Portuguese island of Madeira, the administration turned brief hopes to the interior as a source of labor. The labor crisis coincided with breaches of security in the south.

On the eve of Emancipation in 1833, an Anglican missionary named Thomas Youd reported Brazilian slave raids against the Makushi living in the border town of Pirara and was given permission to establish a mission for their protection. Colonial administrators offered their own solution: they set aside crown lands for Makushi willing to abandon their frontier homelands (Farabee 1967; Riviere 1966–1967). Their goal was clear: by convincing the Makushi to relocate, the colonial government could establish an easily controlled workforce. The Pirara Makushi declined the offer but did not find peace at home. Slaving continued throughout the 1840s and 1850s after Youd's mission failed (Menezes 1977: 157, 164). In 1838, for example, the Brazilian militia enslaved a group of Makushi at Pirara whom they claimed had been taught false religion and the English language. Facing enslavement from the south and spiritual imperialism and the threat of relocation from the north, the Makushi were surely aware of their position as a lever in the struggles of nation building.

Both colonial archives and indigenous oral history record cultural struggle among the Makushi at Youd's mission. According to colonial records, in the mid-1840s, Reverend Youd was confronted by a Makushi man whose sons had stopped dancing the traditional dances. The confrontation became quite serious—Youd's wife was fatally poisoned, and on his return to England, Youd himself died, perhaps of slow poisoning (Menezes 1977: 219). The same Makushi, indigenous consultants told Butt Colson (1960: 85, 105), was subsequently struck down by lightning one Sunday while preaching as if he were a minister.

This episode testifies to the problematics of religious innovation. Although some Makushi resented Youd's well-intentioned intervention, one of his strongest critics apparently patterned a new method of worship on Youd's performative techniques. This proposal received the same fatal verdict as Youd's. The missions were thus centers of ambivalence. As indigenous people weighed the prospects of religious experimentation against cultural struggle, employment against epidemic disease, it is reasonable to imagine that many approached religious instruction as intercultural training, to better allow them to cope with employers and partners. It is little wonder, in any case, that different actors followed different strategies and adhered to different concepts of authentic spiritual experience.

It was in this context of economic and political restructuring after the Emancipation that the beginnings of the Alleluia religion can be found. Labor migration and differing evaluations of missionization were likely concerns for the originators of Alleluia, who may have been stationed at Demerara mission towns such as Muritaro and nearby timber operations (Butt Colson 1985: 113).

Although literary references to Alleluia appear many years later, the Reverend Brett (1868: 180–182, 258–259) gives evidence of a large revitalization movement during 1845 and 1846 that anticipates many features of Alleluia. A Carib catechumen left Brett's Waramuri mission but returned after becoming disillusioned with the prophet and reported to Brett: "A person pretending to be the Lord went into the interior with some deluded followers, and he established himself in the upper part of the Masaruni. From this distant spot, he sent emissaries into the neighborhood of all the missions, calling on the Indians to quit their homes and provision grounds and go to him" (Brett 1868: 180). Brett emphatically states that no baptized Indians from his mission left permanently, but many went temporarily to Akawaio territory to "see God." This countermissionary movement drew hundreds of followers, no doubt more disillusioned than deluded, from several Carib-speaking groups and provided them with spiritual guidance for a year.

Brett's terse denunciation offers glimpses of a social movement that prefigures much of the performance and symbolism of Alleluia. Entire families entered the Upper Mazaruni to hear prophecies of the fire and flood that would end the world; *paiwari* sustained them as they worshiped through song and dance. Promising times of plenty, the leader offered bananas that thrived without cultivation and land on which cassava crops would grow from a single stick. The leader gave Brett's informant paper documents to distribute, a "commission from makonaima, the Almighty, to collect and send to that place all the Indians he could gather" (Brett 1868: 259), probably a version of the "Indian Bible" that Bichiwung received from God.

As he sought to wrest indigenous spirituality from foreign control, the leader of the 1845 revival affirmed cultural features such as dance and folklore recognizable to many of the region's ethnolinguistic groups and therefore created consciousness of the bonds these groups shared. Such unifying discourses were ambitious correctives to intra- and interethnic factionalism caused by colonial policy and developed at a moment when the collapse of the Carib and the comparative inattention of the colonial government made cross-ethnic alliances more viable. This ethnogenetic precursor of Alleluia clearly sought to foster political and spiritual resistance by focusing on the meanings of Amerindian identity shared by all groups in the region.

"Aibilibin Would Sing for You": Resistance and Dialogue

Despite internal disagreements, false starts, and the eventual adoption of a European signifier for the supreme deity, Alleluia followers have consistently presented the religion to travelers, missionaries, and ethnographers as a means of resisting coastal spiritual influence. Their words, usually recorded in English Creole, speak to the strength of ethnic identity in the face of governmental policies and pressure to adopt the beliefs of Roman Catholic and Anglican Churches and especially Protestant evangelicals like Seventh Day Adventists and Pilgrim's Holiness.

This is the case with the earliest evidence. Butt Colson was told that Makushi Alleluia went underground during the 1930s and 1940s as a result of missionaries' criticisms (Butt Colson 1985: 139). Similarly, Friar Cary-Elwes visited the Patamona in 1917 and recorded his conversations with Benjamin, the first Patamona prophet.

> All the people, he told me, wanted to know the doctrine of Jesus Christ, so that they might all go to heaven. He further told me the prayers he said were not his, he had got them from Amokokupai and accepted them without question . . . we actually chose a site together for the church which I intended to build at my next visit. But when I took my departure the very next day, Benjamin began to waver. "You may build your church over there," he said,

"but I will continue with my Alleluia church here" . . . I can see that he is
unwilling to act without the Amokokupai people. (Quoted from Cary-Elwes's
unpublished manuscript in Butt Colson 1971: 29–30)

Benjamin's position suggests a willingness to establish relationships with coastlanders for intercultural learning and most assuredly economic advantages
but at the same time to insist that these affiliations be ones of mutuality and
not domination.

Patamona followers were again pressured to renounce Alleluia by Pilgrim's
Holiness and Roman Catholic missionaries in the early 1960s. A Patamona
Alleluia leader named Henry commented that "other Patamona people lost
it . . . this white priest came from America. He say the people going to burn
in the big fire if they keep up with the Hallelujah. That make them so frightened so they leave off and take up the white man's Bible . . . But I ain't get so
frightened. This place is for the Indians. God give we Hallelujah—the white
man ain't supposed to trouble we" (Henfrey 1964, quoted in Butt Colson
1971: 31).

The Akawaio also coped with missionary interference through a combination of secrecy and selective disclosure. Colin Henfrey's guide to Amokokupai
revealed that he was an Alleluia leader only at the moment an Alleluia dance
started, Henfrey believed, because of his distrust of potential missionaries
(Henfrey 1965: 70). Some past and present Alleluia leaders say that Alleluia
knowledge must be kept secret from non-Amerindians, but as Aibilibin, the
fifth prophet at Amokokupai, told Henfrey, "Once a priest came here to stop
we. He did want to steal Hallelujah and he vexed that we got it. This thing is
for Indian people. But if you come in a right way, if you like this Hallelujah,
Aibilibin would sing for you" (1965: 91).

Religious accommodation finally became mutual: the Anglicans made a
partial rapprochement with the Alleluia Church. Largely owing to the rec-
ommendation of a British Anglican priest based permanently in the Upper
Mazaruni, Father John Dorman, the Anglican Church held an inquiry on the
subject of Alleluia theology (Father C. Roland, personal communication).
Father Dorman traveled to Amokokupai to discuss the matter with Aibilibin,
and the Anglicans' central concerns (whether the referent of Alleluia's "Jesus
Christ" was in fact the Christian deity and the inclusion of a concept of trinity)
were answered to the church's satisfaction in the affirmative. This inquiry was
instrumental in the inclusion of the Alleluia religion in the Guyana Council of
Churches.

At various times and places (essentially whenever statements about Alleluia
were recorded), the religion was a banner of the cultural distinction of indigenous people. The consistent resistance of native peoples suggests that Chris-

tian signifiers are not evidence of succumbing to the power of the dominant society. Clearly aware of their role in the governance of the colonies, of their history of alliance and abandonment, indigenous people may have adopted the symbol of Jesus Christ as an emblem of membership in a multiethnic regional culture that had come to include European, Afro-American, and other immigrants. Certainly Christ was one of the only prominent symbols common among the missionaries, hinterland administrators, and timber operators with whom they had contact. The concept of a multiethnic society united by cultural symbols and practices was not new to people of the circum-Roraima and in fact was of precolonial provenance. The Amerindian Bible of Alleluia folklore and John Winston's baptismal record both index processes through which indigenous people recognize the history that they share with coastlanders without abnegating cultural identity or waiving the option to resist cultural imperialism.

Practice, Poetics, and Performance in a Multiethnic Landscape

The fact that Alleluia has consistently been presented as a resistance movement, rather than a repudiation of tradition, is insufficient to explain the longevity and tenacity the religion has held in Guyana's hinterland. Just as important, the religion has developed flexible means of creating and describing multiethnic relationships.

It would be incorrect to conclude that the Alleluia religion allowed people to transcend all sources of local conflict. Beyond the competitive forces among different religions, indigenous people hold a variety of views on cultural legitimacy and development. Many people follow a mixed economy, including farming, hunting, and small-scale mining, but many others have come to depend primarily on employment in the mining industry to purchase expensive foodstuffs imported from the coast. In the Middle Mazaruni, deciding whether to send children away to the few, widely separated primary schools is quite difficult and creates a great deal of dissension over the future of indigenous culture. Accusations of *kanaima* attacks also disrupt relationships. In this context, the explanatory functions of a religion are perhaps more cogent than the programmatic ones. A religion that sought to limit action in the midst of so many life strategies would likely prove short-lived.

During the late nineteenth and early twentieth centuries, communities across the circum-Roraima took up Alleluia worship. Koch-Grunberg (cited in Butt Colson 1985: 107) noted the participation of Arawakan Wapishana along with Carib groups in a 1911 Alleluia festival. By this time, Alleluia "missionaries" had traveled through nearby parts of Venezuela and Brazil to bring Alleluia to distant villages (Narine 1979: 125). Indeed, as Alleluia spread from Makushi to Kapon and Pemon communities, it reaffirmed indigenous economic relationships that had existed, perhaps tenuously, since precolonial times (Butt Colson 1985). The movement of Alleluia spiritual wealth paralleled that of material wealth by passing through marriage and exchange links at interethnic levels, serving to institutionalize awareness of a regional community. Each June, this community is physically represented at Amokokupai when people from Guyana, Venezuela, and Brazil assemble for the New Crops Festival.

As Alleluia developed a multiethnic purview, it was necessary to develop a means of understanding indigenous life as coherent and unified in spite of linguistic differences, geographical breadth, and memories of interethnic conflict. A common South American motif for the concept of many-in-one draws upon the regenerative power of domestic plants, a trope especially well suited to describe the atomistic but flexible social organization of indigenous groups of the Guianas. For the Barama River Carib, the vegetative propagation of cassava is iconic of egalitarian social organization (Adams 1983–1984: 304–305). Of course, sustaining social life involves equally the political and the edible: the Kapon, Pemon, and the Ye'kuana regard Mount Roraima as the center of the social world, the severed trunk of a tree of life that contributed all the world's cultivars of fruits and vegetables (Thomas 1982: 33; de Civrieux 1980). It is no coincidence that these images combine in the magically productive plants possessed by the leader of the Akawaio movement of 1846. Drawing upon specifically indigenous domains of knowledge, the promise of indigenous independence through abundant sustenance and social equality was powerful political commentary.

It can be appreciated, then, that the miraculous calabash, bananas, and plantains that Bichiwung obtained from God (Butt 1960: 76) were recognizable as folkloric shorthand for social unity and independence, a dynamic metaphor for the reproduction of society. This process is perhaps mirrored in the fate of Bichiwung's body. *Kanaimas* grew jealous of Bichiwung's exuberantly productive gardens and chopped him to pieces. Having been restored to life twice, his final death occurs when the pieces of his body are too widely scattered to be reclaimed. The dispersion and retrieval of Bichiwung's body teach that social differentiation is not deadly unless it is irreconcilably divisive.

The complexities of socially differentiated, multilinguistic landscapes which have just begun to be appreciated by anthropologists have not been ignored in Alleluia expressive culture. The multiethnic group of worshipers has its presence felt in the rules of performance for Alleluia songs. The language of Alleluia songs and prayers differs slightly from ordinary speech, but texts often use conventional phrases, making them interpretable to many people. Performers recognize that some songs use a foreign indigenous language;

Akawaio singers, for example, often know songs in Makushi or Patamona. This multilingual repertoire is the legacy of Abel, who fathered the second generation of Alleluia leaders and who was the first to carry Alleluia across ethnic boundaries:

> Abel, the first Akawaio prophet, used to be a wicked man. He was a blowman— he blew magical spells on people and made them sick. One night, though, he had a dream. He was in heaven and everybody there was singing. The song was so beautiful that when he woke up, he began to sing it to himself over and over again. After a while, he forgot it, but later, in another dream, he went to heaven and caught the song again. This time, God told him that he had to keep singing the song just as he had heard it, in the original language. Abel kept singing the song just so, and later he got more songs. It was Abel who told us that we must never translate Alleluia songs into another language when we sing them. (Akawaio Alleluia leader, Staats field notes, 1994)

Because indigenous language in the circum-Roraima indexes ethnic group, the diversity of the Alleluia congregation was forged in this episode of Abel's life. Instead of social fault lines, distinctions between groups appear as stable boundaries in a confederation of multiple language groups sharing mythic and performative cultural features.

Both narrative symbolism and performance criteria elaborate views of the passage of social groups and practices through time. The social form that receives the most attention is the reproduction of Alleluia knowledge itself, perhaps because Alleluia worship is a totalizing expression of indigenous identity for many followers. More than, say, a blow-by-blow interpretation of historical episodes or an elucidation of religious ideology, Alleluia folklore is highly concerned with delineating modes of transmission of spiritual knowledge. There are two independent and therefore seemingly contradictory pathways through which prophets "get Alleluia."

Through the commemoration of the personalities and interpersonal relationships of learning that brought Alleluia from the Makushi to Akawaio and Patamona communities, Alleluia leaders recall their intellectual lineage with a precision reminiscent of the First-Time knowledge of Saramaka historians (Butt Colson 1971, 1985; Price 1983). The Makushi Wakowyaming taught Alleluia to the Kukui Akawaio. An Akawaio prophet named John William learned Alleluia from Abel and from Poregaman, a Makushi successor to Bichiwung. John William and his younger brother succeeded Abel at Amokokupai and subsequently taught Joseph Grant. Alleluia passed from Grant to a leader named Johnny Bai and from him to Casiano Antoniko and so on, in a complex line of inheritance that can be traced to current leaders.

Alleluia prophets recognize a second mode of transmission of knowledge in which each prophet obtains songs, dances, plants, and papers directly from God during dreams. Certainly, this legitimizes Alleluia leaders' authority and simultaneously renders foreign clergymen superfluous. Divine revelation further insures that Alleluia knowledge, if lost through improper worship, can be regained. But if legitimate spiritual knowledge can only be obtained through God, why then should indigenous people consider it necessary to remember a century-long network of interpersonal learning?

Taken together, this dual genealogy of knowledge is a model of cultural temporality. It represents in a strikingly compact fashion the cogency of both mythic and historical ways of understanding the past (Hill 1988). The mythic axis, obtaining Alleluia directly from God, affirms spiritual distinction and the potentials of the universe open to indigenous people. The historical axis emphasizes agency, the tangible, interpersonal network that brought Alleluia across the region. More important, these two modes of inheritance indicate a convergence of approach between indigenous people and anthropologists in explaining cultural history: "cultural realities are always produced in specific sociohistorical contexts . . . it is necessary to account for the processes that generate those contexts in order to account for both the practice of identity and the production of historical schemes" (Friedman 1992: 837). Alleluia leaders have been on the front lines of intercultural encounters for decades, and the "practice of identity" developed in Alleluia culture informs these contexts of interaction. The emphasis on process in Alleluia origin tales is a model for the past and the future, a theory of history that explains the contemporary meanings of indigenous life.

The Upper Mazaruni Hydroelectric Project

A well-documented case in which the Alleluia religion provided guidance in claiming a position in national culture was the Upper Mazaruni Hydroelectric Project. The homes and livelihood of Akawaio, Arekuna, and Patamona peoples in the Mazaruni and Potaro districts were threatened in the 1970s and 1980s by the plans of former president Forbes Burnham to develop the hydroelectric potential of the area (Bennet, Butt Colson, and Wavell 1978; Henningsgaard 1981; Fournier 1979). Burnham hoped to secure Guyana's claim to the Essequibo, a resource-rich area that is also claimed by Venezuela (Braveboy-Wagner 1984). Had the plan reached completion, the dam would have flooded most of the Akawaio communities in the Upper Mazaruni, including Amokokupai. Alleluia leaders were among the strongest detractors of the plan.

In response to this development program, an old man wrote anonymously to Comrade Burnham:

Long years past it was said we would have to fight to keep our lands . . . but now I partly understand, that Abel received Alleluia from God, and he told us it is an evil to fight and kill one another for we are all brothers. Only now I try to fight in a different way by writing this letter to you. It is my work to tell you how we are living on these lands that God has given to us, and to ask that we can keep the ways the old people taught us. (Bennet, Butt Colson, and Wavell 1978: 9)

It is surely a delicate task to choose a persuasive rhetorical strategy that claims cultural legitimacy in the face of demeaning, exclusionary coastal stereotypes. The letter writer approaches this problem by adopting a historical, developmental framework. After traveling to heaven to get Alleluia, Abel preached against interethnic violence. This criticism of warfare must not be read as self-deprecation. The same development that a coastlander may view as recanting a past identity is, the writer makes clear, a transformation of interethnic conflict into resistance. By "fighting in a different way" he reforms the coastal image of the "wild Indian" into a politically active but ethnically and geographically distinct member of the national scene. He continues:

I do not like it that teachers tell the children it is best to get more money, get diamonds and gold, get job. I want to tell you that alleluia has been given to our people as the ways to pray and we know God taught us how to live in peace and happiness. I do not find that the men with money are able to do this better. I have built my house on the earth and my children are happy around me. I have built our church on the earth and our naked feet have made the earth hard as we dance alleluia. I kneel on the earth to pray. For God has made it good and I am not ashamed.

In this man's powerful assessment, Alleluia is the principle through which native people possessed the earth. The religion is the heart of his claim, fundamental to indigenous rights discourses, of prior occupation and cultural distinction. The author goes on to build up an image of extraordinary stability centered around family and Alleluia worship. He cites the vertical, centered movement whereby Alleluia was received from heaven. He is surrounded by his children, he builds his church, his feet beat the ground into a solid floor. These sequential images of stability, firmness, and cultural integrity contrast sharply with images of futile movement, the casting-about of capitalist expansion: "get more money, get diamonds and gold, get job." This author recognizes that his life has been transformed by long-term encounters with the coast, and yet his ability to critique those with whom he shares a cultural history is uncompromised.

Burnham's administration was unable to raise sufficient funding from international agencies and as a result the Upper Mazaruni Hydroelectric Project was never completed. Plans to relocate Akawaio families to the banks of the Essequibo, to be implemented before building the dam, failed as well. People say that in a vision, Aibilibin had perceived that coastlanders would come to the Upper Mazaruni to flood everybody's homes. He saw that the plan would ultimately fail and told the people that they must not leave their homes. They were encouraged by this prophecy and stayed.

Although incomplete, the project nevertheless transformed indigenous lives enormously. In order to remove valuable resources before flooding, coastal miners were permitted to enter the area to prospect for gold and diamonds. The previous small-scale prospect and dredges were superseded by more extensive dredging operations that clogged the Mazaruni River channel and led to decreased fish yields. Many young people found employment in the business and consequently acquired the pragmatics of mineral work, alcoholism, and prostitution. Most of the coastal miners who entered the area were Afro-Guyanese, primarily because post-Emancipation legislation and labor history have rendered this sector of the population quite mobile. In perhaps its most damaging legacy, this policy inflamed the difficult history of relations between indigenous and Afro-Guyanese peoples and prolonged a centuries-old tactic of bringing these groups into conflict with each other.

Conclusion

Alleluia narrative and ritual reinterpreted the devastating experiences of the post-Emancipation period in British Guiana by strengthening regional ties among indigenous people. The religion did not repudiate traditional culture but rather developed a variety of powerful and compelling representations of the distinct but interconnected ethnolinguistic groups in the circum-Roraima, a vision that fostered resistance against cultural domination. The temporal relations of distinct kin, linguistic, and ethnic groups are a primary preoccupation of Alleluia expressive culture, and the nature of social dynamics is most formally developed in the dual processes of inheritance of Alleluia knowledge through learning and through dreaming. Alleluia cultural temporality is thus both geographical and transcendent, a reminder that social integration is compatible with cultural autonomy.

Notes

1. The symbol *a:* represents a schwa in the original document.
2. Alleluia has a variety of spellings, including Hallelujah, Aleluia, Aleluya, Areruya. Due to the orthography of quoted material, several of these spellings are used within the text.

3. This passage is a condensed version of Butt Colson's published narrative (Butt 1960: 69–71). Butt Colson indicates that she wove together various stories to create this summary but does not clarify her methods further. I have therefore retained as much of the original phrasing as possible in case the wording represents precise translation.

David M. Guss

Cimarrones, Theater, and the State

Despite its celebrity as a center for African traditions and colorful festivals, the small town of Curiepe does not often attract many visitors from beyond the borders of Venezuela. So it was with some surprise that the first two people I met upon arriving for the great San Juan fiesta of 1989 were both Americans, two freshly tanned twenty-eight-year-old women on a tour of northern Latin America. They had arrived early that morning and were still excited at having witnessed what they believed was the inauguration of the festival. I was extremely curious about this, as it is common knowledge that this annual, three-day drum celebration only begins at noon on June 23. But they insisted that it had begun around nine in the morning in the open space in front of the church. In fact, although there were few spectators, it had been filmed by a television crew from Caracas. The "ceremony," as they described it, was the reenactment of a slave rebellion. Hacendados and soldiers, in somewhat tacky costumes, had been overwhelmed by a group of enraged blacks, who, once vanquishing them, stole off into the streets beyond.

This, the women assured me, was exactly what San Juan was about. The tourist agent who had directed them to Curiepe had informed them that the holiday was a celebration of the liberation of the slaves. It was certainly unlike anything I had ever witnessed or read about San Juan, so much so that I began to ask people in the village what they knew of the events of that morning. Most had no idea, but finally someone in a very amused voice told me that what the two American women had seen was the filming of the final episode of a TV miniseries entitled *La Iluminada.* Far behind schedule, the crew from Canal

Ocho had desperately been trying to wrap up production before the town succumbed to three days of uncontainable revelry.

While I too was amused by the Americans' confusion between a colonial soap opera and a complex religious celebration, events occurring the following year led me to recall this odd scenario and to reconsider its possible meanings. At the same hour on June 23, 1990, a large procession of children entered the plaza and circled it several times before finally coming to a halt at the bust of Simón Bolívar in its center. At the head of this procession was a small boy of twelve or thirteen. He was shirtless but wore light tan pants and typical, campesino sandals. In his hands was a lit torch, symbol of hope, freedom, and universality. Behind him marched a girl of the same age, yet she was dressed smartly, with pleated skirt, blouse, socks, and sneakers, all freshly pressed and white. The contrast between these two images of black history could not have been clearer. Now came two more students with the school standard stretched between them—Unidad Educativa Estado Trujillo. Behind them marched a large group of boys dressed identically to the one who led the column. Instead of torches, they carried a large sign constructed of gray cardboard letters attached to sticks. It read "ABAJO CADENAS" [down with chains] and was connected, one letter to the next, by a rope simulating bonds. It was obvious that these children represented slaves, as did the group of girls who followed behind. However, the girls were dressed in colorful full-length skirts and large white blouses and had kerchiefs wrapped around their heads. Each one held a different object, indicating the various tasks which female slaves were forced to carry out. One held a bundle of wash, another firewood, and still others baskets of fruit and agricultural products. Behind this group marched the masters, boys dressed in colonial hats and waistcoats, with boots made of cardboard reaching up above their knees. There were also soldiers, and behind them came the rest of the school. This group, which numbered at least sixty, was divided into three equal parts, each one separated by the color of its shirts—red, yellow, and blue, with seven of the latter pressing white stars against their chests. It was a human flag of Venezuela.

A semicircle was formed around the monument and a wreath carefully laid. Now the principal of the school read a statement acknowledging that this was the bicentennial of General José Antonio Paéz, hero of the War of Independence and first president of the Republic of Venezuela. However, the statement only spoke of Paéz in passing. Its main focus was Negro Primero, a former slave who earned his name by always being the first into battle. It was Negro Primero who when mortally wounded at the critical Battle of Carabobo went to find Paéz before dying. When Paéz reprimanded him for leaving his post, he responded with the statement which every Venezuelan child knows: "General, vengo a decirle adiós, porque estoy muerto."[1] At the end of this presentation, which emphasized the contribution of blacks to the struggle for Venezuelan independence, there was a rousing cheer of "abajo cadenas," and the chain and sign were thrown down. Now the procession reformed and, after marching around the plaza one more time, headed off in the direction of the school.

What did this curious embodiment of history, witnessed by only a handful of people, have to do with the celebration of San Juan, which was still several hours away from beginning? Or was this enactment actually meant to be a beginning, a preamble added onto the festival in an attempt to redirect its meaning? For it had become clear to me, after witnessing several San Juan celebrations in Curiepe, that an attempt was being made to transform this holiday from a simple celebration of saintly devotion to one of historical recuperation, to relocate its center not in a Catholic and European past but in an African and social one. To do so, a host of strategies, both conscious and unconscious, had been employed, not simply in Curiepe but in Afro-Venezuelan communities throughout the country. As various authors have pointed out in other contexts, new social and historical realities often lead to a radical reselection of what a group chooses to remember.[2] Put another way, the most effective means of transforming the present may be through the re-imagining of one's past.

Similar to the experience of other African-descended populations in the Americas, those brought as slaves to Venezuela were quickly severed from all ethnic, linguistic, and familial ties. Yet it was not simply the possibility of creating an autonomous and dignified history that was denied them, for even after manumission their cultural and racial identity continued to be erased. Hence, as part of what Mexican philosopher José Vasconcelos termed *la raza cósmica* (the cosmic race), they were merged (at least ideologically) into a new and greater entity—a mestizo or criollo one wherein Indian, white, and African were no longer said to be distinguished. This "myth of racial democracy," as Winthrop Wright refers to it in his recent book, *Café con Leche: Race, Class, and National Image in Venezuela,* created a double-bind situation wherein despite racial discrimination, blacks were unable to articulate it as the very category responsible, for this oppression was not recognized (Wright 1990: 113). Distinctions, where they did occur, were steadfastly claimed to be the result not of race but of class. Complicating this vicious cycle of marginalization and poverty was the belief that if race did not exist as a recognizable category in this color-blind society, then all who spoke of it must be either foreign or subversive. Statements such as the following by writer and philosopher Arturo Uslar Pietri typify this commonly held view: "Whoever speaks of blacks or whites, whoever invokes racial hatred or privilege, is denying Venezuela. In Venezuela, in political and social matters, there are neither whites nor blacks, neither mestizos nor Indians. There are only Venezuelans" (*El Nacional*, October 20, 1948, quoted in Wright 1990: 122).[3]

This pattern of "nonviolent discrimination," as Solaún and Kronus characterize it, has been recognized in a number of countries, including Brazil, Cuba, the Dominican Republic, and Puerto Rico (Wright 1990: 2).[4] What may distinguish Venezuela from these other examples, however, are the particular patterns of settlement. Unlike Brazil and Cuba, the Africans brought to Venezuela were not from any one dominant group. Many in fact were not brought directly from Africa but rather from islands throughout the Caribbean, where they had already been working. Furthermore, while slaves began arriving in Venezuela from the beginning of the 1500s, almost all importation had ceased by 1800.[5] This fact is important in explaining the greater cultural and historical distance which Venezuelan blacks have experienced in relation to Africa. Unlike in Cuba and Brazil, where the slave trade continued until nearly the end of the nineteenth century, in Venezuela ties were cut much earlier. There are no linguistic memories, no African "nations," no religious cults like Candomblé or Palo monte drawing blacks closer to a motherland distantly remembered. In Venezuela the recuperation of an African past (as well as a present) has faced particular challenges. Yet inhabitants of the small cacao- and sugar-growing communities dispersed along the coast from Yaracuy and Zulia in the west to Barlovento in the east have found strategies to reconstitute a past of both dignity and resistance.[6]

Of all the ties still identifiable with an African heritage, none are so important in Venezuela as the music and drum traditions incorporated into various religious festivals. Although masked within a Catholic liturgy, the *chimbangueles*, *mina*, *culo e' puya*, *curbata*, and *cumaco* played at such celebrations as San Juan and San Benito can be traced to an origin that is clearly African. It is little surprise, therefore, that these drums have become the focus of a movement by many Afro-Venezuelans to recognize the particular place they have played in their country's history and through this recognition to begin redressing many of the injustices heretofore ignored. This is not to say that what began in the small towns of Barlovento in the mid-1970s is simply a black pride movement, insisting on the acknowledgment of the African contribution to the national culture; rather, these festivals, with their cultural core of African drumming and dance, have been used as vehicles for the telling of a new narrative, one in which Africans are not simply victims and slaves but heroes and liberators. It is a story that above all focuses on resistance, with the central character that of the *cimarrón*. In fact, it is the very quality of *cimarronaje* which these local celebrations are now being used to commemorate.

Difficult to translate into English, particularly as the closest word we have, Maroon, is already a Spanish cognate, *cimarronaje* is the quality or ethos of a *cimarrón,* an escaped slave. In Venezuela, as elsewhere in the New World, escaped slaves, whether in a *cumbe, quilombo, palenque,* or free village, were a source of inspiration for those still in bondage. They represented a refusal to submit either physically or culturally to the brutalizing institution of slavery. When invoking the concept of *cimarronaje* today, the Afro-Venezuelan refers not merely to a past history but to a living tradition still determined to resist the domination of a European ruling class. It recognizes that black Venezuelans remain marginalized, economically oppressed citizens who must find solutions within their own community.

Conversely, when elements of Afro-Venezuelan culture have already been absorbed into this centralized system of power, it is claimed that the community must *cimarronear,* or "cimarronize," them, which is to say, they must "re-Africanize" them, repositioning both their control and meaning within the society from which they were generated. This is precisely what the new directors of many of these festivals, such as that of San Juan in the community of Curiepe, were trying to do. They were attempting to cimarronize the festivals by showing their direct links to an ongoing tradition of autonomy and resistance. As much historical events as religious ones, these festivals commemorated the gathering of slaves to organize revolts and plan escapes. Saints and *cimarrones* suddenly became blurred, with famous escaped slaves being credited with the origin of various songs as well as rites. Just as important, the festivals became the occasion for community organizing and education. From simple celebrations of two to three days, they were converted into entire "culture weeks," during which panels, musicians, theater groups, school pageants, and even films and book parties all sought to recontextualize the meaning of the event.[7] Programs were also printed, not simply to give participants a schedule of events but to provide the entire celebration with a new statement of purpose. What follows is part of one such statement, included in the Culture Week Program for Curiepe's 1979 San Juan celebration:

> Curiepe's Culture Week will take place on June 16 to 22, with the purpose of returning these drum festivals to their true meaning, which is nothing less than a call to arms of our ancestors in order to transform their society, which is to say slavery. For that reason, this week is the time to discuss the problems facing the population of Barlovento today. It will not only be the presentation of cultural groups with simple artistic goals, but rather a tool of solidarity and discussion for the mechanisms of solution.

COMRADE

WE INVITE YOU TO PARTICIPATE

IN A FULL WEEK OF WORK AND RECREATION

JOIN AND STRUGGLE

By the mid-1980s many of the leaders in this movement to foment a new Afro-Venezuelan consciousness began to feel that their festival-oriented focus was perhaps too limited. If it was the African origins and meanings masked within these celebrations they were trying to expose, then why not expand this discussion into an ongoing, daily one? To do so, they proposed an ambitious program of investigation, diffusion, and education. In short, they concluded that the real cultural work to be done was in the schools. That bastion of national ideology must now be breached and a curriculum based on the actual Afro-Venezuelan experience offered. It was with these objectives in mind that a group of organizers from throughout Barlovento joined together in 1984 to found CIDOCUB, the Centro de Investigación y Documentación de la Cultura Barloventeña. With Curiepe as a base, they built a library and archive and even helped support a small museum. Seminars with titles like "Escuela e identidad regional barloventeña," "Existe un pensamiento barloventeño," "Barlovento ante su historia," and "El cimarronaje histórico y cultural de Barlovento" were held throughout the region. In addition, special courses were offered to grammar and high school teachers, presenting them with materials for a new curriculum based on the history and culture of the students they were teaching. This attempt to decentralize the educational system was a radical, innovative strategy, yet in 1989 it began to find additional support from a very unlikely source, the newly elected government of the state of Miranda.[8]

Before this time, each of Venezuela's twenty state governors was appointed by the president and hence directly responsible to him. But in 1988, a new national law gave the people of each state the power to choose their own leaders, and in Miranda, where the region of Barlovento is located, this resulted in the election of a man named Arnaldo Arocha from the opposition party COPEI. COPEI, a Christian Democratic Party somewhat to the right of the ruling ADECO government of Carlos Andrés Pérez, seems to be an unusual partner in the promotion of a regional, Afrocentric culture and education program, but consider its need to expand on a chronically limited power base.[9] As Tomás Ponce, one of the founders of CIDOCUB, cynically put it, "The Copeyanos are a small party. This is a good way for them to gain popular support. And it's very cheap. Popular culture, cultural promotion, hardly costs anything. It's good value." And so the Copeyanos, led by an aggressive director of culture named Pilarica Romero, enlisted the members of CIDOCUB and other organizers from around the state in enacting a program entitled "Historia de nuestra identidad regional."

In addition to a comprehensive plan of investigation which would eventually enable citizens to rewrite the curriculums for the schools in their own communities, an ambitious cultural program was also launched. It called for a series of concerts and festivals, all of which would focus on the local musical

Figure 1. "Ocoyta, primer vuelo de libertad," slave uprising. Photo by Victor Turco.

traditions of Miranda itself. Several of these were to be broadcast after a complex series of eliminatory competitions had been held throughout the state. Also to be broadcast was an experimental play, an epic on the subject of *cimarronismo* to be performed in Mango de Ocoyta, the actual village where the events had occurred. An open-air production with the actors selected from members of the community, the play was to be based on the life of Barlovento's most famous *cimarrón*, Guillermo Rivas, and would be called "Ocoyta, primer vuelo de libertad" [Ocoyta, first flight of liberty]. For many, it would be this event that signaled the numerous contradictions unleashed by this strange marriage between a right-of-center state government and a black, grass-roots community movement.

Of course, some had already decided that the compromise in this new alliance was already too great. Jesús García, author of *Africa en Venezuela* (1990) as well as a founding member of CIDOCUB, decided to break with the group, claiming that the new program was inviting the type of intervention they had banded together to combat. Indeed, the language announcing the formal inauguration of "Historia de nuestra identidad regional" was the same populist rhetoric which many Afro-Venezuelans were claiming had denied their identity. As Governor Arocha stated in a formal press conference in February 1990,

Figure 2. "Ocoyta, primer vuelo de libertad," the funeral of Guillermo Rivas. Photo by Victor Turco.

Figure 3. "Ocoyta, primer vuelo de libertad," women mourning the death of Guillermo Rivas. Photo by Victor Turco.

the aims of the program were "to take back that which unites us, to reconsider that which we have in common, and to revive all that is capable of evoking a collective pride and emotion: identity and popular culture."[10] It was also announced that "Ocoyta, primer vuelo de libertad" would be performed in Mango de Ocoyta in two months' time.

The idea of basing a play on Guillermo Rivas had come from CIDOCUB, and in fact an homage had been held for him just a year before. At that time, Rivas was acknowledged as one of Barlovento's great unsung heroes or, as was claimed, "a regional symbol of our history." Participants asked why a government which invested so much money in erecting monuments to the leaders of the War of Independence refused to erect even a single monument to one of the many *cimarrones* who had been fighting for their independence long before.[11] Guillermo Rivas was a freedom fighter just like Bolívar, Miranda, or Paéz. The slave of a powerful landowner named Marcos Rivas, Guillermo had escaped in 1769, establishing a *cumbe* deep inside the mountains of central Barlovento. Before long, Ocoyta, as the new *cumbe* was called, began to attract other *cimarrones*. Yet unlike other *cumbes*, this one was not content to exist isolated from the rest of colonial Venezuela. Instead, Rivas turned his men into a small guerrilla band. Raiding haciendas and villages throughout the area, they liberated slaves, secured supplies, and, whenever warranted, punished overseers and *hacendados*. For three years they terrorized the coast, until finally, in November 1771, a special army raised with funds from the crown destroyed Ocoyta and killed Guillermo Rivas. As a warning to all future rebels, they cut off his head and one hand and hung them over the entrance to the village of Panaquire (Acosta Saignes 1967: 285–296). It was this story which the present inhabitants of Ocoyta, with the assistance of the Dirección de Cultura, now prepared to tell. As part of the state's new program, Pilarica Romero, director of culture, had hired her own director and crew to write a script and prepare the play.[12]

Many of those who arrived on April 30 to see the play had left Caracas at dawn, traveling for hours in chartered buses or old beat-up Chevies. I had come from Curiepe with Tomás Ponce and his family. We thought we would be late, but the many people already there were still lined up on both sides of the single main street waiting for the play to begin. In fact, the only activity so far was the frantic movement of Pilarica Romero and her crew, all of whom wore white T-shirts with the words "Ocoyta, primer vuelo de libertad" written in red on the front and a message from the governor on the back:

> "La Cultura es lo que une
> a los Pueblos"
> Arnaldo Arocha

Of course, Pilarica was not wearing one of these shirts but rather a flowing white cotton top with an enormous pair of matching harem pants. It was unclear as we all hovered as close to the walls as possible, searching for the smallest bit of shade, why the play was not beginning. Suddenly a helicopter appeared, flew down the main street, and vanished. "The governor," said Tomás Ponce with a big smile. "It must be the governor." Sure enough, ten minutes later a Land Rover came roaring down the main street and stopped at the very center. The door swung open and Arnaldo Arocha, silver-haired and in a cream-colored summer suit, stepped out on the running board and with a bull horn began to speak. He reminded us of the importance of this event, the need to "recover, revive, and revalue," and of course the fact that it was his government, that of COPEI, which had come to the aid of the community, had come to support its culture and its history. He spoke of the glories of Miranda and Barlovento and the search for meaning through cultural identity. Then he uttered his famous phrase, "La cultura es lo que une a los pueblos," waved farewell, and drove away.[13]

Now the rebels took over the town, exploding onto the main street dressed in loincloths and painted like Indians. Wild with rage, they pushed through the crowds and, breaking through the doors of several homes, dragged a group of *hacendados* and their wives out into the street. Once bound, the way slaves had formerly been, they moved their captives off to the town square, the spectators close behind. There, on a specially prepared stage, they conducted a trial, listing all the crimes the slaveowners had committed against their workers. From here the action moved down to the river, where a replica of the original Ocoyta *cumbe* had been set up. With the actors on one side and the audience on the other, the daily rhythms of *cimarrón* life were shown. Women washed clothes in the river, singing and telling stories. Men went off to hunt, prepared game, and talked of rumors and danger. There were ceremonies and dances, a communal meal, and small bands of children playing in the water with canoes and wooden weapons. All the time, the feeling of a cloud rising over this bucolic scene became greater and greater until finally the inevitable happened and a group of soldiers burst through the woods and began to fire.

This was the third act, or, as it said in the program, *estación*. It was called "La destrucción de un Cumbe, el nacimiento de muchos." It began with confusion and terror, the screams of women and children, the shots and commands of the soldiers, the resistance of Guillermo Rivas and his men. Then after a long lull, a figure with his head covered by red cloth was seen crawling up the bed of the river. This was Rivas, who when he finally arrived at the site of the destroyed *cumbe* died in the arms of his weeping comrades. Lifting him onto their shoulders, they carried him in a long procession through all the streets of the village. By now it was already dusk, and as we followed solemnly behind, it was clear to everyone that Rivas was being borne through the streets exactly as a saint in a religious celebration.

When the procession disappeared, there was a long break until finally the actors reappeared on the plaza stage for the fourth and final station, "El Mango de Ocoyta, fruta sabrosa y amarga, 1990." They had changed their clothes and were now dressed in simple blue jeans and T-shirts. Sitting on folding chairs lined up across the stage, each actor now spoke one after another. They talked of their daily lives, of the poverty and difficulty of their existence. They spoke of the marginalization and oppression they felt as black people and as *campesinos*, of the problems in health and education, of the high prices for food and the low prices for their produce. All the time, they emphasized that they were the *cimarrones* of today, the forgotten ones, living in the hills and still resisting the oppression which had not stopped since the days of Guillermo Rivas.

It was a powerful moment, but the final applause was quickly interrupted by Pilarica Romero, who had leapt onto the stage and was now standing with her arms outstretched, calling for silence. The last words, like the first, would be those of her party. "We have shown that the people of Ocoyta can fulfill what they set out to do," she said. "They can complete and carry out whatever they want to. And with our help, they will. And you can continue to count on the support of this government. And on me, Pilarica Romero, personally!" Then there was music and everyone danced.

Two months later "Ocoyta, primer vuelo de libertad" was performed a second time as the opening act in Curiepe's annual San Juan Culture Week. While it has not appeared on television yet, there is talk of another open-air work, this one to be based on the life of Juan del Rosario Blanco, captain of the Free Black Militia and founder of Curiepe.[14] In the meantime, the "Historia de nuestra identidad regional" program continues to move ahead with the same contradictions between national appropriation and a regionally inspired agenda, between the populism that Britto García has called "the language of domination" and an authentic Afro-Venezuelan voice (1990). Yet despite the conflicting interests of each group, the story which those in Barlovento wish to tell is indeed starting to be heard. The recovery of a past based not in slavery and suffering but rather in resistance and dignity is being realized with each procession and performance. Figures such as Guillermo Rivas are being integrated into a new pantheon not simply of Afro-Venezuelan but of national heroes. As the members of CIDOCUB have claimed, it is time to acknowledge that the great contribution of African peoples to the Americas is the struggle for freedom, beginning in 1514 with the very first rebellion in Puerto Rico (García 1990: 51). It is the *cimarrón* then who must be respected as the real precursor in the fight for liberty. Thus, any curriculum which does not place the *cimarrón* at its center is not teaching the true history of Venezuela or honoring its actual cultural and ethnic diversity.

Notes

1. The translation of Negro Primero's famous statement is "General, I've come to tell you good-bye, because I am dying." Negro Primero's real name was Pedro Camejo. Born a slave in the southern plains state of Apure, he originally fought on the side of the Spanish. Upon switching to Paéz's Republican forces in 1816, he quickly rose to the rank of lieutenant in the cavalry. The Battle of Carabobo, in which Camejo was killed, took place on June 24, the Día de San Juan, 1821, and was the decisive victory in the War of Independence against the Spanish. As such it is annually celebrated as a national holiday. The 1990 ceremony observed in Curiepe's Plaza Bolívar has skillfully collapsed several powerful events together, therefore. Not only is it the bicentennial of José Antonio Paéz's birth but it is also the anniversary of Negro Primero's death, the end of the War of Independence, and the beginning of a holiday dedicated to Afro-Venezuelan liberation.

2. The literature on what might be called "the selective uses of the past" has been growing exponentially over the last several years. For examples, see Appadurai (1981), Boissevain (1992), Brow (1990), Chapman, McDonald, and Tonkin (1989), Dirks (1994), Handler (1988), Handler and Linnekin (1984), Hobsbawm and Ranger (1983), Lincoln (1989), and Williams (1977). Also see Guss (1993, 1994a, 1994b, 1995) for specific discussions of how this has occurred not only in the Día de San Juan but in other Venezuelan celebrations as well.

3. It is interesting to note that the same accusations of subversive, unpatriotic behavior have been used against indigenous leaders in Latin America who have attempted to call attention to their plight.

4. For examples of the way the myth of racial democracy has functioned in various areas of Latin America, see Burdick (1992), Hanchard (1994), and Skidmore (1974) for Brazil; Wade (1993) for Colombia; Stutzman (1981) and Whitten (1981, 1986 [1974]) for Ecuador; García (1990) and Wright (1990) for Venezuela; and Guss (1994c) and Whitten and Torres (1992) for a general overview of the continent.

5. While slavery was officially abolished in Venezuela in 1854, it had clearly disappeared as an important social and economic force some time before then. In fact, estimates are that at the time of manumission the number of slaves, most of whom were described as elderly, was down to several thousand (see Acosta Saignes 1967; Lombardi 1974).

6. Small pockets of African-descended communities exist throughout the coastal area of northern Venezuela. However, the strongest concentration of these communities exists in a region known as Barlovento. Located several hours east of Caracas, Barlovento is a 4,500-square-kilometer, pie-shaped piece of land bounded by the Caribbean on the north and mountains on the south and east. While its proximity to Caracas has made it vulnerable to land speculation and

tourism, its major source of income remains that of its small *conucos* (small garden plots) and cacao orchards. The village of Curiepe, with nearly 5,000 inhabitants, has long been considered its spiritual and cultural center.

7. For a detailed discussion of how this recontextualization took place, see Guss (1993).

8. During the presidency of Luis Herrera Campíns, a program known as PASIN (Pensamiento, Acción Social e Identidad Nacional) was briefly instituted in order to give more regional control over school curriculums. However, after the naming of many panels and much heated discussion, the program was abandoned and no concrete action taken. For a brief discussion of PASIN and other government attempts to redirect the education system away from its predominantly modernizing and centralizing mission, see Ortiz (1994).

9. COPEI is an acronym for Comité Pro Elecciones Independiente and ADECO for Acción Democrática. Since the first popular elections in Venezuela in 1948, COPEI has only occupied the presidency twice, once during the government of Rafael Caldera (1968–1973) and a second time under Luis Herrera Campíns (1978–1983).

10. *Nacional,* February 17, 1990.

11. To the best of my knowledge the only monument in the entire country honoring an African-Venezuelan is the bust of Lieutenant Pedro Camejo (Negro Primero), which stands in the Parque Carabobo in Caracas.

12. The person hired to write and direct the play was a well-known theater figure named Fernando Yvosky Morales. Although nationally respected for his work with the Caracas-based Thespis Company, Yvosky had done little regional theater and was completely unacquainted with the Afro-Venezuelan communities of Barlovento. He was able in a very short time, however, to create a theater company from untrained members of the Ocoyta community and stage a play filled with spontaneity and local concerns. He also asserted that Pilarica Romero had not interfered with the production in any way.

13. While the governor's slogan can be translated as "Culture is what unites the people," attacks upon local history and regional culture programs have often claimed that they subvert a cohesive national identity. Yet Arocha's message is less a commitment to multiculturalism than it is a strategy with which to use culture to unite people in support of his party.

14. Since the completion of this article, a second piece focusing on Juan del Rosario Blanco and the founding of Curiepe was completed and performed at the annual San Juan Culture Week. Like the first play, it was written and directed by Fernando Yvosky Morales and acted and staged by local members of the community.

Norman E. Whitten, Jr.

The Ecuadorian Levantamiento Indígena of 1990 and the Epitomizing Symbol of 1992

Reflections on Nationalism,
Ethnic-Bloc Formation, and Racialist
Ideologies

In the mid-1970s I argued for a perspective that could encompass processes called ethnocide and ethnogenesis. These processes were taken to be complementary features in systems of radical change. My focus was on the Canelos Quichua people of Amazonian Ecuador who were among the first indigenous people in the moist tropics of South America to "accept" Christianity (Pierre 1983: 188) and who today sustain a rich indigenous cosmology and cosmogony (see, e.g., Whitten 1976, 1985; Whitten and Whitten 1988, 1993; Sullivan 1988). In the late twentieth century they are also at the forefront of movements of political self-assertion as part of an indigenous nation of native Quichua speakers in ideological alliance with all other indigenous nations. Between mid-April and May 12, 1992, the Canelos Quichua people marched from Amazonian Puyo to Andean Quito to claim legal rights to ancient indigenous territory. I explore the Caminata, as the march was called by indigenous participants, in a larger work which is now in preparation.[1]

This essay continues my interest in ethnogenesis: the public, historical emergence of culture (Hill, introduction; Whitten 1996). To express this in technical language, processes of ethnogenesis subsume both the expansion and condensation of contrast sets among and between human aggregates. These processes manifest all of the structural properties of symbols, as set forth by Victor Turner (1973, 1974), including multivocality, condensation, associational unification, and polarization. Consciousness of an ethnic-bloc formation, as manifest in public discourse focused on us/other (or us/them), is fundamental to ethnogenetic processing of aggregate contrast sets into culturally meaningful systems of social movement.

Ethnogenetic processes are profoundly symbolic and value laden; however we conceive of them, we must always bear in mind that these cultural processes move people to action. To come to grips with ethnogenesis in the late twentieth century, we must strive for a broad frame of reference that includes nation-state nationalist domination and hegemony, ethnic-bloc nationalism as a culturally constitutive process, strife between peoples over ethnic-bloc agency of development and survival, processes of counterhegemony, and enduring structures of racism and racialism. The resulting frame of reference that encompasses these processes should provide a basis for understanding oppositional processing and patterning of discourse formations and social movements. The general purpose of this contribution is to work toward such a framework.

The specific purpose of this essay is to explore, in a preliminary way, dimensions of ideologies of interethnicity manifest in racialist discourse and in collective action. As a conceptual guide to what follows, please consider these two quotations:

> Whatever else ideologies may be—projections of unacknowledged fears, disguises for ulterior motives, phatic expressions of group solidarity—they are, most distinctively, maps of problematic social reality and matrices for the creation of collective conscience. (Geertz 1973: 220)

> Practice . . . has its own dynamics—"a structure of the conjuncture"—which meaningfully defines the persons and the objects that are parties to it. And these contextual values, if unlike the definitions culturally presupposed, have the capacity then of working back on the conventional values. Entailing unprecedented relations between the acting subjects, mutually and by relation to objects, practice entails unprecedented objectifications of categories. (Sahlins 1981: 35)

Nation-State Sociocultural Structure of Ecuador

The Republic of Ecuador in western South America is a modern OPEC/ NOPEC nation that won its independence from colonial rule in 1822 and became in 1830 El Ecuador (the equator). Salient features of its tumultuous history are sustained ethnic clashes and equally sustained domination by a white minority. Mainland Ecuador is divided into three parts, Coast, Sierra (or Andes), and Upper Amazonia (Región Amazónica); the vast majority of its twelve to thirteen million people live in the Coast and Sierra. Ecuador is now, as it has been since at least the early nineteenth century and perhaps since the sixteenth century, in the ongoing process of social reproduction and cultural transformation of strongly represented ethnic categories that signify segments of its ever-expanding population (e.g., Salomon 1986; Whitten 1976, 1981, 1985, 1986 [1974]). To even begin considering these processes, it is necessary to sketch the well-known, highly dynamized concepts of *indio* and *negro* as set against the national hypostasis of supremacy of the *blanco* and ideological redemption of the middle and lower classes and the "masses" through an elitist imagery of *mestizaje*.

Ecuadorian social structure may be considered as a class pyramid within which the siphon economy of center-periphery developmentalist capitalism operates. An oligarchy, known in the upper classes as *la sociedad* and internally as *gente de bién* (or *gente bién*, "good, proper, right kind of" and, by extension, righteous people), constitutes the pinnacle of political power, economic control, and social esteem. The *sociedad* is complemented by what we might call a parallel oligarchy, or *gente de bienes*, those whose position is a direct result of accumulated wealth. All members of these oligarchies self-identify, and are usually identified unconditionally, as *blanco*. Ecuador has a significant "middle class" of professional, commercial, and service people who also generally self-identify as *blanco*. The ways by which they represent other people depend on varied contexts and situations. It is from the elite that the concept of a united body of mixed people, *el mestizaje*, emanates.[2]

Further down the class hierarchy we find people dependent for their livelihood on commercial transactions of varying scale, none of whom self-identify as mestizo, except under exceptional circumstances, but who are politely tagged with various labels meaning "mixed" by those above them or with the labels of the antipodes— *indio, negro*—when discourses reflect interaggregate or interpersonal anger signaling open conflict. Sometimes, under conditions of severe stress, those in superordinate positions use common metonymic associations for the ethnic antipode terminology— *salvaje*, "savage," or *alzado*, "out of control"—in heated discussion reflecting social conflict. Upward mobility is conceived of by those in superordinate positions of power and wealth as a process often called *blanqueamiento*, "whitening," in Ecuador, as in Colombia and Venezuela. Within what some call the "masses" processes of *mestizaje* are often called by the vulgar term *cholificación* in Ecuador, as in Peru and Bolivia.

At the real antipodes of class-status relationships are those aggregates of people represented by power wielders as *negro*, on the one side, and *indio*, on the other. I have noted elsewhere (e.g., Whitten 1985) that, in power politics, the endeavor is made by indigenous leaders to move a discourse about the *indio* potential for revolt directly into the realm of the status-conscious rhetoric of the oligarchies. Spokesmen and spokeswomen of the *negro* potential for insurrection aim their discourse of pending disorder at middle levels of the class and status hierarchy. When discourses of ethnic "disorder" or "revolt" reach the mass media all subtleties of ethnic categorization are dropped in favor of condensed, multivocalic, polarized, and associationally unified representations of human beings. In this process synthetic symbolic units of racialist ideology that emerged in the Americas soon after its European "discovery"—*blanco, negro,* and *indio*—bring forth a predicative link that carries the double act of assertion and denial. I explore this proposition below.

An Ethnic-Enacted Sociocultural Event of National and Regional Salience

My wife, Dorothea Scott Whitten, and I arrived in Quito, Ecuador, Sunday evening, May 27, 1990. We had a research grant from the Wenner-Gren Foundation for Anthropological Research to study the ethnointerpretation of salient features of Canelos Quichua and Achuar Jivaroan culture in the Amazonian region, and we planned to work through materials suggested to us by indigenous people from Pastaza Province. On the day of our arrival, Quichua-speaking indigenous people from various Andean provinces occupied the Catholic church of Santo Domingo (built between 1581 and 1650) in the colonial part of Quito. Just before the occupation the Instituto Nacional de Patrimonio Cultural del Ecuador, which until recently had its offices across the street from the church, announced that under the Plaza Santo Domingo was an ancient indigenous burial site of the first urban Ecuadorians, those who predated the Inca and took the initial steps toward genuine indigenous Quiteño urbanity.

June and July in Andean Ecuador is a period of intense indigenous festival activity. A central feature of indigenous ritual during this period is an ongoing, highly stylized (but sometimes violent) battle for the sacred urban spaces of regional administrative centers (Weismantel 1988; Fine 1991). Additionally, national elections for Congress were upcoming in two weeks, and the indigenous vote was considered to be critical to the fate of contending parties throughout the Sierra and Upper Amazonia.

When the president of the Republic of Ecuador, Dr. Rodrigo Borja Cevallos, refused to enter into a dialogue with those occupying the church or with their clerical spokesmen, eleven indigenous protesters (three women and eight men) announced on Saturday, June 2, that they would begin a hunger strike in the church on Monday.

On Sunday, June 3, Ecuador experienced the first nationwide indigenous uprising in its history.[3] The uprising itself began about 3:00 A.M. in Salasaca (just east of Ambato) and had spread throughout the Sierra by late Sunday night. By Monday morning Riobamba and Latacunga were "occupied" by indigenous people. Ambato was sealed off, and there was no access by major or minor roads between Coast, Sierra, and Upper Amazonia. Word came on the radio at 10:00 A.M. that there was a *paro* (national strike, standstill) and that the president of the Republic would not enter into a dialogue with anyone disrupting national life. By 7:00 P.M. of the same day the nationwide special news network (La Cadena Nacional) of television and radio announced to all Ecuadorians that according to the Confederation of Indigenous Nationalities of Ecuador (Confederación de Nacionalidades Indígenas del Ecuador, hereafter CONAIE) a Levantamiento Indígena (indigenous uprising) had begun and was taking place on a national scale. The national television and radio network also announced that the president of the Republic would be "dialoguing" with the leaders of indigenous organizations as soon as the "strikers" allowed traffic to pass on the major highways (the Panamerican and its branches to Coast and Upper Amazonia) and left the "Sacred Quiteño Temple" (as it was now being called) of Santo Domingo.

By Tuesday things were really getting rough: thirty military and police were held hostage by indigenous people in Riobamba; one indigenous leader was shot and killed in Riobamba by the military; haciendas were ransacked throughout the Sierra and the southwestern coastal region; hacendados were physically abused in a number of ways (one was held without clothes during the subfreezing night). Part of the Ambato market was sacked by indigenous people. In Upper Amazonia road-construction machinery was confiscated, and the only plane to fly that day was also confiscated. The president of the Republic, who had steadfastly refused to dialogue with indigenous people up to noon Tuesday, suddenly agreed to a national dialogue to address the sixteen points of the Acuerdo de Sarayacu (the Sarayacu agreement) presented to him in 1989 by CONAIE as a condition to resume transformed relationships between indigenous Ecuadorians and other Ecuadorians. The points had been drawn up initially in a confrontational setting in the Amazonian region and the president of the Republic had not acted on them, or even mentioned them, for slightly more than a year. These points included (among others):

1. delivery (surrender) without charge of appropriated land to the indigenous nationalities;
2. end of property taxes for indigenous people;
3. cancellation of all debts owed by indigenous people;
4. a constitutional change to designate Ecuador as a multinational, multiethnic state;
5. federal allocation of funds for the indigenous nationalities to allow them to develop their own priorities and to carry them through by sustained indigenous agency;

    6. tax- and duty-free import and export for indigenous artisans and artists;

    7. legalization of indigenous medical and curing practices;

    8. the placing of all archaeological investigations and the wherewithal to carry them out in the hands of CONAIE and affiliated indigenous organizations;

    9. expulsion of the Summer Institute of Linguistics;

    10. recognition of the Acuerdo de Sarayacu and implementation of the points of the *acuerdo*.[4]

Discourse Structures, Reference Points, and Interethnic Salience

Throughout our three and a half months in Ecuador in 1990, the most salient features of indigenous discourse involved the Levantamiento Indígena,[5] which came to be called *el alzamiento indio* by most of the media commentators and by political analysts. The contrast in terminology is instructive. Whereas *levantamiento* carries the meanings of conscious raising and sublimity, and even rebirth, as well as insurrection, *alzamiento* means unruly behavior, as well as insurrection. There is no sense of consciousness in the term *alzamiento*; loss of control is implied, and the term may be used for animal behavior. Indigenous people perceived in their *levantamiento* (or, in Quichua, *jatari*, though it was in Spanish discourse that the macrocategories were utilized and contrasted) a raising of culture to a new level; those using the term *alzamiento* saw indigenous peoples as "lowering" their cultural potential to that bordering on animality, and they saw and described indigenous behavior as "like sheep." An *alzamiento* implies that, by definition, the indigenous peoples do not have the cultural potential to engage in a *levantamiento*; therefore, they are *fuera de su lugar*, "out of their proper place," or *indios alzados*, "unruly Indians."

    For indigenous people the fundamental public pronouncement in the Andes and Amazonia was "¡Después de 500 años de dominación, autodeterminación indígena en 1992!" [After 500 years of domination, indigenous self-determination in 1992!]. 1992 was chosen as the epitomizing symbol of a raising up, in a cultural as well as political-economic sense, in clear and confrontational opposition to the elitist rhetoric of the quincentennial celebratory activities to be undertaken in that year to commemorate the European "discovery" and conquest of ancient indigenous territory and the establishment of hegemony over contemporary indigenous people. That territory included, according to indigenous discourse reflecting on recent scientific and humanistic pronouncements, the colonial center of Quito, which was also taken to be the precolonial and pre-Incaic center of indigenous civilization. As the polarities increased between nonindigenous ideologues in very active and sustained public discourse (which was reported daily in newspapers, magazines, and tabloids and on radio and television), black spokesmen and spokeswomen of Esmeraldas and Carchi Provinces also joined the national debate through the communicative vehicle of *négritud*, a concept developed in the Francophonic Caribbean and recently adopted by some leaders in the Ecuadorian *comunidades negras* directly from Colombian racialist politics. The term *mestizo* is not one normally heard in intraindigenous discourse or in indigenous discourse directed to nonindigenous audiences. But during and after the Levantamiento Indígena it was commonly used by indigenous and black spokespersons to refer to cultural barriers to ethnic, social, economic, and political advancement.

In the rhetoric of the Levantamiento Indígena, including as it did the central postulates of *autodeterminación indígena* and *autogestión indígena*, and in the rhetoric of *négritud, liberación de las comunidades negras,* and *liberación del pueblo negro,* discourses that could be described as racialist continued (and continue) to swirl and eddy within the Republic of Ecuador. From nonindigenous and nonblack standpoints, the media and political analysts stepped up the rhetoric centering on the conjoined concepts of *el problema indio* and *el problema negro.* As such, commentators on both sides of the escalating confrontational discourse presented rich racialist imagery in a paradigmatic way: mention in any context of any of the key racialist signifiers such as *blanco, negro, indio,* mestizo, among others, automatically evoked imagery of the opposites and the syntagmatic associations with these opposites (see also for background Whitten 1981, 1985; Fine 1991; Weismantel 1988).

The field of racialist discourse in this modern Latin American nation, in other words, became central to both nation-state nationalist discourse and ethnic-bloc nationalist discourse, just as the denial of such discourse became located in the same centralities. For example, the president of the Cámara de Agricultura del Primer Sector, Ignacio Pérez, said that "los indígenas están cayendo en el nazismo de la raza pura" [the indigenes are falling into the Nazism of pure race], to which the president of CONAIE, Cristobal Tapuy, responded, "Quien habla de racista es el primer racista" [he who speaks of racism (racist) is the primary (or first) racist].[6]

Let us consider for a moment the concept of *el problema* as it is used in Ecuador. Mary Weismantel (1988) has recently argued that *problema* in Ecuador suggests the concept elaborated upon by Victor Turner as a cultural "arena," "the concrete settings in which cultural paradigms become transformed into metaphors and symbols with reference to which political power is mobilized [and] in which there is a trial of strength between influential paradigm bearers" (1974: 16). " 'Social dramas' represent the phased process of their contestation." A social arena has the following explicit characteristics:

(1) a framework, a "setting for antagonistic interaction aimed at arriving at a publicly recognized decision"; (2) "an explicit frame; nothing is left merely implied" (Turner 1976: 134); (3) "a scene for the making of a decision . . . There is a moment of truth when a major decision is made, even if it is the decision to leave things temporarily undecided" (Turner 1976: 135).

An illustration of this *problema* as arena within a larger setting of charged symbolic fields occurred in the Gold Room (Salón Amarillo, also called the Reception Hall) of the National Palace on August 22, 1990. There, in the well-appointed room where foreign diplomats are received by the president, the president of the Republic of Ecuador received a *planteamiento histórico* (a document in the form of a proposal with the implication of history in the making [Quichua, *cayamanda*]) from the regional indigenous organization of indigenous peoples of Pastaza (Organización de Pueblos Indígenas de Pastaza, OPIP).

Prior to the meeting with indigenous leaders from Sierra and Upper Amazonia, the president had met with his unofficial but very prominent advisor on indigenous affairs, Alfonso Calderón Cevallos, who then left the building. Then President Borja met with the assembled indigenous leaders. There followed a public confrontation carried live on all the national news channels (La Cadena Nacional). The president was clearly angry and quite authoritative about a serious legal and political breach that he and his technical advisor on indigenous affairs perceived to be caused by the explicit language of the document presented to him.

The basis of the perceived indigenous breach of national sovereignty was especially evident in the third chapter of the report submitted on the territorial rights of the Quichua, Shuar, Achuar, and Shiwiar people of Pastaza Province. The key terms singled out were *autodeterminación, autogestión,* and *autonomía* of the indigenous people of Pastaza Province, together with the proposition of *autogobierno* and claim to the wealth of their territory, including all rights to the revenues to be reclaimed from the exploitation of all subsurface deposits, including petroleum.

It appeared that the president, on the righteous nation-state nationalist side, and the Amazonian indigenous people, who seemed to call for an ethnic-bloc nationalist state in Pastaza Province, were not previously aware of each other's positions. But a little probing reveals that a key role in this confrontation was played by Alfonso Calderón Cevallos, first cousin of the president (their mothers are sisters), informal but highly influential technical advisor to the president on indigenous affairs and informal technical advisor to OPIP and the Confederation of Indigenous Peoples of Amazonian Ecuador (CONFENAIE) during the writing of the indigenous proposal.

Much of the "indigenous rhetoric" that so infuriated the president was taken directly from Calderón's own well-known book, *Reflexiones en las culturas orales.*[7] Moreover, Alfonso Calderón had been at the confrontational meeting in 1989 in Upper Amazonia when the controversial Acuerdo de Sarayacu was drawn up, and he had worked with the president of CONFENAIE, Luis Vargas Canelos, on the very document presented to the president by OPIP.

Prior to his election as president of the Republic of Ecuador, Rodrigo Borja Cevallos had stated in public campaign speeches that the nation-state of Ecuador was most clearly one of "multiple nationalities, multiple cultures, and multiple ethnic peoples" (Serrano 1993). The rhetoric of Ecuador as a multinational, multiethnic state emanated directly from the espoused ideology of the then-aspiring presidential hopeful, Rodrigo Borja Cevallos. One finds the very same rhetoric in all five editions of the small but influential book of his first cousin, Alfonso Calderón Cevallos.

We can conclude from this that elitist rhetoric (as manifested by Borja at the presidential pinnacle of power of the ethnically entitled white *gente de bién*) is not transformable or transferable to the indigenous (or black) antipode of discourse of the indigenous social movements. Borja's own rhetoric could not be used, as the elite and wealthy saw the matter, in the polarized arena wherein indigenous discourse appropriated a paradigm of liberation from the charged field of nation-state nationalist political ideology. Borja, prior to his election, engaged in a persuasive discourse of ethnic gratuities; his appropriated rhetoric, as part of ethnogenetic processing by indigenous people from Amazonian Ecuador, was repulsed with a presidential self-righteous fury born in and backed by nation-state power, domination, and hegemony.

For their part, the indigenous people from Pastaza Province perceived a serious breach within the National Palace, a breach of social contract inscribed in the enduring relationships of kinship and bureaucracy. They had worked on that critical chapter with future historic implications for more than two years, grounding it in the principles set forth in *Reflexiones en las culturas orales*. Indeed, sections of this history-making document are taken word for word from Calderón's book, with only specific geographic locations inserted.

This dramaturgical event of the televised confrontation in the presidential Gold Room, as an Ecuadorian *problema*, and the terminal incident reflected in the president's public negative reaction to chapter 3 of the *planteamiento histórico* brought negotiations between indigenous people and representatives of the central government to an end. This event and public reaction indicate that Ecuador is characterized by a system of vertical articulation of conflict that complements that of horizontal articulation of conflict. By this I mean that schisms at the highest levels of government ramify systemically to grass-roots sociopolitical movements. In the process of downward ramification, the liberal-leftist rhetoric of ethnogratuities confronts, at the grass-roots and at the ethnic antipodes, the same symbols. But these symbols move people to action as an ethnogenetic counterrhetoric, thereby feeding the process of oppositional processing and contributing to the paradigms that become increasingly rigid in the charged field of racialist discourse.

When, it seems, the pinnacle spokesman for nationalist pride, propriety, and righteousness, the president of the republic, encounters in indigenous discourse the familiar conflict generated in his own discourse (or that of Calderón Cevallos, his cousin and advisor on indigenous affairs) about democratic reform and recognition of multiple nationalities within a nation-state, severe conflict between his office and that of the indigenous nationalities is again sparked.

The charged fields of cultural paradigms electrifying Ecuador in 1990 that influenced the oppositional processing within clear-cut sociopolitical arenas of conflict were denied to indigenous people. In turn, it was precisely to those fields of symbolic- and metaphoric-laden discourse that indigenous people turned. The replication of a system of oppositions across the antipodes of ethnic and class awareness in Ecuador in 1990, as in previous years (see Whitten 1981) and in the present, continues to motivate systems of ethnogenesis just as it motivates increased forms of domination and hegemony.

Ideologies of racialism that spawn such vertical articulation force unending oppositional processing between the white spokesmen for one nation and the indigenous and black spokesmen and spokeswomen for ethnic freedom. Such ideological forces undergird discourses in many Latin American nations. Such discourses have led to hemispherewide paradigmatic imagery focused on the highly charged and evocative epitomizing symbol of "1492–1992" (e.g., Rivera Cusicanqui 1991).

Culture and Agency

Between 1990 and 1991 the symbol of 1992 and the praxis of the Levantamiento Indígena in Ecuador conjoined discourse structures from the highest level of Ecuadorian society to the dynamic antipodes of blackness and indigenousness. The processes this essay has considered, though illustrated by events in Ecuador, should allow us to think more broadly about indigenous and black autogenous "uprising" ongoing throughout the Western Hemisphere. Ideologies of racialism that have framed discourse in many Latin American nations have led to hemispherewide paradigmatic imagery focused, through 1992, on the highly charged and evocative epitomizing symbol of 1992. What is unfolding subsequent to the passing of 1992, and its international prolongation during the 1993 International Year of Indigenous People, is beyond the scope of this essay. The foci in 1993 changed, but the ethnogenetic processes discussed are expressed in myriad public performances and in countless genres with common paradigmatic underpinnings.

What I would like to do now is reflect on culture, ethnicity, race, domination, hegemony, resistance, and related concepts that emerge in considering the highly charged epochal epitome of the 1992 "celebration" of people throughout the Americas of the "discovery" or "encounter" of the New World by Cristóbal Colón. Colón, as the "Bearer of Christ" and the "Admiral of the Ocean Sea," insisted to his death that he had arrived in India in 1492. The black and indigenous perspectives on 1492 focused on an epochal event nearly 500 years ago when all native people were tagged with the image *indios* with lands to be conquered and commodified and souls to be appropriated and turned into ecclesiastical commodities.

The commercial conquest of the Americas itself, stemming from this focal ideological event, was undertaken by trafficking in *negros bozales* (black bondsmen) from the *negrería* (black land) brought by *negreros* (slavers in black people) (see Rout 1976; Hyatt and Nettleford 1995; Forbes 1993; Whitten and Torres 1992, in press). As such, the epitomizing symbol of 1992 signaled a public, transnational cultural contest between the celebration of European hegemony for the *blancos* and the spontaneity of a rising up of indigenous and black people and a raising of indigenous and black cultures with a new imaging of a future for a new millennium.

Let us turn again to "Culture," not so much for disciplinary reasons but because it is a tremendously important concept to indigenous and black people throughout the Americas. Clifford Geertz tells us that "cultural phenomena should be treated as significative systems posing expositive questions" (1983: 3). To this let us add the definition recently deployed effectively by Greg Urban: "culture is localized in concrete, publicly accessible signs, the most important of which are actually occurring instances of discourse" (1991: 1). So let us begin with *cultura*. In Spanish, the feminine article *la*, as in *la cultura*, elevates the concept to something refined, European, civilized. When one goes to an expensive opera in Bogotá, Colombia, for example, wearing fine clothes and speaking in a refined manner, one is participating in *la cultura* and one is *muy culto*, very civilized. The *gente de bién* (or *gente bién*), Ecuador's old social oligarchy, regard themselves as "the most civilized." Today, in most Latin American societies, to affix *cultura* to blackness or Indianness without the article *la* is to demean traditions and lifeways to something vernacular or popular, worthy of study by folklorists but insignificant in the processes leading to higher and higher levels of Latin American civilization.

Still worse, *cultura indígena* or *una cultura indígena, cultura negra* or *una cultura negra* is something to be viewed as unrefined, inchoate, confused, fragmented, stagnant, and static. One studies *una cultura popular* or *una cultura vernacular* to find something of antiquity retained and an enormous amount of culture lost. During the 1990 Levantamiento Indígena in Ecuador indigenous people·insisted on the concept of *las nacionalidades indígenas* (the indigenous nationalities) as the appropriate designation of representation for their collectivity. In each indigenous language the concept of "our culture" (e.g., *ñucanchi yachai, ñaupa yachai* in Quichua) is embedded—by a juxtaposition of signs—within the Spanish concept of *la Nación. La Nación* implies culture, sovereignty, and viable territoriality. *Las nacionalidades* is an older term of respect for indigenous cultures ("high civilizations") of the Americas. Attributes of *las nacionalidades* included differentiation of humanity according to language and territory; shared status in terms of exploitation beginning, ideologically, with the arrival of Cristóbal Colón in 1492; and a continuous strain toward hemispherewide indigenous cultural advancement truncated by *mestizaje* thereafter.

A hemispherewide black movement, similar to the indigenous one, began in a centralized fashion at the First Congress of Black Culture in the Americas held in Cali, Colombia, in 1977 (which I attended) and continued through the Fourth Congress held in 1991 in Paris. At all four congresses black people, well aware of the power of racist symbols and stereotypes, insisted (and insist) on the article *la*, as *la cultura negra*, for black cultures: black, sophisticated, existential, experiential, and adaptable—entwined processes of tradition, history, and modernity moving toward higher and higher levels of black civilization in the Americas.

Geertz's concept of cultural phenomena as something to be treated as "significative systems posing expositive questions" can be combined with one derived by the historian Daniel J. Boorstin (1983) that resonates well with the insistence of Latin American indigenous and black spokesmen and spokeswomen for *las nacionalidades indígenas* and *la cultura negra*: "'Culture' (from Latin cultus for 'worship') originally meant reverential homage. Then it came to describe the practices of cultivating the soil, and later it was extended to the cultivating and refinement of mind and manners. Finally, by the nineteenth century *'culture' had become a name for the intellectual and aesthetic side of civilization*" (Boorstin 1983: 647, emphasis mine).

Indigenous and/or black culture, as I am coming to understand the polarization of the signification of confrontational discourse, is that which is worthy of reverential homage by indigenous people and by black people within their communities, regions, and nation-states; it is also the means by which the cultivation and refinement of mind and manners has been nurtured, developed, and adapted in the New World for nearly 500 years. It is an aesthetic side of the raising of civilization which may be found explicitly or implicitly in any domain or context of social life. Survival itself, as in the cultivation of the soil, figuratively and literally, is a critical concept contributing to the sense and reference of indigenous culture (undergirding the concept of *nacionalidades indígenas*) and black culture (undergirding the concepts of *négritud* and *las comunidades negras*).

Black culture and indigenous culture, as such concepts are manifest in practical and spiritual conflict, are characterized by reverential webs of signification that are illuminating to black people and to indigenous people in any given time and place, and through them to others who will read, reflect, and think about ethnic-bloc formations and ethnic transformations and reproductions in settings of white domination. This concept of culture is also reflected in, and contributes to, subsistence and commercial survival strategies and is adaptive to a myriad of structures of domination encountered and overcome in the Americas.

In coming to understand racialist rhetoric in Ecuador and elsewhere, one finds that the same terminology transcends the polarities in the symbolic fields where paradigms develop and are elaborated. For the moment, I would like to discuss some relatively invariant postulates of racialist discourse in charged political settings, separating the macrosymbols of "race" as they seem to emerge in nation-state nationalist discourse and in ethnic-bloc nationalist discourse.

Nationalism, Ethnic-Bloc Formation, and Ideologies of Racial Cultures

Let us begin with the idea of nation-state nationalism. Although clearly rife with ambiguity, the term refers to the identity of the majority of people within a nation-state with the republic, nation, or national society as the primary reference group. A nation-state must, above all else, retain all power of sovereignty and all power of territoriality. Ideologies of nation-state nationalism are located within the cultural space of nation-state control. In Latin America and the Caribbean in the 1990s we find two complementary and one competing nationalist ideology of racial culture, often denoted by one of these symbols: racial mixture, Indianism, blackness. I present each of them briefly, by reference to the terms in the language with which they are most commonly associated (i.e., *négritude*, in French, which has become a Spanish term, *négritud*), but always with a focus on the ways by which they are currently used as signs and symbols in Spanish.

Mestizaje, the ideology of racial intermingling, is an explicit master symbol in all Latin American countries. *Indigenismo* is a dual concept reflecting, on the one hand, a search for the creative dimensions of nationalism through the symbolism of an indigenous past and, on the other hand, a sociopolitical-literary symbol that conveys the mood of remorse over the living conditions of contemporary "acculturated Indians." Both of these meanings seem to run through American Romanticism and American Realism (e.g., Sacoto 1967). The ideology of *mestizaje* embraces both senses of *indigenismo* (e.g., Bourri-caud 1962; Pitt-Rivers 1967, 1973). Indeed, *indigenismo* may be thought of as a key support for the exclusion of contemporary native peoples from nation-state affairs. A related component of *mestizaje* (*blanqueamiento*) is discussed below because it is not an explicit component of nationalist ideology.

Négritude is a concept that denotes the positive features of blackness among people classed as, or self-identifying as, black. This specific term was intro-duced into French literary usage in 1947 by the black Martiniquan poet Aimé Césaire (Coulthard 1962: 58; see especially Trouillot 1990: 124–136). It pro-vides a single term by which to assert the positive power inherent in, and the positive aesthetic forces of, "blackness," leaving many avenues open for the definition of what and who is, and what and who is not, to be considered black. Within the Americas only Haiti has adopted an explicit nationalist ide-ology of *négritude*, and the literary and artistic roots of this concept provide the basis for Césaire's and others' (such as Frantz Fanon) literary and political creativity (Coulthard 1962: 58–70).

Nationalist ideologies develop not only symbols of internal oneness based on concepts of racial classification but also ideas of oppositions using the criterion of "cultural exaggeration" as discussed by James Boon (1982). It is perhaps the case that, throughout the Americas, the *mestizaje/négritude* contrast represents a symbolic opposition reflecting cultural exaggeration of ideologically conjoined social constructs of race, civilization, nationalist pat-rimony, and social movement. There is, perhaps, no room in explicit nation-state nationalist discourse for *autodeterminación étnica* or for *autogestión ét-nica* except as an elitist political ploy.

Let us now turn for a moment from nationalist ideologies with key racialist symbols to ethnic-bloc nationalist formation. The New Nations program at the University of Chicago turned up information that sustained ethnic-bloc nationalist formation characterized the consolidation of nation-state nation-alism (Geertz 1973: 234–310). An ethnic bloc constitutes a conscious refer-ence group for those who share recurrent processes of self-identification.

Ethnic-bloc formation is a political-economic manifestation of cultural ethnogenesis. Ethnic blocs, and expressions of ethnic-bloc nationalism, may be based on any criteria such as common residence, language, tradition, and custom. Indeed, the bases for bloc identity may sort of slip and slide around the criteria themselves, as the bloc itself becomes increasingly strong. The concept "bloc" is taken from politics (as in a political bloc); whatever its bases, power of identity, power of representation, and power of discourse structuring are crucial. Such powers come into being when ethnic exclusion takes place, as when indigenous people or black people are ethnically disfranchised from full participation in the dominant society.

Such powers within ethnic blocs also derive from a collective, inner sense of the oneness of a people, in contradistinction to nation-state racialist hegemony. The two generative power sources are related, but the nature of such a dynamic relationship requires careful, empirical study. Ethnic-bloc nationalist formation may be seen as a process of contra-nation-state nationalism, and the symbolic processes of ethnic-bloc formation seem similar to, or the same as, those identified as fundamental in processes of nation-state nationalist consolidation. The relationships created by these generative powers permeate the political-economic fabric of any social order. Ethnic-bloc formation, and hence ethnogenesis, in other words, is as international in scope as it is local in origin.

One would anticipate that black-based ethnic-bloc formations would use the ideology of *négritude* and, in so doing, be perceived as a threat to nationalist sovereignty and nationalist territoriality. This certainly seems to be the case in Venezuela, Guyana, and Colombia (e.g., Wright 1990; Williams 1993; Friedemann and Arocha 1995; Wade 1993). In the processes of ethnic-bloc nationalist formation in the Americas, three master symbols of racialist ideology emerge, the latter two of which are potentially complementary: phenotypical, cultural, or ethnic lightening (or whitening); black liberation; and indigenous self-determination.

Blanqueamiento refers to the processes of becoming increasingly acceptable to those classified as and/or self-identified as "white" or "light." This is an ethnic strategy (however unconscious it may be) now coterminous with socioeconomic advancement governed by the ideology of "development" that depends upon socioeconomic and political assistance and loans from the developed (i.e., highly industrialized, high-energy-dependent) countries. *Blanqueamiento* essentially accepts the implicit hegemonic rhetoric of the United States with regard to white supremacy and often blames those classed as black people and indigenous people for the worsening state of the nation.

Ethnic or cultural lightening may occur as an ideological feature among people self-identifying as black (e.g., Wade 1993; Williams 1993). One example of the former would be in nineteenth-century Haitian literary circles, wherein the positive attributes of blackness (via Egypt and the Sudan) were juxtaposed to French civilization. *Blanqueamiento*, an enduring ethnic-bloc complement to the nationalist ideology of *mestizaje*, is an ephemeral feature of enduring *négritude*. To the extent that people in the Americas accept, however implicitly, standards of whiteness as attached to "developmental potential," the phenomenon of hegemony may be said to exist.

Négritude may express the same sets of meanings in ethnic-bloc rhetoric that it does in nation-state rhetoric, as discussed above. Indeed, the Haitian ethnologist Jean Price-Mars (1928), during the extended U.S. occupation of Haiti from 1915 to 1934, conscientiously turned to the voices of Haitians for concepts of blackness, Africanness, and being Haitian. Price-Mars sought to liberate nationalist ideology from its European Francophonic bases in "whitening," where the powerful, literate elite of Haiti saw themselves as mulatto (analogous here to *mestizo*; for an extended analysis of such terminology see Trouillot 1990; Whitten and Torres in press). *Négritude*, and its implicit and explicit cognates, from the writing of Price-Mars (1928) onward, must be considered to have two senses: in its nationalist sense it may or may not reflect a process of lightening, but in its ethnic-bloc sense it is profoundly populist and rejecting of nonblackness as a criterion for sophisticated self-awareness (see especially Trouillot 1990: 124–136).

Autodeterminación indígena is predicated on the assertion that indigenous people, who were deposed and disfranchised by the Euramerican conquest of the Americas, must articulate to New World nation-states in modern, indigenous ways which they themselves will determine. It is a proclamation of indigenous sovereignty and territoriality. *Autogestión* adds indigenous agency as the central ethnogenetic dynamic to sovereignty and territoriality. This multivocalic, condensed symbol of liberation (self-determination) specifically looks to contemporary indigenous cultures in multiple communities and societies across the Americas. It rejects the literary-based ideological components of *indigenismo*, just as early-twentieth-century ethnographers such as Price-Mars in Haiti and Fernando Ortiz in Cuba turned away from elite academician definitions of national culture and sought out the voices of the culturally rich black poor in both urban and rural areas. Today indigenous self-determination appeals to black people in many areas. *Négritude* and *autodeterminación indígena* are complementary constructs of ethnic-bloc ideology, both of which are contrary to *mestizaje* as nation-state nationalist ideology and ethnic-bloc nationalist ideology (see Whitten and Torres in press).

To return to nationalism and racialist ideology for a moment, in the non-Anglophonic world today, Peru-Ecuador-Colombia-Venezuela, on one side, and Haiti, on the other, constitute polar nationalist opposites. In the former nations the colonial dream of overcoming the barriers of racialist classification linked to economic opportunities became transformed into a nationalist, democratic ideology of racial mixture. In the latter, blackness inundated a formative New World gene pool to create the first self-liberated democratic island republic in the Americas with collective, self-conscious roots in its African and European past.

Structures of Domination

Nationalism represents, for indigenous and black people in nation-states governed by any racialist ideology, a structure of domination (e.g., Dolgin, Kemnitzer, and Schneider 1977). Structures of domination intensify culturally by simple rhetorical devices. The first of these is simile. When a person says, "S/he sure doesn't look like a *negro*" [El (ella) no parece como negroide(a)] or "S/he sure doesn't talk like an Indian" [Seguro que el (ella) no habla como indio(a)], a powerful statement has been made that some other people will "look like" someone who "is" black or "talk like" someone who is "Indian." The "like" (*como*), in other words, signals a conscious or unconscious awareness that there are agreed-upon commonalities or properties that attach symbolically to the salient cultural representations of *indio* and *negro*. Put another way, the symbolic denial, by simile, of an individual's adherence to dimensions of a putative racial category is a powerful assertion of the enduring existence of the synthetic category itself.

Metaphor is the second rhetorical strategy, as when someone says, "S/he is Indian"; "S/he is black"; "S/he is mestizo[a]"; "S/he is mulatto[a]." With metaphor the person, class, aggregate, group, community, or region is tagged with the cognitive and symbolic associations of a nonwhite or culturally "darkened" resemblance. These symbolic associations constitute properties of Indianness and blackness that convey meaning. Metaphor concretizes properties that are categorical and provides the rhetorical wherewithal to all people to label other people with such properties, as though physical features, genealogy, and heritage have some real correspondences among people, representations, and categories. People who "are" *negro* or *indio*, in other words, are signified by qualities and resemblances that belong to signifiers that stem from racialist and racist cultural constructs. These constructs, to repeat, carry the twin predications of affirmation and denial in public discourse.

Structures of domination are given form, meaning, and power of repression by the rhetorical strategy of reification. Reification occurs when people consciously read symbolic, religious, moral, or ideological properties into categorical social relationships, as though these properties actually exist. In a chapter on "Humanity and Animality," Edmund Leach put it this way: "The naming of relationships marks the beginnings of moral sanctions" (1982: 107). This is the process of signification wherein meaning is constructed by strengthening the relationship between the signified (individuals, aggregates, groups, or categories of people) and the signifier (cognitive and symbolic associations that constitute the properties of representations and categories).

When nation-state nationalist ontology and ideology reify racial mixture not only as an ideal but as a reality, they create objectifications of outsidership (*los otros* as opposed to *nosotros*) among indigenous and black populations within the nation-state. People in communities and regions so objectified and morally sanctioned by undesirable attributes self-consciously reflect on such reifications and attempt to overcome the barriers imposed by racialist structures of domination. This involves symbolic as well as practical dimensions of actions of moral inversion in society. The result is a reordering of visions that people hold of humanity and spirituality in the world perceived and in the world imagined. When such actions spark social movements of self-liberation and cultural resistance, they may be said to raise the issue of nation-state national*ist* domination to one of transcendentalist ethnic-bloc national*ist* formation.

In the process of formation and strengthening of structures of domination and the inevitable forces of resistance to them, we must consider the phenomenon of hypostasis. This concept, which entered the English language in 1529, literally means "that which stands under"; that is, a support or foundation (for other concepts). If we take structure to be a set of relatively invariant reference points that remain after a series of transformations has occurred, hypostatized structures are those that are taken to be enduring realities. They are structures with deep historical underpinnings and supports that unite concepts of humanity and divinity and separate both from animality (see Leach 1982). In the ethnic formation of New World structures of European domination, three relatively invariant reference points were the categories of the white (European) in superior relationship over the black (African) and the native ("Indian").

When a structure of domination—such as a pyramidal class structure of a given nation-state with white people on top, masses of pluralized mestizo, mulatto, and white people in the middle, and poor, pluralized black, mestizo, and indigenous people on the bottom—is assumed to be an unchanging, static reality by people at the pinnacle and middle of the structure, then the full power of bureaucracy is wielded to "solve the black problem," find new ways to overcome the "Indian problem," and accelerate the processes of *mestizaje*. While such solutions to hypostatized problems are being sought, national, regional, and local political, social, and economic resources flow to the top, are partially redistributed in the middle, and deprive those on the bottom of the class-ethnic hierarchy. This is a process of reproduction of underdevelopment of Fourth World people in underdeveloping Third World nations and the production of increased distance between Third World poverty and First World wealth (see Worsley 1984; Comaroff 1985).

Processes of ethnogenesis flow from the structures of oppression and also subvert such structures. In the processes of downward flow from elite, *blanco* control, through those represented by upper echelons as striving toward whiteness, and in the processes of populist and ethnic subversion, the paradigm of *blanco, negro, indio,* and mestizo that emerged 500 years ago in the Americas is strengthened.

Within any given structure of domination, we seem to find that those in power endeavor to maintain hegemony over those immediately below them by blaming those on the bottom (especially ethnically distinct indigenous and black people) for the lowly "undeveloped" condition of regions and communities which can be easily designated by reified ethnic terminology. The hypostatized "reality" is often inscribed in developmental reports, plans, and educational materials and in scholarly publications. At the same time, this symbolic but negatively concretized "reality" is challenged by powerful, dynamic counterideologies and social movements that seek to spark recognition of the falsity of the hypostatic ideological racialist structures.

Ethnic-bloc formation undertaken under the ideological aegis of *négritude* and/or *autodeterminación indígena* strongly illustrates the challenges mounted in the late twentieth century to false yet hypostatized "reality" that has been with the New World since 1492. No wonder, then, that many black people (and mestizo people) in Latin America joined their indigenous congeners in the cry, "¡Después de 500 años de dominación, autodeterminación en 1992!"

Processes of Liberation

The Levantamiento Indígena that took place in Ecuador in 1990 may be understood, at least in part, as a process of liberation from structures of domination that are bundled into the epitomizing symbol of 1492. Understanding processes of liberation involves us with dominance formations that constitute structures of power. Structures of domination and the ways by which class, ethnicity, and political blocs coalesce, change, and are expressed, maintained, and transformed are dynamic and volatile. While hegemony may come into being, it is extremely difficult to maintain, for people are conscious actors attuned to their life situations.

When discussing structures of domination I introduced the idea that people are signified by signifiers as they become parts of categorical webs of signification in modern nations. Rhetoric attendant on the Ecuadorian Levantamiento Indígena, which rapidly reached the national congress and the office of the president of the republic, Dr. Rodrigo Borja Cevallos, contained a rich embodiment of enlightened and insightful indigenous representation of the entwined histories, presents, and futures of conquest, domination, and self-liberation. It reminds us of Michael Taussig's phrase, "From the represented shall come that which overturns the representation" (1987: 135). This statement relates directly to the idea of people remaking the world and being in a world refashioned from the conquered one that the European "discovery" or "encounter" of 1492 began.

In the concept of the unity of *las nacionalidades indígenas*, within Ecuador and across the Americas, one finds the embodiment of the transcendental concept of being indigenous as *bound to survival for nearly 500 years*. The ultimate transcendence, or transformation, or cultural metamorphasis, is to reproduce, in an entirely new manner, indigenous unity of the coming twenty-first century.

In July 1990, while the president of Ecuador was still engaged in public "dialogue" with indigenous spokesmen and spokeswomen, a Pan-Indigenous Congress was held in Quito. The theme of the congress, which had been established a year before in Bogotá, Colombia, was manifest in its title: Primer Encuentro Continental: 500 Años de Resistencia India (First Continental Encounter: 500 Years of Indian Resistance). The unity resulting from the sustained resistance was expressed as a reuniting of the condor and the eagle, symbolizing the union of the inner essence of Latin American indigenous spirituality, bound to shamanism, with the outer essence of North American indigenous spirituality, bound to public indigenous ceremony. The key to the unity lies in the collective sense of indigenous healing of foreign-inflicted illness. The identity of the power to heal serves as one of many reverential symbols worthy of macro-indigenous identity. This is an aesthetic quality that people self-identifying with human indigenousness find and appreciate across the boundaries of specific communities, regions, nations, and traditions.

Blackness at the Primer Congreso de la Cultura Negra de las Américas in Cali in 1977, and at the three subsequent congresses of black culture, also referred (and continues to refer) to that epitomizing symbol worthy of a macro-identity to which communities, regions, and even nations could aspire. Such a referent is also transcendental; it comes from black people in black communities but it is the polar opposite of popular culture. In the United States, and elsewhere in the Americas, the epitomizing symbol of blackness in its transcendental character is expressed as "soul." This is an aesthetic quality that people self-identifying with human blackness and/or with black cultures find and appreciate across the boundaries of specific communities, regions, nations, and traditions (Whitten and Torres in press).

1492–1992 as Epitomizing Symbol

The tripartite ideological structure of white power and moral righteousness, a coverlet of *mestizaje* to cloak flagrant racism, and the enduring praxis of forced *indio/negro* subservience to the church, state, and secular holders of land and people was established in the early sixteenth century in Europe and in the Americas. The epitomizing symbol "1492" expresses the inherent evil of this foreign hegemony to black and indigenous people in the Western Hemisphere.

For a while, the symbol "1992" represented the movement to counter this evil, to raise blackness and indigenousness to new counterhegemonic levels of civilized discourse in multiple languages within relatively old modern states. These nation-states, of which Ecuador is clearly one, are constituted of complementary and contradictory ideological processes of transformation and reproduction that reveal, in their sparked interethnic oppositional rhetoric, a concern with emergent and traditional "culture" as sets of structures of conjuncture. The emergence of cultures within and between these sets fits well the definition of ethnogenesis offered by Hill in his introduction to this book. It is my intent to complement his introduction and the other contributions with this extended set of reflections and provide a comprehensive fresh beginning to understand cultural processes of ethnogenesis that intensify as the year 2000 approaches.

Jean Comaroff (1985: 196; following Hebdige 1979: 17) has put forth a persuasive perspective which strikes me as especially helpful in understanding these processes. This is the sense that we may continue to understand more and more about ideological clashes within and between the structures of conjuncture (and disjuncture) in history and in ethnography, and especially by their combination, by reference to *"an unending struggle for the possession of the sign"* (my emphasis).

Much of the public rhetoric of the Levantamiento Indígena in Ecuador in 1990 focused on making 1992 the year when the tragedy of Euramerican conquest would become transformed into a triumph wherein a new nation of indigenous peoples, including all peoples with indigenous backgrounds and all people who identified as indigenous, would regain their lost freedom and assert their cultural and political autonomy.

From about 1989 through the first half of 1992 the symbolism of "1492–1992: 500 Years of Resistance!" in indigenous and black discourse in Ecuador was framed by the cosmogonic polarities that Lawrence Sullivan (1988) calls the "Primordium" and the "Eschaton." These concepts pertain to the pre-beginning of everything (the Primordium) and the end of everything, with new life occurring out of death (the Eschaton). Midway through 1992 the public rhetoric of ethnic and class schism shifted from millennial to practical, from cosmic-nationalist (hemispherewide) to local and regional.

In Ecuador a shift toward local-level violence occurred wherein indigenous and black people appropriated land by force, pledged alliance to one another's movements, and became pitted against one another in an arena of increasingly violent local-level political-economic maneuvering by power-wielders.

Nationalist rhetoric as manifest by the public statements by the new president, Sixto Durán Ballén, from August 10, 1992, on has vigorously stressed the ideology of *mestizaje* and the black and indigenous "problems" that only governmental agencies (often unspecified) can "solve." The major change in national praxis has been the denial of direct access by indigenous people to the president of the republic and to his immediate advisors. Indigenous people, under the regime of Durán Ballén, have become increasingly analogous to their black congeners.

Current ethnic and class clashes in the Americas define a structure of conjuncture entailing "unprecedented objectifications of [ethnic] categories" (Sahlins 1981: 35) cast in increasingly rigid racialist terms (see also Sahlins 1993). Ethnogenetic processes and the discourses that emerge from such conjunctures provide a profound cultural critique on Western thought. Dimensions of such a critique have been recently set forth with learned elegance by the comparative religion specialist Lawrence Sullivan (1988) and by the anthropologist Michael Taussig (1987). In this essay I have endeavored to embed a sense of such a cultural critique within my overall specific theme of interethnicity manifest in racialist discourse and in collective action.

Acknowledgments and Notes as to Context

This essay draws, in part, from two collaborative projects and reflects ongoing research and interpretation of radical change and pluralist cultural endurance in Ecuador. One of these projects, joint with Arlene Torres, focuses on blackness in Latin America and the Caribbean. For a brief statement of the first phase of this project, see Whitten and Torres (1992); the larger framework is offered in our introductions to Whitten and Torres (in press).

The second project, joint with Dorothea (Sibby) Scott Whitten, focuses on the Ecuadorian cultural continuities and radical changes within a research framework that has developed over a number of years. This framework includes intensive work with indigenous people in Puyo, capital of Pastaza Province (see Whitten and Whitten 1993), and informal but intensive communication with friends and colleagues in Salasaca, Otavalo, and Quito about the meaning of the Levantamiento Indígena of 1990 and other cognate events. Additionally, Sibby and I have collected whatever public-domain information we could from newspapers, magazines, pamphlets, radio, and television focusing on the Levantamiento Indígena, the Caminata de Puyo a Quito (1992), the symbolism of 1492–1992 in Ecuador, and a myriad of related political-economic, socioeconomic, and ideological issues. We are currently engaged in a content analysis of the published material.

Work on concepts of *négritud* and *liberación de las comunidades negras* in

Ecuador has taken place through the auspices of the Centro Cultural Afro-Ecuatoriano and with the extensive collaboration of P. Rafael Savoia, director of the *centro*, and of Dr. Diego Quiroga of the Universidad San Francisco de Quito. The principal sponsor of our research in Ecuador has been, since 1989, the Universidad San Francisco de Quito. I am grateful to colleagues there, especially Santiago Gangotena, María del Carmen Molestina, and Diego Quiroga, for sustained collegiality and assistance.

Papers containing materials in this chapter were presented at the symposium Andean Crises: Traditional Dilemmas and Contemporary Challenges (March 26–29, 1992) in Gainesville, Florida (read by Paul Doughty); at the regular Monday Afternoon Advanced Seminar in Anthropology at the University of Chicago (April 1, 1992); in the symposium De-Mythologizing the Political Cultures of Coercion and Terror in Latin America at the Latin American Studies Association Meetings in Washington, D.C. (April 5, 1991, read by Jonathan Hill); and at the Friday Forum series focused on 1492–1992 at the University of Illinois at Urbana-Champaign (January 31, 1992).

Funds for research leading to this essay were provided by a grant from the Wenner-Gren Foundation for Anthropological Research (number 5232) in 1990 and by a National Endowment for the Humanities Summer Fellowship in 1992. Subsequent funding in 1993 and 1994 was provided by my appointment as Senior University Scholar at the University of Illinois at Urbana-Champaign.

For substantive and analytical background to the interpretation presented in this essay, see Whitten (1965, 1976, 1981, 1985, 1988, 1986 [1974]), Whitten and Whitten (1993), and Whitten and Whitten, eds. (1993). After I completed this essay, several books and pamphlets focused on the Levantamiento Indígena of 1990 appeared. I have read all of them, and they complement this presentation without altering my interpretation. The references are included in the bibliography but are not incorporated into the text. In 1992 a dramatic march by long-time indigenous associates (among others) of ours took place from Puyo to Quito to gain concessions from the national government. Ideas, interpretations, and observations from the Caminata are incorporated in this essay. A larger work, now in progress, will make all this material available.

I am most grateful to Arlene Torres, Diego Quiroga, and Sibby Whitten for critical and productive readings of early drafts of this essay and for the collaborative work that made the essay possible. Although the essay reflects joint research and joint publication, only I am to be faulted for any errors of omission or commission, and I am entirely responsible for flaws in interpretation.

Notes

1. In this work my concern is to deal with the cultural, ethnic, discursive, and symbolic dimensions of the Ecuadorian Levantamiento Indígena of 1990. My analysis applies equally to the Caminata. Indeed, the Caminata manifests many features far more dramatic than anything known to me to have occurred in the Levantamiento Indígena. The materials on these movements will be combined with other illustrations of processes herein sketched in a larger work, now in progress. There is no room here to discuss many other highly salient features of the Levantamiento, most of which are discussed elsewhere (Almeida et al. 1991; Albán 1993; Bolívar Torres 1993; Comisión por la Defensa de los Derechos Humanos 1990; Macas 1991; Rosero 1990; Serrano 1993), often in confrontational manners. Such features include:

> The role of Catholic liberation theologists in providing and sustaining an economic, social, political and ideological infrastructure for the Levantamiento.
> The role of foreign governments, especially European, in providing substantial funding and infrastructural support for the Levantamiento.
> The role of foreign governments and revolutionary movements in training people for specialized roles in the Levantamiento.
> The role of Ecuadorian political parties and other political forces in supporting specialized activities by participants in the Levantamiento.

2. See, for example, Whitten (1981, 1985) and Tomoeda and Millones (1992).

3. For a history of local-level indigenous uprisings beginning in the sixteenth century, see Newson (1995), Albórnez (1976), Garcés (1961), Oberem (1971), and especially Santos (1993). Segundo Moreno (1976) wrote his doctoral dissertation on the subject of *sublevaciones indígenas* in Ecuador's history under the direction of the late Andeanist-Amazonianist ethnohistorian, archaeologist, and ethnographer Udo Oberem. Although many social movements by indigenous people (and by black people) have had repercussions throughout the nation (and, previously, colony), there has never been a nationwide uprising before. Indeed, the Levantamiento of 1990 was probably the most organized movement of people to make policy in a public arena in all of Ecuador's history. No political movement has been of this magnitude. In reworking his book for popular consumption after the Levantamiento, and in subsequent pronouncements, Moreno has changed from the focus on *sublevación* (uprising, rebellion, revolution)—the most neutral term available for an uprising—to *alzamiento*, which means, in all social contexts dealing with human beings, people out of control. The concept of "inferior human" is part of the concept of *alzamiento*, for *blancos* cannot, by definition, be *alzado*; usually, only *indios* and *negros* are so represented. Like his colleague Alfonso Calderón Cevallos, Dr. Moreno also worked with both the president of the republic and indigenous people to further develop the Janus-like system of vertical articulation that has led to increased misunderstanding and conflict across the ethnic antipodes of Ecuadorian modernization and developmentalism.

4. There are many renditions of all of the points of the Levantamiento. I give here those that seem most salient in public discourse from 1990 through the present. Often some points are embedded in others, and some points are elaborated to constitute several points.

5. By 1992 the most salient discourse focused on the Caminata. Our discussions and studies of the Caminata have contributed to our understanding of the Levantamiento. In 1994 another "uprising" occurred when the president of the republic, Sixto Durán Ballén, essentially signed into law a new agrarian program that would plunge rural people back into the system of peonage from which the agrarian programs of the 1960s promised liberation but provided oppression. With the legal specter of any "businesses" having the right to move onto subsistence or fallow land, indigenous and nonindigenous people alike went on strike throughout much of the Andes and Amazonian regions (but not Imbabura-Carchi) and literally shut the metropoles (Quito, Latacunga, Ambato, Cuenca) down for a minimum of nine days. The most popular word for the 1994 uprising was "strike" (*paro*) and that of the urban critics, *indios revolucionando* (Indians revolutionizing [i.e., in revolt]).

6. *Vistazo* (September 1990): 78, 79.

7. Alfonso Calderón Cevallos, *Reflexiones en las culturas orales*, 4th ed., 1987, 5th ed., 1992 (Quito: Abya-Yala).

Notes on Contributors

Patricia C. Albers received her Ph.D. at the University of Wisconsin-Madison. She is professor of anthropology and acting director of the American West Center at the University of Utah. Her publications include an edited book, *The Hidden Half: Studies of Plains Indian Women*, and various articles on ethnicity, gender, intergroup relations, and visual anthropology. Currently she is writing a book on postcard imagery of American Indians.

Kenneth Bilby is a research associate in the Department of Anthropology at the Smithsonian Institution. He holds an M.A. in anthropology from Wesleyan University and a Ph.D. in anthropology from Johns Hopkins University. He has carried out extensive ethnographic research in Jamaica, French Guiana, and Surinam, with a special focus on contemporary Maroon societies. In addition to having produced several ethnomusicological recordings and a film, he is the author of numerous articles on Caribbean folklore, expressive culture, linguistics, and ethnohistory. Among his recent publications are "Oral Traditions in Two Maroon Societies: The Windward Maroons of Jamaica and the Aluku Maroons of French Guiana and Suriname" (in Wim Hoogbergen, *Born out of Resistance* and (with Peter Manuel and Michael Largey) *Caribbean Currents: Caribbean Music from Rumba to Reggae*. He is currently preparing the first comprehensive dictionary of a Guianese Maroon language, the *Dictionary of Aluku (Boni)*.

David M. Guss is a member of the faculty in the Department of Sociology and Anthropology at Tufts University. He has lived and worked in Venezuela and other Latin American countries. His forthcoming book, *The Festive State: Race, Ethnicity, and Nationalism as Cultural Performance*, explores the ways in which festive behavior is used to negotiate, challenge, and constitute identity. His most recent publication is a study of the Ye'kuana Indians of Venezuela, *To Weave and Sing: Art, Symbol, and Narrative in the South American Rain Forest*. He is also the translator of this tribe's creation epic into English, *Watunna: An Orinoco Creation Cycle*.

Nancy P. Hickerson is a member of the anthropology faculty at Texas Tech University. She is the author of *Linguistic Anthropology* and has publications on color terms, place-names, and other ethnolinguistic topics. Her interest in ethnohistory has resulted in a book, *The Jumanos: Hunters and Traders of the South Plains*, and articles on South Plains history and ethnogenesis. Her current research project focuses on Cabeza de Vaca and the Indians of Texas.

Jonathan D. Hill is professor of anthropology at Southern Illinois University at Carbondale. He has served as contributing editor for lowland South American ethnology, the *Handbook of Latin American Studies*, and as advisory editor for the *American Anthropologist*. His publications include an edited volume, *Rethinking History and Myth: Indigenous South American Perspectives on the Past*, a book called *Keepers of the Sacred Chants: The Poetics of Ritual Power in an Amazonian Society*, and essays on ethnohistory, ethnomusicology, social organization, and ecology among indigenous peoples of lowland South America.

Richard A. Sattler received his Ph.D. in anthropology from the University of Oklahoma and is currently on the staff of the D'Arcy McNickle Center for the History of the American Indian at the Newberry Library and an instructor at Barat College, both in Chicago. He has conducted extensive ethnographic and ethnohistorical research and published on the Seminole and Creek Indians. His current research focuses on their articulation to the European world economy and the sociopolitical transformations among these groups in the eighteenth and early nineteenth centuries.

Susan K. Staats earned an M.S. in mathematics at Ohio State University and an M.A. in anthropology from Southern Illinois University at Carbondale. She conducted nine months of fieldwork among the Akawaio and neighboring peoples of the middle Mazaruni River in Guyana in 1994 and 1995 and is currently making plans to return to the region for additional fieldwork in 1996 and 1997. She is a doctoral student in anthropology at Indiana University.

Neil Lancelot Whitehead holds undergraduate and graduate degrees in philosophy, psychology, and social anthropology from Oxford University. He has been a research fellow of the University of London and the Ecole des Hautes Etudes in Paris and a visiting professor at Leiden University. His major publications include *Lords of the Tiger Spirit, War in the Tribal Zone, Wild Majesty,* and *Wolves from the Sea.* He is currently associate professor of anthropology at the University of Wisconsin-Madison.

Norman E. Whitten, Jr., is professor of anthropology and Latin American studies and affiliate of Afro-American studies at the University of Illinois at Urbana-Champaign. He is past editor of the *American Ethnologist* and past head of the Department of Anthropology at the UIUC, where he is currently a Senior University Scholar. His major publications, based on extensive field research in Ecuador, include *Black Frontiersmen: Afro-American Culture of Ecuador and Colombia, Sacha Runa: Ethnicity and Adaptation of Ecuadorian Jungle Quichua, Cultural Transformations and Ethnicity in Modern Ecuador, Sicuanga Runa: The Other Side of Development in Amazonian Ecuador,* and, with Dorothea S. Whitten, *From Myth to Creation: Art from Amazonian Ecuador* and *Imagery and Creativity: Ethnoaesthetics and Art Worlds in the Americas.*

Bibliography

Abel, Annie Heloise, ed.
   1932 *Chardan's Journal at Fort Clark, 1834–1839: Descriptive of Life on the Up-per Missouri of a Fur Trader's Experience among the Mandans, Gros Ventres, and Their Neighbors of the Ravages of the Small-Pox Epidemic of 1837.* Pierre, S.D.: Lawrence Fox, History Department, State of South Dakota.

Acosta Saignes, Miguel
   1967 *Vida de los esclavos negros en Venezuela.* Caracas: Hesperides.

Adams, Kathleen J.
   1983–1984 "The Premise of Equality in Carib Societies." *Antropológica* 59–62: 299–308.

AGISD
   Archivo General de las Indies: Santo Domingo. Ayer Collection, Newberry Library, Chicago, Illinois.

Albán, Gómez Ernesto, et al.
   1993 *Los indios y el estado-pais: pluriculturalidad y multietnicidad en el Ecuador: contribuciones al debate.* Quito: Abya-Yala.

Albers, Patricia
   1974 "The Regional System of the Devil's Lake Sioux." Ph.D. dissertation, University of Wisconsin, Madison.
   1993 "Symbiosis, Merger, and War: Contrasting Forms of Intertribal Relationship among Historic Plains Indians." In *Political Economy of North American Indians,* ed. John Moore. Norman: University of Oklahoma Press, 94–134.

Albers, Patricia, Janet Ahlers, and James Howard
in press "The Plains Ojibwa." *The Handbook of American Indians*, vol. 14: *The Plains*, ed. R. Demallie.

Albers, Patricia, and William James
1986 "On the Dialectics of Ethnicity: To Be or Not To Be Santee." *Journal of Ethnic Studies* 14: 1–27.
1991 "Horses without People: A Critique of Neoclassical Ecology." In *Explorations in Political Economy: Essays in Criticism*, ed. R. K. Kanth and E. K. Hunt. Savage, Md.: Rowman and Littlefield Publishers, 5–31.

Albers, Patricia, and Jeanne Kay
1987 "Sharing the Land: A Study in American Indian Territoriality." In *A Cultural Geography of North American Indians*, ed. T. E. Ross and T. G. Moore. Boulder, Colo.: Westview Press, 47–91.

Albórnoz P., Oswaldo
1976 *Las luchas indígenas en el Ecuador.* Guayaquil: Editorial Claridad

Alderson
1873–1875 "Fort Belknap Journal." Unpublished manuscript. Montana Historical Society.

Allaire, L.
1980 "On the Historicity of Carib Migrations in the Lesser Antilles." *American Antiquity* 45 (2): 232–245.

Almeida, José, et al.
1993 *Sismo étnico en el Ecuador: varias perspectivas.* Quito: Abya-Yala.

Almeida, Leana, et al.
1991 *Indios: una reflexión sobre el Levantamiento Indígena de 1990.* Quito: Instituto Latinoamericano de Investigaciones Sociales (ILDIS), Abya-Yala, and El Duende.

Anastasio, Angelo
1972 "The Southern Plateau: An Ecological Analysis of Intergroup Relations." *Northwest Anthropological Research Notes* 6: 109–229.

Anderson, David G.
1990 "Stability and Change in Chiefdom-Level Societies: An Examination of Mississippian Political Evolution on the South Atlantic Coast." In *Lamar Archaeology: Mississippian Chiefdoms in the Deep South*, ed. M. Williams and G. Shapiro. Tuscaloosa: University of Alabama Press, 187–213.

Anonymous
1940 "Fort Sarpy Journal, 1855–1856." *Contributions to the Historical Society of Montana*, no. 10.

Anonymous
1763 "Some Account of the Government of East and West Florida; with a Map of the Country; According to the Limits Laid Down by the Royal Proclamation." *Gentleman's Magazine and Historical Chronicle* 33 (November): 552–554.

Appadurai, Arjun
1981 "The Past as a Scarce Resource." *Man* 16 (n.s.): 201–219.
Arens, William, and Ivan Karp
1989 *Creativity of Power.* Washington, D.C.: Smithsonian Press.
Auxiliary Bishop of Florida
1736 "Letter to the King, August 31, 1735." AGISD 843 SC.
Ayala, Enrique Mora
1989 *Los partidos políticos en el Ecuador: síntesis histórica.* 2d ed. Quito: Ediciones La Tierra.
Ayala y Escobar, Juan de
1718 "Letter to the King, January 28, 1718." AGISD 843 SC.
Ayer, Mrs. E. G., trans.
1900–1901 *The Memorial of Fray Alonso de Benavides, 1630. Land of Sunshine,* 13 & 14.
Babcock, Barbara, ed.
1978 *The Reversible World: Symbolic Inversion in Art and Society.* Ithaca, N.Y.: Cornell University Press.
Bakhtin, M. M.
1981 *The Dialogic Imagination,* ed. Michael Holquist, trans. Caryl Emerson and Michael Holquist. Austin: University of Texas Press.
Bandelier, Adolph F. A.
1890 *Final Report of Investigations among Indians of the Southwestern United States.* Papers of the Archaeological Institute of America 3. Washington, D.C.: American Anthropological Association.
Barcía Carballido y Zuñiga, Andres Gonzalez
1951 *Barcía's Chronological History of the Continent of Florida,* trans. A. Kerrigan. Introduction by H. E. Bolton. Gainesville: University of Florida Press.
Barker, Alex W., and Timothy R. Pauketat, eds.
1992 *Lords of the Southeast: Social Inequality and the Native Elites of Southeastern North America.* Archeological Papers of the American Anthropological Association 3. Washington, D.C.: American Anthropological Association.
Barth, F.
1969 "Introduction." In *Ethnic Groups and Boundaries: The Social Organization of Cultural Difference,* ed. F. Barth. London: Allen & Unwin, 9–38.
Bartram, William
1848 "Observations on the Creek and Cherokee Indians." *Transactions of the American Ethnological Society* 3: 1–81.
1927 *Travels through North and South Carolina, Georgia, East and West Florida,* ed. Mark Van Doren. New York: Dover.
Bateman, Rebecca
1990 "Africans and Indians: A Comparative Study of Black Carib and Black Seminole." *Ethnohistory* 37 (1): 1–24.

Bemrose, John
  1966 *Reminiscences of the Second Seminole War*, ed. John K. Mahon. Gainesville: University of Florida Press.
Benavides, Antonio de
  1726 "Testimony of the Investigation Made during the Visitation of the Indian
  Settlements near St. Augustine, December 1, 1726." AGISD 865 SC.
Bennet, Gordon, Audrey Butt Colson, and Stewart Wavell
  1978 *The Damned: The Plight of the Akawaio Indians of Guyana*. London: Survival International.
Bennett, John
  1969 *Northern Plainsmen: Adaptive Strategy and Agrarian Life*. Chicago: Aldine
  Press.
Bentley, G. Carter
  1983 "Theoretical Perspectives on Ethnicity and Nationality." *Sage Race Relations Abstracts* 8 (2): 1–53, 8 (3): 1–26.
Besson, Jean
  1984 "Family Land and Caribbean Society: Toward an Ethnography of Afro-
  Caribbean Peasantries." In *Perspectives on Caribbean Regional Identity*, ed. Elizabeth M. Thomas-Hope. Liverpool: Center for Latin American Studies, University of Liverpool, 57–83.
  1987 "A Paradox in Caribbean Attitudes to Land." In *Land and Development
  in the Caribbean*, ed. Jean Besson and Janet Momsen. London: Macmillan,
  13–45.
  1988 "Agrarian Relations and Perceptions of Land in a Jamaican Peasant Village." In *Small Farming and Peasant Resources in the Caribbean*, ed. John S.
  Brierley and Hymie Rubenstein. Winnipeg: Department of Geography, University of Manitoba, 39–61.
Biersack, Aletta
  1989 "Local Knowledge, Local History: Geertz and Beyond." In *The New Cultural History*, ed. Lynn Hunt. Berkeley: University of California Press, 72–96.
Bilby, Kenneth
  1981 "The Kromanti Dance of the Windward Maroons of Jamaica." *Nieuwe
  West-Indische Gids* 55 (1–2): 52–101.
  1984a "The Treacherous Feast: A Jamaican Maroon Historical Myth." *Bijdragen tot de Taal-, Land- en Volkenkunde* 140: 1–31.
  1984b "'Two Sister Pikni': A Historical Tradition of Dual Ethnogenesis in
  Eastern Jamaica." *Caribbean Quarterly* 30 (3–4): 10–25.
  1988 "Ethnogenesis, Historical Consciousness, and Historical Depth: The Case
  of Cenogenic Societies." Paper presented at the 87th Annual Meeting of the
  American Anthropological Association, Phoenix, Ariz.
  1990 "The Remaking of the Aluku: Culture, Politics, and Maroon Ethnicity in
  French South America." Ph.D. dissertation, Johns Hopkins University, Baltimore, Md.

1992 *Drums of Defiance: Maroon Music from the Earliest Free Black Communities of Jamaica.* Notes to Smithsonian/Folkways compact disc SF 40412. Washington, D.C.: Smithsonian Institution.

1994a "Swearing by the Past, Swearing to the Future: Oath-Taking and Alliances among the Guianese and Jamaican Maroons." Paper presented at the 48th International Congress of Americanists, Uppsala, Sweden, July 7.

1994b "Time and History among a Maroon People: The Aluku." In *Time in the Black Experience*, ed. Joseph Adjaye. Westport, Conn.: Greenwood Press, 141–160.

1995 "Oral Traditions in Two Maroon Societies: The Windward Maroons of Jamaica and the Aluku Maroons of French Guiana and Suriname." In *Born out of Resistance: On Caribbean Cultural Creativity*, ed. Wim Hoogbergen. Utrecht: ISOR, 169–180.

Bilby, Kenneth, and Diana Baird N'Diaye

1992 "Creativity and Resistance: Maroon Culture in the Americas." In *1992 Festival of American Folklife*, ed. Peter Seitel. Washington, D.C.: Smithsonian Institution, 54–61.

Bilby, Kenneth, and Filomina Chioma Steady

1981 "Black Women and Survival: A Maroon Case." In *The Black Woman Cross-Culturally*, ed. Filomina Chioma Steady. Cambridge, Mass.: Schenkman Publishing Co., 451–467.

Biord Castillo, Horacio

1985 "El contexto multilingüe del sistema de interdependencia regional del Orinoco." *Antropológica* 63–64: 83–101.

Bishop, Charles

1987 "Coast-Interior Exchange: The Origins of Stratification in Northwestern North America." *Arctic Anthropology* 24: 72–83.

Bishop of Cuba

1728 "Letter to the King, Havana, September 1, 1728." AGISD 865 SC.

Bittle, William

1971 "A Brief History of the Kiowa Apache." *Papers in Anthropology* 12: 1–32.

Blu, Karen

1980 *The Lumbee Problem: The Making of an American Indian People.* Cambridge, Eng.: University of Cambridge Press.

Blyth, Joseph

1916 "Affidavit of Joseph Blyth, 24 November 1756." *Colonial Records of the State of Georgia* 7 (1): 427–428.

Bogy, Thomas

1874–1879 "Journal." Unpublished manuscript. Montana Historical Society.

Boissevain, Jeremy, ed.

1992 *Revitalizing European Rituals.* London: Routledge.

Bolívar Torres, César

1993 *La revolución arco iris.* Quito: Editorial Parra.

Boller, Henry

1972 *Among the Indians: Four Years on the Upper Missouri, 1858–1862*, ed. M. Quaife. Lincoln: University of Nebraska Press.

Bolton, Herbert E.

1911 "The Jumano Indians, 1650–1771." *Texas Historical Association Quarterly* 15: 66–84.

Bolton, Herbert E., ed.

1908 *Spanish Explorations in the Southwest, 1542–1706.* New York: Scribner's.

1925 *Arrendondo's Historical Proof of Spain's Title to Georgia: A Contribution to the History of One of the Spanish Borderlands.* Berkeley: University of California Press.

Bonar, William

1757 "A Draught of the Creek Nation." Manuscript map.

Boomert, A.

1980 "Hertenrits: An Arauquinoid Complex in North West Suriname." *Archaeology and Anthropology* 3 (2): 68–104.

1984 "The Arawak Indians of Trinidad and Coastal Guiana, ca. 1500–1650." *Journal of Caribbean History* 19 (2): 123–188.

1986 "The Cayo Complex of St. Vincent: Ethnohistorical and Archaeological Aspects of the Island Carib Problem." *Antropológica* 66:3–68.

1987 "Gifts of the Amazons: 'Green Stone' Pendants and Beads as Items of Ceremonial Exchange in Amazonia and the Caribbean." *Antropológica* 67: 33–54.

1995 "Island Carib Archaeology." In *Wolves from the Sea: Readings in the Anthropology of the Native Caribbean*, ed. Neil L. Whitehead. Leiden: KITLV Press, 23–36.

Boon, James A.

1982 *Other Tribes, Other Scribes: Symbolic Anthropology in the Comparative Study of Cultures, Histories, Religions, and Texts.* Cambridge, England: Cambridge University Press.

Boorstein, Daniel J.

1983 *The Discoverers: A History of Man's Search to Know His World and Himself.* New York: Random House.

Bottineau, J. B.

1900 "The Turtle Mountain Band of Chippewa Indians." 5th Cong., 1st sess. S. Doc. 444.

Bourricaud, François

1962 *Changements à Puno.* Paris: Institut de Hautes Ètudes de l'Amérique Latine.

Bowers, Alfred

1950 *Mandan Social and Ceremonial Organization.* Chicago: University of Chicago Press.

1965 *Hidatsa Social and Ceremonial Organization.* Washington, D.C.: Smithsonian Institution, Bureau of American Ethnology, Bulletin 194.

Boyd, Mark F.

1934 "Apalachee during the British Occupation." *Florida Historical Quarterly* 12: 114–122.

1937 "Events at Prospect Bluff on the Apalachicola River, 1808–1818: An Introduction to Twelve Letters of Edmund Doyle, Trader." *Florida Historical Quarterly* 16: 55–96.

1941a "From a Remote Frontier: San Marcos de Apalache, 1763–1769, Part 1." *Florida Historical Quarterly* 19: 179–212, 402–412.

1941b "From a Remote Frontier: San Marcos de Apalache, 1763–1769, Part 2." *Florida Historical Quarterly* 20: 82–90, 203–205, 293–308, 382–388.

1941c "From a Remote Frontier: San Marcos de Apalache, 1763–1769, Part 3." *Florida Historical Quarterly* 21: 44–50, 136–146.

1949 "Diego Peña's Expedition to Apalachee and Apalachicolo in 1716." *Florida Historical Quarterly* 28: 1–27.

1952 "Documents Describing the Second and Third Expeditions of Lieutenant Diego Peña to Apalachee and Apalachicolo." *Florida Historical Quarterly* 31: 109–139.

1958 "Horatio S. Dexter and Events Leading to the Treaty of Moultrie Creek with the Seminole Indians." *Florida Anthropologist* 11 (3): 65–95.

Boyd, Mark F., and Jose N. Latorre

1953 "Spanish Interest in British Florida and in the Progress of the American Revolution, I: Relations with the Spanish Faction of the Creek Indians." *Florida Historical Quarterly* 32: 92–130.

Boyd, Maurice, ed.

1981 *Kiowa Voices*, vol. 1. Fort Worth: Texas Christian University Press.

Braveboy-Wagner, Jacqueline

1984 *The Venezuela-Guyana Border Dispute: Britain's Colonial Legacy in Latin America.* Boulder, Colo.: Westview Press.

Brett, Rev. W. H.

1868 *The Indian Tribes of Guiana.* London: Bell and Daldy.

Britto García, Luis

1990 "Fin de populismo." Paper presented at the Casa de Titeres, Ciudad Bolívar, Venezuela, September 3.

Brose, David S.

1984 "Mississippian Period Cultures in Northwestern Florida." In *Perspectives on Gulf Coast Prehistory*, ed. D. D. Davis. Gainesville: University Presses of Florida, 165–197.

1989 "From the Southeastern Ceremonial Complex to the Southern Cult: You Can't Tell the Players without a Program." In *The Southeastern Ceremonial Complex: Artifacts and Analysis*, ed. P. Galloway. Lincoln: University of Nebraska Press, 27–44.

Brow, James

1990 "Notes on Community, Hegemony, and the Uses of the Past." *Anthropological Quarterly* 63 (1): 1–6.

Brown, Michael

1991 "Beyond Resistance: Utopian Renewal in Amazonia." *Ethnohistory* 38 (4): 363–387.

Brown, Michael, and Eduardo Fernandez

1991 *War of Shadows: The Struggle for Utopia in the Peruvian Amazon.* Berkeley: University of California Press.

Burdick, John

1992 "The Myth of Racial Democracy." *NACLA: Report on the Americas* 25 (4): 40–43.

Burpee, J. L., ed.

1927 *Journals and Letters of Pierre Gaultier de Varennes de la Verendrye and His Sons.* Toronto: Champlain Society.

Butt, Audrey

1960 "Birth of a Religion." *Journal of the Royal Anthropological Institute* 90: 66–106.

Butt Colson, Audrey

1971 "Hallelujah among the Patamona Indians." *Antropológica* 28: 25–28.

1977 "The Akawaio Shaman." In *Carib-Speaking Indians: Culture, Society and Language*, ed. Ellen Basso. Tucson: University of Arizona Press, 43–65.

1983–1984 "The Spatial Component in the Political Structure of the Carib Speakers of the Guiana Highlands: Kapon and Pemon." *Antropológica* 59–62: 73–124.

1985 "Routes of Knowledge: An Aspect of Regional Integration in the Circum-Roraima Area of the Guiana Highlands." *Antropológica* 63–64: 103–149.

Buve, R.

1966 "Gouverneur Johannes Heinsius: de rol van van Aerssen's voorganger in de Surinaamse Indianeroorlog." *Nieuwe West-Indische Gids* 45: 14–26.

Calderón Cevallos, Alfonso

1987 *Reflexiones en las culturales orales.* 4th ed. Quito: Abya-Yala.

Campbell, Mavis C.

1977 "Marronage in Jamaica: Its Origins in the Seventeenth Century." In *Comparative Perspectives on Slavery in New World Plantation Societies*, ed. Vera Rubin and Arthur Tuden. New York: New York Academy of Sciences, 389–419.

1988 *The Maroons of Jamaica 1655–1796: A History of Resistance, Collaboration and Betrayal.* Granby, Mass.: Bergin and Garvey.

Campbell, Robert

1963 *The Private Journal of Robert Campbell*, ed. G. Brooks. Missouri Historical Society Bulletin 20.

Campbell, Robert G.
N.d. "Some Possible Kiowa Origins." Paper delivered at Kiowa Symposium, Texas Tech University, Lubbock.

Candler, Allen D.
1910 *Original Papers: Correspondence, Trustee, General Ogelthorpe and Others.* Colonial Records of the State of Georgia, 1735–1737, vol. 21.

Carnegie, Charles V.
1987 "Is Family Land an Institution?" In *Afro-Caribbean Villages in Historical Perspective*, ed. Charles V. Carnegie. ACIJ Research Review No. 2. Kingston: African-Caribbean Institute of Jamaica, 83–99.

Carter, Clarence Edwin, ed.
1956 *The Territorial Papers of the United States.* Vol. 22, *The Territory of Florida, 1821–1824.* Washington, D.C.: U.S. Government Printing Office.

Casiño, Eric S.
1985 "The Parameters of Ethnicity Research: Intentionality, Content and Classification." In *Ethnicity: Intercocta Glossary*, ed. Fred W. Riggs. Paris: International Social Science Council, UNESCO, 3–46.

Caughey, John Walton, ed.
1938 *McGillivray of the Creeks.* Norman: University of Oklahoma Press.

CDI
1864–1885 *Collección de documentos inéditos, relativos al descubrimiento, conquista y colonización de las posesiones españolas en América y Oceanía.* 42 vols. Madrid: Real Academia de la Historia.

Chapman, Malcolm, Maryon McDonald, and Elizabeth Tonkin, eds.
1989 *History and Ethnicity.* Association of Social Anthropology Monographs 27. London: Routledge.

Chernela, Janet
1983 "Hierarchy and Economy of the Uanano (Kotiria)-Speaking Peoples of the Middle Uaupés Basin." Ph.D. dissertation, Columbia University.
1988 "Righting History in the Northwest Amazon." In *Rethinking History and Myth*, ed. Jonathan Hill. Urbana: University of Illinois Press, 35–49.
1993 *The Wanano Indians of the Brazilian Northwest Amazon: A Sense of Space.* Austin: University of Texas Press.

Clarke, Edith
1966 *My Mother Who Fathered Me: A Study of the Family in Three Selected Communities of Jamaica.* 2d ed. London: Allen and Unwin.

Cohen, M. M.
1836 *Notices of Florida and the Campaigns, by an Officer of the Left Wing.* Charleston, S.C.: Burges & Honour.

Comaroff, Jean
1985 *Body of Power, Spirit of Resistance: The Culture and History of a South African People.* Chicago: University of Chicago Press.

Comisión por la Defensa de los Derechos Humanos
1990 *El Levantamiento Indígena y la cuestión nacional.* Quito: Comisión por la Defensa de los Derechos Humanos and Abya-Yala.

CONAIE
1989 *1991: 500 años de resistencia india: las nacionalidades indígenas en el Ecuador.* 2d ed. Quito: Tincui/CONAIE and Abya-Yala.

Cook, Noble David
1981 *Demographic Collapse: Indian Peru, 1520–1620.* Cambridge, England: Cambridge University Press.

Coues, Elliott, ed.
1897 *New Light on the Early History of the Northwest,* vols. 1 and 2. Minneapolis: Ross and Haines.
1965 [1893] *History of the Expedition under the Command of Lewis and Clark.* 3 vols. New York: Dover Publications.

Coulthard, G. R.
1962 *Race and Colour in Caribbean Literature.* London: Oxford University Press.

Covey, Cyclone, ed.
1961 *Cabeza de Vaca's Adventures in the Unknown Interior of America.* New York: Collier Books.

Covington, James W.
1961 "The British Meet the Seminoles: Contributions of the Florida State Museum." *Social Sciences* 7.
1963 "Apalachicola Seminole Leadership, 1820–1833." *Florida Anthropologist* 16 (2): 57–62.

Cowie, Isaac
1913 *The Company of Adventurers on the Great Buffalo Plains: A Narrative of Seven Years in the Service of the Hudson's Bay Company during 1867–1874.* Toronto: William Briggs.

Cox, Isaac Joselin, ed.
1922 *The Journeys of Rene Robert Cavalier Sieur de La Salle.* New York: Allerton Books.

Craig, Alan K., and Christopher S. Peebles
1974 "Ethnoecologic Change among the Seminoles, 1740–1840." *Geoscience and Man* 5 (June 10): 83–96.

Crane, Verner W.
1928 *The Southern Frontier, 1670–1732.* Durham, N.C.: Duke University Press.

CSP
1661–1668 *Calendar of State Papers,* Colonial Series, America and West Indies. London: HMSO.

Dallas, Robert Charles
1803 *The History of the Maroons.* London: T. N. Longman and O. Rees.

Davis, Irvine
  1979 "The Kiowa-Tanoan, Keresan, and Zuni Languages." In *The Languages of North America*, ed. L. Campbell and M. Mithune. Austin: University of Texas Press, 390–443.
Davis, James T.
  1974 *Trade Routes and Economic Exchange among the Indians of California.* Ramona, Calif.: Ballena Press.
Davis, T. Frederick
  1930 "United States Troops in Spanish East Florida, 1812–1813." *Florida Historical Quarterly* 9 (1): 390–443, (2): 96–116, (3): 135–155, (4): 259–278.
de Beet, Chris
  1984 *De eerste Boni-Oorlog, 1765–1778.* Bronnen voor de Studie van Bosneger Samenlevingen 9. Utrecht: Centrum voor Caraïbische Studies, State University of Utrecht.
de Civrieux, Marc
  1980 *Watunna: An Orinoco Creation Cycle*, ed. and trans. David Guss. San Francisco: North Point Press.
de Groot, Silvia W.
  1975 "The Boni Maroon War 1765–1793, Surinam and French Guyana." *Boletín de Estudios Latinoamericanos y del Caribe* 18: 30–48.
Delahaye, Guillame-Nicolas
  1740 "Map of Florida Peninsular." In A. H. Phinney, "Florida's Spanish Missions." *Florida Historical Quarterly* 4 (1): 15–21.
Delgado, Marcos
  1686 "Report of Marcos Delgado, Tuave Village, Cosate Province, October 30, 1686." In "The Expedition of Marcos Delgado from Apalachee to the Upper Creek Country in 1686," ed. Mark F. Boyd. *Florida Historical Quarterly* 16 (1937): 21–28.
Delorme, David
  1955 "History of the Turtle Mountain Band of Chippewa Indians." *North Dakota History* 22: 121–134.
Dempsey, Hugh
  1972 "Western Plains Trade Ceremonies." *Western Canadian Journal of Anthropology* 3: 29–33.
  1984 *Big Bear: The End of Freedom.* Lincoln: University of Nebraska Press.
Denevan, W.
  1992 "The Pristine Myth: The Landscape of the Americas in 1492." *Annals of the Association of American Geographers* 82 (3): 369–385.
Denevan, William, ed.
  1976 *The Native Population of the Americas in 1492.* Madison: University of Wisconsin Press.

Denig, Edwin
1961 *Five Indian Tribes of the Upper Missouri*, ed. J. Ewers. Norman: University of Oklahoma Press.

DePratter, Chester B.
1991 *Late Prehistoric and Early Historic Chiefdoms in the Southeastern United States*. New York: Garland Publishing.

Dexter, Horatio S.
1823 [1958] "Observations on the Seminole Indians." In "Horatio S. Dexter and Events Leading to the Treaty of Moultrie Creek with the Seminole Indians," ed. Mark F. Boyd. *Florida Anthropologist* 11: 81–85.

Dillon, Mary, and Thomas Abercrombie
1988 "The Destroying Christ: An Aymara Myth of Conquest." In *Rethinking History and Myth*, ed. Jonathan Hill. Urbana: University of Illinois Press, 50–77.

Dirks, Nicholas B.
1994 "Ritual and Resistance: Subversion as a Social Fact." In *Culture/Power/History: A Reader in Contemporary Social Theory*, ed. Nicholas B. Dirks, G. Eley, and Sherry B. Ortner. Princeton, N.J.: Princeton University Press, 483–503.

Dobyns, Henry F.
1966 "Estimating Aboriginal American Population: An Appraisal of Techniques with a New Hemisphere Estimate." *Current Anthropology* 7: 395–416.

Dolgin, Janet L., David S. Kemnitzer, and David M. Schneider, eds.
1977 "As People Express Their Lives, So They Are . . ." In *Symbolic Anthropology: A Reader in the Study of Symbols and Meanings*, ed. J. Dolgin, D. Kemnitzer, and D. Schneider. New York: Columbia University Press, 3–44.

Drennan, R. D., and Carlos A. Uribe, eds.
1987 *Chiefdoms in the Americas*. Lanham, Md.: University Press of America.

Dusenberry, Verne
1954 "The Rocky Boy Indians." *Montana, the Magazine of Western History* 4: 1–15.
1962 *The Montana Cree: A Study in Religious Persistence*. Uppsala, Sweden: Almquvist and Wiksells Boktryckeri.
1985 "Waiting for a Day That Never Comes." In *The New Peoples: Being and Becoming Métis in North America*, ed. J. Peterson and J. Brown. Lincoln: University of Nebraska Press, 119–136.

Duval, William P.
1824 "Receipt by Seminole Chiefs of Payments for Transportation, November 12, 1824." In *The Territorial Papers of the United States*, vol. 23, *The Territory of Florida, 1824–1828*, ed. Clarence E. Carter. Washington, D.C.: U.S. Government Printing Office, 1958.

Dye, David H.
1990 "Warfare in the Sixteenth Century Southeast: The de Soto Expedition in

the Interior." In *Columbian Consequences*, vol. 2, *Archaeological and Historical Perspectives on the Spanish Borderlands East*, ed. D. H. Thomas. Washington, D.C.: Smithsonian Institution Press, 211–222.

Earle, Timothy, ed.
1991 *Chiefdoms: Power, Economy, and Ideology*. School of American Research Advanced Seminar Series. New York: Cambridge University Press.

Edmundson, G.
1906 "Early Relations of the Manoas with the Dutch, 1606–1732." *English Historical Review* 21: 229–253.

Edwards, Bryan
1796 *Observations on the Disposition, Character, Manners, and Habits of Life of the Maroons*. London: John Stockdale.

Elmendorf, William W.
1971 "Coast Salish Status Ranking and Intergroup Ties." *Southwestern Journal of Anthropology* 27: 353–380.

Evans, Clifford, and Betty Meggers
1960 *Archaeological Investigations in British Guiana*. Bureau of American Ethnology Bulletin 177. Washington, D.C.: Smithsonian Institution.

Ewers, John
1968 "The Indian Trade on the Upper Missouri before Lewis and Clark." In *Indian Life on the Upper Missouri*. Norman: University of Oklahoma Press.
1974 *Ethnological Report on the Chippewa Cree Tribe of the Rocky Boy Reservation and the Little Shell Band of Indians, Chippewa Indians*, vol. 6. New York: Garland Press.
1975 "Intertribal Warfare as the Precursor of Indian-White Warfare on the Northern Great Plains." *Western Historical Quarterly* 5: 397–410.

Fabian, Johannes
1983 *Time and the Other: How Anthropology Constructs Its Object*. New York: Columbia University Press.

Fairbanks, Charles H.
1974 *Ethnohistorical Report on the Florida Indians*. Florida Indians 3. New York: Garland Publishing.
1978 "The Ethno-Archeology of the Florida Seminole." In *Tacachale: Essays on the Indians of Florida and Southeastern Georgia during the Historic Period*, ed. J. T. Milanich and S. Proctor. Gainesville: University Presses of Florida, 163–194.

Falassi, Alessandro, ed.
1987 *Time out of Time: Essays on the Festival*. Albuquerque: University of New Mexico Press.

Farabee, W. C.
1924 *The Central Caribs*. Philadelphia: University of Pennsylvania, University Museum.

1967 [1918]. *The Central Arawaks.* Oosterhaut N.B., The Netherlands: Anthropological Publications.

Farmar, Robert

1764 [1911] "Creek Villages and Their Population, 24 January 1764." In *Mississippi Provincial Archives, 1763–1766,* vol. 1, *English Dominion,* ed. Dunbar Rowland. Nashville, Tenn.: Press of the Brandon Printing Company, 94–97.

Ferguson, R. Brian

1990 "Blood of the Leviathan: Western Contact and Warfare in Amazonia." *American Ethnologist* 17 (2): 237–257.

Fernandez, James W.

1986 *Persuasions and Performances: The Play of Tropes in Culture.* Bloomington: Indiana University Press.

1991 *Beyond Metaphor: The Theory of Tropes in Anthropology.* Stanford, Calif.: Stanford University Press.

Fine, Kathleen

1991 *Cotocollao: Ideología, Historia y Acción en un Barrio de Quito.* Quito: Abya-Yala.

Fitch, Tobias

1916 "Tobias Fitch's Journal to the Creeks, 1726." In *Travels in the American Colonies, 1690–1783,* ed. N. D. Mereness. New York: Macmillan Company, 176–212.

Flannery, Regina

1953 *The Gros Ventres of Montana. Part I. Social Life.* Washington, D.C.: Catholic University of America Anthropological Series No. 15.

Forbes, Jack D.

1993 *Africans and Native Americans: The Language of Race and the Evolution of Red-Black Peoples.* Urbana: University of Illinois Press.

Ford, Lawrence Carroll

1939 *The Triangular Struggle for Spanish Pensacola, 1689–1739.* Washington, D.C.: Catholic University of America Press.

Ford, Richard

1983 "Inter-Indian Exchange in the Southwest." In *Handbook of American Indians, Vol. 10: The Southwest,* ed. A. Ortiz. Washington, D.C.: Smithsonian Institution, 711–722.

Forte, Janette, and Ian Melville, eds.

1989 *Amerindian Testimonies.* Boise, Idaho: Boise State University Press.

Fournier, Alain, ed.

1979 *Waramadong: A Case Study for Amerindian Resettlement in Upper Mazaruni Area, Guyana.* Georgetown, Guyana: Upper Mazaruni Development Authority.

Fox, Irene

1983 Interview. August. Notes in author's possession.

Fraser, William
1963 "Plains Cree, Assiniboin and Saulteaux (Plains) Bands, 1874–84." Unpublished manuscript, Glenbow Museum Archives (M4379).

Freeman, W. B.
1872 "Letter to Acting Assistant Adjunct General, Fort Shaw (Nov. 27)." RG 75 M234, MF Roll 493. Washington, D.C.: National Archives.

Fried, Morton H.
1967 *The Evolution of Political Society: An Essay in Political Anthropology.* New York: Random House.

Friedemann, Nina S. de, and Jaime Arocha
1995 "Colombia." In *No Longer Visible: Afro-Latin Americans Today,* ed. Minority Rights Group. London: Minority Rights Publications, 47–76.

Friedman, Jonathan
1992 "The Past in the Future: History and the Politics of Identity." *American Anthropologist* 94 (4): 837–859.

Friedrich, Paul
1986 *The Language Parallax.* Austin: University of Texas Press.

Fromhold, J.
1981 "Inter-Tribal Influences in Plains Cree Societies." In *Networks of the Past: Regional Interaction in Archaeology,* ed. P. Francis, F. Kense, and P. Duke. Calgary: University of Calgary Archaeological Association, 411–424.

Garcés, Enrique
1961 *Daquilema, rex: biografía de un dolor indio.* Quito: Casa de la Cultura Ecuatoriana.

García, Jesús
1990 *Africa en Venezuela, pieza de Indias.* Caracas: Cuadernos Lagoven.

Gatschet, Albert S.
1969 *A Migration Legend of the Creek Indians, with Linguistic, Historic and Ethnographic Introduction.* Reprint edition. New York: Kraus Reprint Co.

Geertz, Clifford
1973 *The Interpretation of Culture.* New York: Basic Books.
1983 *Local Knowledge: Further Essays in Interpretive Anthropology.* New York: Basic Books.

Georgia Council
1761 "List of the Real Creek Towns in the Lower Country with the Number of Hunters, July 3, 1761." In *Colonial Records of the State of Georgia,* ed. Allen D. Candler. Vol. 8: 522–524.

Giddings, Joshua R.
1858 *The Exiles of Florida, or, The Crimes Committed by Our Government against the Maroons, Who Fled from South Carolina and the Other Slave States, Seeking Protection under Spanish Laws.* Columbus, Ohio: Follett, Foster and Company.

Giraud, Marcel
1945 *Le Métis canadien: son rôle dans l'histoire de l'ouest.* Paris: Institut d'Ethnologie.

Glazer, Nathan, and Daniel P. Moynihan, eds.
1975 *Ethnicity: Theory and Experience.* Cambridge, Mass.: Harvard University Press.

Glover, Captain
1725 "Account of Indian Tribes, 15 Mar. 1725." In *The Creek Indian Tribes in 1725,* ed. Alexander S. Salley. *South Carolina Historical and Genealogical Magazine* 32 (1931): 241–242.

Goeje, C. H. de
1931–1932 "Oudheden uit Suriname: op zoek naar de Amazonen." *Nieuwe West-Indische Gids* 13: 449–482, 497–530.

Gold, Robert L.
1969 *Borderland Empires in Transition: The Triple-Nation Transfer of Florida.* Carbondale: Southern Illinois University Press.

Goldman, Irving
1963 *The Cubeo: Indians of the Northwest Amazon.* Urbana: University of Illinois Press.

Gonzalez, Nancie L.
1970 "The Neoteric Society." *Comparative Studies in Society and History* 12: 1–13.

Gonzalez Ñ., Omar
1980 *Mitología warequena.* Caracas: Monte Avila Editores.
1986 "Sexualidad y rituales de iniciación entre los indígenas Warekenas del Rio Guainía–Rio Negro, TFA." *Montalban* 17: 103–138.

Goslinga, C.
1971 *The Dutch in the Caribbean and on the Wild Coast, 1580–1680.* Assen: Van Gorcum.

Grant, C. L., ed.
1980 *Letters, Journals, and Writings of Benjamin Hawkins.* 2 vols. Savannah: Beehive Press.

Grau, Pedro Cunill
1987 *Geografía del poblamiento venezolano en el siglo XIX.* 3 vols. Caracas: Ediciones de la Presidencia de la República.

Green, Michael D.
1982 *The Politics of Indian Removal: Creek Government and Society in Crisis.* Lincoln: University of Nebraska Press.

Greenberg, Adolf, and James Morrison
1981 "Group Identities in the Boreal Forest: The Origin of the Northern Ojibwa." *Ethnohistory* 29: 75–102.

Guss, David M.

1993 "The Selling of San Juan: The Performance of History in an Afro-Venezuelan Community." *American Ethnologist* 20 (3): 451–473.

1994a "Historias ocultas: relatos afroamericanos de resistencia y llegada." *Revista de Investigaciones Folklóricas* 9: 47–53.

1994b "Syncretic Inventions: 'Indianness' and the Day of the Monkey." In *Syncretism/Anti-Syncretism: The Politics of Religious Synthesis*, ed. Charles Stewart and Rosalind Shaw. London: Routledge, 145–160.

1994c "Re-imaginando la comunidad imaginada: la política de la diversidad cultural en América Latina y el Caribe." In *Teoría y política de la construcción de identidades y diferencias en América Latina y el Caribe*, ed. Daniel Mato. Caracas: Nueva Sociedad.

1995 "'Indianness' and the Construction of Ethnicity in the Day of the Monkey." Latin American Studies Center Series No. 9. College Park: University of Maryland.

Haas, Mary R.

1978 "The Position of Apalachee in the Muskogean Family." In *Language, Culture, and History: Essays by Mary R. Haas*. Stanford, Calif.: Stanford University Press, 282–293.

Hackett, Charles W., ed.

1922, 1926, 1937 *Historical Documents Relating to New Mexico, Nueva Vizcaya, and Approaches Thereto*. Washington, D.C.: Carnegie Institution.

1931, 1934, 1946 *Pichardo's Treatise on the Limits of Louisiana and Texas*. Austin: University of Texas Press.

Hafen, Leroy R., ed.

1982 *Mountain Men and Fur Traders of the Far West*. Lincoln: University of Nebraska Press.

Haines, Francis

1938 "The Northward Spread of Horses among the Plains Indians." *American Anthropologist* 40: 429–436.

Halbert, H. S., and T. H. Ball

1969 *The Creek War of 1813 and 1814*, ed. F. L. Owsley. Reprint of 1895 edition. University: University of Alabama Press.

Hambly, William, and Edmund Doyle

1818 "Deposition of William Hambly and Edmund Doyle, Ft. Gadsden, 2 May 1818." In *Message from the President in Relation to the Seminole War, etc., 3 December 1818*. 15th Cong., 2d sess. H. Doc. 14.

Hamilton, J. A.

1834a "Letter to K. McKenzie (September 17)." In *Fort Union Letterbook*. North Dakota Historical Society Microfilm.

1834b "Letter to K. McKenzie (November 15)." *Fort Union Letterbook*.

1835a "Letter to Chardan (March 24)." *Fort Union Letterbook*.

1835b "Letter to Agent Sanford (March 24)." *Fort Union Letterbook.*

1835c "Letter to K. McKenzie (March 29)." *Fort Union Letterbook.*

1835d "Letter (July 4)." *Fort Union Letterbook.*

Hammond, G. P., and A. Rey, eds.

1953 *Don Juan Oñate: Colonizer of New Mexico 1595–1628.* 2 vols. Albuquerque: University of New Mexico Press.

Hanchard, Michael

1994 *Orpheus and Power: The Movimento Negro of Rio de Janeiro and São Paulo, Brazil, 1945–1988.* Princeton, N.J.: Princeton University Press.

Handler, Richard

1988 *Nationalism and the Politics of Culture in Quebec.* Madison: University of Wisconsin Press.

Handler, Richard, and Joyce Linnekin

1984 "Tradition, Genuine or Spurious." *Journal of American Folklore* 97: 273–290.

Hann, John H.

1988 *Apalachee: The Land between the Rivers.* Gainesville: University Presses of Florida.

Hanson, Jeffery

1986 "Kinship, Residence and Marriage Patterns in Hidatsa Village Composition." In *The Origins of Hidatsa Indians: A Review of Ethnohistorical and Traditional Data,* vol. 32, ed. R. Wood. Lincoln, Nebr.: J & L Reprint Co., 43–76.

1987 *Hidatsa Culture Change, 1780–1845: A Cultural Ecological Approach,* vol. 34. Lincoln, Nebr.: J & L Reprint Co.

Harlow, V. T.

1925 *Colonising Expeditions to the West Indies and Guiana, 1623–1667.* London: Hakluyt Society.

Harmon, Daniel W.

1911 *A Journal of Voyages and Travels in the Interior of North America.* New York: Allerton Book Company.

Harney, Lt. Col.

1837 "Letter to General Thomas Jesup, May, 1837." In *American State Papers: Documents Legislative and Executive of the Congress of the United States.* Class V: *Military Affairs,* vol. 6. Washington, D.C.: U.S. Government Printing Office, 870–871.

Hart, Richard

1985 *Slaves Who Abolished Slavery: Blacks in Rebellion.* Kingston: Institute of Social and Economic Research, University of the West Indies.

Hawkins, Benjamin

1848 "A Sketch of the Creek Country in the Years 1798 and 1799." Georgia Historical Society, *Collections* 3 (1).

1916 "Letters of Benjamin Hawkins, 1796–1806." Georgia Historical Society, *Collections* 9.

Hebdige, D.
1979 *Subculture: The Meaning of Style*. New York: Methuen.
Henfrey, Colin
1964 *Through Indian Eyes: A Journey among the Indian Tribes of Guiana*. New York: Holt, Rinehart and Winston.
1965 *The Gentle People*. London: Hutchinson.
Henningsgaard, William
1981 *The Akawaio, the Upper Mazaruni Hydroelectric Project and National Development in Guyana*. Cultural Survival Occasional Paper 4. Cambridge, Mass.: Cultural Survival.
Hewitt, J. N. B.
1939 "Notes on the Creek Indians," ed. John R. Swanton. Bureau of American Ethnology, *Bulletin* 123.
Hickerson, Harold
1956 "The Genesis of a Trading Post Band: The Pembina Chippewa." *Ethnohistory* 3: 289–345.
1970 *The Chippewa and Their Neighbors: A Study in Ethnohistory*. New York: Holt, Rinehart and Winston.
1974 *The Mdewakanton Band of Sioux Indians: Sioux Indians*, vol. 1. New York: Garland Press.
Hickerson, Nancy P.
1988 "The Linguistic Position of Jumano." *Journal of Anthropological Research* 44: 311–326.
1990 "Jumano: The Missing Link in South Plains History." *Journal of the West* 29 (4): 5–12.
1994 *The Jumanos: Hunters and Traders of the South Plains*. Austin: University of Texas Press.
Hill, Jonathan
1983 "Wakuénai Society: A Processual-Structural Analysis of Indigenous Cultural Life in the Upper Rio Negro Basin, Venezuela." Ph.D. dissertation, Indiana University.
1985 "Agnatic Sibling Relations and Rank in Northern Arawakan Myth and Social Life." In *Working Papers on South American Indians*, no. 7, ed. J. Shapiro. Bennington, Vt.: Bennington College, 25–33.
1987 "Wakuénai Ceremonial Exchange in the Northwest Amazon." *Journal of Latin American Lore* 13 (2): 183–224.
1989 "Demystifying Structural Violence." *Latin American Anthropology Review* 1 (2): 42–48.
1992 "Contested Pasts and the Practice of Anthropology." *American Anthropologist* 94 (4): 809–815.
1993 *Keepers of the Sacred Chants: The Poetics of Ritual Power in an Amazonian Society*. Tucson: University of Arizona Press.
1994 "Alienated Targets: Military Discourses and the Disempowerment of In-

digenous Amazonian Peoples in the Venezuelan Amazon." *Identities: Global Studies in Culture and Power* 1 (1): 7–34.

Hill, Jonathan, ed.

1988 *Rethinking History and Myth: Indigenous South American Perspectives on the Past.* Urbana: University of Illinois Press.

Hill, Jonathan, and Robin Wright

1988 "Time, Narrative, and Ritual: Historical Interpretations from an Amazonian Society." In *Rethinking History and Myth: Indigenous South American Perspectives on the Past,* ed. Jonathan Hill. Urbana: University of Illinois Press, 78–105.

Hind, Henry

1971 [1860] *Narrative of the Canadian Red River Exploring Expedition of 1857 and of the Assiniboine and Saskatchewan Expedition of 1858.* Edmonton: M. G. Hurtig.

Hitchcock, Captain E. A.

1837 "Testimony of Captain E. A. Hitchcock, January 12–14, 1837." 24th Cong., 1st sess. H. Doc. 271.

Hlady, Walter

1970 "Southwestern Manitoba Resurveyed." In *Ten Thousand Years: Archaeology in Manitoba,* ed. W. M. Hlady. Winnipeg: Manitoba Archaeological Society, 278–279.

Hobsbawm, Eric, and Terence Ranger, eds.

1983 *The Invention of Tradition.* Cambridge, England: Cambridge University Press.

Hodge, F. W.

1911 "The Jumano Indians." *Proceedings of the American Antiquarian Society* 20 (n.s.): 249–268.

Hoff, B.

1995 "Language Contact, War, and Amerindian Historical Tradition: The Special Case of the Island Carib." In *Wolves from the Sea: Readings in the Anthropology of the Native Caribbean,* ed. N. L. Whitehead. Leiden: KITLV Press, 37–60.

Hoijer, Harry

1938 "The Southern Athapaskan Languages." *International Journal of American Linguistics* 34: 165–175.

1971 "The Position of the Apachean Languages in the Athapaskan Stock." In *Apachean Culture History and Ethnology,* ed. Keith H. Basso and Morris E. Opler. Anthropological Papers of the University of Arizona, no. 21. Tucson: University of Arizona Press, 3–6.

Hoogbergen, Wim

1984 *De Boni's in Frans-Guyana en de tweede Boni-Oorlog, 1776–1793.* Bronnen voor de Studie van Bosneger Samenlevingen 10. Utrecht: Centrum voor Caraïbische Studies, State University of Utrecht.

1985 *De Boni-Oorlogen 1757–1860: Marronage en Guerilla in Oost-Suriname.* Bronnen voor de Studie van Afro-Amerikaanse Samenlevingen in de Guyana's 11. Utrecht: Centrum voor Caraïbische Studies, State University of Utrecht.

1990 *The Boni Maroon Wars in Suriname.* Leiden: E. J. Brill.

Howard, James

1961 "The Identity and Demography of the Plains-Ojibwa." *Plains Anthropologist* 6: 171–178.

1977 "The Plains-Ojibwa or Bungi: Hunters and Warriors of the Northern Prairies with Special Reference to the Turtle Mountain Band." *Reprints in Anthropology*, vol. 7. Lincoln, Nebr.: J & L Reprint Co.

Hudson, Charles

1976 *The Southeastern Indians.* Knoxville: University of Tennessee Press.

1990 *The Juan Pardo Expeditions: Explorations of the Carolinas and Tennessee, 1566–1568.* Washington, D.C.: Smithsonian Institution Press.

Hugh-Jones, Christine

1979 *From the Milk River.* Cambridge, England: Cambridge University Press.

Hugh-Jones, Stephen

1979 *The Palm and the Pleiades.* Cambridge, England: Cambridge University Press.

1988 "The Gun and the Bow: Myths of White Men and Indians." *L'Homme* 106 (7): 138–158.

Hurault, Jean

1960 "Histoire des noirs réfugiés Boni de la Guyane française." *Revue Française d'Histoire d'Outre-Mer* 47: 76–137.

1961 *Les Noirs Réfugiés Boni de la Guyane française.* Mémoires de l'Institut Français d'Afrique Noire 63. Dakar: IFAN.

Hurtado, Osvaldo

1977 *El poder político en el Ecuador.* Quito: Prensa de la Pontificia Universidad Católica del Ecuador.

1980 *Political Power in Ecuador,* trans. Nick D. Mills, Jr. Albuquerque: University of New Mexico Press.

Hyatt, Vera Lawrence, and Rex Nettleford, eds.

1995 *Race, Discourse, and the Origin of the Americas.* Washington, D.C.: Smithsonian Institution Press.

Hyde, George E.

1959 *Indians of the High Plains.* Norman: University of Oklahoma Press.

Im Thurn, Everard

1883 *Among the Indians of Guiana.* London: Kegan Paul.

1885 "Roraima." *Timehri* 4 (2): 256–267.

Innerarity, James

1931 "The Forbes Purchase: A Letter from James Innerarity to William Simpson, Partners of John Forbes and Company." *Florida Historical Quarterly* 10: 102–108.

Jackson, Jean
   1983 *The Fish People: Linguistic Exogamy and Tukanoan Identity in Northwest Amazonia.* New York: Cambridge University Press.
Jackson, John
   1982 "The Branden House and the Mandan Connection." *North Dakota History* 49: 11–19.
James, Edwin, ed.
   1956 [1830] *A Narrative of Captivity and Adventure of John Tanner during Thirty Years Residence among the Indians of the Interior of North America.* Minneapolis: Ross and Haines.
Jefferys, Thomas
   1761 *The Natural and Civil History of the French Dominions in North and South America.* Parts 1–2. London.
Jenness, Diamond
   1932 *The Sarcee Indians of Alberta.* Bulletin No. 90 of the Publications of the National Museum of Canada. Anthropological Series 23.
Jordan, Phyllis
   1980 "Hallelujah Religion." In *Focus on Amerindians,* ed. Walter F. Edwards. Georgetown: Amerindian Languages Project, University of Guyana.
Journet, Nicolas
   1988 "Les Jardins de paix." Ph.D. dissertation, Université de Paris.
Juricek, John T., ed.
   1987 *Georgia Treaties, 1733–1763: Early American Indian Documents, Treaties and Laws 1607–1789,* vol. 11, ed. A. T. Vaughn. Frederick, Md.: University Publications of America.
Kane, Paul
   1968 [1859] *Wanderings of an Artist among the Indians of North America, from Canada to Vancouver's Island and Oregon through the Hudson's Bay Company's Territory and Back Again.* Edmonton: Hurtig.
Kaplan, Joanne
   1981 "Amazonian Anthropology." *Journal of Latin American Studies* 13 (1): 151–164.
Kennedy, Michael, ed.
   1961 *The Assiniboines: From the Accounts of the Old Ones Told to First Boy (James Larpenteur Long).* Norman: University of Oklahoma Press.
Kertzer, David I.
   1988 *Ritual, Power, and Politics.* New Haven, Conn.: Yale University Press.
Key, M. R.
   1979 *The Grouping of South America Indian Languages.* Tubingen: Gunter Harr Verlag.
Keymis, L.
   1596 *A Relation of the Second Voyage to Guiana.* London.

Kinnaird, Lawrence
1931a "The Significance of William Augustus Bowles's Seizure of Panton's Apalachee Store in 1792." *Florida Historical Quarterly* 9: 156–192.
1931b "International Rivalry in the Creek Country, Part 1, the Ascendency of Alexander McGillivray, 1783–1789." *Florida Historical Quarterly* 10: 59–85.
1946 *Spain in the Mississippi Valley, 1765–1794: Translations of Materials from the Spanish Archives in the Bancroft Library.* American Historical Association, *Annual Report for 1945,* vols. 2–4.
Kinnaird, Lawrence, and Lucia B. Kinnaird
1983 "War Comes to San Marcos." *Florida Historical Quarterly* 62: 25–43.
Kline, Ben
1882 "Letter to Lieut. R. F. Bates (April 4)." Washington, D.C.: National Archives.
Köbben, A. J. F.
1967 "Unity and Disunity: Cottica Djuka Society as a Kinship System." *Bijdragen tot de Taal-, Land- en Volkenkunde* 123: 10–52.
Kopytoff, Barbara K.
1973 "The Maroons of Jamaica: An Ethnohistorical Study of Incomplete Polities, 1655–1905." Ph.D. dissertation, University of Pennsylvania.
1976a "The Development of Jamaican Maroon Ethnicity." *Caribbean Quarterly* 22 (2–3): 33–50.
1976b "Jamaican Maroon Political Organization: The Effects of the Treaties." *Social and Economic Studies* 25: 87–105.
1978 "The Early Political Development of Jamaican Maroon Societies." *William and Mary Quarterly* 35 (3d series): 287–307.
1979 "Colonial Treaty as Sacred Charter of the Jamaican Maroons." *Ethnohistory* 26: 45–64.
Kurz, Rudolph
1937 *Journal of Rudolph Friedrich Kurz: An Account of His Experiences among Fur Traders and American Indians on the Mississippi and Missouri Rivers during the Years 1846 to 1852,* ed. J. N. Hewitt. Washington, D.C.: Bureau of American Ethnology Bulletin 115.
Landaburu, Jon, and Roberto Piñeda Camacho
1984 *Tradiciones de la gente del Hacha: mitología de los indios andoques del Amazonas.* Yerbabuena: Instituto Patriótica del Instituto Caro y Cuervo.
Larpenteur, Charles
1898 *Forty Years a Fur Trader on the Upper Missouri: The Personal Narrative of Charles Larpenteur,* ed. Mailo Quaife.
Las Casas, Bartolomé de
1951 *Historia de las Indias,* ed. A. Millares Carlos. Mexico City.
Leach, Edmund J.
1982 *Social Anthropology.* New York: Oxford University Press.

Lenoir, John D.
    1975 "Surinam National Development and Maroon Cultural Autonomy." *Social and Economic Studies* 24: 308–319.
Lichtveld, U. M., and J. Voorhoeve
    1980 *Suriname: Spiegel der vaderlandse Kooplieden.* The Hague: Martinus Nijhoff.
Lincoln, Bruce
    1989 *Discourse and the Construction of Society: Comparative Studies of Myth, Ritual, and Classification.* New York: Oxford University Press.
Lincoln, W. W.
    1878 "Letter to E. A. Hoyt, Commissioner of Indian Affairs (Aug. 20)." RG 75 M234 Roll 511 L610. Washington, D.C.: National Archives.
    1879 "Letter to Gen. John Brooke (Jan. 4)." Washington, D.C.: National Archives.
Littlefield, David
    1980a *The Chickasaw Freedmen: A People without a Country.* Westport, Conn.: Greenwood Press.
    1980b *The Cherokee Freedmen: From Emancipation to American Citizenship.* Westport, Conn.: Greenwood Press.
Lockey, Joseph B.
    1949 *East Florida, 1783–1785: A File of Documents Assembled, and Many of Them Translated.* Foreword by J. W. Caughey. Berkeley: University of California Press.
Lombardi, John V.
    1974 "The Abolition of Slavery in Venezuela: A Nonevent." In *Slavery and Race Relations in Latin America,* ed. Robert Brent Toplin. Westport, Conn.: Greenwood Press, 228–252.
Lowie, Robert
    1909 "The Assiniboin." *Anthropological Papers of the American Museum of Natural History* 4: 3–101.
    1953 "Alleged Kiowa-Crow Affinities." *Southwestern Journal of Anthropology* 9: 357–368.
Macas, Luis
    1991 *El Levantamiento Indígena visto por sus protagonistas.* Quito: Instituto Científico de Culturas Indígenas, Amauta Runacunapac Yachai.
Mandelbaum, David
    1979 *The Plains Cree: An Ethnographic, Historical, and Comparative Study.* Canadian Plains Studies No. 9. Regina: Canadian Plains Research Center, University of Regina.
    1989 *Customs in Conflict: The Anthropology of a Changing World.* Lewiston, N.Y.: Broadview Press.
Margry, Pierre
    1974 [1879] *Découvertes et établissements des français dans l'ouest et dans le*

sud de l'Amérique Septentrionale (1613–1754). 5 vols. New York: AMS Press.

Martin, Leann
1973 "Maroon Identity: Processes of Persistence in Moore Town." Ph.D. dissertation, University of California, Riverside.

Masson, L. R.
1960 [1890] *Les Bourgeois de la compagnie du Nord-Ouest.* 2 vols. New York: Antiquarian Press.

Matos Arvelo, Martin
1912 *Vida indiana.* Barcelona: Casa Editorial Maucci.

Maximillian, Alexander, Prince of Wied-Neuwied
1906 *Travels in the Interior of North America,* vols. 22 and 23, ed. R. Thwaites. Cleveland: Arthur M. Clark.

Mayhall, Mildred P.
1962 *The Kiowas.* Norman: University of Oklahoma Press.

McCall, George A.
1974 [1868] *Letters from the Frontier.* Gainesville: University of Florida Press.

McDowell, W. L., Jr., ed.
1958 *Colonial Records of South Carolina.* Series 2: *Documents Relating to Indian Affairs, May 21, 1750-August 7, 1754.* Columbia: South Carolina Archives Department.

McGuire, Randall
1992 "Archeology and the First Americans." Contemporary Issues Forum on Contested Pasts and the Practice of Anthropology, ed. J. Hill. *American Anthropologist* 94 (4): 816–836.

McKay, John
1858 "Indian Summer Debt Book." Saskatchewan Archives Board (BBH869J).

McKenzie, K.
1835a "Letter to Major Fulkerson (December 10)." *Fort Union Letterbook.* North Dakota Historical Society Microfilm.
1835b "Letter to P. Choteau (December 10)." *Fort Union Letterbook.* North Dakota Historical Society Microfilm.

McReynolds, Edwin C.
1957 *The Seminoles.* Norman: University of Oklahoma Press.

Meggers, B.
1992 "Prehistoric Population Density in the Amazon Basin." In *Disease and Demography in the Americas,* ed. J. W. Verano and D. H. Ubelaker. Washington, D.C.: Smithsonian Institution Press, 197–205.

Meggers, Betty, and Clifford Evans
1957 *Archaeological Investigations at the Mouth of the Amazon.* Bureau of American Ethnology Bulletin 167. Washington, D.C.: Smithsonian Institution.

Menezes, Sister Mary Noel
1977 *British Policy towards Amerindians in British Guiana 1803–1873.* Oxford: Clarendon Press.

Merritt, W.

1876 "Letter to Adjunctant General Military Division of the Missouri (Feb. 8)." RG 393 Post Records, Fort Logan, Montana. Washington, D.C.: National Archives.

Milanich, Jerald T.

1990 "The European Entrada into la Florida: An Overview." In *Columbian Consequences*, vol. 2: *Archaeological and Historical Perspectives on the Spanish Borderlands East*, ed. D. H. Thomas. Washington, D.C.: Smithsonian Institution Press, 3–29.

Milanich, Jerald T., and Charles Hudson

1993 *Hernando de Soto and the Florida Indians.* Gainesville: University Press of Florida.

Miller, Bruce

1989 "Centrality and Measurements of Regional Structure in Aboriginal Western Washington." *Ethnology* 28: 265–276.

Miller, Bruce, and Daniel Boxberger

1994 "Creating Chiefdoms: The Puget Sound Case." *Ethnohistory* 41: 267–293.

Miller, Kerby

1985 *Emigrants and Exiles: Ireland and the Irish Exodus to North America.* New York: Oxford University Press.

Milloy, John

1972 "The Plains Cree: A Preliminary Trade and Military Chronology, 1670–1870." M.A. thesis, Carleton University, Ottawa.

1988 *The Plains Cree: Trade, Diplomacy, and War 1790 to 1870.* Winnipeg: University of Manitoba Press.

Mintz, Sidney W., and Richard Price

1992 *The Birth of African-American Culture: An Anthropological Perspective.* Boston: Beacon Press.

Mitchell, John

1755 "A Map of the British and French Dominions in North America." Ayer Collection, Newberry Library, Chicago.

Montiano, Manuel de

1738 "Letter to the King of Spain, 2 Mar 1738." Archivo General de las Indies, Santo Domingo 86-6-5. Transcript, Ayer Collection, Newberry Library, Chicago.

1747 "Letter to the King, August 3, 1747." AGISD 2584 NCC reel 17–46.

Mooney, James

1979 [1898] *Calendar History of the Kiowa Indians.* Washington, D.C.: Smithsonian Institution Press.

Moore, John

1974 "Cheyenne Political History, 1829–1894." *Ethnohistory* 21: 329–359.

1987 *The Cheyenne Nation: A Social and Demographic History.* Lincoln: University of Nebraska Press.

Moore, Sally F., and Barbara G. Myerhoff, eds.
1977 *Secular Ritual.* Amsterdam: Van Gorcum.

Morales, Escopia
1802 "List of the Leading Men, Captains, Warriors, Women and Children of the Indian Nations Attending the Peace Conference with the Seminoles and Others, 13 December 1802." AGISD 2619.

Moreno Yánez, Segundo
1976 *Sublevaciones indígenas en la audiencia de Quito desde comienzos del siglo XVIII hasta finales de la colonia.* Bonn: Bonner Amerikanistische Studien/Estudios Americanistas de Bonn.

Morey, Robert C., and Nancy C. Morey
1975 *Relaciones comerciales en el pasado en los llanos de Colombia y Venezuela.* Caracas: Instituto de Investigaciones Históricas.

Morris, R. T.
1881 "Letter to AAG, Fort Snelling (Nov. 4)." RG 75 LR/OIA. Washington, D.C.: National Archives.

Morton, A.
1929 *The Journal of Duncan McGillivray of the Northwest Company.* Toronto: Macmillan Company.

Mowat, Charles L.
1943 *East Florida as a British Province, 1763–1784.* University of California Publications in History 32. Berkeley: University of California Press.

Muga, David
1984 "Academic Sub-Cultural Theory and the Problematic of Ethnicity: A Tentative Critique." *Journal of Ethnic Studies* 12: 1–51.
1988 "Native Americans and the Nationalities Question: Premises for a Marxist Approach to Ethnicity and Self-Determination." *Journal of Ethnic Studies* 16: 31–51.

Mulroy, Kevin
1993 *Freedom on the Border: The Seminole Maroons in Florida, the Indian Territory, Coahuila, and Texas.* Lubbock: Texas Tech University Press.

Murdoch, Richard K.
1957 "Indian Presents: To Give or Not to Give: Governor White's Quandary." *Florida Historical Quarterly* 35: 326–346.

Murdock, George P.
1967 *Ethnographic Atlas.* Pittsburgh: University of Pittsburgh Press.

NACLA
1991 "Inventing America, 1492–1992." *North American Congress on Latin America* 14 (5), February.
1992 "The Black Americas, 1492–1992." *North American Congress on Latin America* 125 (4), February.

Nairne, Thomas

1708 [1947] "Letter to Unidentified Lord, 10 July 1708." In *Records of the British Public Records Office Relating to South Carolina,* ed. Alexander S. Salley, vol. 5: 193–202.

1988 *Nairne's Muskhogean Journals: The 1708 Expedition to the Mississippi River,* ed. and introduction by Alexander Moore. Jackson: University of Mississippi Press.

Narine, Dhanpaul

1979 "A Brief Review of the History of the Upper Mazaruni." In *Waramadong: A Case Study for Amerindian Resettlement in Upper Mazaruni Area, Guyana,* ed. Alain Fournier. Georgetown, Guyana: Upper Mazaruni Development Authority.

Newcombe, W. W., Jr.

1969 *The Indians of Texas.* Austin: University of Texas Press.

Newson, Linda A.

1995 *Life and Death in Early Colonial Ecuador.* Norman: University of Oklahoma Press.

Nye, Wilbur S.

1962 *Bad Medicine and Good: Tales of the Kiowa.* Norman: University of Oklahoma Press.

Oberem, Udo

1971 *Los Quijos: historia de la transculturación de un grupo indígena en el Oriente Ecuatoriano (1538–1956).* 2 vols. Madrid: Memorias del Departamento de Antropología y Etnología de América.

O'Connell, Samuel

n.d. Unpublished papers. Sc597. Helena: Montana Historical Society.

Oliver, Symmes

1962 *Ecology and Cultural Continuity as Contributing Factors in the Social Organization of the Plains Indian.* University of California Publications in American Archaeology and Ethnology 48 (1).

Olivier, Pedro

1793 "Letter to Carondelet, December 1, 1793." In Lawrence Kinnaird, *Spain in the Mississippi Valley, 1765–1794* (1946), vol. 3: 229–233.

Ortiz, Manuel Antonio

1994 "El país se reinventa en el aula." *Revista Bigott* 32: 13–17.

Palliser, John

1863 *The Journals, Detailed Report and Observations Relative to the Exploration, by Captain John Palliser of That Portion of British North America . . . during the Years 1857, 1858, 1859, and 1863.* London: G. E. Eyre and W. Spottiswoode.

Parker, John, ed.

1976 *The Journal of Jonathan Carver and Related Documents, 1766–1770.* St. Paul: Minnesota Historical Society Press.

Parker, Susan R.
N.d. "The Cattle Trade in East Florida, 1784–1821." Ms. prepared for the St. Augustine Historical Commission.

Parris, Scott V.
1981 "Alliance and Competition: Four Case Studies of Maroon-European Relations." *Nieuwe West-Indische Gids* 55 (3–4): 174–224.

Peers, Laura
1987 "An Ethnohistory of the Western Ojibway, 1780–1830." Master's thesis, University of Winnipeg and University of Manitoba.
1994 *The Ojibwa of Western Canada: 1780–1870.* St. Paul: Minnesota Historical Society.

Peña, Diego
1716 "Journal of the Journey to Apalachee and to the Province of Apalachicolo Ordered Made by the Governor and Captain General Don Pedro de Oliver y Fullana, Major General of the Presidio of San Agustin and of All the Provinces of Its Jurisdiction, by His Majesty, August 4, 1716." In "Diego Peña's Expedition to Apalachee and Apalachicolo in 1716," ed. Mark F. Boyd. *Florida Historical Quarterly* 28: 12–27.

Perryman, George
1817 "Letter to R. Sands, February 24, 1817." In *Message from the President in Relation to the War with the Seminoles, March 25, 1818.* 15th Cong., 1st sess. H. Doc. 173.

Pierre, Françoise
1983 [1889] *Viaje de exploración al Oriente Ecuatoriano 1887–1888.* Quito: Abya-Yala.

Pilcher, Joshua
1824 "Answers to Questions Put to Him by the Committee of the Senate on Indian Affairs, Feb. 10, 1824." *American State Papers, Indian Affairs*, vol. 2.
1838 *Report to Commissioner of Indian Affairs.* 25th Cong., 3d sess. H. Doc. 2.

Pitt-Rivers, Julian
1967 "Race, Color, and Class in Central America and the Andes." *Daedalus* 96 (2): 542–559.
1973 "Race in Latin America: The Concept of 'Raza.'" *Archives Européens de Sociologie* 14 (1): 3–31.

Porter, Kenneth W.
1945 "Negroes and the East Florida Annexation Plot, 1811–1813." *Journal of Negro History* 30: 9–29.
1946a "John Caesar: Seminole Negro Partisan." *Journal of Negro History* 31 (2): 190–207.
1946b "The Negro Abraham." *Florida Historical Quarterly* 25: 1–43.
1948 "Negroes on the Southern Frontier, 1670–1763." *Journal of Negro History* 33: 53–78.

1949 "The Founder of the 'Seminole Nation': Secoffee or Cowkeeper?" *Florida Historical Quarterly* 27: 362–384.

1951a "Negroes and the Seminole War, 1817–1818." *Journal of Negro History* 36: 249–280.

1951b "Origins of the St. John's River Seminole: Were They Mikasuki?" *Florida Anthropologist* 4 (3–4): 39–45.

1952 "The Cowkeeper Dynasty of the Seminole Nation." *Florida Historical Quarterly* 30: 341–349.

Posey, D., and W. Balée

1989 *Resource Management in Amazonia: Indigenous and Folk Strategies.* Advances in Economic Botany Series no. 7. New York: New York Botanical Garden.

Potter, Woodburne

1836 *The War in Florida: Being an Exposition of Its Causes, and an Accurate History of the Campaigns of Generals Clinch, Gaines, and Scott.* Baltimore: Lewis & Coleman.

Price, Richard

1973 "Avenging Spirits and the Structure of Saramaka Lineages." *Bijdragen tot de Taal-, Land- en Volkenkunde* 129: 86–107.

1975 *Saramaka Social Structure.* Caribbean Monograph Series 12. Rio Piedras: Institute of Caribbean Studies, University of Puerto Rico.

1976 *The Guiana Maroons: A Historical and Bibliographical Introduction.* Baltimore: Johns Hopkins University Press.

1983 *First-Time: The Historical Vision of an Afro-American People.* Baltimore: Johns Hopkins University Press.

Price, Richard, ed.

1979 *Maroon Societies: Rebel Slave Communities in the Americas,* 2d ed. Baltimore: Johns Hopkins University Press.

Price-Mars, Jean

1928 *Ainse parla l'oncle.* Paris: Imprimerie de Compliègne.

Primo de Rivera, Jose

1718 "Letter to Governor Juan de Ayala y Escobar, San Marcos de Apalachee, April 28, 1718." AGISD 843 SC.

Purcell, Joseph

1772 "A Map of the Southern Indian District of North America. Compiled under the Direction of John Stuart, Esq., His Majesty's Superintendent of Indian Affairs." Ms. Map, Ayer Collection, Newberry Library, Chicago.

Purchas, S.

1906 *Hakluytus Posthumus or His Pilgrimes.* Vol. 16. London: Hakluyt Society.

Quinn, William

1993 "Intertribal Integration: The Ethnological Argument in Duro v. Reina." *Ethnohistory* 40: 34–69.

Rabinow, Paul, and William M. Sullivan, eds.
1979 *Interpretive Social Science: A Reader.* Berkeley: University of California Press.

Rangles Lara, Rodrigo
1995 *Venturas y desventuras de poder.* Quito: Carvajal, S.A.

Rasnake, Roger
1988 "Images of Resistance to Colonial Domination." In *Rethinking History and Myth: Indigenous South American Perspectives on the Past,* ed. Jonathan Hill. Urbana: University of Illinois Press, 136–156.

Rausch, Jane
1984 *A Tropical Plains Frontier: The Llanos of Colombia 1531–1831.* Albuquerque: University of New Mexico Press.

Ray, Arthur
1974 *Indians in the Fur Trade: Their Role as Hunters, Trappers and Middlemen in the Lands Southwest of Hudson Bay, 1660–1870.* Toronto: University of Toronto Press.

Read, O. B.
1883 "Letter to AAG DD (April 6)." RG 393, Camp Poplar River Post Records. Washington, D.C.: National Archives.

Reichel-Dolmatoff, Gerardo
1971 *Amazonian Cosmos.* Chicago: University of Chicago Press.
1975 *The Shaman and the Jaguar.* Philadelphia: Temple University Press.
1985 "Tapir Avoidance in the Colombian Northwest Amazon." In *Animal Myths and Metaphors in South America,* ed. G. Urton. Salt Lake City: University of Utah Press, 107–144.

Reynolds, George A.
1867 "Letter to the Commissioner of Indian Affairs, August 28, 1867." In *Annual Report of the Commissioner of Indian Affairs for 1867.* Washington, D.C.: U.S. Government Printing Office.

Ricoeur, Paul
1976 *Interpretation Theory: Discourse and the Surplus of Meaning.* Fort Worth: Texas Christian University Press.

Riggs, Fred W., ed.
1985 *Ethnicity: Intercocta Glossary. Concepts and Terms Used in Ethnicity Research,* pilot ed. Paris: International Social Science Council, UNESCO.

Rivera Cusicanqui, Silvia
1991 "Aymara Past, Aymara Future." In NACLA, *Report on the Americas: The First Nations, 1492–1992.* New York: North American Congress on Latin America 25, December, vol. 3: 18–23.

Rivers, William J.
1874 *A Chapter in the Early History of South Carolina.* Charleston, S.C.: Walker, Evans, & Cogswell, Printers.

Riviere, P. G.

1966–1967 "Some Ethnographic Problems of Southern Guyana." *Folk* 8–9: 301–312.

Rodnick, David

1938 *The Fort Belknap Assiniboin: A Study in Culture Change.* New Haven, Conn.: Yale University Publications in Anthropology.

Romans, Bernard

1775 *A Concise Natural History of East and West Florida.* New York.

Roosevelt, A. C.

1989 "Resource Management in Amazonia before the Conquest: Beyond Ethnographic Projection." In *Resource Management in Amazonia: Indigenous and Folk Strategies*, ed. D. Posey and W. Balée. Advances in Economic Botany Series no. 7. New York: New York Botanical Garden, 30–62.

Rosaldo, Renato

1980 *Ilongot Headhunting, 1883–1974: A Study in Society and History.* Stanford, Calif.: Stanford University Press.

Rosero, Fernando

1990 *Levantamiento Indígena: tierra y precios.* Quito: Serie Movimiento Indígena en el Ecuador Contemporáneo, No. 1.

Ross, Alexander

1957 [1854] *The Red River Settlement: Its Rise, Progress, and Present State.* Minneapolis: Ross & Haines.

Rout, Leslie B., Jr.

1976 *The African Experience in Spanish Americas: 1502 to the Present Day.* New York: Cambridge University Press.

Russell, Dale

1991 *Eighteenth-Century Western Cree and Their Neighbors.* Hull, Quebec: Canadian Museum of Civilization.

Sacoto, Antonio

1967 *The Indian in the Ecuadorian Novel.* New York: Las Américas Publishing Company.

Sahlins, Marshall

1976 *Culture and Practical Reason.* Chicago: University of Chicago Press.

1981 *Historical Metaphors and Mythical Realities: Structure in the Early History of the Sandwich Islands Kingdom.* Ann Arbor: University of Michigan Press.

1993 "Goodbye to Tristes Tropes: Ethnography in the Context of Modern World History." In *Assessing Cultural Anthropology*, ed. Robert Borofsky. New York: McGraw Hill, 377–395.

Salley, Alexander S.

1926 *Journal of the Commissioners of the Indian Trade of South Carolina, September 20, 1710–April 12, 1715.* Columbia: Historical Commission of South Carolina.

1939 *Journal of the Commons House of Assembly of South Carolina, November 20, 1706–February 8, 1706/7*. Columbia: Historical Commission of South Carolina.

Salomon, Frank

1981 "Killing the Yumbo: A Ritual from North Quito." In *Cultural Transformations and Ethnicity in Modern Ecuador*, ed. Norman E. Whitten, Jr. Urbana: University of Illinois Press, 162–208.

1986 *Native Lords of Quito in the Age of the Incas: The Political Economy of North Andean Chiefdoms*. New York: Cambridge University Press.

Santos, Fernando

1993 *Etnohistoria de la alta Amazonía: siglos XV–XVIII*. Quito: Abya-Yala.

Sattler, Richard A.

1985 "The Politics of Trade among the Seminoles." Paper presented at the Annual Meeting of the American Society for Ethnohistory, Chicago, Ill., November 7–10.

1987 "*Siminoli Italwa*: Sociopolitical Change among the Oklahoma Seminoles from Removal to Allotment, 1835–1905." Ph.D. dissertation, University of Oklahoma.

1988 "Women's Status among the Muskogee and Cherokee." Paper presented at the Annual Meeting of the American Anthropological Association, Phoenix, Ariz., November 16–20.

1989 "The Politics of Kinship: Dynastic Marriage and Patterns of Succession among the Alachua Seminoles." Paper presented at the Annual Meeting of the American Society for Ethnohistory, Chicago, Ill., November 2–5.

1992 "Ethnic Transformations on the Gulf Coast: The Apalachi Case." Paper presented at the Annual Meeting of the American Association for the Advancement of Science, Chicago, Ill., February 6–11.

Sauer, Carl O.

1934 *The Distribution of Aboriginal Tribes and Languages in Northwestern Mexico*. Ibero-Americana, no. 5. Berkeley: University of California Press.

Scarry, John F.

1992 "Political Offices and Political Structure: Ethnohistoric and Archaeological Perspectives on the Native Lords of Apalachee." In *Lords of the Southeast: Social Inequality and the Native Elites of Southeastern North America*, ed. Alex W. Barker and Timothy R. Pauketat. American Anthropological Association, Archaeological Papers, No. 3.

Schafer, Daniel Lee

1973 "The Maroons of Jamaica: African Slave Rebels in the Caribbean." Ph.D. dissertation, University of Minnesota.

Schilz, Thomas

1988 "The Gros Ventres and the Canadian Fur Trade: 1754–1831." *American Indian Quarterly* 12: 41–56.

Schnell, Frank T.

1971 "A Comparative Study of Some Lower Creek Sites." *Southeastern Archaeological Conference Bulletin* 13: 133–136.

Schnell, Frank T., Vernon J. Knight, Jr., and Gail S. Schnell

1981 *Cemochechobee: Archaeology of a Mississippian Ceremonial Center on the Chattahoochee River*. Gainesville: University Presses of Florida.

Scholes, F. V., and H. P. Mera

1940 *Some Aspects of the Jumano Problem: Contributions to American Anthropology and History*. Washington, D.C.: Carnegie Institution.

Searcy, Martha C.

1985 *The Georgia-Florida Contest in the American Revolution, 1776–1778*. Tuscaloosa: University of Alabama Press.

Secoy, Frank

1953 *Changing Military Patterns on the Great Plains*. Monographs of the American Ethnological Society, 21. Seattle: University of Washington Press.

Serrano, Fernando

1993 "The Transformation of the Indian People of the Ecuadorian Amazon into Political Actors and Its Effects on the State's Modernization Policies." M.A. thesis, University of Florida.

Service, Elman

1962 *The Origins of the State and Civilization: The Process of Cultural Evolution*. New York: W. W. Norton & Company.

Seymour-Smith, Charlotte

1988 *Shiwiar: identidad étnica y cambio en el Río Corrientes*. Quito: Abya-Yala.

Sharp, Paul

1954 "Massacre at Cypress Hills." *Montana, the Magazine of Western History* 4: 21–36.

1955 *Whoop-Up Country*. Norman: University of Oklahoma Press.

Sharrock, Floyd, and Susan Sharrock

1974 *History of the Cree Indian Territorial Expansion from the Hudson Bay Area to the Interior Saskatchewan and Missouri Plains, Chippewa Indians*, vol. 6. New York: Garland Press.

Sharrock, Susan

1974 "Cree, Cree-Assiniboines, and Assiniboines: Interethnic Social Organization on the Northern Plains." *Ethnohistory* 21: 95–122.

1977 "Cross-Tribal Ecological Categorization of Far Northern Plains Cree and Assiniboin by the Late Eighteenth and Early Nineteenth Century." *Western Canadian Journal of Anthropology* 4: 7–21.

Sider, Gerald

1994 "Identity as History: Ethnohistory, Ethnogenesis and Ethnocide in the Southeastern United States." *Identities* 1 (1): 109–122.

Silverblatt, Irene

1988 "Political Memories and Colonizing Symbols: Santiago and the Mountain Gods of Colonial Peru." In *Rethinking History and Myth: Indigenous South American Perspectives on the Past*, ed. Jonathan Hill. Urbana: University of Illinois Press, 174–194.

Simmons, A. J.

1871 *Annual Report of the Commissioner of Indian Affairs*. Washington, D.C.: U.S. Government.

Simmons, William H.

1973 [1822] *Notices of East Florida*. Gainesville: University of Florida Press.

Skidmore, Thomas E.

1974 *White into Black: Race and Nationality in Brazilian Thought*. New York: Oxford University Press.

Skinner, Alanson

1914 "Political and Ceremonial Organization of the Plains-Ojibway." *Anthropological Papers of the American Museum of Natural History*, vol. 11.

Skinner, Elliott

1975 "Resource Competition and Inter-ethnic Relations in Nigeria." In *Ethnicity and Resource Competition in Plural Societies*, ed. L. Despres. The Hague: Mouton, 119–130.

Smith, James G. E.

1981 "Western Woods Cree." In *Handbook of American Indians: Subarctic*, vol. 6, ed. June Helm. Washington, D.C.: Smithsonian Institution, 257–259.

Smith, M. G.

1969 "Some Developments in the Analytic Framework of Pluralism." In *Pluralism in Africa*, ed. L. Kuper and M. G. Smith. Berkeley: University of California Press, 27–66.

Smith, Marvin T.

1987 *Aboriginal Culture Change in the Interior Southeast: Depopulation during the Early Historic Period*. Gainesville: University Presses of Florida.

1989 "Aboriginal Population Movements in the Early Historic Period Interior Southeast." In *Powhatan's Mantle: Indians in the Colonial Southeast*, ed. P. H. Wood, G. A. Waselkov, and M. T. Hartley. Lincoln: University of Nebraska Press, 21–34.

Southall, Aidan

1988 "The Segmentary State in Africa and Asia." *Comparative Studies in Society and History* 30: 52–82.

1991 "The Segmentary State: From the Imaginary to the Material Means of Production." In *Early State Economics*, ed. H. J. M. Claessen and P. van de Velde. Political and Legal Anthropology Series 8. New Brunswick, N.J.: Transaction Publishers.

Spicer, Edward

1992 "The Nations of a State." Special issue, *1492–1992: American Indian Persistence and Resurgence*, ed. K. Kroeber. *Boundary 2* 19 (3): 26–48.

Sprague, John T.

1847 *The Origin, Progress, and Conclusion of the Florida War.* New York: D. Appleton & Company.

Sprenger, G. Herhan

1972 "An Analysis of Selective Aspects of Metis Society, 1810–1870." M.A. thesis, University of Manitoba.

Stedman, John Gabriel

1988 *Narrative of a Five Years Expedition against the Revolted Negroes of Surinam, Transcribed for the First Time from the Original 1790 Manuscript,* ed. Richard Price and Sally Price. Baltimore: Johns Hopkins University Press.

Stevens, Isaac

1859 "Reports of the Explorations and Surveys, from the Mississippi River to the Pacific Ocean." 35th Cong., 2d sess. S. Doc. 46. Washington, D.C.: Wm. A. Harris.

Steward, Julian H.

1955 *Theory of Culture Change: The Methodology of Multilinear Evolution.* Urbana: University of Illinois Press.

Stuart, John, and Joseph Purcell

1778 "A Map of the Road from Pensacola in West Florida to St. Augustine in East Florida in 1778." Photocopy. Ayer Collection, Newberry Library, Chicago.

Sturtevant, William

1971 "Creek into Seminole: North American Indians." In *Historical Perspective,* ed. E. Leacock and N. Lurie. New York: Random House, 92–128.

1983 "Tribe and State in the Sixteenth and Twentieth Centuries." In *The Development of Political Organization in Native North America,* ed. E. Tooker. Washington, D.C.: Proceedings of the American Ethnological Society, 3–16.

Stutzman, Ronald

1981 "*El Mestizaje*: An All-Inclusive Ideology of Exclusion." In *Cultural Transformations and Ethnicity in Modern Ecuador,* ed. Norman Whitten. Urbana: University of Illinois Press, 45–94.

Sullivan, Lawrence

1988 *Icanchu's Drum: An Orientation to Meaning in South American Religions.* New York: Macmillan.

Swan, Caleb

1791 "Position and State of Manners and Arts in the Creek or Muskogee Nation in 1791." In *Historical and Statistical Information Respecting the History, Condition and Prospects of the Indian Tribes of the United States,* ed. H. R. Schoolcraft. Philadelphia: Lippincott, Granbo, 251–283.

Swanton, John R.

1922 *Early History of the Creeks and Their Neighbors.* Washington, D.C.: U.S. Government Printing Office.

1928a "Social Organization and Social Usages of the Indians of the Creek Confederacy." Bureau of American Ethnology, *Annual Report* 42: 23–472.

1928b "Religious Beliefs and Medical Practices of the Creek Indians." Bureau of American Ethnology, *Annual Report* 42: 473–672.

Syms, E. Leigh

1977 *Cultural Ecology and Ecological Dynamics of the Ceramic Period in Southwestern Manitoba. Plains Anthropologist,* Memoir 12.

1979 "The Devil's Lake–Souirisford Burial Complex on the Northern Plains." *Plains Anthropologist* 24: 283–308.

Taitt, David

1916 "Journal of David Taitt's Travels from Pensacola, West Florida, to and through the Country of the Upper and the Lower Creeks, 1772." In *Travels in the American Colonies, 1690–1783,* ed. N. D. Mereness. New York: Macmillan Company, 493–565.

Tanner, Helen

1987 *Atlas of Great Lakes Indian History.* Norman: University of Oklahoma Press.

Taussig, Michael

1978 *Destrucción y resistencia campesina: el caso del litoral pacífica.* Bogotá: Punta de Lanza.

1980 *The Devil and Commodity Fetishism in South America.* Chapel Hill: University of North Carolina Press.

1987 *Shamanism, Colonialism and the Wild Man: A Study in Terror and Healing.* Chicago: University of Chicago Press.

Taylor, John F.

1977 "Sociocultural Effects of Epidemics on the Northern Plains: 1734–1850." *Western Canadian Journal of Anthropology* 7: 55–72.

TePaske, John J.

1964 *The Governorship of Spanish Florida, 1700–1763.* Durham, N.C.: Duke University Press.

Thistle, Paul

1986 *Indian-European Trade Relations in the Lower Saskatchewan River Region to 1840.* Winnipeg: University of Manitoba Press.

Thoden van Velzen, H. U. E.

1966 "Het Geloof in Wraakgeesten: Bindmiddel en Splijtzwam van de Djuka Matri-Lineage." *Nieuwe West-Indische Gids* 45: 45–51.

Thomas, A. B., ed.

1982 *Alonso de Posada Report, 1686.* Spanish Borderlands Series, 4. Pensacola: Perdido Bay Press.

Thomas, David Hurst, ed.

1990 *Columbian Consequences,* vol. 2: *Archaeological and Historical Perspectives on the Spanish Borderlands East.* Washington, D.C.: Smithsonian Institution Press.

Thomas, David John
  1976 "El movimiento religioso de San Miguel entre los Pemon." *Antropológica*
  33: 3–57.
  1982 *Order without Government: The Society of the Pemon Indians of Venezuela.*
  Urbana: University of Illinois Press.
Thornton, Russell
  1987 *American Indian Holocaust and Survival: A Population History since 1492.*
  Norman: University of Oklahoma Press.
Thwaites, Rueben, ed.
  1904–1905 *Original Journal of the Lewis and Clark Expedition, 1804–1806.*
  New York: Dodd and Mead Co.
Tomoeda, Hiroyasu, and Luis Millones, eds.
  1992 *500 años de mestizaje en los Andes.* Osaka: Museo Etnológico Nacional de
  Japon, and Lima: Biblioteca Peruana de Psicoanálisis.
Toro, Alonso Marques del
  1738 "Letter, San Marcos de Apalachee, April 18, 1738." AGISD 2593 SC.
  Microfilm copy in P. K. Yonge Library of Florida History, University of Florida.
Trigger, Bruce
  1976 *The Children of Aataentsic: A History of the Huron People to 1660,* vol. 1.
  Montreal: McGill–Queens University Press.
Trimble, Michael
  1986 *An Ethnohistorical Interpretation of the Spread of Smallpox in the Northern
  Plains: Utilizing Concepts of Disease Ecology.* Vol. 33. Lincoln, Nebr.: J & L Re-
  print Co.
Trouillot, Michel-Rolph
  1990 *Haiti, State against Nation: The Origins and Legacy of Duvalierism.* New
  York: Monthly Review Press.
Trouwborst, Albert A.
  1991 "The Political Economy of the Interlacustrine States in East Africa." In
  Early State Economics, ed. H. J. M. Claessen and P. van de Velde. Political and
  Legal Anthropology Series 8. New Brunswick, N.J.: Transaction Publishers.
Tsing, Anna Lowenhaupt
  1994 "From the Margins." *Cultural Anthropology* 9 (3): 279–297.
Tucker, Sara Jones
  1942 *Indian Villages of the Illinois Country. Part I: Atlas.* Scientific Papers of the
  Illinois State Museum, 2. Springfield, Illinois.
Turner, Terence
  1988 "Commentary: Ethno-Ethnohistory: Myth and History in Native South
  American Representations of Contact with Western Society." In *Rethinking
  History and Myth: Indigenous South American Perspectives on the Past,* ed. Jona-
  than Hill. Urbana: University of Illinois Press, 235–281.
Turner, Victor
  1973 "Symbols in African Ritual." *Science* 179 (March): 1100–1105.

1974 *Dramas, Fields, and Metaphors: Symbolic Action in Human Societies.* Ithaca: Cornell University Press.

1985 *On the Edge of the Bush: Anthropology as Experience.* Tucson: University of Arizona Press.

Tyrrell, J. B., ed.

1968 [1916] *David Thompson's Narrative of His Explorations in Western America, 1784–1812.* New York: Green Wood Press.

Urban, Greg

1991 *A Discourse-Centered Approach to Culture: Native South American Myths and Rituals.* Austin: University of Texas Press.

Urban, Greg, and Joel Sherzer, eds.

1992 *Nation-States and Indians in Latin America.* Austin: University of Texas Press.

U.S. Congress

1832–1861 *American State Papers: Documents Legislative and Executive of the Congress of the United States.* Class 2: *Indian Affairs,* vols. 1–2; class 5: *Military Affairs,* vols. 1, 6, 7. Washington, D.C.: U.S. Government Printing Office.

Vail, J. A.

1872 *Report of the Commissioner of Indian Affairs.* Washington, D.C.: U.S. Government.

van den Berghe, Pierre

1973 "Pluralism." In *Handbook of Social and Cultural Anthropology,* ed. J. Honigman. Chicago: Rand McNally & Co., 959–978.

Versteeg, A. H.

1985 *The Prehistory of the Young Coastal Plain of West Suriname.* Rijksdienst voor het Oudheidkundig Bodemonderzoek.

Vidal, Silvia

1987 "El modelo del proceso migratorio prehispanico de los Piapoco: hipótesis y evidéncias." M.S. thesis, Instituto Venezolano de Investigaciones Científicas.

1993 "Reconstrucción de los procesos de etnogénesis y de reproducción social entre los Baré de Rio Negro (siglos XVI–XVIII)." Ph.D. dissertation, Instituto Venezolano de Investigaciones Científicas.

Vogelin, E. W.

1933 "Kiowa-Crow Mythological Affiliations." *American Anthropologist* 35: 470–474.

Vogelin, Ermine, and Harold Hickerson

1974 *The Red Lake and Pembina Chippewa, Chippewa Indians,* 1. New York: Garland.

Wade, Peter

1993 *Blackness and Race Mixture: The Dynamics of Racial Identity in Colombia.* Baltimore: Johns Hopkins University Press.

Warren, G.

1667 *An Impartial Description of Surinam.* London.

Wavell, Stewart, Audrey Butt, and Nina Epton
1966 *Trances.* London: George Allen and Unwin.
Weber, David J.
1971 *The Taos Trappers: The Fur Trade in the Far Southwest, 1540–1846.* Norman: University of Oklahoma Press.
Weismantel, Mary J.
1988 *Food, Gender and Poverty in the Ecuadorian Andes.* Philadelphia: University of Pennsylvania Press.
Weist, Katherine
1977 "An Ethnohistorical Analysis of Crow Political Alliances." *Western Canadian Journal of Anthropology* 7: 34–54.
Wenhold, Lucy L., and A. C. Manucy, eds.
1957 "The Trials of don Isidoro de Leon." *Florida Historical Quarterly* 35: 246–265.
Westcott, James D., Jr.
1833a "Letter to E. Herring, November 5, 1833." 24th Cong., 1st sess. H. Doc. 271.
1833b "Letter to E. Herring, November 13, 1833." In *Correspondence of the Office of Indian Affairs (Central Office), Letters Received, 1824–1881, Seminole Emigration.* M 234. Washington, D.C.: National Archives Microfilm Publications.
White, Richard
1991 *The Middle Ground: Indians, Empires and Republics in the Great Lakes Region, 1650–1815.* New York: Cambridge University Press.
Whitehead, Neil L.
1988 *Lords of the Tiger-Spirit: A History of the Caribs in Colonial Venezuela and Guyana, 1498–1820.* KITLV, Caribbean Studies Series no. 10. Dordrecht, Holland: Foris Publications.
1990a "Carib Ethnic Soldiering in Venezuela, the Guianas and Antilles, 1492–1820." *Ethnohistory* 37 (4): 357–385.
1990b "The Snake Warriors—Sons of the Tiger's Teeth: A Descriptive Analysis of Carib Warfare ca. 1500–1820." In *The Anthropology of War*, ed. Jonathan Haas. Cambridge, England: Cambridge University Press.
1992 "Tribes Make States and States Make Tribes: Warfare and the Creation of Colonial Tribe and State in Northeastern South America." In *War in the Tribal Zone: Expanding States and Indigenous Warfare*, ed. R. B. Ferguson and N. L. Whitehead. Santa Fe: SAR Press, 127–150.
1993a "Native American Cultures along the Atlantic Littoral of South America, 1499–1650." *Proceedings of the British Academy* 81: 197–231.
1993b "Historical Discontinuity and Ethnic Transformation in Native Amazonia and Guayana." *L'Homme* 28: 289–309.
1994 "The Ancient Amerindian Polities of the Lower Orinoco, Amazon and Guayana Coast: A Preliminary Analysis of Their Passage from Antiquity to

Extinction." In *Amazonian Indians: From Prehistory to the Present*, ed. A. C. Roosevelt. Tucson: University of Arizona Press, 19–31.

1995 "Ethnic Plurality and Cultural Continuity in the Native Caribbean: Remarks and Uncertainties as to Data and Theory." In *Wolves from the Sea: Readings in the Anthropology of the Native Caribbean*, ed. N. L. Whitehead. Leiden: KITLV Press, 91–112.

Whitehead, Neil L., and R. B. Ferguson, eds.

1992 *War in the Tribal Zone: Expanding States and Indigenous Warfare*. Santa Fe: SAR Press.

Whitten, Dorothea, and Norman E. Whitten, Jr.

1988 *From Myth to Creation: Art from Amazonian Ecuador*. Urbana: University of Illinois Press.

1993 "The Canelos Quichua." In *Amazonian Worlds*, ed. Catalina Sosa and Noemi Paymal. Quito: Mariscal, 100–110.

in press "Poder cultural y la fuerza estética en la Amazonía ecuatoriana." In *Las culturas amazónicas en el siglo veinte*, ed. Fernando Santos and Federica Barclay. Quito: FLACSO.

Whitten, Dorothea, and Norman E. Whitten, Jr., eds.

1993 *Imagery and Creativity: Ethnoaesthetics and Art Worlds in the Americas*. Tucson: University of Arizona Press.

Whitten, Norman E., Jr.

1965 *Class, Kinship, and Power in an Ecuadorian Town: The Negroes of San Lorenzo*. Stanford, Calif.: Stanford University Press.

1976 *Ecuadorian Ethnocide and Indigenous Ethnogenesis: Amazonian Resurgence amidst Andean Colonization*. Copenhagen: International Work Group for Indigenous Affairs (IWGIA).

1985 *Sicuanga Runa: The Other Side of Development in Amazonian Ecuador*. Urbana: University of Illinois Press.

1986 [1974] *Black Frontiersmen: Afro-Hispanic Culture of Ecuador and Colombia*. Prospect Heights: Waveland Press.

1988 "Historical and Mythic Evocations of Chthonic Power in South America." In *Rethinking History and Myth: Indigenous South American Perspectives on the Past*, ed. Jonathan Hill. Urbana: University of Illinois Press, 282–306.

1992 *Pioneros negros: la cultura afro-Latinoamericana del Ecuador y de Colombia*. Quito: Prensa del Centro Cultural Afro-Ecuatoriano.

1994 "The Canelos Quichua." In *Encyclopedia of World Cultures*, ed. Johannes Wilbert. New Haven, Conn.: Human Relations Area Files Press.

1996 "Ethnogenesis." In *The Encyclopedia of Cultural Anthropology*, ed. D. Levinson and M. Ember. New York: Henry Holt.

Whitten, Norman E., Jr., ed.

1981 *Cultural Transformations and Ethnicity in Modern Ecuador*. Urbana: University of Illinois Press.

1993 *Tranformaciones culturales y etnicidad en la sierra ecuatoriana.* Quito: Prensa de la Universidad San Francisco de Quito.

Whitten, Norman E., Jr., and Diego Quiroga

1994 "The Black Pacific Lowlanders of Ecuador and Colombia." In *Encyclopedia of World Cultures,* ed. Johannes Wilbert. New Haven, Conn.: Human Relations Area Files Press.

1995 "Ecuador." In *No Longer Invisible: Afro-Latin Americans Today,* ed. Minority Rights Group. London: Minority Rights Publications, 287–317.

Whitten, Norman E., Jr., and Arlene Torres

1992 "Blackness in the Americas." NACLA, *Report on the Americas: The Black Americas, 1492–1992.* New York: North American Congress on Latin America 25, February, vol. 4: 18–23.

Whitten, Norman E., Jr., and Arlene Torres, eds.

in press *To Forge the Future in the Fires of the Past: Blackness in Latin America and the Caribbean.* 2 vols. New York: Carlson Publishing.

Williams, Brackette F.

1993 *Stains on My Name, War in My Veins: Guyana and the Politics of Cultural Struggle.* Durham, N.C.: Duke University Press.

Williams, John Lee

1837 *The Territory of Florida: or Sketches of the Topography, Civil and Natural History, of the Country, the Climate, and the Indian Tribes, from the First Discovery to the Present Time, with a Map, Views, etc.* New York: A. T. Goodrich.

Williams, Joseph J.

1938 "The Maroons of Jamaica." *Anthropological Series of the Boston College Graduate School* 3 (4): 379–471.

Williams, Raymond

1977 *Marxism and Literature.* Oxford, England: Oxford University Press.

Williamson, J. A.

1923 *English Colonies in Guiana and on the Amazon.* Oxford, England: Oxford University Press.

Wissler, Clark

1927 "Distribution of Moccasin Decorations among the Plains Tribes." *Anthropological Papers of the American Museum of Natural History* 29: 1–23.

Wolf, Eric

1982 *Europe and the People without History.* Berkeley: University of California Press.

Wood, W. Raymond

1971 *Biesterfeldt: A Post-Contact Coalescent Site on the Northeastern Plains.* Smithsonian Contributions to Anthropology 15.

1980 "Plains Trade in Prehistoric and Protohistoric Intertribal Relations." In *Anthropology on the Great Plains,* ed. W. R. Wood and M. Liberty. Lincoln: University of Nebraska Press, 98–109.

Wood, W. Raymond, and Alan Downer
1977 "Notes on the Crow-Hidatsa Schism." In *Trends in Middle Missouri Prehistory: A Festschrift Honoring the Contributions of Donald J. Lehmer*, ed. R. Wood. *Plains Anthropologist*, Memoir 13: 83–100.

Worsley, Peter
1984 *The Three Worlds: Culture and World Development*. Chicago: University of Chicago Press.

Wright, J. Leitch
1986 *Creeks and Seminoles: Destruction and Regeneration of the Muscogulge People*. Lincoln: University of Nebraska Press.

Wright, James
1965 "A Regional Examination of Ojibwa Culture History." *Anthropologia* 7: 189–227.
1981 "Prehistory of the Canadian Shield." In *Handbook of American Indians: Subarctic*, vol. 6, ed. June Helm. Washington, D.C.: Smithsonian Institution, 86–96.

Wright, Robin
1981 "History and Religion of the Baniwa Peoples of the Upper Rio Negro Valley." Ph.D. dissertation, Stanford University.

Wright, Robin, and Jonathan Hill
1986 "History, Ritual, and Myth: 19th Century Millenarian Movements in the Northwest Amazon." *Ethnohistory* 33 (1): 31–54.

Wright, Winthrop
1990 *Café con Leche: Race, Class, and National Image in Venezuela*. Austin: University of Texas Press.

Young, Hugh
1934 "A Topographical Memoir on East and West Florida with Itineraries of General Jackson's Army, 1818," ed. M. F. Boyd and G. M. Ponton. *Florida Historical Quarterly* 13: 16–50, 82–104, 128–164.

Index